W9-CJM-768

Global Social Change

Global Social Change

Historical and Comparative Perspectives

Edited by Christopher Chase-Dunn and Salvatore J. Babones

The Johns Hopkins University Press · Baltimore

© 2006 The Johns Hopkins University Press
All rights reserved. Published 2006
Printed in the United States of America
on acid-free paper
9 8 7 6 5 4 3 2 1

The Johns Hopkins University Press
2715 North Charles Street
Baltimore, Maryland 21218-4363
www.press.jhu.edu

Library of Congress Cataloging-in-Publication Data
Global social change : historical and comparative perspectives / edited by
Christopher Chase-Dunn and Salvatore J. Babones.
    p. cm.
  Includes bibliographical references and index.
  ISBN 0-8018-8423-3 (alk. paper)—ISBN 0-8018-8424-1 (pbk. : alk. paper)
  1. Social change. 2. Globalization. I. Chase-Dunn, Christopher K.
II. Babones, Salvatore J.
HM831.G495 2006
303.48'2—dc22   2005032615

A catalog record for this book is available from the British Library.

CONTENTS

This book is composed of contemporary classics by social scientists who do research on global social change in historical and comparative perspective. The chapters provide an accessible introduction for students who are interested in globalization. Most of the popular and scholarly literature presumes that globalization consists of social features and processes that are uniquely new. The extent to which this is true can be determined only by careful comparisons with the past. The chapters in this book study how social structures and institutions have experienced cycles of change, and they allow us to understand the long-run continuities of globalization as well as the emergent new features.

Many of the chapters in this volume were previously published as articles in the *Journal of World-Systems Research* and have been revised for a more general audience. The collection focuses on contemporary and historical global social change, with contributions from prominent social scientists from the United States, England, and Sweden.

The book includes an introductory chapter that discusses the connections between the main topics and locates the study of global social change in world-historical perspective. It also includes a chapter on methodological issues that must be confronted in studying global social change. Part I presents and examines contending conceptualizations of globalization and the long-term expansion (and contraction) of human interaction networks. Part II reviews studies of global inequalities and presents new results regarding income and energy usage. Part III addresses interactions between human societies and the environment in long-term perspective—so-called world-systems ecology—and also summarizes research on the more recent aspects of the relationship between globalization and environmental degradation. Part IV examines recent changes in the structures of world economic, political, and military power in the light of comparisons with the nineteenth century. The trajectory of U.S. hegemony is compared with the rise and fall of British hegemony in the nineteenth century, and the recent literature on "neoimperialism" is examined. Part V focuses on several contemporary transnational social movements and their relations with one another, as well as their prospects for playing an important role in future global governance and in challenging contemporary arrangements. Part VI assesses the past trajectory of and future prospects for democracy on a global scale. The future of world society is considered, as well.

This book is designed primary for advanced undergraduate and graduate courses in the social sciences dealing with issues of globalization and large-scale social change. It should also appeal to students in courses on particular themes such as the environment, global social movements, and democratic global governance. We hope it will be read by readers everywhere who seek a representative introduction to current social science on globalization and global social change.

Global Social Change

1

Introduction

CHRISTOPHER CHASE-DUNN AND SALVATORE J. BABONES

Social change is the restructuring of human social institutions: culture, consciousness, technology, organizations, settlement systems, forms of exchange, and structures of authority and decision-making. It is commonly observed that some aspects of human social change, especially those connected with technology, have greatly accelerated over the past few centuries, and the very speed of change produces new problems as people need to spend much time and energy adapting to and resisting change. Over this same period of time, the spatial scale and population size of social units, in particular the regional world-systems in which social relations have been embedded, have expanded to the point where it is necessary to analyze social change in the context of a single, globe-spanning world-system. Today, in addition to studying social change in a global context, social scientists study globalization itself as an important form of social change.

Social change has always been a central concern of sociological study, but the sheer pace and scale of social change associated with globalization challenge classical sociological perspectives on change. Emile Durkheim, Karl Marx, and Max Weber all grappled with social problems arising from the (then unprecedented) social changes occurring in nineteenth-century Europe, but today's rapid, large-scale social changes are creating problems that classical sociologists could never have imagined. Increased specialization continues at the same time that some observers note the blurring of formerly separate realms of life and the promiscuous appropriation of symbols for new and unintended purposes—a condition that has gone far beyond Emile Durkheim's concern about the emergence of normlessness. Commodification and the glorification of consumption as well as the construction of huge megamall "temples of consumption" seem to dwarf Karl Marx's observations about the "fetishism of commodities." Max Weber's concerns about the demystification of life seem quaint in the light of further massive extension of formally rational calculation and models of rational decision-making into all the remaining precontractual realms. Today's social problems are not so much different from those studied by the classical sociologists but bigger —so much bigger as to be qualitatively distinct. Understanding them requires not just bigger tools but new tools.

Social Change in Global Perspective

A global society is being formed, and to understand contemporary social change, even in the most "advanced" regions, it is necessary to understand the whole global system. Most of the chapters of this book proceed from a point of view in which national societies have been importantly affected by a larger intersocietal system for centuries and so the model of independent national societies has always been a false ideological construction produced by nationalism. The intersocietal space in which not just nations but organizations and individual people interact and form relationships is called a world-system. Premodern world-systems were bounded by limits to transportation and communication; today's modern world-system is global in scope, embracing every human being and political unit on the planet. Nationalism has been the most important form of collective identification in the modern world-system, allowing states to mobilize their populations for production and for war and reinforcing the institutional structures in which most people define their social, political, and economic realities in national terms.

The latest wave of globalization strongly challenges this institutionalized ideology of nation-states as separate worlds. More and more people have become aware that their lives are strongly affected by forces that are operating on a global scale—global markets for goods, money, and securities; global transportation and communications flows; global environmental issues; and global inequalities and issues of justice. The insight behind most of the chapters in this book contends that this recent recognition of the importance of global forces and processes is popular consciousness catching up with a reality that has long been present. Social change became world historical in the centuries after Europeans sailed to the "New World." During the nineteenth century what had formerly been largely independent "international systems" of competing and allying states in the East and the West became joined into a single global system of states.

The need to focus research questions at a global level of analysis is the subject of Chapter 2, in which "global" phenomena are distinguished from those that are merely cross-national or widespread in scope. A global phenomenon is defined as "one that represents a single, interacting system on a global scale that does not respect international borders." The physical science archetype of a global phenomenon is the atmosphere; in the sphere of social science, markets, information, and pop culture are all examples of global phenomena. Descriptions and determinants of change in global social systems of these kinds are the foci of later substantive chapters in this volume: in Part II, the trajectory of global inequalities in income and energy; in Part III, the evolution of global ecology and the physical environment; in Part IV, the dynamics of the global economic and political systems; in Part V, the mobilization of popular forces into social movements to shape or resist processes of globalization; and in Part VI, the emergence of and prospects for social, political, and economic democracy. None of these issues can be fully understood without taking a global perspective in analyzing them.

The clearest example of a kind of social change that can be studied only at a global level of analysis is the process of globalization itself (Part II). Understanding contemporary globalization requires us to compare the wave of globalization since World War II with earlier waves, especially the one in the last half of the nineteenth century, when international trade as a proportion of the whole world-economy was nearly as high as it is now. One reason why many see the contemporary wave of globalization as a completely new stage of global capitalism is that nationalism and Keynesian national development policies have been powerfully institutionalized and centrally propagated since World War II. The Keynesian national development project (the Global New Deal) was itself a world-historical response to the "Age of Extremes" (Hobsbawm 1994) and the deglobalization of the 1930s. It never created a world of separate national economies but rather focused attention on the problem of national import substitution and the development of the national welfare state.

A profit squeeze and accumulation crisis occurred in the 1970s when Japan and Germany caught up with the United States in the production of important core commodities (Brenner 2002). This crisis took place in the wake of the "world revolution of 1968," a global mobilization of radical college students who were the politically unincorporated generation produced by the massification of higher education all around the world during the 1950s and 1960s. The reactionary response to the accumulation crisis and the critiques of the radical students was Reaganism-Thatcherism, also called the "Washington Consensus" and the "globalization project" (McMichael 2004).

This response was a revival of the nineteenth-century ideology of "market magic" and an attack on the welfare state and organized labor. It borrowed the antistatist ideology of the New Left and used new communications and information technologies to globalize capitalist production, undercutting nationally organized trade unions and attacking the entitlements of the welfare state as undeserved and inefficient rents. This "global stage of capitalism" is what has brought globalization into the popular consciousness, but rather than being the first time that the world has experienced strong global processes, it is a response to the problems of capitalist accumulation as they emerged from the prior Global New Deal, which was itself a response to the earlier Age of Extremes and deglobalization. This is what we mean by saying that social change is world historical.

Social Change in World-Historical Perspective

Global social change did not begin in the late twentieth century with the latest wave of globalization. Social change, of course, has been around for as long as there have been human societies. Some forms of social change began to take on global aspects as early as the sixteenth century. The Age of Discovery, which led to regular European contact with and exploitation of Asia, sub-Saharan Africa, and the Americas, ushered in massive, global-scale changes in human society and regional ecosystems. To take one major example, aggressive Spanish exploitation of New World silver and gold resulted in the devastation of indigenous American cultures, a century of wars accompanied by massive price inflation in Europe, the economic decline of West Africa as it shifted from exporting gold to exporting slaves, and the opening up of cash-and-carry trade with China, which had no interest in European goods as such. From the sixteenth century forward, few humans have been unaffected by forces of social change operating at a global level.

The pace of global social change accelerated dramatically with the late eighteenth-century Industrial Revolution, culminating in the first wave of what can properly be called "globalization." The United Kingdom of Great Britain was the world leader in industrialization, an exporter of the key technologies (railroads, steamships, and telegraph communications), and the advocate of free trade policies and the gold standard (O'Rourke and Williamson 2000). As Germany, Belgium, France, and the United States began to catch up with and surpass the British in the production of highly profitable goods, Britain turned to high finance as a source of profits and continued to make money on money in the "beautiful" Edwardian Indian summer of the early twentieth century. The centrality of London in the global financial system was a valuable asset that prolonged the hegemony of Britain (Silver and Arrighi 2005). The British also played their other remaining card—control of a large empire in the periphery and an edge in military technology—in order to try to have their way in international matters. The Boer War in South Africa, in which they put down the resistance of Dutch farmers at great cost, was a clear example of what has been called "imperial overstretch."

The decline of British hegemony was accompanied by a decline of economic globalization from 1880 to 1900 and then by a period of imperial rivalry—two world wars with Germany. The deglobalization of the late nineteenth century and the first half of the twentieth has been called the "Age of Extremes" by the historian Eric Hobsbawm (1994). The Bolshevik Revolution of October 1917 was part of a larger challenge to the social injustices of the global order that included the Mexican Revolution of 1910, the Boxer Rebellion in China, and radical labor and national movements in most of the other countries. World War I and World War II were two long and massively destructive battles in a single struggle over who would perform the role of hegemon. Between the wars was a short wave of economic globalization in the 1920s followed by the stock market crash of 1929 and a retreat to economic nationalism and protectionism during the depression of the 1930s. Fascism was a virulent form of zealous nationalism that spread widely in the second-tier core and the semiperiphery during the Age of Extremes. This was deglobalization.

The point here is that globalization is not just a long-term trend. It is also a cycle. Waves of globalization have been followed by waves of deglobalization in the past, and this is also an entirely plausible scenario for the future. The momentum for trade globalization, for example, reached a high point with the 1995 formation of the World Trade Organization (WTO). As Part V of this volume underscores, the successes of antiglobalization movements in the past ten years have blunted the WTO's effectiveness. Similarly, Part IV questions the economic sustainability of the recent trajectory of the world-system, as Part III questions its environmental sustainability. While conventional wisdom dictates that globalization will continue to be the dominant force in global social change well into the future, it is not impossible that the process of globalization will stall or even reverse. As a case in point, an entire session at the 2002 World Congress of Sociology in Brisbane, Australia, was devoted to the open question "After Globalization?" It is difficult to detect an inflection point when you are in the midst of a transition, which is very well where we may be today.

The Future of Global Social Change

Whether or not the current wave of globalization continues, it is certain that many important processes of social change will continue to occur primarily at a global level. So long as we live in an integrated world-economy, the competition among the people and countries of the world for scarce resources (Part II) will continue. Domestic political change within the countries of the world (Part VI) will continue to be influenced by supernational forces. The physical environment we live in (Part III) will continue to be shared and shaped by all of us. All humans will continue to contribute to—and be affected by—global forces of social change.

The continuing decline of U.S. hegemony and emerging challenges to the policies of neoliberalism and neoconservativism that have been the responses of global elites to the contradictions of the most recent wave of globalization are likely to lead to a new period of deglobalization. Understanding the dynamics of uneven development and the repeated patterns of the global system in the past can be helpful tools for preventing the return to collapse and crisis that gripped the world during the last Age of Extremes.

In the United States, demographic changes and slow economic growth are going to result in important political reorganizations that will test the abilities of Americans to get along with one another in a trying time. The contemporary wave of global industrialization based on fossil fuels may have already led to a substantial overshoot in the ability of human society to sustain the biosphere. If this is the case, we may encounter environmental disasters that require global cooperation in order to restore the balance between human society and the natural systems upon which it depends. Another round of conflict over global hegemony may be forthcoming despite the current monopolization of serious military power by the United States. The "global gamble" by the neoconservatives to prop up the U.S. hegemony by playing the military card to control the world's oil supplies is likely to pour gasoline on the coals of resistance in those regions that have been left out of the wonders of globalization (Gowan 1999; Harvey 2003).

If this sounds gloomy, we should point out that the coming period of contestation is also an opportunity to create global democratic cooperative institutions that set up a more sustainable relationship between human society and the natural environment and more humane and just relationships among the peoples of the world. A global democratic and collectively rational commonwealth will probably emerge eventually unless we manage to completely extinguish ourselves (Wagar 1999). With intelligence and political action based on a world-historical understanding of global social change, it is possible that this will emerge sooner rather than later. The chimes of freedom (and necessity) are ringing.

References

Brenner, Robert. 2002. *The Boom and the Bubble: The U.S. in the World Economy*. London: Verso.

Gowan, Peter. 1999. *The Global Gamble: Washington's Faustian Bid for World Dominance*. London: Verso.

Harvey, David. 2003. *The New Imperialism*. New York: Oxford University Press.

Hobsbawm, Eric. 1994. *The Age of Extremes: A History of the World, 1914–1991*. New York: Pantheon.

McMichael, Phillip. 2004. *Development and Social Change*. Thousand Oaks, CA: Pine Forge.

O'Rourke, Kevin H. and Jeffrey G. Williamson. 2000. *Globalization and History*. Cambridge, MA: MIT Press.

Silver, Beverly and Giovanni Arrighi. 2005. "Polanyi's 'Double Movement': The *Belle Époques* of British and U.S. Hegemony Compared." In *Hegemonic Declines: Present and Past*, edited by Jonathan Friedman and Christopher Chase-Dunn. Boulder, CO: Paradigm Press.

Wagar, Warren W. 1999. *A Short History of the Future*. Chicago: University of Chicago Press.

2

Conducting Global Social Research

SALVATORE J. BABONES

The ubiquitous admonition to "think globally" has become a cliché in virtually every sphere of international endeavor, in business and government as well as in academia. Researchers are implored to develop a "scope and depth of consciousness of the world as a single place" (Robertson 1992:183). Holton (1998:35) elaborates that "it is not so much the sense of the world as a single place that matters as a sense of the interconnections that exist within that space." Taking things one step further, Robertson (1995) encourages researchers to suffuse even locally oriented work with a global perspective, creating a global-local blend: "glocalization."

In response to this call, over the past decade literally thousands of books and articles have been published that take an ostensibly global perspective in analyzing their research questions. In sociology alone, the number of journal articles published that have the word "global" in the title has risen from fewer than 50 to an average of around 200 annually in recent years (fig. 2.1). This number is a count of articles that, according to their titles, are global in orientation; it does not include the larger number of articles on the process of globalization. Any advocate of globally oriented research should be pleased, and quite satisfied, by these figures.

Globally oriented researchers, however, might wonder how it is possible that such a high level of research productivity exists in global studies, considering that we do not have reliable aggregate income, education, or even population data for most of the 200-odd countries of the world. Below the aggregate level, individual-level data are almost entirely lacking for most countries. Although data collection and collation are improving, thanks in part to the recent effort to evaluate progress toward the United Nations' Millennium Development Goals, this does not help the situation for historical data. It is puzzling that so much research productivity could be based on so little actual data.

This conundrum provokes one to ask: Just what is global social research? The intuitive answer to this is that global social research is social research

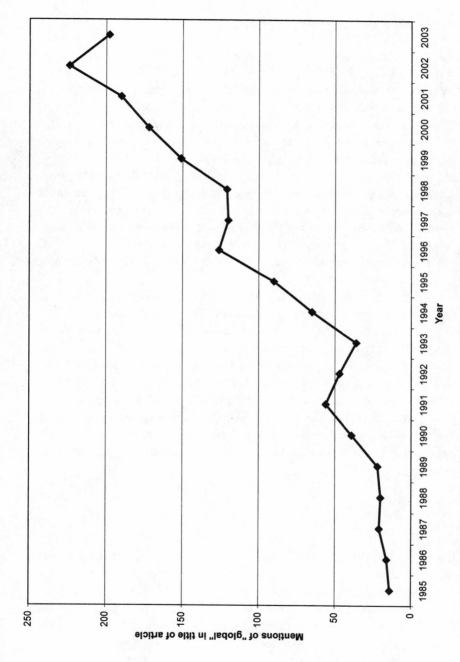

Fig. 2.1. Mentions of "Global" in the Titles of Sociology Articles. *Source: Sociological Abstracts*

based on a target population including all the countries or all the people of the world. Holding to this inclusive standard, however, implies that no existing social research is truly global in scope. This definition, then, is not adequate. A common fudge to the inclusive definition of "global" is to define broadly cross-national research as "global" when the countries included in the analyses reach some arbitrary threshold, such as accounting for greater than 90 percent of the world's population. This approach fails on two counts. First, studies may include or sample from cases representing the majority of world's population without addressing any globally oriented theme. For example, the empirical growth literature in the tradition of Barro (1991) uses data on a wide panel of countries to investigate the effects of variables such as educational policies, government consumption, private investment, and average fertility on rates of economic growth. The research is broadly cross-national, including countries that represent most of the world's population, but it does not address any mechanism that is hypothesized to operate at a global level.

Second, studies may in fact address mechanisms that operate at a global level without using data from a wide panel of countries. For example, Dolan (2004) investigates the allocation of income to structural positions in global commodity chains using data on producers in only one country, Kenya. The fact that the cases underlying her analysis are all Kenyan does not change the fact that they are being used to answer questions about global allocation processes. The research is fundamentally concerned with the operation of global, not Kenyan, phenomena. The study should thus be considered part of the body of "global" research. Clearly, a more nuanced definition of global social research than one based solely on population or number of countries is required.

"Global" as a Level of Analysis

A more productive approach is to define "global" as a level of analysis. The level of analysis of a research study is defined by the scope of the research questions underlying the study. Research that is designed to answer questions about social phenomena that operate at a global level can reasonably be labeled global social research. This is true even if the range of the cases used in analysis does not span the entire globe. So, for example, research on how a country's position in the world-economy is related to its output of greenhouse gasses (Roberts, Grimes, and Manale 2003) is pitched at a global level of analysis—it attempts to answer a research question that ties a global system of economic allocation to a global environmental problem. The fact that 154 countries are included in the analysis buttresses the case for labeling this global research but is not central to it. For example, a study covering only 66 developing countries but similarly relating global economic and environmental processes (Grimes and Kentor 2003) would also represent global social research.

By this definition much research that purports to apply to all of humanity would be excluded from the "global" label. For example, most medical research is universal in application, in the sense that human anatomy, cytology, genetics, and so on apply equally well to all people regardless of where they live. Nonetheless, typical medical research is pitched at an individual level of analysis, as the mechanisms at work in most medical models operate at the individual level. The conclusions of medical research may be universal in application, but the research questions they answer generally do not involve phenomena that operate on a global scale.

Similarly, sociological models, such as the status attainment model (Blau and Duncan 1967) linking parents' education and income to their children's education and income, may describe processes that are near universal in application. The status attainment model, for example, has been applied in Germany and Poland (Krymkowski 1991), Hungary (Luijkx et al. 2002), Japan (Kim 2003), Australia (Marjoribanks 1996), and elsewhere. Yet in its general form the level of analysis of the status attainment model is the society—it is a model that describes how a society allocates resources based on people's places within that society. A status attainment model typically would not take into account an individual's location in, for example, a global commodity chain. If it did, it would be an example of global social research, even if the model was estimated in one country only.

Defining "global" as a level of analysis distinguishes "global" as a meaningful descriptor distinct from "international" (involving a country other than one's own), "cross-national" (involving more than one country), and "comparative" (explicitly comparing countries). Relative to the term "cross-national" and its cousins, the term "global" as used here is not a subset but an oblique concept. While there is certainly some overlap between research that is cross-national in terms of the cases studied and research that is global in terms of the research questions asked, the two terms are conceptually distinct.

In his typology of comparative cross-national research designs, Kohn (1987:715–716) defines a subset of "transnational" research studies that "treat nations as components of larger international systems." This is not so different in its implications from the definition of "global" as a level of analysis, but it differs dramatically in its conceptual origins. "Global" as a level of analysis refers to the scope of the research questions asked; the research and analyses undertaken to answer those questions may be very local indeed: thus "glocalization." In an extreme example of the intersection of the local with the global, Macleod (1999) traces the impact of global business networks and the embeddedness of the tourism industry in the global economy on morality, gender roles, and cultural identity in the port city of Vueltas (population 350), on the island of Gomera in the Canary Islands.

On the other hand, for Kohn, as for Tilly (1984), Ragin (1989), and others, the "transnational" category (Tilly: "encompassing comparison"; Ragin: "larger unit formed by cases") is a subset of the universe of comparative cross-national research designs. Where cross-national comparisons are used to elucidate the influence of larger, systemic-level forces, a new supernational category is required. Generally the system-level variable is modeled as primarily exogenous and objective, as in Wallerstein's (1974) world-systems approach and the world society approach of Meyer et al. (1997); more recently, it has also been modeled as endogenous and emergent, as in McMichael's (1990) world-historical approach of incorporating comparisons. In either situation, the motivation for the creation of a new label is to account for research that is comparative but transcends the label "comparative" by incorporating systemic factors.

In contrast, global research, defined in terms of the level of analysis of the research questions addressed, need not be comparative at all, as Macleod (1999) demonstrates. While it is true that most of the research literature that Kohn labels "transnational" would also be considered "global" in terms of its level of analysis, the reverse is not true. "Transnational," as defined by Kohn, is a type of cross-national research; "global," as defined here, only sometimes involves countries. Consider, for example, the literature on global cities (Sassen 1994) and global slums (United Nations 2003): Nations, as such, are not under comparison, yet the research questions are definitely global. Similarly, recent work on global income allocation among all of the individuals of the world, reviewed in Babones and Turner (2004), is global but explicitly not cross-national.

As these examples illustrate, although the level of analysis of global social research is broadly cross-national in perspective, the units of analysis used to answer globally oriented research questions range from the smallest (individual human beings) to the largest (in the extreme case, the world as a whole). This helps explain how there can be so much research that is self-consciously "global" even though so little internationally consistent data are available with which to compare countries. Global social research encompasses much of the transnational comparative literature, but it also includes much more. Data sources and research strategies for conducting global social research depend on the units of analysis used in answering the research questions posed. While much attention has been given to globally oriented research designs that take the country as the unit of analysis, research based on data collected at the individual, regional, area, and world levels are important as well. The key to differentiating global social research as a distinct category lies in the questions asked, not in the evidence amassed to answer those questions.

Asking Global Research Questions

If global social research is to be defined in terms of the level of analysis of the research questions addressed, then the practice of global social research must begin with the formulation of research questions that are global in scope. Some topics, such as the time-series relationship between fossil fuel consumption and average world temperatures (Kerr 2004), can be addressed only at a global level. For other topics, the decision to pose questions at a global level is a choice rather than a necessity. For most topics in social research, global forces and mechanisms, while perhaps relevant, are not central. There is no virtue in introducing a global perspective on a problem when none is called for. In some research areas, however, a global (as opposed to merely international, cross-national, or even comparative) perspective is becoming increasingly indispensable: the sociology of culture, environmental sociology, and political economics, to name a few. In other fields of social research, global research questions are emerging as important subfields; for example, global social movements. Given the steady march of "globalization" in (seemingly) every field, the secular trend is undoubtedly toward more rather than less globally oriented research.

Most social research questions are about processes that operate at a regional or societal level. This is reflected in the fact that most sample surveys are keyed to a regional (metropolitan area, state, province) or national target population. By way of review, the target population of a study is the group to which the researchers intend to generalize their findings. So long as every individual in the target population has an equal probability of being sampled for inclusion in the study, the study's sample-based results can be generalized to answer questions posed at the level of the target population. Typical social problems research topics, such as the effects of poverty, race, or gender on program participation, crime, or divorce are generally studied at the level of the country or region. The implication is that while the forces determining individual outcomes in each of these areas might be similar across countries, those forces operate in the context of a specific country's social system. Concepts like "poverty," "race," and "gender" are constructed differently in different societies.

Thus survey-based studies tend to be based on national or regional samples because the research questions typically answered using sample surveys tend to be pitched at those levels. Even the few international surveys that exist (such as the World Values Survey) are constructed to be variously representative of each of the participating countries, not representative of the world as a whole. Researchers typically use the World Values Survey to compare stratification and opinion-formation systems in different countries, rather than to construct global systems. For example, Cao and Hou (2001) use the World Values Survey to compare attitudes toward police in the United States and China. They model each country's system of beliefs separately; there is no implication in the article that individual attitudes toward authority are shaped by global-level forces.

Nonetheless, one could imagine a study that is designed to model attitudes toward authority at a global level of analysis. Certainly the protest movements of the 1960s and 1970s operated at a global level to encourage individuals to question authority. When Abbie Hoffman (1971) exhorted readers to "Steal This Book," the advice had a global impact on culture, even if that advice was focused on "Amerikan" examples. Similarly, Corinne Maier (2004) is now encouraging the world to say "Hello to Laziness," despite the fact that her essay on working as little as possible is written for a French audience. Can one measure the impact of global cultural forces on individual attitudes? Surveys like the World Values Survey could be used to trace across multiple countries corresponding movements in attitudes toward authority that are attributable to global cultural change.

Something like this has been done by Tsutsui (2004), using not individual persons but individual social movements as the units of analysis. Taking a global society perspective (Meyer et al. 1997) to the study of social movements, Tsutsui found that the intensity of ethnic social movements mobilization is influenced by local social movements' ties to global nongovernmental organizations. In Tsutsui's theoretical model, global legitimization of local social movements affects their individual chances of success. This is a prime example of a global-level force (in this case, global civil society) affecting individual-level outcomes, that is, "glocalization" (Robertson 1995).

If the examples above illustrate how global forces can affect local phenomena, it is also true that local forces can affect global phenomena. For example, national elections that are decided primarily on domestic issues can still have a profound impact on the global governance system. Regional terrorist movements can affect the global security system. Municipal tax policies can shift the loci of production in global commodity chains. Whether social research involves global phenomena as inputs or outcomes, the resulting studies are global in their level of analysis. Of course, if both sides of the causal arrow are global phenomena, the research question is also global. This suggests a simple four-square typology of global research questions (fig. 2.2).

Given global-level phenomena, it is clear that research questions involving them must be pitched at a global level or at least involve some degree of global orientation. All social research, however, involves some phenomena that, at a stretch, can be construed as subject to global influences. What kind of social phenomena truly operate at a global level, such that questions about them are unambiguously "global"? As Boli, Elliot, and Bieri (2004:396) point out, "theories to explain why particular types of social problems are seen as global while most types have yet to be constructed as arenas for global moral combat are notable by their absence." The perspective taken here is that "global" should be defined in terms of the level of analysis; what does this imply for the types of problems that raise inherently global research questions? Just what are "global" social phenomena?

Perhaps the ideal type of a global phenomenon is atmospheric pollution. The atmosphere pays no regard to international boundaries; it is a single global system in which changes at any one point will eventually work their way through to affect the entire system. These two criteria read like the core

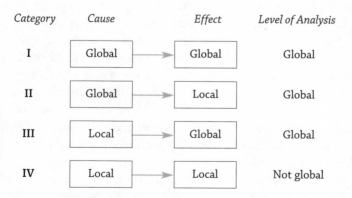

Category	Cause	Effect	Level of Analysis
I	Global →	Global	Global
II	Global →	Local	Global
III	Local →	Global	Global
IV	Local →	Local	Not global

Fig. 2.2. Components of Globally Oriented Research Questions

of a reasonable definition for global (social or other) phenomena. Thus, a global social phenomenon may be defined as one that represents a single, interacting system on a global scale that does not respect international borders. The first criterion specifies that to be considered "global" a social phenomenon must in some sense be unified at a global level. It must present the same face from many different perspectives. In concrete terms, it is meaningful to speak of "the atmosphere" as a single, undifferentiated unit, whether one is in Atlanta or Addis Ababa.

Though less obvious, the second qualifying criterion is at least as important as the first. A social phenomenon that respects national boundaries is not "global" in nature. Otherwise, nearly every aspect of a society's economic and cultural systems would be labeled global. Consider labor markets. Owing to immigration restrictions and low labor mobility, labor markets operate primarily at the national and regional levels. Every labor market does, however, have an attenuated effect on labor markets throughout the world. Oversupply of labor will spur emigration, and undersupply of labor will spur immigration. Thus, to some extent, the world's labor market can be thought of as a single, interacting system. Nonetheless, labor markets do respect international boundaries. Except perhaps in a few highly specialized areas such as investment banking or intellectual property law, it is not meaningful to speak of a "global labor market." People discussing "the labor market" in Atlanta are unlikely to care much about events in Addis Ababa or even Albuquerque.

What kinds of social phenomena should be labeled global? The social phenomena that are closest to the ideal type are probably the global commodity markets. Commodities like coffee, soybeans, oil, gold, and steel, to name a few, are each sold in a single global market where, for all practical purposes, one can imagine that all the world's output is concentrated in a single auction and sold to the highest bidder, regardless of nationality. Markets for other tradable, but less fungible, goods, such as picture tubes and computer memory chips, are very close to this ideal type, though prices are set through direct negotiations between buyers and sellers, rather than on an organized auction market. In general, the markets for all goods that can be shipped and sold easily in bulk across borders can be thought of as global markets. For similar reasons, many markets for services (especially wholesale financial services) are global as well.

Beyond markets, many other economic phenomena, such as the commodity chains (Hopkins and Wallerstein 1986; Gereffi and Korzeniewicz 1994) through which raw materials are transformed into finished products, are also global in scope. Global social phenomena, however, are not limited to economic phenomena. Many aspects of "the media" are globally oriented, and many electronic media (such as the Internet) are primarily global in scope. Information itself is increasingly being construed in global terms. There are no national border posts on the "information superhighway."

Systems of human organization can also be global in scope. At opposite (and often opposing) ends of the spectrum of global organizations are, on the one hand, multinational corporations (MNCs) and intergovernmental organizations (IGOs) and, on the other hand, global social movements (GSMs) and international nongovernmental organizations (INGOs). The individual trees in this forest of acronyms may appear to be planted in one country, but under the ground and overhead their spread does not respect international borders. For example, a typical MNC headquartered in the United States raises capital from shares and bonds issued simultaneously in many countries and owned by a global investor base (roots) and has operating subsidiaries branching out to cover both developed and developing countries (leaves). The "company" may appear to be American, but ultimately the American headquarters operates somewhat like the stem of a tree, taking in capital and passing it along to the MNC's various operations. Similarly, at the opposite pole GSMs build networks of support across many countries to support action in many (potentially other) countries.

The definition of a global social phenomenon as a single interacting system on a global scale that does not respect international borders is inclusive enough to cover a variety of phenomena ranging from markets to the environment to social movements. It also draws boundaries that are exclusive enough to eliminate phenomena that are only partially or casually global in nature. Research questions involving global social phenomena as either cause or effect (or both) can reasonably be defined as being global in scope, and social research based on these questions can reasonably be defined as global social research. Global social research, however, does not necessarily require global evidence. The units of analysis in global social research may range from the unambiguously local to the truly global, as discussed in the next section.

Units of Analysis in Global Research

Even when the research question asked is global in scope, the units of analysis used in answering that questions need not be. Units of analysis used in global social research can range from the smallest (the individual human or sensor) to the largest (the world itself at different points in time). Data sources used for globally oriented research correspond to these units of analysis. Thus, for a study using individuals as its units of analysis, the data source may be field interviews, while for a study using the world as its unit of analysis, the data source might be published aggregate statistics (fig. 2.3). What ties together all global research, regardless of the units of analysis, are the nature of the research question and the nature of its solution. Where these are global in scope, the specific units used to study them are not particularly relevant in distinguishing the research as global. On the contrary: the best global social research might use a variety of units of analysis to tackle different aspects of a globally oriented research question.

In figure 2.3 and in the subsections below, five specific "levels" (so to speak) of units of analysis are discussed: the individual, the region, the country, the area, and the world. This list is meant to be illustrative, rather than exhaustive. The theme that unifies these five subsections is that global social research can be conducted in sometimes surprising ways, as evidenced by units that differ wildly in scale. Specific research studies are cited for each unit of analysis to make this point concrete.

The Individual as a Unit of Analysis

It is tempting to view "the world" as a collection of individual human beings and any study that incorporates all those human beings (collectively or via probability sampling) as a global study. Representative data on all the human beings in the world are, however, nonexistent. The World Values Survey does come close, having been conducted at different times in as many as 65 countries. Unfortunately, most of the published research based on the World Values Survey to date has focused on comparing countries rather than on integrating individuals at a global level without regard to their citizenship status. A serious debate has even surfaced over whether it is meaningful to use cross-national survey data to study individual (as opposed to country-average) attitudes (Seligson 2002; Inglehart and Welzel 2003). Of course, once individual-level data have been aggregated for a comparison of national averages, the individual is no longer the unit of analysis.

More common than studies that attempt to include all individual humans in their target populations are studies conducted on individuals in one locale that nonetheless attempt to shed light on global-level research questions. For example, Inhorn (2003) uses fieldwork among Egyptian couples and clinic doctors to study infertility as a global phenomenon. Her objective is to understand how various factors that cut across national and cultural borders affect global demand for new reproductive technologies. Interviews with indi-

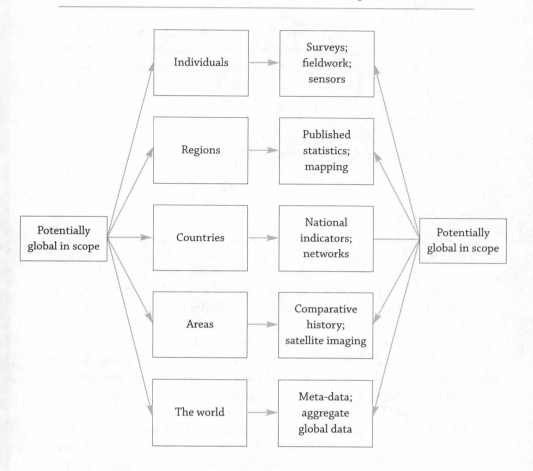

Fig. 2.3. Schematic of the Process of Conducting Global Social Research

viduals and couples are used to shed light on the driving forces behind the global expansion of new technologies, such as in vitro fertilization, even in areas of the world for which these technologies are prohibitively expensive. While the research itself is emphatically local, its implications, in terms of the research questions it is designed to answer, are explicitly global.

It is sometimes meaningful to speak of research at an individual level of analysis when the cases being studied are not individual human beings but rather organizations (which are "legal individuals"), sensors (such as weather buoys), newspaper articles, or events. An example of the last is Wood's (2004) study of antiglobalization movements. Wood's unit of analysis was the individual protest event; she studied 467 such events occurring in 432 cities around the world. Her objective was to better understand evolving patterns in the targeting of antiglobalization protests before and after the September 11 terrorist attacks. Even though she studied specific events, each of which occurred in a single, local context, the phenomena she investigated were global in scope—she found that protest targets and strategies across many locales varied in unison in response to global forces. Changes in antiglobalization protest tactics in the United States following the September 11 attacks quickly diffused through GSM networks to affect protest events worldwide.

The Region as a Unit of Analysis

Saskia Sassen's (1994) well-known work on cities in a global economy has been alluded to above. A more recent example of a study that uses city data to investigate globally oriented research questions is Wilkinson's (2002) study of the structure of the Old World world-system(s) from 1360 BC to AD 1900. Wilkinson uses the location of the world's largest city by population as an indicator of the level of development of each of the competing world-systems. He also uses the relative sizes of leading cities across the Old World as an indicator of the level of differentiation among world-systems. Though the units of analysis themselves are cities, the phenomena being studied are global in scope (or as global as could be before the Old World's intrusion on the New in 1492).

In addition to cities, counties, metropolitan areas, states/provinces, and similar regional units of analysis can provide the data for global research. Nor are political units the only kinds of regions that can serve as units of analysis in global research. Wimmer (2001) shows how uniform global forces can have widely differing local effects in his comparative-historical study of river valleys in Mexico and Iraq. What distinguishes research designs that use regions as opposed to individuals as the units of analysis is the need for aggregation. This need is also evident in studies based on countries, but these are differentiated by the special character of the sovereign country as the basic building block of the international system.

Many would argue that regional units (whether human settlements like cities or natural zones like watersheds) are a more "natural" unit of analysis than the country. When appropriately defined, regions are far more comparable to one another than are countries, making regions more suitable as multiple cases in a single analysis. On the other hand, while regions may be inherently more comparable than countries, the data collected on them are less standardized. So although regions are often more comparable, countries are generally easier to compare, and much (if not most) global social research uses the countries as the units of analysis.

The Country as a Unit of Analysis

As the basic political unit in today's world, the country is in many respects the basic statistical unit as well. A plethora of internationally comparable data exist at the country level. The World Bank's (2004) World Development Indicators database alone contains 550 data fields, each a multiyear time series, based on the country as the unit of analysis. The United Nations agencies and many other IGOs and INGOs also publish data at the country level. In addition, as noted above, studies based on international surveys such as the World Values Survey often aggregate individual-level data to the country level. While virtually none of these data are truly global in scope, all of them can be used to support national and cross-national research designs that address globally oriented research questions.

Illustrating this point, Alderson and Nielsen (2002) examine recent trends in income inequality in 16 Organisation for Economic Co-operation and Development (OECD) countries. A main driver of their model of changes in inequality in these rich, developed countries is the changing structure of the world-economy: The shift of manufacturing jobs from developed to developing countries affects the income structures of the developed countries themselves (and also those of developing countries, though this is not examined). The globalization of the world-economy (a global phenomenon, as defined above) is their main independent variable of interest, even though their data are drawn from only a thin, elite layer of the world-economy.

Since countries are the fundamental units of the world polity, they share many traits in common with individuals as units of analysis. Indeed, they are commonly anthropomorphized as actors. This sense of countries-as-individuals creates interesting possibilities for research design, though it also introduces subtle pitfalls, as discussed in the next section. One major class of analytical strategies designed for individuals that has been applied to countries is social network analysis.

In network analyses of countries, countries are generally modeled as the nodes of the social network, while the various treaties and trading relationships that connect them are modeled as the edges. Research in this methodological tradition has been used to elucidate the economic (Smith and White 1991) and political (Kick 1987) structures of the modern world-system, as well as to attempt to discredit those perceived structures (Van Rossem 1996).

One objective of these network analytical studies is to classify countries by position in the world-system (an objective at the country level of analysis), but a second, more important objective is to understand the structure of the global world-system as a whole and how it evolves over time. Here, in the interstitial ether within which countries exist, is the essential subject matter of global social research.

Countries are especially important as units of analysis for global social research because it is statistically feasible to aggregate countries into a picture of the world as a whole. This is generally not possible with the existing individual- and regional-level data. While it is certainly true that the world is the sum of its individuals or the sum of its regions, statistically it is not currently possible to take those sums. With country-level data, it is possible. Thus, whether or not it is always appropriate, global social research is most often conducted using countries as the units of analysis.

The Area as a Unit of Analysis

Much less common is the use of supernational areas as units of analysis in global social research. Only in world-systems analysis is this done routinely, and even there most scholars find it more convenient to use countries, rather than world-systems or their zones, as the units of analysis. A recent study that does use world-systems in toto as its units of analysis is Turchin and Hall (2003). Turchin and Hall study the timing of cycles of hegemony across all the Old World world-systems, examining potential theoretical explanations for the observed synchronicities, such as global climate change and global epidemics. These global phenomena simultaneously affect supernational systems across the world.

World-systems as area-level units of analysis are meaningful only for the premodern era, since the modern era is characterized by a single, global world-system. The modern world-system, however, is generally modeled as being composed of three interacting zones: the core, the semiperiphery, and the periphery of the world-system. Some studies in the world-systems tradition take these zones as their units of analysis, notably Arrighi and Drangel (1986). Arrighi and Drangel are mainly concerned with the creation and maintenance of the boundaries that distinguish the middle, semiperipheral zone of the world-economy. They aggregate from country data to create synthetic units of analysis representing each of the three zones at different points in time. In their model, the (largely internal) dynamics of each zone create the emergent structure of the global world-economy.

The World as a Unit of Analysis

While many global phenomena can be studied using subglobal (and indeed very local) units of analysis, some require a broader view, in which the world as a whole becomes the unit of analysis. A recent example is Chase-Dunn, Kawano, and Brewer (2000), who chart the progress of global trade integration over the past 200 or more years. Although a single country's (or even individual's) integration into the global trading system could be studied using subglobal units of analysis, studying the evolution of the trading system as a whole requires data on the system as a whole. Chase-Dunn and his collaborators find evidence for two great waves of global integration, one peaking at the end of the nineteenth century and the second ongoing today. The data series they use to support this conclusion is the annual average level of international trade as a percentage of world economic output, an aggregation of national data to a world level.

A similar use of aggregated national data to represent an attribute of a global system is found in the debate over the trajectory of international income inequality (Korzeniewicz and Moran 1997; Firebaugh 1999; Babones 2002). Here national output data are used to compute a summary global measure of inequality, which is then tracked over time. Interestingly, in this literature the global measure, typically a Gini coefficient, is more than the sum of its parts; the Gini coefficient depends on the overall shape of the global income distribution and is not a simple sum or average. In other words, while aggregate world output is simply a sum of many country outputs, aggregate world inequality is not a simple sum of local inequalities. It is an emergent quality of the world-economy itself.

To date, most social research that uses the world as its unit of analysis is focused on economic statistics. This is unlikely to remain the case much longer. Increasing interest in noneconomic global processes, such as global energy usage, global environmental change, and global social movements, is increasing the use of the world itself as an analytical unit in a variety of fields. As a perception of the world as a single, interacting system becomes more widespread, it is likely that in the next decade social researchers will make more use of world-level data from the physical and biological sciences as both dependent and independent variables. Average temperature, average rainfall, temperature and rainfall variability, air and water pollution, species diversity, human genetic diversity, and the like will be familiar measures for global social researchers in the not-so-distant future.

Challenges in Conducting Global Research

The study of global social phenomena raises several difficulties that are not commonly encountered when research questions are posed at less comprehensive levels. Problems of arising from aggregation, diffusion, and path dependence, to name three, plague any attempt at answering questions that are posed at a global level. Ultimately, all these problems arise from the fact that there is only one world available for us to study, and when the world itself is the scope of the analysis, additional worlds are not available for validating initial results. Similarly, since the number of competing interpretations of global phenomena generally exceeds one, it is often impossible to evaluate the relative merits of competing theories. The one-world problem permeates all global research, in the social sciences as well as in the physical and biological sciences.

Specific challenges can sometimes be met through careful attention to research methods. For example, a common problem in global social research is inappropriate aggregation. Goesling (2001), for example, in studying global income inequality, appropriately aggregates national income levels to compute summary inequality measures, such as the Gini coefficient. The Gini coefficient (like other measures of inequality) is based on an transfer principle that any income transfer from a richer to a poorer individual reduces the measured level of inequality. This makes sense for national income, which (in some models at least) is allocated across the countries of the world by forces in the world-economy operating at a global level.

Goesling goes on, however, to apply the same models to the global distribution of health (Goesling and Firebaugh 2004), operationalized as national average life expectancy. There is no meaningful sense in which years of life are directly transferable from high-health to low-health countries. In the absence of a careful and well-documented theoretical model, Gini coefficients should not be applied to life expectancy data. In other words, while the world-economy clearly represents a single, interacting system on a global scale, the world distribution of health does not. A better way to attack the problem would be to model health as an indicator of some phenomenon that is appropriate to measure at the global level: for instance, income, natural resources, or environmental degradation.

Some difficulties with conducting global social research cannot be solved but can be recognized and managed. The classic example is cultural diffusion: Galton's problem. Nineteenth-century British geneticist Francis Galton posed the problem with regard to marriage customs in different cultures. Did customs originate independently in each culture, or did multiple cultures share a common source for their customs? Galton's problem was illustrated on a grand scale in the twentieth century by Norwegian anthropologist Thor Heyerdahl. Heyerdahl's dramatic transoceanic voyages using aboriginal materials, designs, and navigational technologies demonstrated the possibility of cultural diffusion between widely dispersed populations, first from Peru to Polynesia and later from Egypt to Central America. Of course, today no culture is free of the impact of the modern world, but Heyerdahl showed that Galton's problem applied well before the modern era.

Because of Galton's problem, even when the units of analysis in global social research are subglobal, making it possible to compare multiple cases, it is often difficult to distinguish the effects of global forces from those of cultural diffusion. For example, when firms around the world scramble to adopt a uniform global set of practices of corporate governance, is this evidence of concerted action at the global level of a small group of controllers of the global economy (Carroll and Carson 2003), or is it merely Galton's problem of cultural diffusion at work? Galton's problem is at the heart of the debate between the world-systems and world society approaches to understanding the phenomenon of globalization.

Can Galton's problem be controlled, or is it always fatal? Naroll (1968) suggested that researchers compare cases for which diffusion would have been impossible, but as Heyerdahl demonstrated, this is a difficult proposition for the ancient world, and of course it is not applicable to the modern world whatsoever. Chase-Dunn (1989:311) suggests a better way to mitigate Galton's problem: endogenize it. Accounting for cultural diffusion in the conceptual models underlying global social research helps analysts avoid the pitfalls of ignoring its role as a potential confounder. While it may not be possible to control for diffusion statistically, it should be possible to take diffusion into account and to make adjustments for it.

Complementary to Galton's problem of diffusion in space is the problem of diffusion in time, or path dependency. In the technical literature, this is known as temporal autocorrelation— the correlation of observations in adjacent time periods. A researcher might hypothesize, for example, that global greenhouse gas emission is tied to the levels of the world's population and industrial output, but the one-world problem implies that the only way to correlate these quantities is by using multiple time points for the same unit of analysis (the world). The problem is that levels of each of these three variables are strongly path-dependent.

Ideally, this problem is solved through differencing: Instead of studying the levels of a global phenomenon (like income inequality or energy use) at a given point in time, the researcher studies changes in that phenomenon over time. However, this dramatically reduces the power of any statistical analysis. Moreover, the question arises as to the appropriate period over which data should be differenced, what Chase-Dunn (1989:321–322) calls the "width of a time point." It is not clear that annual changes in population will be tied to annual changes in pollution; nor is a thousand-year interval likely justified. The appropriate period is somewhere in the middle, but where? There is no good theoretical guidance for answering this or other, similar questions.

A Manifesto for Global Studies

Global social research can profitably be defined in terms of levels of analysis: Global social research is research that is designed to answer questions about social phenomena that operate at a global level. What distinguishes truly global research from broadly cross-national or human-universal research is its focus on unified global-scale systems that do not respect international borders. The emphasis on scale distinguishes global social research from research on universal human institutions that might be found everywhere in the world, such as the family. The disrespect for international borders distinguishes global social research from cross-national research more broadly, though much global research is implicitly cross-national as well.

If the qualifier "social" is dropped from the foregoing passage, the term "global research," whether social, biological, physical, or a combination of all three, is equally meaningful. Global research is research that is designed to answer questions about social phenomena that operate at a global level, and what distinguishes global phenomena from the merely universal is their nature as global-scale systems that do not respect international borders. Given current trends in academia and wider society, it is likely that coming years will witness an explosion in explicitly global research. Much of this research, particularly in the physical sciences, will take the world as its unit of analysis, a trend that will only slowly be followed by the social sciences. On the other hand, the physical sciences will begin to learn from the social sciences how to address globally oriented research questions with subglobal data. In this area, the social sciences excel.

Ideally, the future will bring more research collaboration among social, biological, and physical scientists. Cross-citation is no substitute for active collaboration; even researchers in adjacent disciplines are generally a decade out of date on one another's literatures. Social, biological, and physical scientists are far enough apart in training and temperament that their ability to cross-cite is virtually nil. Active collaboration among scholars conducting global research from widely divergent angles is the necessary solution. It is not in doubt that the future will bring more collaboration, since any amount of collaboration is more than none, and today we have none. In the future, collaborative global research, bringing social, biological, and physical scientists together in multidisciplinary study teams, will creatively address problems that we have not yet even identified.

Note

The author would like to thank Prof. Burkart Holzner for a close reading of and comments on an earlier draft of this chapter.

References

Alderson, Arthur S. and François Nielsen. 2002. "Globalization and the Great U-Turn: Income Inequality Trends in 16 OECD Countries." *American Journal of Sociology* 107:1244–1299.

Arrighi, Giovanni and Jessica Drangel. 1986. "The Stratification of the World-Economy: An Exploration of the Semiperipheral Zone." *Review* 10:9–74.

Babones, Salvatore J. 2002. "Population and Sample Selection Effects in Measuring International Income Inequality." *Journal of World-Systems Research* 8:1–22.

Babones, Salvatore J. and Jonathan H. Turner. 2004. "Global Inequality." Pp. 101–120 in *Handbook of Social Problems: A Comparative International Perspective,* edited by George Ritzer. Thousand Oaks, CA: Sage Publications.

Barro, Robert J. 1991. "Economic Growth in a Cross-Section of Countries." *Quarterly Journal of Economics* 106:407–443.

Blau, Peter M. and Otis Dudley Duncan. 1967. *The American Occupational Structure.* New York: Wiley.

Boli, John, Michael A. Elliot, and Franziska Bieri. 2004. "Globalization." Pp. 389–415 in *Handbook of Social Problems: A Comparative International Perspective,* edited by George Ritzer. Thousand Oaks, CA: Sage Publications.

Cao, Liqun and Charles Hou. 2001. "A Comparison of Confidence in the Police in China and in the United States." *Journal of Criminal Justice* 29:87–99.

Carroll, William K. and Colin Carson. 2003. "Forging a New Hegemony? The Role of Transnational Policy Groups in the Network and Discourses of Global Corporate Governance." *Journal of World-Systems Research* 9:67–102.

Chase-Dunn, Christopher K. 1989. *Global Formation: Structures of the World-Economy.* Cambridge, MA: Basil Blackwell.

Chase-Dunn, Christopher K., Yukio Kawano, and Benjamin D. Brewer. 2000. "Trade Globalization since 1975: Waves of Integration in the World-System." *American Sociological Review* 65:77–95.

Dolan, Catherine S. 2004. "On Farm and Packhouse: Employment at the Bottom of a Global Value Chain." *Rural Sociology* 69:99–126.

Firebaugh, Glenn. 1999. "Empirics of World Income Inequality." *American Journal of Sociology* 104:1597–1630.

Gereffi, Gary and Miguel Korzeniewicz, eds. 1994. *Commodity Chains and Global Capitalism*. Westport, CT: Praeger.

Goesling, Brian. 2001. "Changing Income Inequalities within and between Nations: New Evidence." *American Sociological Review* 66:745–761.

Goesling, Brian and Glenn Firebaugh. 2004. "The Trend in International Health Inequality." *Population and Development Review* 30:131–146.

Grimes, Peter and Jeffrey Kentor. 2003. "Exporting the Greenhouse: Foreign Capital Penetration and CO2 Emissions 1980–1996." *Journal of World-Systems Research* 9:261–275.

Hoffman, Abbie. 1971. *Steal This Book*. New York: Grove Press.

Holton, Robert J. 1998. *Globalization and the Nation-State*. London: Macmillan Press.

Hopkins, Terence and Immanuel Wallerstein. 1986. "Commodity Chains in the World Economy Prior to 1800." *Review* 10:157–170.

Inglehart, Ronald and Christian Welzel. 2003. "Political Culture and Democracy: Analyzing Cross-Level Linkages." *Comparative Politics* 36:61–79.

Inhorn, Marcia C. 2003. "Global Infertility and the Globalization of New Reproductive Technologies: Illustrations from Egypt." *Social Science and Medicine* 56:1837–1851.

Kerr, Richard A. 2004. "Three Degrees of Consensus." *Science* 305:932–935.

Kick, Edward L. 1987. "World-System Structure, Nationalist Development, and the Prospects for a Socialist World Order." Pp. 127–155 in *America's Changing Role in the World-System*, edited by Terry Boswell and Albert Bergesen. New York: Praeger.

Kim, Myungsoo. 2003. "Ethnic Stratification and Inter-Generational Differences in Japan: A Comparative Study of Korean and Japanese Status Attainment." *International Journal of Japanese Sociology* 12:6–16.

Kohn, Melvin L. 1987. "Cross-National Research as an Analytic Strategy." *American Sociological Review* 52:713–731.

Korzeniewicz, Roberto Patricio and Timothy Patrick Moran. 1997. "World-Economic Trends in the Distribution of Income, 1965–1992." *American Journal of Sociology* 102:1000–1039.

Krymkowski, Daniel H. 1991. "The Process of Status Attainment among Men in Poland, the U.S., and West Germany." *American Sociological Review* 56:46–59.

Luijkx, Ruud, Peter Robert, Paul M. de Graaf, and Harry B.G. Ganzeboom. 2002. "Changes in Status Attainment in Hungary between 1910 and 1989: Trendless Fluctuation or Systematic Change?" *European Societies* 4:107–140.

Macleod, Donald V. L. 1999. "Tourism and the Globalization of a Canary Island." *Journal of the Royal Anthropological Institute* 5:443–456.

Maier, Corinne. 2004. *Bonjour Paresse, De l'Art et de la Nécessité d'en Faire le Moins Possible en Entreprise.* Paris: Éditions Michalon.

Marjoribanks, Kevin A. 1996. "Family Environment Model and Australian Young Adults' Social-Status Attainment: A Follow-Up Analysis." *International Journal of Sociology of the Family* 26:101–112.

McMichael, Philip. 1990. "Incorporating Comparison within a World-Historical Perspective: An Alternative Comparative Method." *American Sociological Review* 55: 385–397.

Meyer, John W., John Boli, George M. Thomas, and Francisco Ramirez. 1997. "World Society and the Nation-State." *American Journal of Sociology* 103:144–181.

Naroll, Raoul. 1968. "Some Thoughts on Comparative Method in Cultural Anthropology." Pp. 236–277 in *Methodology in Social Research,* edited by Hubert M. Blalock Jr. and Ann B. Blalock. New York: McGraw-Hill.

Ragin, Charles. 1989. "New Directions in Comparative Research." Pp. 57–76 in *Cross-National Research in Sociology,* edited by Melvin L. Kohn. Newbury Park, CA: Sage Publications.

Roberts, J. Timmons, Peter E. Grimes, and Jodie L. Manale. 2003. "Social Roots of Global Environmental Change: A World-Systems Analysis of Carbon Dioxide Emissions." *Journal of World-Systems Research* 9:277–315.

Robertson, Roland. 1992. *Globalization: Social Theory and Global Culture.* London: Sage Publications.

———. 1995. "Glocalization: Time-Space and Homogeneity-Heterogeneity." Pp. 25–44 in *Global Modernities,* edited by Mike Featherstone, Scott Lash, and Roland Robertson. Thousand Oaks, CA: Sage Publications.

Sassen, Saskia. 1994. *Cities in a World Economy.* Thousand Oaks, CA: Pine Forge Press.

Seligson, Mitchell A. 2002. "The Renaissance of Political Culture or the Renaissance of the Ecological Fallacy?" *Comparative Politics* 34:273–292.

Smith, David A. and Douglas R. White. 1991. "Structure and Dynamics of the Global Economy Network Analysis of International Trade 1965–80." *Social Forces* 70:857–893.

Tilly, Charles. 1984. Big Structures, Large Processes, Huge Comparisons. New York: Russell Sage Foundation.

Tsutsui, Kiyoteru. 2004. "Global Civil Society and Ethnic Social Movements in the Contemporary World." *Sociological Forum* 19:63–87.

Turchin, Peter and Thomas D. Hall. 2003. "Spatial Synchrony among and within World–Systems: Insights from Theoretical Sociology." *Journal of World-Systems Research* 9:37–64.

United Nations. 2003. *The Challenge of Slums: Global Report on Human Settlements.* London: Earthscan Publications.

Van Rossem, Ronan. 1996. "The World-System Paradigm as General Theory of Development: A Cross-National Test." *American Sociological Review* 61:508–527.

Wallerstein, Immanuel. 1974. *The Modern World-System*. Vol. 1: *Capitalist Agriculture and the Origins of the European World-Economy in the Sixteenth Century*. New York: Academic Press.

Wilkinson, David. 2002. "The Status of the Far Eastern Civilization/World System: Evidence from City Data. *Journal of World-Systems Research* 8:292–328.

Wimmer, Andreas. 2001. "Globalizations Avant la Lettre: A Comparative View of Isomorphization and Heteromorphization in an Inter-Connecting World." *Comparative Studies in Society and History* 43:435–466.

Wood, Lesley J. 2004. "Breaking the Bank and Taking to the Streets: How Protesters Target Neoliberalism." *Journal of World-Systems Research* 10:69–89.

World Bank. 2004. *World Development Indicators 2004*. Washington, DC: World Bank.

I | What Is Globalization?

3

Global Social Change in the Long Run

THOMAS D. HALL AND CHRISTOPHER CHASE-DUNN

The comparative world-systems perspective is a strategy for explaining social change that focuses on whole intersocietal systems rather than single societies. The main insight is that important interaction networks (trade, information flows, alliances, and fighting) have woven polities and cultures together since the beginning of human social evolution. Explanations of social change need to take intersocietal systems (world-systems) as the units that evolve. But intersocietal interaction networks were rather small when transportation was mainly a matter of hiking with a pack. Globalization, in the sense of the expansion and intensification of larger interaction networks, has been increasing for millennia, albeit unevenly and in waves.

World-systems are systems of societies. Systemness means that these societies are interacting with one another in important ways—interactions are two-way, necessary, structured, regularized, and reproductive. Systemic interconnectedness exists when interactions importantly influence the lives of people within societies and are consequential for social continuity or social change. World-systems may not cover the entire surface of the planet. Some extend over only parts of the Earth. The word *world* refers to the importantly connected interaction networks in which people live, whether these are spatially small or large.

Only the modern world-system has become a global (Earth-wide) system composed of national societies and their states. It is a single economy composed of international trade and capital flows, transnational corporations that produce goods and services on several continents, and all the economic transactions that occur within countries and at local levels. The whole world-system is more than just international relations. It is the whole system of human interactions. The world economy is all the economic interactions of all the people on Earth, not just international trade and investment.

The modern world-system is structured politically as an interstate system—a system of competing and allying states. Political scientists commonly call this the international system, and it is the main focus of the field of international relations. Some of these states are much more powerful than others, but the main organizational feature of the world political system is that it is multicentric. There is no world state. Rather, there is a system of states. This is a fundamentally important feature of the modern system and of many earlier regional world-systems as well.

When we discuss and compare different kinds of world-systems, it is important to use concepts that are applicable to all of them. "Polity" is a more general term that means any organization with a single authority that claims sovereign control over a territory or a group of people. Polities include bands, tribes, and chiefdoms as well as states. All world-systems are politically composed of multiple interacting polities. Thus we can fruitfully compare the modern interstate system with earlier systems in which there were tribes or chiefdoms but no states.

In the modern world-system it is important to distinguish between nations and states. Nations are groups of people who share a common culture and a common language. Conationals identify with one another as members of a group with a shared history, similar food preferences, and ideas of proper behavior. To a varying extent nations constitute a community of people who are willing to make sacrifices for one another. States are formal organizations such as bureaucracies that exercise and control legitimate violence within a specific territory. Some states in the modern world-system are nation-states, in which a single nation has its own state. But others are multinational states, in which more than one nation is controlled by the same state. Ethnic groups are subnations, usually minorities within states in which there is a larger national group. Ethnic groups and nations are sociologically similar in that they are both groups of people who identify with one another and share a common culture, but they often differ with regard to their relationship with states. Ethnic groups are minorities, whereas nations are majorities within a state.

The modern world-system is also importantly structured as a core-periphery hierarchy in which some regions contain economically and militarily powerful states while other regions contain polities that are much less powerful and less developed. The countries that are called "advanced, " in the sense that they have high levels of economic development, skilled labor forces, high levels of income, and powerful, well-financed states, are the core powers of the modern system. The modern core includes the United States, the European countries, Japan, Australia, and Canada.

In the contemporary periphery we have relatively weak states that are not strongly supported by the populations within them and have little power relative to other states in the system. The colonial empires of the European core states have dominated most of the modern periphery until recently. These colonial empires have undergone decolonization, and the interstate system of formally sovereign states was extended to the periphery in a series of waves of decolonization that began in the last quarter of the eighteenth century with American independence, followed in the early nineteenth century by the independence of the Spanish American colonies and in the twentieth century by the decolonization of Asia and Africa. Peripheral regions are also economically less developed in the sense that their economy is composed of subsistence producers and industries that have relatively low productivity and that employ unskilled labor. Agriculture in the periphery is typically performed using simple tools, whereas agriculture in the core is capital-intensive, employing machinery and nonhuman, nonanimal forms of energy. Some industries in peripheral countries, such as oil extraction or mining, may be capital-intensive, but these sectors are often controlled by core capital.

In the past, peripheral countries have been primarily exporters of agricultural and mineral raw materials. But even when they have developed some industrial production, it has usually been less capital-intensive and has used less skilled labor than production processes in the core. The contemporary peripheral countries are most of the countries in Asia, Africa, and Latin America—for example Bangladesh, Senegal, and Bolivia.

The core-periphery hierarchy in the modern world-system is a system of stratification in which socially structured inequalities are reproduced by the institutional features of the system (fig. 3.1). The periphery is not "catching up" with the core. Rather, both core and peripheral regions are developing, but most core states are staying well ahead of most peripheral states. There is also a stratum of countries that we call the semiperiphery: countries that are in between the core and the periphery. The semiperiphery in the modern system includes countries that have intermediate levels of economic development or a balanced mix of developed and less developed regions. The semiperiphery includes large countries that have political-military power as a result of their large size and smaller countries that are relatively more developed than those in the periphery.

The exact boundaries between the core, semiperiphery, and periphery are unimportant because the main point is that there is a continuum of economic and political-military power that constitutes the core-periphery hierarchy. It does not matter exactly where we draw lines across this continuum in order to categorize countries. Indeed, we could just as well make four or seven categories instead of three. The categories are only a convenient termi-

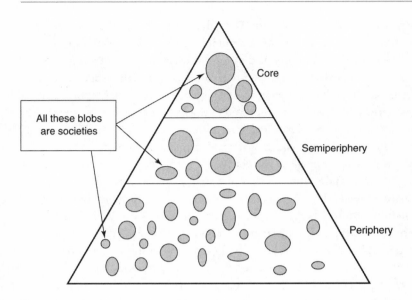

Fig. 3.1. Core-Periphery Hierarchy

nology for pointing to the fact of international inequality and for indicating that the middle of this hierarchy may be an important location for processes of social change.

There have been a few cases of upward and downward mobility in the core-periphery hierarchy, though most countries simply run hard to stay in the same relative positions that they have long occupied. A most spectacular case of upward mobility is the United States. Over the past 300 years the territory that became the United States has moved from outside the Europe-centered system (a separate continent containing several regional world-systems), to the periphery, to the semiperiphery, to the core, to the position of hegemonic core state (see below), and now its hegemony is slowly declining. An example of downward mobility is the United Kingdom of Great Britain, the hegemon of the nineteenth century and now just another core society.

The global stratification system is a continuum of economic and political-military power that is reproduced by the normal operations of the system. In such a hierarchy there are countries that are difficult to categorize. For example, most oil-exporting countries have very high levels of GNP per capita, but their economies do not produce high-technology products that are typical of core countries. They have wealth but not development. The point here is that the categories (core, periphery, and semiperiphery) are just a convenient set of terms for pointing to different locations on a continuous and multidimensional hierarchy of power. It is not necessary to have each case fit neatly into a box. The boxes are only conceptual tools for analyzing the unequal distribution of power among countries.

When we use the idea of core-periphery relations for comparing very different kinds of world-systems, we need to broaden the concept a bit and to make an important distinction (see below). But the most important point is that we should not assume that all world-systems have core-periphery hierarchies just because the modern system does. It should be an empirical question in each case as to whether core-periphery relations exist. Not assuming that world-systems have core-periphery structures allows us to compare very different kinds of systems and to study how core-periphery hierarchies themselves emerged and evolved.

In order to do this it is helpful to distinguish between core-periphery differentiation and core-periphery hierarchy. Core-periphery differentiation means that societies with different degrees of population density, polity size, and internal hierarchy are interacting with one another. As soon as we find village dwellers interacting with nomadic neighbors, we have core-periphery differentiation. Core-periphery hierarchy refers to the nature of the relationship between societies. This kind of hierarchy exists when some societies are exploiting or dominating other societies. Examples of intersocietal domination and exploitation would be the British colonization and deindustrialization of India and the conquest and subjugation of Mexico by the Spaniards. Core-periphery hierarchy is not unique to the modern Europe-centered world-system of recent centuries. Both the Roman and the Aztec empires conquered and exploited peripheral peoples as well as adjacent core states.

Distinguishing between core-periphery differentiation and core-periphery hierarchy allows us to deal with situations in which larger and more powerful societies are interacting with smaller ones but are not exploiting them. It also allows us to examine cases in which smaller, less dense societies may be exploiting or dominating larger societies. This latter situation definitely occurred in the long and consequential interaction between the nomadic horse pastoralists of Central Asia and the agrarian states and empires of China and West Asia. The most famous case was that of the Mongol Empire of Chingis Khan, but confederations of Central Asian steppe nomads managed to extract tribute from agrarian states long before the rise of Mongols.

So the modern world-system is now a global economy with a global political system (the interstate system). It also includes all the cultural aspects and interaction networks of the human population of the Earth. Culturally the modern system is composed of several civilizational traditions (e.g., Islam, Christendom, Hinduism), nationally defined cultural entities—nations (and these are composed of class and functional subcultures, e.g., lawyers, technocrats, bureaucrats), and the cultures of indigenous and minority ethnic groups within states. The modern system is multicultural in the sense that important political and economic interaction networks connect people who have rather different languages, religions, and other cultural aspects. Most earlier world-systems have also been multicultural.

Interaction networks are regular and repeated interactions among individuals and groups. Interaction may involve trade, communication, threats, alliances, migration, marriage, gift giving, or participation in information networks such as radio, television, telephone conversations, and e-mail. Important interaction networks are those that affect people's everyday lives, their access to food and necessary raw materials, their conceptions of who they are, and their security from or vulnerability to threats and violence. World-systems are fundamentally composed of interaction networks.

One of the important systemic features of the modern system is the rise and fall of hegemonic core powers—the so-called hegemonic sequence. A hegemon is a core state that has a significantly greater amount of economic power than any other state and that takes on the political role of system leader. In the seventeenth century the Dutch Republic performed the role of hegemon in the Europe-centered system, while Great Britain was the hegemon of the nineteenth century, and the United States has been the hegemon in the twentieth century. Hegemons provide leadership and order for the interstate system and the world economy. But the normal operating processes of the modern system—uneven economic development and competition among states—make it difficult for hegemons to sustain their dominant positions, and so they tend to decline. Thus the structure of the core oscillates back and forth between hegemony and a situation in which several competing core states have a roughly similar amount of power and are contending for hegemony—that is, hegemonic rivalry (fig. 3.2).

The modern world-system, then, is composed of states that are linked to one another by the world economy and other interaction networks. Earlier world-systems were also composed of polities, but the interaction networks that linked these polities were not intercontinental in scale until the expansion of Europe in the fifteenth century. Before that world-systems were smaller regional affairs. But these had been growing in size for millennia with the expansion of trade networks and long-distance military campaigns.

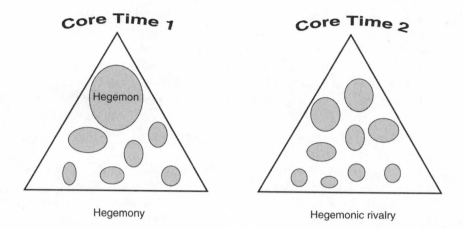

Fig. 3.2. Hegemony and Hegemonic Rivalry

Spatial Boundaries of World-Systems

One big difference between the modern world-system and earlier systems is the spatial scale of different types of interaction networks. In the modern global system most of the important interaction networks are themselves global in scale. But in earlier, smaller systems there was a significant difference in spatial scale between networks in which food and basic raw materials were exchanged and networks in which prestige goods or luxuries were exchanged, the latter networks being much larger. Food and basic raw materials we call "bulk goods" because they have a low value per unit of weight. Indeed, it is uneconomical to carry food very far under premodern conditions of transportation.

Imagine that the only type of transportation available is people carrying goods on their back (or head). This situation actually existed everywhere until the domestication of beasts of burden. Under these conditions a person can carry, say, 30 kilograms of food. Imagine that this carrier is eating the food as he or she goes. So after a few days of walking all the food will be consumed. Human carrying capacity determines the economic limit of food transportation under these conditions. This does not mean that food will never be transported farther than this distance, but there would have to be an important reason for moving it beyond its economic range.

A prestige good (e.g., jewels, bullion, or a very valuable food, such as spices) has a much larger spatial range than a bulk good because a small amount of such a good may be exchanged for a great deal of food. This is why prestige goods networks are normally much larger than bulk goods networks. A network does not usually end as long as there are people with whom one might trade. Indeed, most early trade was what is called down-the-line trade, in which goods are passed from group to group. For any particular group the effective extent of its trade network is that point beyond which nothing that happens will affect the group of origin.

In order to bound interaction networks, we need to pick a place from which to start—a so-called place-centric approach. If we go looking for actual breaks in interaction networks, we will usually not find them because almost all groups of people interact with their neighbors. But if we focus on a single settlement, for example, the precontact indigenous village of Onancock on the Eastern Shore of the Chesapeake Bay (near the boundary between what are now the states of Virginia and Maryland), we can determine the spatial scale of the interaction network by finding out how far food moved to and from our focal village. Food came to Onancock from some maximum distance. A bit beyond that were groups that were trading food to groups that were directly sending food to Onancock. If we allow two indirect jumps, we are probably far enough from Onancock so that no matter what happened (e.g., a food shortage or surplus), it would not have affected the supply of food in Onancock. This outer limit of Onancock's indigenous bulk goods network probably included villages at the very southern and northern ends of the Chesapeake Bay.

Onancock's prestige goods network was much larger than its bulk goods network because prestige goods move farther distances. Indeed, copper that was in use by the indigenous peoples of the Chesapeake may have come from as far away as Lake Superior. In between the size of bulk goods networks (BGNs) and prestige goods networks (PGNs) are the interaction networks in which polities make war and ally with one another. These are called political-military networks (PMNs). In the case of the Chesapeake world-system at the time of the arrival of the Europeans in the sixteenth century, Onancock was part of a district chiefdom in a system of multivillage chiefdoms. Across the bay on the western shore were at least two larger polities, the Powhatan and the Conoy paramount chiefdoms. These were core chiefdoms that were collecting tribute from a number of smaller district chiefdoms. Onancock was part of an interchiefdom system of allying and war-making polities. The boundaries of that network included some indirect links, just as the trade network boundaries did. Thus the PMN of which Onancock was the focal place extended to the Delaware Bay in the north and into what is now the state of North Carolina to the south.

Information, like a prestige good, is light relative to its value. Information may travel far along trade routes and beyond the range of goods. Thus information networks (INs) are usually as large as or even larger than PGNs.

A general picture of the spatial relationships between different kinds of interaction networks is presented in figure 3.3. The actual spatial scale of important interaction networks needs to be determined for each world-system we study, but figure 3.3 shows what is generally the case—that BGNs are smaller than PMNs and that PMNs are in turn smaller than PGNs and INs.

Defined in the way that we have above, world-systems have grown from small to large over the past 12 millennia as societies and intersocietal systems have gotten larger, more complex, and more hierarchical. This spatial growth of systems has involved the expansion of some and the incorporation of some into others. The processes of incorporation have occurred in several ways as systems distant from one another have linked their interaction networks. Because interaction nets are of different sizes, it is the largest ones that come into contact first. Thus information and prestige goods link dis-

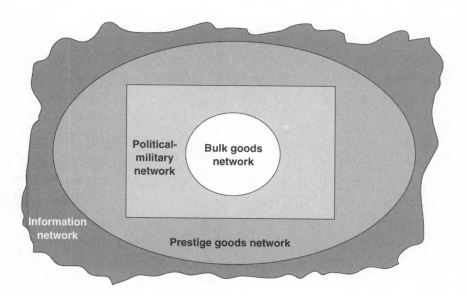

Fig. 3.3. The Spatial Boundaries of World-Systems

tant groups long before they participate in the same political-military or bulk goods networks. The processes of expansion and incorporation brought different groups of people together and made the organization of larger and more hierarchical societies possible. It is in this sense that globalization has been going on for thousands of years.

Using the conceptual apparatus for spatially bounding world-systems outlined above, we can construct spatio-temporal chronographs for how the interaction networks of the human population changed their spatial scales to eventuate in the single global political economy of today. Figure 3.4 uses PMNs as the unit of analysis to show how a "Central" PMN, composed of the merging of the Mesopotamian and Egyptian PMNs in about 1500 BCE, eventually incorporated all the other PMNs into itself.

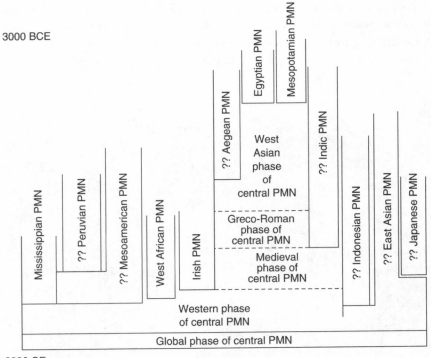

Fig. 3.4. Chronograph of Political-Military Networks (PMNs).
Adapted from Wilkinson 1987.

World-System Cycles: Rise and Fall, and Pulsations

Comparative research reveals that all world-systems exhibit cyclical processes of change. There are two major cyclical phenomena: the rise and fall of large polities, and pulsations in the spatial extent and intensity of trade networks. "Rise and fall" corresponds to changes in the centralization of political-military power in a set of polities—an "international" system. It is a question of the relative size and distribution of power across a set of interacting polities. The term "cycling" has been used to describe this phenomenon as it operates among chiefdoms (Anderson 1994).

All world-systems in which there are hierarchical polities experience a cycle in which relatively larger polities grow in power and size and then decline. This applies to interchiefdom systems as well as interstate systems, to systems composed of empires, and to the modern rise and fall of hegemonic core powers (e.g., Britain and the United States). Though very egalitarian and small-scale systems such as the sedentary foragers of northern California (Chase-Dunn and Mann 1998) do not display a cycle of rise and fall, they do experience pulsations.

All systems, including even very small and egalitarian ones, exhibit cyclical expansions and contractions in the spatial extent and intensity of exchange networks. We call this sequence of trade expansion and contraction pulsation. Different kinds of trade (especially bulk goods trade vs. prestige goods trade) usually have different spatial characteristics. It is also possible that different sorts of trade exhibit different temporal sequences of expansion and contraction. It should be an empirical question in each case as to whether changes in the volume of exchange correspond to changes in its spatial extent. In the modern global system large trade networks cannot get spatially larger because they are already global in extent.[1] But they can get denser and more intense relative to smaller networks of exchange. A good part of what has been called globalization is simply the intensification of larger interaction networks relative to the intensity of smaller ones. This kind of integration is often understood to be an upward trend that has attained its greatest peak in recent decades of so-called global capitalism. But research on trade and investment shows that there have been two recent waves of integration, one in the last half of the nineteenth century and the most recent since World War II (Chase-Dunn, Kawano, and Brewer 2000).

The simplest hypothesis regarding the temporal relationships between rise and fall on the one hand and pulsation on the other is that they occur in tandem. Whether or not this is so, and how the relationships might differ in distinct types of world-systems, are problems that are amenable to empirical research.

Chase-Dunn and Hall (1997) have contended that the causal processes of rise and fall differ depending on the predominant mode of accumulation. One big difference between the rise and fall of empires and the rise and fall of modern hegemons is in the degree of centralization achieved within the core. Tributary systems alternate back and forth between a structure of multiple and competing core states on the one hand and corewide (or nearly corewide) empires on the other. The modern interstate system experiences the rise and fall of hegemons, but these never take over the other core states to form a corewide empire. This is the case because modern hegemons are pursuing a capitalist, rather than a tributary, form of accumulation.

Analogously, rise and fall works somewhat differently in interchiefdom systems because the institutions that facilitate the extraction of resources from distant groups are less fully developed in chiefdom systems. David G. Anderson's (1994) study of the rise and fall of Mississippian chiefdoms in the Savannah River valley provides an excellent and comprehensive review of the anthropological and sociological literature about what Anderson calls "cycling," the processes by which a chiefly polity extended control over adjacent chiefdoms and erected a two-tiered hierarchy of administration over the tops of local communities. At a later point these regionally centralized chiefly polities disintegrated back toward a system of smaller and less hierarchical polities.

Chiefs relied more completely on hierarchical kinship relations, control of ritual hierarchies, and control of prestige goods imports than do the rulers of true states. These chiefly techniques of power are all highly dependent on normative integration and ideological consensus. States developed specialized organizations for extracting resources that chiefdoms lacked—standing armies and bureaucracies. And states and empires in the tributary world-systems were more dependent on the projection of armed force over great distances than modern hegemonic core states have been. The development of commodity production and mechanisms of financial control and further development of bureaucratic techniques of power have allowed modern hegemons to extract resources from faraway places with much less overhead cost.

The development of techniques of power has made core-periphery relations ever more important for competition among core powers and has altered the way in which the rise-and-fall process works in other respects. Chase-Dunn and Hall (1997, chap. 6) argued that population growth in interaction with the environment and changes in productive technology and social structure produce social evolution that is marked by cycles and periodic jumps. This is because each world-system oscillates around a central tendency (mean) owing to both internal instabilities and environmental fluctuations. Occasionally, on one of the upswings, people solve systemic problems in a new way that allows substantial expansion. We want to explain expansions, evolutionary changes in systemic logic, and collapses. That is the point of comparing world-systems.

The multiscalar regional method of bounding world-systems as nested interaction networks outlined above is complementary to a multiscalar temporal analysis of the kind suggested by Fernand Braudel's work. Temporal depth, the *longue durée*, needs to be combined with analyses of short-run and middle-run processes to fully understand social change. The shallow presentism of most social science and contemporary culture needs to be denounced at every opportunity.

A strong case for the very *longue durée* is made by Jared Diamond's (1997) study of original zoological and botanical wealth. The geographical distribution of those species that could be easily and profitably domesticated explains a huge portion of the variance regarding which world-systems expanded and incorporated other world-systems thousands of years hence. Diamond also contends that the diffusion of domesticated plant and animal species occurs much more quickly in the latitudinal dimension (east-west) than in the longitudinal dimension (north-south), and so this explains why domesticated species spread so quickly to Europe and East Asia from West Asia, while the spread south into Africa was much slower, and the north-south orientation of the American continents made diffusion much slower than in the Old World island of Eurasia.

Figure 3.5 depicts the coming together of the East Asian and the West Asian–Mediterranean systems. Both the PGNs and the PMNs are shown, as are the pulsations and rise-and-fall sequences. The PGNs linked intermittently and then joined. The Mongol conquerors linked the PMNs briefly in the thirteenth century, but the Eastern and Western PMNs were not permanently linked until the Europeans and Americans established Asian treaty ports in the nineteenth century.

Modes of Accumulation

In order to comprehend the qualitative changes that have occurred with the processes of social evolution, we need to conceptualize different logics of development and the institutional modes by which socially created resources

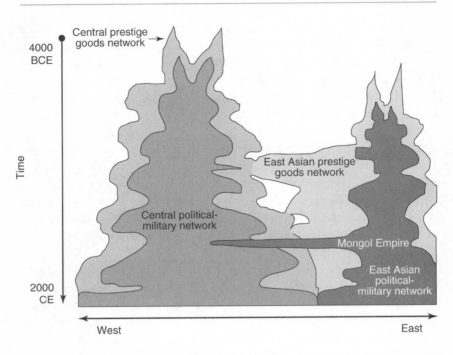

Fig. 3.5. East-West Pulsations and Merger

are produced and accumulated. All societies produce and distribute the goods that are necessary for everyday life. But the institutional means by which human labor is mobilized are very different in different kinds of societies. Small and egalitarian societies rely primarily on normative regulation organized as commonly shared understandings about the obligations that members of families have toward one another. When a hunter returns with his game, there are definite rules and understandings about who should receive shares and how much. All hunters in foraging societies want to be thought of as generous, but they must also take care of some people (those for whom they are the most responsible) before they can give to others.

The normative order defines the roles and the obligations, and the norms and values are affirmed or modified by the continual symbolic and nonsymbolic action of the people. This socially constructed consciousness is mainly about kinship, but it is also about the nature of the universe, of which the human group is understood as a part. This kind of social economy is called a kin-based mode of production and accumulation. People work because they need food and have obligations to provide food for others. Accumulation mainly involves the preservation and storage of food supplies for the season in which food will become scarce. Status is based on the reputation that one has as a good hunter, a good gatherer, a good family member, or a talented speaker. Group decisions are made by consensus, which means that the people keep talking until they have come to an understanding of what to do. The leaders have authority that is mainly based on their ability to convince others that they are right. These features are common (but not universal) among societies and world-systems in which the kin-based modes of accumulation are the main logic of development.

As societies become larger and more hierarchical, kinship itself becomes hierarchically defined. Clans and lineages become ranked so that members of some families are defined as senior or superior to members of other families. Classical cases of ranked societies were those of the Pacific Northwest, in which the totem pole represents a hierarchy of clans. This tendency toward hierarchical kinship resulted in the eventual emergence of class societies (complex chiefdoms) in which a noble class owned and controlled key resources and a class of commoners was separated from the control of important resources and had to rely on the nobles for access to these. Such a society existed in Hawaii before the arrival of the Europeans.

The tributary modes of accumulation emerged when institutional coercion became a central form of regulation for inducing people to work and for the accumulation of social resources. Hierarchical kinship functions in this way when commoners must provide labor or products to chiefs in exchange for access to resources that chiefs control by means of both normative and coercive power.

Normative power does not work well by itself as a basis for the appropriation of labor or goods by one group from another. Those who are exploited have a great motive to redefine the situation. The nobles may have elaborated a vision of the universe in which they were understood to control natural forces or to mediate interactions with the deities and so commoners were supposed to be obligated to support these sacred duties by turning over their produce to the nobles or contributing labor to sacred projects. But the commoners would have had an incentive to disbelieve unless they had only worse alternatives. Thus the institutions of coercive power were invented to sustain the extraction of surplus labor and goods from direct producers. The hierarchical religions and kinship systems of complex chiefdoms became supplemented in early states by specialized organizations of regional control—groups of armed men under the command of the king and bureaucratic systems of taxation and tribute backed up by the law and by institutionalized force. The tributary modes of accumulation developed techniques of power that allowed resources to be extracted over great distances and from large populations. These are the institutional bases of the states and the empires.

The third mode of accumulation is based on markets. Markets can be defined as any situation in which goods are bought and sold, but we use the term here to denote what are called price-setting markets, in which the competitive trading by large numbers of buyers and sellers is an important determinant of the price. This is a situation in which supply and demand operate on the price because buyers and sellers are bidding against one another. In practice there are very few instances in history or in modern reality of purely price-setting markets because political and normative considerations quite often influence prices. But the price mechanism and resulting market pressures have become more important. These institutions were completely absent before the invention of commodities and money.

A commodity is a good that is produced for sale in a price-setting market in order to make a profit. A pencil is an example of a modern commodity. It is a fairly standardized product; the conditions of production, the cost of raw materials, labor, energy, and pencil-making machines are important forces acting on the price of the pencil. Pencils are also produced for a rather competitive market, and so the necessary costs given the current level of technology, plus a certain amount of profit, sum to the cost of the pencil.

The idea of the commodity is an important element of the definition of the capitalist mode of accumulation. Capitalism is the concentrated accumulation of profits by the owners of major means of the production of commodities in a context in which labor and the other main elements of production are commodified. Commodification means that things are treated like commodities, even though they may have characteristics that make this somewhat difficult. So land can be commodified—treated like commodity—even though it is a limited good that has not originally been produced for profitable sale. There is only so much land on Earth. We can divide it up into sections with straight boundaries and price it based on supply and demand. But it will never be a perfect commodity. This is also the case with human labor time.

The commodification of land is a historical process that began when "real property" was first legally defined and sold. The conceptualization of places as abstract, measurable, substitutable, and salable space is an institutional redefinition that took thousands of years to develop and to spread to all regions of the Earth.

The capitalist modes of production also required the redefinition of wealth as money. The first storable and tradable valuables were probably prestige goods. These were used by local elites in trade with adjacent peoples and eventually as symbols of superior status. Trade among simple societies is primarily organized as gift giving among elites in which allegiances are created and sustained. Originally prestige goods were used only in specific circumstances by certain elites. This "proto-money" was eventually redefined and institutionalized as the so-called universal equivalent that serves as a general measure of value for all sorts of goods and that can be used by almost anyone to buy almost anything. The institution of money has a long and complicated history, but suffice it to say here that it has been a prerequisite for the emergence of price-setting markets and capitalism as increasingly important forms of social regulation. Once markets and capital become the predominant form of accumulation, we can speak of capitalist systems.

Patterns and Causes of Social Evolution

It is important to understand the similarities but also the important differences between biological and social evolution. These are discussed by Chase-Dunn and Lerro (2005, chap. 1). This section describes a general causal model that explains the emergence of larger hierarchies and the development of productive technologies. It also points to a pattern that is noticeable only when we study world-systems rather than individual societies. The pattern is called semiperipheral development. This means that those innovations that transform the logic of development and allow world-systems to get larger and more hierarchical come mainly from semiperipheral societies. Some semiperipheral societies are unusually fertile locations for the invention and implementation of new institutional structures. And semiperipheral societies are not constrained to the same degree as older core societies by having invested huge resources in doing things in the old way. So they are freer to implement new institutions. There are several different important kinds of semiperipheries, and these not only transform systems but also often take over and become new core societies. We have already mentioned semiperipheral marcher chiefdoms. The societies that conquered and unified a number of smaller chiefdoms into larger paramount chiefdoms were usually from semiperipheral locations. Peripheral peoples did not usually have the institutional and material resources that would allow them to make important inventions and to implement these or to take over older core regions. It was in the semiperiphery that core and peripheral social characteristics could be recombined in new ways. Sometimes this meant that new techniques of power or political legitimacy were invented and implemented in semiperipheral societies.

Much better known than semiperipheral marcher chiefdoms is the phenomenon of semiperipheral marcher states. The largest empires have been assembled by conquerors who have come from semiperipheral societies. The following semiperipheral marchers are well known: the Achaemenid Persians, the Macedonians led by Alexander the Great, the Romans, the Ottomans, the Manchus, and the Aztecs.

Some semiperipheries, however, transform institutions but do not take over. The semiperipheral capitalist city-states operated on the edges of the tributary empires, where they bought and sold goods in widely separate locations, encouraging people to produce a surplus for trade. The Phoenician cities (e.g., Tyre and Carthage), as well as Malacca, Venice, and Genoa, spread commodification by producing manufactured goods and trading them across great regions. In this way the semiperipheral capitalist city-states were agents of the development of markets and the expansion of trade networks, and so they helped to transform the world of the tributary empires without themselves becoming new core powers.

In our discussion of the modern world-system we have already mentioned the process of the rise and fall of hegemonic core states. All the cases we cited—the Dutch Republic, Great Britain, and the United States—were countries that had formerly been in semiperipheral positions relative to the regional core-periphery hierarchies within which they existed. And indeed, the rise of Europe within the larger Afroeurasian world-system was also a case of semiperipheral development, one in which a formerly peripheral and then semiperipheral region rose to become the new core of what had been a huge multicore world-system.

The idea of semiperipheral development does not claim that all semiperipheral societies perform transformational roles; nor does it contend that every important innovation came from the semiperiphery. The point is rather that semiperipheries have been unusually prolific sites for the invention of those institutions that have expanded and transformed many small systems into the particular kind of global system that we have today. This observation would not be possible without the conceptual apparatus of the comparative world-systems perspective.

But what have been the proximate causes that led semiperipheral societies to invent new institutional solutions to problems? Some of the problems that needed to be solved were new, unintended consequences of earlier inventions, but others were very old problems that kept emerging again and again as systems expanded—for example, population pressure and ecological degradation. It is these basic problems that make it possible for us to specify a single underlying causal model of world-systems evolution. Figure 3.6 shows what is called the "iteration model, which links demographic, ecological, and interactional processes with the emergence of new production technologies, bigger polities, and greater degrees of hierarchy.

This is called an iteration model because it has an important positive feedback mechanism in which the original causes are themselves consequences of the things that they cause. Thus the process goes around and around, which is what has caused the world-systems to expand to the global level. Starting at the top we see population growth. The idea here is that all human societies contain a biological impetus to grow that is based on sexuality. This impetus is both controlled and encouraged by social institutions. Some societies try to regulate population growth by means of, for instance, infanticide, abortion, and taboos on sexual relations during nursing. These institutional means of regulation are costly, and when greater amounts of food are available, these types of regulation tend to be eased. Other kinds of societies

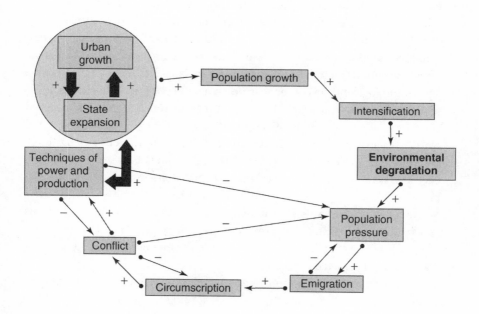

Fig. 3.6. Basic Iteration Model of World-System Evolution

encourage population growth by means of channeling sexual energy toward reproduction, pronatalist ideologies, and support for large families. All societies experience periodic "baby booms" when social circumstances are somewhat more propitious for reproduction, and thus, over the long run, the population tends to grow despite institutional mechanisms that try to control it.

Intensification is caused by population growth. This means that when the number of mouths to feed increases greater efforts are needed to produce food and other necessities of life and so people exploit more intensively the resources they have been exploiting. This usually leads, in turn, to ecological degradation because all human production processes use up the natural environment. More production leads to greater environmental degradation. This occurs because more resources are extracted and because of the polluting consequences of production and consumption activities. Nomadic hunter-gatherers depleted the herds of big game, and Polynesian horticulturalists deforested many a Pacific island. Environmental degradation is not a new phenomenon. Only its global scale is new.

As Jared Diamond (1997) points out, all continents around the world did not start with the same animal and plant resources. In West Asia both plants (barley and wheat) and animals (sheep, goats, cows, and oxen) were more easily domesticated than the plants and animals of Africa and the New World. Since domesticated plants and animals can more easily diffuse latitudinally (east and west) than longitudinally (north and south), these inventions spread more quickly to Europe and East Asia than they did to Africa. These exogenous factors affect the timing and speed of hierarchy formation and technological development, as do climate change and geographical obstacles that affect transportation and communications. It is widely believed that the emergence of an early large state on the Nile was greatly facilitated by the ease of controlling transportation and communications in that linear environment, while the more complicated geography of Mesopotamia stabilized the system of city-states and slowed the emergence of a corewide empire. Patrick Kirch (1984, 1991) contends that it was the difficult geography of the Marquesas Islands (short steep valleys separated by high mountains and treacherous coasts) that prevented the emergence of islandwide paramount chiefdoms and kept the Marquesas in the messy bottom end of the iteration model depicted in figure 3.7.

The consequences of the above-mentioned processes are that the economics of production change for the worse. According to Joseph Tainter (1988), after a certain point increased investment in complexity does not result in proportionate increasing returns. This occurs in the areas of agricultural pro-

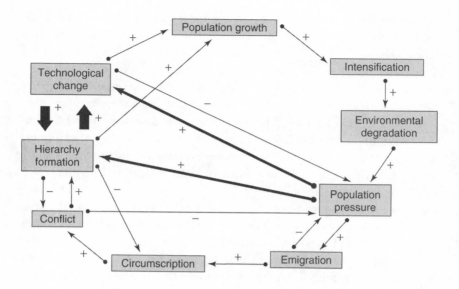

Fig. 3.7. Temporary Institutional Shortcuts in the Iteration Model

duction, information processing, and communication, including education and maintenance of information channels. Sociopolitical control and special-ization, such as military and the police, also develop diminishing returns. Tainter points out that marginal returns can occur in at least four instances: benefits constant, costs rising; benefits rising, costs rising faster; benefits falling, costs constant; benefits falling, costs rising.

When herds are depleted, the hunters must go farther to find game. The combined sequence from population growth to intensification to environ-mental degradation leads to population pressure, the negative economic ef-fects on production activities. The growing effort needed to produce enough food is a big incentive for people to migrate. And so humans populated the whole Earth. If the herds in this valley are depleted, we may be able to find a new place where they are more abundant.

Migration eventually leads to circumscription. Circumscription is the con-dition that no new desirable locations are available for emigration. This can be because all the herds in all the adjacent valleys are depleted, or because all the alternative locations are deserts or high mountains, or because all adja-cent desirable locations are already occupied by people who will effectively re-sist immigration.

The condition of social circumscription in which adjacent locations are already occupied is, under conditions of population pressure, likely to lead to a rise in the level of intergroup and intragroup conflict. This is because more people are competing for fewer resources. Warfare and other kinds of conflict are more prevalent under such conditions. All systems experience some warfare, but warfare becomes a focus of social endeavor that often has a life of its own. Boys are trained to be warriors, and societies make decisions based on the presumption that they will be attacked or will be attacking other groups. Even in situations of seemingly endemic warfare the amount of conflict varies cyclically. Figure 3.6 shows an arrow with a negative sign going from conflict back to population pressure. This is because high levels of conflict reduce the size of the population as warriors are killed off and noncombatants die because their food supplies have been destroyed. Some systems get stuck in a vicious cycle of population pressure and warfare.

But situations such as this are also propitious for the emergence of new institutional structures. It is in these situations that semiperipheral development is likely to occur. People get tired of endemic conflict. One solution is the emergence of a new hierarchy or a larger polity that can regulate access to resources in a way that generates less conflict. The emergence of a new larger polity usually occurs as a result of successful conquest of a number of smaller polities by a semiperipheral marcher. The larger polity creates peace by means of an organized force that is greater than any force likely to be brought against it. The new polity reconstructs the institutions of control over territory and resources, often concentrating control and wealth for a new elite. And larger and more hierarchical polities often invest in new technologies of production that change the way in which resources are utilized. They produce more food and other necessaries by using new technologies or by intensifying the use of old technologies. New technologies can expand the number of people that can be supported in the territory. This makes population growth more likely, and so the iteration model is primed to go around again.

The iteration model has kept expanding the size of world-systems and developing new technologies and forms of regulation, but, at least so far, it has not permanently solved the original problems of ecological degradation and population pressure. What has happened is the emergence of institutions such as states and markets that articulate changes in the economics of production more directly with changes in political organization and technology. This allows the institutional structures to readjust without having to go through short cycles at the messy bottom end of the model.

Another way to say this is that political and market institutions allow for some adjustments to occur without greatly increasing the level of systemic conflict. This said, the level of conflict has remained quite high because the rate of expansion and technological change has increased. Even though institutional mechanisms of articulation have emerged, these have not permanently lowered the amount of systemic conflict because the rates of change in the other variables have increased.

It is also difficult to understand why and where innovative social change emerges without a conceptualization of the world-system as a whole. New organizational forms that transform institutions and that lead to upward mobility most often emerge from societies in semiperipheral locations. Thus all the countries that became hegemonic core states in the modern system had formerly been semiperipheral (the Dutch Republic, Great Britain, and the United States). This is a continuation of the long-term pattern of social evolution that Chase-Dunn and Hall (1997) have called "semiperipheral development." Semiperipheral marcher states and semiperipheral capitalist city-states had acted as the main agents of empire formation and commercialization for millennia. This phenomenon arguably also includes organizational innovations in contemporary semiperipheral countries (e.g., Mexico, India, South Korea, Brazil) that may transform the now global system.

This approach requires that we think structurally. We must be able to abstract from the particularities of the game of musical chairs that constitutes uneven development in the system to see the structural continuities. The core-periphery hierarchy remains, though some countries have moved up or down. The interstate system remains, though the internationalization of capital has further constrained the abilities of states to structure national economies. States have always been subjected to larger geopolitical and economic forces in the world-system, and as is still the case, some have been more successful at exploiting opportunities and protecting themselves from liabilities than others.

In this perspective many of the phenomena that have been called "globalization" correspond to recently expanded international trade, financial flows, and foreign investment by transnational corporations and banks. Much of the globalization discourse assumes that until recently there were separate national societies and economies and that these have now been superseded by an expansion of international integration driven by information and transportation technologies. Rather than a wholly unique and new phenomenon, globalization is primarily international economic integration, and as such it is a feature of the world-system that has been oscillating as well as increasing for centuries. Recent research comparing the nineteenth and twentieth centuries has shown that trade globalization is both a cycle and a trend.

The Great Chartered Companies of the seventeenth century were already playing an important role in shaping the development of world regions. Certainly the transnational corporations of the present are much more important players, but the point is that "foreign investment' is not an institution that became important only since 1970 (or since World War II). Giovanni Arrighi (1994) has shown that finance capital has been a central component of the commanding heights of the world-system since the fourteenth century. The current floods and ebbs of world money are typical of the late phase of very long systemic cycles of accumulation.

Most world-systems scholars contend that leaving out the core-periphery dimension or treating the periphery as inert is a grave mistake, not only for reasons of completeness but also because the ability of core capitalists and their states to exploit peripheral resources and labor has been a major factor in deciding the winners of the competition among core contenders. And the resistance to exploitation and domination mounted by peripheral peoples has played a powerful role in shaping the historical development of world orders. Thus world history cannot be properly understood without attention to the core-periphery hierarchy.

Philip McMichael (2000) has studied the "globalization project"—the abandoning of Keynesian models of national development and a new (or renewed) emphasis on deregulation and opening national commodity and financial markets to foreign trade and investment. This approach focuses on the political and ideological aspects of the recent wave of international integration. The term many prefer for this turn in global discourse is "neoliberalism," but it has also been called "Reaganism/Thatcherism" and the "Washington Consensus." The worldwide decline of the political Left predated the revolutions of 1989 and the demise of the Soviet Union, but it was certainly also accelerated by these events. The structural basis of the rise of the globalization project is the new level of integration reached by the global capitalist class. The internationalization of capital has long been an important part of the trend toward economic globalization. And there have been many claims to represent the general interests of business before. Indeed, every modern hegemon has made this claim. But the real integration of the interests of capitalists all over the world has very likely reached a level greater than at the peak of the nineteenth-century wave of globalization.

This is the part of the theory of a global stage of capitalism that must be taken most seriously, though it can certainly be overdone. The world-system has now reached a point at which both the old interstate system based on separate national capitalist classes and new institutions representing the global interests of capital exist and are powerful simultaneously. In this light each country can be seen to have an important ruling-class faction that is allied with the transnational capitalist class. The big question is whether this new level of transnational integration will be strong enough to prevent competition among states for world hegemony from turning into warfare, as it has always done in the past, during a period in which a hegemon (now the United States) is declining.

The insight that capitalist globalization has occurred in waves and that these waves of integration are followed by periods of globalization backlash has important implications for the future. Capitalist globalization increased both intranational and international inequalities in the nineteenth century, and it has done the same thing in the late twentieth century (O'Rourke and Williamson 2000). Those countries and groups that are left out of the "belle epoque" either mobilize to challenge the hegemony of the powerful or retreat into self-reliance, or both.

Globalization protests emerged in the noncore with the anti–International Monetary Fund (IMF) riots of the 1980s. The several transnational social movements that participated in the 1999 protest in Seattle brought globalization protest to the attention of observers in the core, and this resistance to capitalist globalization has continued and grown despite the setback that occurred in response to the terrorist attacks on New York and Washington in 2001.

There is an apparent tension between those who advocate deglobalization and delinking from the global capitalist economy and the building of stronger, more cooperative, and self-reliant social relations in the periphery and semiperiphery, on the one hand, and those who seek to mobilize support for new or reformed institutions of democratic global governance. Self-reliance by itself, though an understandable reaction to exploitation, is not likely to solve the problems of humanity in the long run. The great challenge of the twenty-first century will be the building of a democratic and collectively rational global commonwealth. World-systems theory can be an important contributor to this effort.

Notes

1. If we manage to get through several sticky wickets looming in the twenty-first century, the human system will probably expand into the solar system, and so "globalization" will continue to be spatially expansive.

References

Anderson, David G. 1994. *The Savannah River Chiefdoms: Political Change in the Late Prehistoric Southeast.* Tuscaloosa, AL: University of Alabama Press.

Arrighi, Giovanni. 1994. *The Long Twentieth Century.* London: Verso.

Chase-Dunn, Christopher and Thomas D. Hall. 1997. *Rise and Demise: Comparing World-Systems.* Boulder, CO: Westview Press.

Chase-Dunn, Christopher, Yukio Kawano, and Benjamin Brewer. 2000. "Trade Globalization since 1795: Waves of Integration in the World-System." *American Sociological Review* 65:77–95.

Chase-Dunn, Christopher and Bruce Lerro. 2005. *Social Change: World Historical Social Transformations.* Boston: Allyn and Bacon.

Chase-Dunn, Christopher and Kelly M. Mann. 1998. *The Wintu and Their Neighbors: A Very Small World-System in Northern California.* Tucson, AZ: University of Arizona Press.

Chase-Dunn, Christopher and Alice Willard. 1993. "Systems of Cities and World-Systems: Settlement Size Hierarchies and Cycles of Political Centralization, 2000 BC–1988 AD." Paper presented at the International Studies Association meeting, March 24–27, Acapulco, Mexico.

Diamond, Jared. 1997. *Guns, Germs and Steel: The Fates of Human Societies.* New York: Norton.

Kirch, Patrick V. 1984. *The Evolution of Polynesian Chiefdoms.* Cambridge, MA: Cambridge University Press.

———. 1991. "Chiefship and Competitive Involution: The Marquesas Islands of Eastern Polynesia." Pp. 119–145 in *Chiefdoms: Power, Economy and Ideology,* edited by Timothy Earle. Cambridge, MA: Cambridge University Press.

McMichael, Philip. 2000. *Development and Social Change: A Global Perspective.* Thousand Oaks, CA: Pine Forge.

O'Rourke, Kevin H. and Jeffrey G. Williamson. 2000. *Globalization and History.* Cambridge, MA: MIT Press.

Tainter, Joseph A. 1988. *The Collapse of Complex Societies.* Cambridge, MA: Cambridge University Press.

4

Competing Conceptions of Globalization

LESLIE SKLAIR

Globalization is a relatively new idea in the social sciences, although people who work in and write about the mass media, transnational corporations, and international business have been using it for some time. Jacques Maisonrouge, the French-born former president of IBM World Trade, was an early exponent of the view that the future lies with global corporations that operate as if the world had no real borders rather than organizations tied to a particular country. The influential U.S. magazine *Business Week* (May 14, 1990) summed up this view in the evocative phrase "The Stateless Corporation." The purpose of this chapter is to critically review the ways in which sociologists and other social scientists use ideas of globalization and to evaluate the fruitfulness of these competing conceptions.

The central feature of the idea of globalization is that many contemporary problems cannot be adequately studied at the level of nation-states, that is, in terms of each country and its inter-national relations, but instead need to be seen in terms of global processes. Some globalists have even gone so far as to predict that global forces—by which they usually mean transnational corporations and other global economic institutions, global culture or globalizing belief systems/ideologies of various types, or a combination of all of these—are becoming so powerful that the continuing existence of the nation-state is in serious doubt. This is not a necessary consequence of most theories of globalization, though many argue that the significance of the nation-state is declining (even if the ideology of nationalism is still strong in some places).

There is no single agreed-on definition of globalization; indeed, some scholars argue that its significance has been much exaggerated, but as the ever increasing numbers of books and articles discussing different aspects of it suggest, it appears to be an idea whose time has come in sociology in particular and in the social sciences in general. The author of the first genuine textbook on globalization suggests that it may be "the concept of the 1990s" (Waters 1995:1; see also Robertson 1992; Albrow 1996).

The argument of this chapter is that the central problem in understanding much of the globalization literature is that not all those who use the term distinguish it clearly enough from internationalization, and some writers appear to use the two terms interchangeably. I argue that a clear distinction must be drawn between the inter-national and the global. The hyphen in "inter-national" is to signify confusing conceptions of globalization founded on the existing, even if changing, system of nation-states, while the "global" signifies the emergence of processes and a system of social relations not founded on the system of nation-states.

This difficulty is compounded by the fact that most theory and research in sociology are based on concepts of society that identify the unit of analysis with a particular country (e.g., sociology of Britain, of Japan, of the United States, of Russia, of India), subsystems within countries (British education, the Japanese economy, American culture, politics in Russia, religion in India), or comparisons between single countries and groups of them (modern Britain and traditional India, declining America and ascendant Japan, rich and poor countries, the West and the East). This general approach, usually called state-centrism, is still useful in many respects, and there are clearly good reasons for it. Not the least of these is that most historical and contemporary sociological data sets have been collected on particular countries.[1] However, most globalization theorists argue that the nation-state is no longer the only important unit of analysis. Some even argue that the nation-state is now less important in some fundamental respects than other, global forces; examples of such forces are the mass media and the corporations that own and control them, transnational corporations (some of which are richer than the majority of nation-states in the world today), and even social movements that spread ideas such as universal human rights, global environmental responsibility, and the worldwide call for democracy and human dignity. Yearley (1996, chap. 1) identifies two main obstacles to making sociological sense of globalization, namely, "the tight connection between the discipline of sociology and the nation-state" (p. 9) and the fact that countries differ significantly in their geographies. Despite these difficulties (really elaborations of the local-global problem, which is discussed below), he makes the telling point that a focus on the environment encourages us to "work down to the global" from the universal, a necessary corrective to state-centrist conceptions, which work up to the global from the nation-state or even, as we shall see, from individualistic notions of "global consciousness."

The study of globalization in sociology revolves primarily around two main classes of phenomena that have become increasingly significant in the past few decades. These are (1) the emergence of a globalized economy based on new systems of production, finance, and consumption and (2) the idea of "global culture." While not all globalization researchers entirely accept the existence of a global economy or a global culture, most accept that local, national, and regional economies are undergoing important changes as a result of processes of globalization even where there are limits to globalization (see, e.g., Scott 1997).

Researchers on globalization have focused on two phenomena, increasingly significant in the past few decades:

1. The ways in which transnational corporations (TNCs) have facilitated the globalization of capital and production (Dunning 1993; Barnet and Cavanagh 1994; Dicken 1998)

2. Transformations in the global scope of particular types of TNCs, those that own and control the mass media, notably television channels and the transnational advertising agencies. This phenomenon is often connected with the spread of particular patterns of consumption and a culture and ideology of consumerism at the global level (Featherstone 1990; Dowmunt 1993; Barker 1997; Sklair 2002).

The largest TNCs have assets and annual sales far in excess of the GNPs of most of the countries in the world. In the first year of the new millennium (2000–2001) the World Bank annual publication *World Development Report* reported that fewer than 60 countries out a total of around 200 for which there are data had GNPs of more than US$20 billion. By contrast, the Fortune Global 500 list of the biggest TNCs by turnover in 2001 reported that 245 TNCs had annual revenues greater than $20 billion. Thus, in this important sense, such well-known names as Wal-Mart, General Motors, Shell, Toyota, Unilever, Volkswagen, Nestle, Sony, Pepsico, Coca-Cola, Kodak, Xerox, and the huge Japanese trading houses (and many other corporations most people have never heard of) have more economic power at their disposal than the majority of the countries in the world. These figures prove little in themselves; they simply indicate the gigantism of TNCs relative to most countries.

Not only have TNCs grown enormously in size in recent decades, but their "global reach" has expanded dramatically. Many companies, even from large rich countries, regularly earn a third or more of their revenues from "foreign" sources (see Sklair 2001). Not all Fortune Global 500 corporations are headquartered in the First World; some come from what was called the Third World or those parts of it known as the newly industrializing countries (NICs).[2] Examples of these are the "national" oil companies of Brazil, India,

Mexico, Taiwan, and Venezuela (some owned by the state but most run like private corporations), banks in Brazil and China, an automobile company from Turkey, and the Korean manufacturing and trading conglomerates (*chaebol*), a few of which have attained global brand-name status, for example, Hyundai and Samsung (see Sklair and Robbins 2002).

Writers who are skeptical about economic globalization argue that because most TNCs are legally domiciled in the United States, Japan, and Europe and they trade and invest mainly between themselves, the world-economy is still best analyzed in terms of national corporations and the global economy is a myth (see, e.g., Hirst and Thompson 1996). But this deduction entirely ignores the well-established fact that an increasing number of corporations operating outside their "home" countries see themselves as developing global strategies, as is obvious if we read their annual reports and other publications rather than focus exclusively on aggregate data on foreign investment.[3] One cannot simply assume that all "U.S.," "Japanese," and other "national" TNCs somehow express a "national interest." They do not. They primarily express the interests of those who own and control them, even if historical patterns of TNC development have differed from place to place, country to country, and region to region. Analyzing globalization as a relatively recent phenomenon, originating in the 1960s, allows us to see more clearly the tensions between traditional "national" patterns of TNC development and the new global corporate structures and dynamics. It is also important to realize that, even in state-centrist terms, a relatively small investment for a major TNC can result in a relatively large measure of economic presence in a small, poor country or a poor region or community in a larger and less poor country.

The second crucial phenomenon for globalization theorists is the global diffusion and increasingly concentrated ownership and control of the electronic mass media, particularly television (Barker 1997). The number of TV sets per capita has grown so rapidly in Third World countries in recent years (from fewer than 10 per 1,000 population in 1970 to 60 per 1,000 in 1993, according to UNESCO) that many researchers argue that a "globalizing effect" due to the mass media is taking place even in the Third World (Sussman and Lent 1991; Sklair 2002).

Ownership and control of television, including satellite and cable systems, and associated media like newspaper, magazine, and book publishing, films, video, records, tapes, compact discs, and a wide variety of other marketing media are concentrated in relatively few very large TNCs. The predominance of U.S.-based corporations is being challenged by others based in Japan, Europe, and Australia and even by "Third World" corporations like the media empires of TV Globo, based in Brazil, and Televisa, based in Mexico (Nordenstreng and Schiller 1993; Herman and McChesney 1997).

Main Approaches to Globalization

As with other topics in sociology, there are several ways to categorize theory and research on globalization. One common approach is to compare monocausal with multicausal explanations of the phenomenon, as does McGrew (1992). This is a useful way of looking at the problem, but it has two main drawbacks. First, it ends up by putting thinkers with entirely different types of explanations—for example, those who see globalization as a consequence of the development of material-technological forces and those who see it as a consequence of ideological or cultural (or both) forces—in the same bag. Second, few thinkers present an entirely monocausal explanation of anything; most of the thinkers McGrew identifies as monocausal do try to show the relevance of a variety of factors even if they tend to prioritize some factors over others, while those he identifies as multicausal do not always argue that everything causes everything else. Globalization, by its very nature, is a big and complex subject.

A second approach is to compare the disciplinary foci of globalization studies. This is certainly an interesting and fruitful avenue to explore—several disciplines have made distinctive contributions to the study of globalization (to some extent all the social sciences have contributed to the debate, but anthropology, geography, and international political economy, in addition to sociology, can be singled out). These contributions are commonly borrowed by sociologists of globalization, and vice versa, and this is reflected in my own categorization. I have chosen to categorize globalization studies on the basis of four research clusters in which groups of scholars are working on similar research problems, either in direct contact with one another or, more commonly, in rather indirect contact. Accordingly, globalization studies can be categorized on the basis of four clusters of theory and research:

1. The world-systems approach
2. The global culture approach
3. The global society approach
4. The global capitalism approach

The World-Systems Approach

This approach is based on the distinction between core, semiperipheral, and peripheral countries in terms of their changing roles in the international division of labor dominated by the capitalist world-system. The world-systems model in social science research, inspired by the work of Immanuel Wallerstein, has been developed in a large and continually expanding body of literature since the 1970s (see Wallerstein 1979 and Shannon 1989 for a good overview).

The world-systems approach is, unlike the others to be discussed, not only a collection of academic writings but also a highly institutionalized academic enterprise. It is based at the Braudel Center at the State University of New York, Binghamton; supports various international joint academic ventures; and publishes the journal *Review*. Though the work of world-systems theorists cannot be said to be fully a part of the globalization literature as such (see King 1991), the institutionalization of the world-systems approach undoubtedly prepared the ground for globalization in the social sciences.

In some senses, Wallerstein and his school could rightly claim to have been "global" all along—after all, what could be more global than the "world-system"? However, there is no specific concept of the "global" in most world-systems literature. Reference to the "global" comes mainly from critics and, significantly, can be traced to the long-standing problems that the world-systems model has had with "cultural issues." Wallerstein's essay "Culture as the Ideological Battleground of the Modern World-System," its critique by Boyne, and Wallerstein's attempt to rescue his position under the title "Culture Is the World-System" (all in Featherstone 1990) illustrate the problem well.

Chase-Dunn, in his suggestively titled book *Global Formation* (1989), does try to take the argument a stage further by proposing a dual logic approach to economy and polity. At the economic level, he argues, a global logic of the world-economy prevails, whereas at the level of politics a state-centered logic of the world-system prevails. However, as the world-economy is basically still explicable only in terms of national economies (countries of the core, semiperiphery, and periphery), Chase-Dunn's formulation largely reproduces the problems of Wallerstein's state-centrist analysis.

There is, therefore, no distinctively "global" dimension in the world-systems model apart from the inter-national focus that it has always emphasized. Wallerstein himself rarely uses the word "globalization." For him, the economics of the model rests on the inter-national division of labor that distinguishes core, semiperiphery, and periphery countries. The politics are mostly bound up with antisystemic movements and "superpower struggles." And the cultural, insofar as it is dealt with at all, covers debates about the "national" and the "universal" and the concept of "civilization(s)" in the social sciences. Many critics are not convinced that the world-systems model, usually considered to be "economistic" (i.e., too locked into economic factors), can deal with cultural issues adequately. Janet Wolff tellingly comments on the way in which the concept of "culture" has been inserted into Wallerstein's world-systems model: "An economism which gallantly switches its attentions to the operations of culture is still economism" (in King 1991:168). Wallerstein's attempts to theorize "race," nationality, and ethnicity in terms of what he refers to as different types of "peoplehood" in the world-system (Wallerstein 1991) might be seen as a move in the right direction, but few would argue that cultural factors are an important part of the analysis.

While it would be fair to say that there are various remarks and ideas that do try to take the world-systems model beyond state-centrism,[4] any conceptions of the global that world-systems theorists have tend to be embedded in the world-economy based on the system of nation-states. The "global" and the "inter-national" are generally used interchangeably by world-systems theorists. This is certainly one possible use of "global," but it seems quite superfluous, given that the idea of the "inter-national" is so common in the social science literature. Whatever the fate of the world-systems approach, it is unlikely that ideas of globalization would have spread so quickly and deeply in sociology without the impetus it gave to looking at the whole world.

Global Culture Model

A second model of globalization derives specifically from research on the "globalization of culture." The global culture approach focuses on the problems that a homogenizing mass media–based culture poses for national identities. As we shall see below, this approach is complementary to, rather than in contradiction with, the global society approach, which focuses more on ideas of an emerging global consciousness and their implications for global community, governance, and security.

This complementarity is well illustrated in a collection of articles from the journal *Theory, Culture and Society* (*TCS*) published in book form under the title *Global Culture,* edited by Featherstone (1990). *TCS* has brought together groups of like-minded theorists through the journal and conferences, which has resulted in an institutional framework and an intellectual critical mass for the development of a culturalist approach to globalization. Of the writers associated with *TCS* who have made notable contributions to this effort, Robertson—who has been credited with introducing the term "globalization" into sociology (Waters 1995:2)—is probably the most influential.

Although these researchers cannot be identified as a school in the same way that world-systems researchers can be, their works do constitute a relatively coherent whole. First, they tend to prioritize the cultural over the political or the economic (or both). Second, these researchers have a common interest in the question of how individual or national identity (or both) can survive in the face of an emerging "global culture."

A distinctive feature of this model is that it problematizes the existence of "global culture" as a reality, a possibility, or a fantasy. This is based on the very rapid growth that has taken place over the past few decades in the scale of the mass media of communication and the emergence of what Marshall McLuhan famously called "the global village." The basic idea is that the spread of the mass media, especially television, means that everyone in the world can be exposed to the same images, almost instantaneously. This, the argument goes, turns the whole world into a sort of "global village."

Of considerable interest to sociologists theorizing and researching globalization is the distinctive contribution of anthropologists to these debates. Jonathan Friedman, a Swedish anthropologist, argues, for example, that "ethnic and cultural fragmentation and modernist homogenization are not two arguments, two opposing views of what is happening in the world today, but two constitutive trends of global reality. The dualist centralized world of the double East-West hegemony is fragmenting, politically, and culturally, but the homogeneity of capitalism remains as intact and as systematic as ever" (in Featherstone 1990:311). While not all would agree either that capitalism remains intact and systematic or that it is, in fact, the framework of globalization, the fragmentation of "the double East-West hegemony" is beyond doubt. Ideas such as hybridization and creolization have been proposed in the effort to try to conceptualize what happens when people and items from different (sometimes, but not always, dominant and subordinate) cultures interact.[5] Since the early 1990s the voices of a growing number of scholars from outside Europe and North America have been heard in these debates (see, e.g, some of the contributions to Jameson and Miyoshi 1998).

Some "globalization of culture" theorists have also contributed to current debates on postmodernity in which transformations in the mass media and media representations of reality and so-called hyperreality play a central role. Indicative of similar interests is a compilation of articles edited by Albrow and King (1990) that raised several central issues relevant to the ideas of global sociology, global society, and globalization as new problem areas in the social sciences. One important emphasis has been the "globalization" of sociology itself as a discipline. While the classical sociological theorists, notably Marx, Weber, and Durkheim, all tried to generalize about how societies changed and tried to establish some universal features of social organization, none of them saw the need to theorize on the global level. This connects in some important ways with the debate about the integrity of national cultures in a globalizing world, particularly the influence of "Western" economic, political, military, and cultural forms on non-Western societies.

A subset of the global culture approach, characterized as "globo-localism," derives from a group of scholars from various countries and social science traditions whose main concern is to try to make sense of the multifaceted and enormously complex web of local-global relations. There is a good deal of overlap between this and the "globalization of culture" model, but the globo-local researchers tend to emphasize the "territorial" dimension.

This view has been actively developed within the International Sociological Association (ISA). The ISA's 12th World Congress of Sociology in Madrid in 1990 was organized around the theme "Sociology for One World: Unity and Diversity." Mlinar (1992) reports that the issue of globalization was readily accepted, and his edited volume of papers from the conference illustrates the variety of issues raised in Madrid. The 1994 ISA World Congress in Bielefeld, Germany, continued the theme under the title "Contested Boundaries and Shifting Solidarities," and again discussions of globalization were quite prominently featured on the agenda, and the 1998 conference in Montreal continues the trend. It is not surprising that globalization and territory attracted attention, for in the background to the 1990 and 1994 conferences the wars in the former Yugoslavia were raging (Mlinar himself is from Slovenia, formerly part of Yugoslavia) and, of course, the first shocks of the end of the communist state system were giving way to new territorial issues created by an explosive mix of local and global forces.

If Mlinar is a European progenitor of the globo-local model, then the American progenitor is Alger (1988), who developed the concept of the "local-global nexus." No single common theoretical position in the work of Mlinar, Alger, and the others is involved in this enterprise. What unites them is the urge to theorize and research questions of what happens to territorial identities (within and across countries) in a globalizing world. Thus, the globo-local model is part of the more general global culture model, but with a distinct territorial focus.

The main research question for all these writers is the autonomy of local

cultures in the face of an advancing "global culture." Competing claims of local cultures against the forces of "globalization" have forced themselves onto
sociological, cultural, and political agendas all over the world. Since the early
1990s issues of globalization have penetrated deeply into studies of culture
at all levels. This is largely continuous with the focus of the third globalization model, based on the idea of global society.

Global Society Models

Inspiration for this general conception of globalization is often located in the
pictures of planet Earth sent back by space explorers. A classic statement of
this was the report of *Apollo XIV* astronaut Edgar Mitchell in 1971: "It was a
beautiful, harmonious, peaceful-looking planet, blue with white clouds, and
one that gave you a deep sense . . . of home, of being, of identity. It is what I
prefer to call instant global consciousness."[6]

Had astronaut Mitchell penetrated a little through the clouds, he would
also have seen horrific wars in Vietnam and other parts of Asia, bloody repression by various dictatorial regimes in Africa and Latin America, and dead
and maimed bodies as a result of sectarian terrorism in Britain and Ireland,
as well as a terrible toll of human misery from hunger, disease, drug abuse,
and carnage on roads all around the world as automobile cultures intensified
their own peculiar structures of globalization. Nevertheless, some leading
globalization theorists, for example, Giddens (1991) and Robertson (1992),
do attribute great significance to ideas like "global awareness" and "planetary
consciousness."

Historically, global society theorists argue that the concept of world or
global society has become a believable idea only in the modern age and, in
particular, science, technology, industry, and universal values are increasingly creating a twentieth-century world that is different from any past age.
The globalization literature is full of discussions of the decreasing power and
significance of the nation-state and the increasing significance (if not actually power) of supranational and global institutions and systems of belief.
Ideas of space-time distanciation (see Giddens 1991) and of time-space compression (see Harvey 1989) illustrate how processes of globalization com-
press, stretch, and deepen space-time for people all over the world, thus creating some of the conditions for a global society.

In his attempt to order the field of globalization studies, Spybey (1995)
contrasts the view that "modernity is inherently globalizing" (Giddens 1991:
63) with the view that globalization predates modernity (Robertson 1992).
While Spybey comes down in favor of Giddens's thesis that globalization is

best conceptualized as "reflexive modernization," he is less clear about why these differences matter, and in the end, as with so many debates in the social sciences, the main protagonists seem to be saying more or less the same things in rather different languages. However, it is important to establish whether globalization is a new name for a relatively old phenomenon (which appears to be the argument of Robertson), or whether it is relatively new, a phenomenon of late modernity (the argument of Giddens), or whether it is very new and primarily a consequence of post-1960s capitalism (the argument of Sklair). Why does this matter? It matters because if we want to understand our own lives and the lives of those around us, in our families, communities, local regions, countries, and supranational regions, and, ultimately, how we relate to the global, then it is absolutely fundamental that we are clear about the extent to which the many different structures within which we live are the same in the most important respects as they have been or are different. Two critics, in their attempt to demonstrate that globalization is a myth because the global economy does not really exist, argue that there is "no fundamental difference between the international submarine telegraph cable method of financial transactions [of the early twentieth century] and contemporary electronic systems (Hirst and Thompson 1996:197). They are entirely mistaken. The fundamental difference is, precisely, in the way that the electronics revolution (a post-1960s phenomenon) has transformed the quantitative possibilities of transferring cash and money capital into qualitatively new forms of corporate and personal financing, entrepreneurship, and, crucially, the system of credit on which the global culture and ideology of consumerism largely rests. Some globalization theorists argue forcefully that these phenomena are all new and fundamental for understanding what is happening not only in the rich countries but in social groups anywhere that have a part to play in this global system. In this sense the idea of a global society is a very provocative one, but while it is relatively easy to establish empirically the objective dimensions of globalization as they involve the large majority of the world's population, the idea of a global society based on subjective relationships to globalization, planetary consciousness, and the like is highly speculative.[7]

There appears to be, however, a real psychological need for many writers to believe in the possibilities of a global society (which I share).[8] As McGrew (1992) shows, this theme is elaborated by scholars grappling with the apparent contradictions between globalization and local disruption and strife based on ethnic and other particularistic loyalties. It is in this type of approach that a growing appreciation of the ethical problems of globalization is particularly to be found. The reason for this is simple: Now that humankind has the capacity to destroy itself through war and toxic accidents of various types, a democratic and just human society on the global level, however utopian, seems to be the best long-term guarantee of the continued survival of humanity (Held 1995).

Global Capitalism Model

A fourth model of globalization locates the dominant global forces in the structures of an ever more globalizing capitalism (e.g., Ross and Trachte 1990; McMichael 1996; Sklair 2002; see also Robinson 1996). While all these writers and others who could be identified with this approach develop their own specific analyses of globalization, they all strive toward a concept of the "global" that involves more than the relations between nation-states and state-centrist explanations of national economies competing against one another.

Ross and Trachte focus specifically on capitalism as a social system that is best analyzed on three levels, namely, the level of the internal logic of the system (inspired by Marx and Adam Smith), the structural level of historical development, and the level of the specific social formation, or society. They explain the deindustrialization of some of the heartland regions of capitalism and the transformations of what we still call the Third World in these terms and argue that the globalization of the capitalist system is deeply connected to the capitalist crises of the 1970s and after (oil price shocks, rising unemployment, and increasing insecurity as the rich countries experience problems in paying for their welfare states). This leads them to conclude that "we are only at the beginning of the global era" (Ross and Trachte 1990:230).

Sklair proposes a more explicit model of the global system based on the concept of transnational practices, practices that originate with nonstate actors and cross state borders. They are analytically distinguished in three spheres: economic, political, and cultural-ideological. Each of these practices is primarily, but not exclusively, characterized by a major institution. The transnational corporation is the most important institution for economic transnational practices, the transnational capitalist class (TCC) for political transnational practices, and the culture-ideology of consumerism for transnational cultural-ideological practices (Sklair 1991, 1995, 2002). The research agenda of this theory is concerned with how TNCs, TCCs, and the culture-ideology of consumerism operate to transform the world in terms of the global capitalist project.

In global system theory, under certain circumstances the TCC may act as a "global ruling class." Table 4.1 suggests how the TCC fits into the global system in terms of its transnational practices, its leading institutions, and its integrating agents.

The culture-ideology of consumerism prioritizes the exceptional place of consumption and consumerism in contemporary capitalism, increasing consumption expectations and aspirations without necessarily ensuring the income to buy. The extent to which economic and environmental constraints on the private accumulation of capital challenge the global capitalist project in general and its culture-ideology of consumerism in particular is a central issue for global system theory (thus Sklair 2001, chap. 7, on the corporate capture of sustainable development; see also Durning 1992).

McMichael (1996) focuses on the issue of Third World development and provides both theoretical and empirical support for the thesis that globalization is a qualitatively new phenomenon and not simply a quantitative expansion of older trends. He contrasts two periods. The first is the "Development Project" (late 1940s to early 1970s), when all countries tried to develop their

Table 4.1. The Transnational Capitalist Class

Transnational Practices	Leading Institutions	Integrating Agents
Economic Sphere	*Economic Forces*	*Global business elite*
Transnational capital	Global TNCs	
International capital	World Bank, IMF, BIS	
State capital	State TNCs	
Political Sphere	*Political Forces*	*Global political elite*
TNC executives	Global business organizations	
Globalizing bureaucrats	Open-door agencies (WTO)	
Politicians and professionals	Parties and lobbies	
Regional blocs	EU, NAFTA, ASEAN	
Emerging transnational states	UN, NGOs	
Culture-Ideology Sphere	*Culture-Ideology Forces*	*Global cultural elite*
Consumerism	Shops, media	
Transnational neoliberalism	Think tanks, elite social movements	

national economies with the help of international development agencies and institutions. The second period he labels the "Globalization Project" (1980s onward), when development is pursued through attempts to integrate economies into a globalized world market and the process is directed by a public-private coalition of "Global Managers." He explains: "As parts of national economies became embedded more deeply in global enterprise through commodity chains, they weakened as national units and strengthened the reach of the global economy. This situation was not unique to the 1980s, but the mechanisms of the debt regime institutionalized the power and authority of global management within states' very organization and procedures. This was the turning point in the story of development" (p. 135). This contribution to the debate is notable for its many telling empirical examples of the effects of globalization on Third World communities.

To these writers on globalization and capitalism we can add other Marxist and Marx-inspired scholars who see capitalism as a global system but do not have any specific concepts of globalization. The most important of these is the geographer David Harvey, whose Marxist analysis of modernity and postmodernity is significant for the attempt to build a bridge between the debates around economic and cultural globalization (Harvey 1989, esp. chap. 15).

Summing up the Approaches

Each of the four approaches to globalization has its own distinctive strengths and weaknesses. The world-systems model tends to be economistic (minimizing the importance of political and cultural factors), but as globalization is often interpreted in terms of economic actors and economic institutions, this does seem to be a realistic approach. The globalization of culture model, on the other hand, tends to be culturalist (minimizing economic factors), but as much of the criticism of globalization comes from those who focus on the negative effects of homogenizing mass media and marketing on local and indigenous cultures, the culturalist approach has many adherents. The world society model tends to be both optimistic and all-inclusive, an excellent combination for the production of worldviews but less satisfactory for social science research programs. Finally, the global capitalism model, by prioritizing the global capitalist system and paying less attention to other global forces, runs the risk of appearing one-sided. However, the question remains: How important is that "one side" (global capitalism)?[9]

Resistances to Globalization

Globalization is often seen in terms of impersonal forces wreaking havoc on the lives of ordinary and defenseless people and communities. It is not coincidental that interest in globalization over the past two decades has been accompanied by an upsurge in what has come to be known as New Social Movements (NSM) research (Spybey 1995, chap. 7; Sklair 2002, chap. 10; Smith and Johnston 2002). NSM theorists, despite their substantial differences, argue that the traditional response of the labor movement to global capitalism, based on class politics, has generally failed and that a new analysis based on identity politics (of gender, sexuality, ethnicity, age, community, belief systems) is necessary to mount effective resistance to sexism, racism, environmental damage, warmongering, capitalist exploitation, and other forms of injustice.

The globalization of identity politics involves the establishment of global networks of people with similar identities and interests outside the control of international, state, and local authorities. There is a substantial volume of research and documentation on such developments in the women's, peace, and environmental movements, some of it in direct response to governmental initiatives (e.g., alternative and nongovernmental organizations shadowing official United Nations and other conferences), but most theorists and activists tend to operate under the slogan "think global, act local" (Ekins 1992).

The main challenges to global capitalism in the economic sphere have also come from those who "think global and act local." This normally involves disrupting the capacity of TNCs and global financial institutions to accumulate private profits at the expense of their workforces, their consumers, and the communities that are affected by their activities. An important part of economic globalization today is the increasing dispersal of the manufacturing process into many discrete phases carried out in many different places. Being no longer so dependent on the production of one factory and one workforce gives capital a distinct advantage, particularly against the strike weapon, which once gave tremendous negative power to the working class. Global production chains can be disrupted by strategically planned stoppages, but these generally act more as inconveniences than as real weapons of labor against capital. The international division of labor and its corollary, the globalization of production, build flexibility into the system so that not only can capital migrate anywhere in the world to find the cheapest reliable productive sources of labor but also few workforces can any longer decisively "hold capital to ransom" by withdrawing their labor. At the level of the production process, globalizing capital has all but defeated labor. In this respect, the global organization of the TNCs and allied institutions like globalizing government agencies and the World Bank have, so far, proved too powerful for the local organization of labor and communities.

Nevertheless, the global capitalists, if we are to believe their own propaganda, are continuously beset by opposition, boycott, legal challenge, and moral outrage from the consumers of their products and by disruptions from their workers. There are also many ways to be ambivalent or hostile about global capitalism and cultures and ideologies of consumerism, some of which have been successfully exploited by the green movement (see Mander and Goldsmith 1996).

The issue of democracy is central to the advance of the forces of globalization and the practices and the prospects of social movements that oppose them, both local and global. The rule of law, freedom of association and expression, and freely contested elections, as minimum conditions and however imperfectly sustained, are as necessary in the long run for mass market–based global consumerist capitalism as they are for alternative social systems.[10]

This account of the state of globalization studies to date has focused on what distinguishes global from inter-national forces, processes, and institutions. It is almost exclusively based on the European and North American literature and does not preclude the possibility of other and quite different conceptions of globalization being developed elsewhere. Despite the view, particularly evident in the accounts of "global culture" theorists, that globalization is more or less the same as Westernization or Americanization or McDonaldization (Ritzer 1995), more and more critics are beginning to question this one-way traffic bias in the globalization literature. This critique is well represented in the empirical cases and analytical points of those who are "Interrogating Theories of the Global" (in King 1991, chap. 6) and the work of "non-Western" scholars represented in Albrow and King (1990) and Jameson and Miyoshi (1998), all of whom provide some necessary correctives to European–North American orthodoxies. These scholars, and others, are doing important research relevant for the study of globalization, and their work does not necessarily fit into the four approaches identified above. It is very likely that an introduction to globalization studies to be written 10 years from now will reflect non-Western perspectives much more strongly. Further, the time is ripe for distinctions between generic, capitalist, and alternative globalizations to be more systematically theorized and researched (see Sklair, 2004).

Although of quite recent vintage compared with many of the key concepts of the social sciences, globalization as a theoretical issue and an object of research is undeniably now firmly on the intellectual and political agenda.

Notes

This chapter, an updated version of Sklair, "Competing Conceptions of Globalization" (*Journal of World-Systems Research* 5 [1999]: 143–162), borrows from Sklair (2001, 2002).

1. For some extremely interesting examples of cross-cultural data presented in forms that are not state-centrist, see United Nations Development Programme (1993) and subsequent annual volumes.

2. On the NICs, see Dicken (1998) and Sklair (1994).

3. All parts of all economies are clearly not equally globalized. However, there does appear to be increasing evidence that production and marketing processes within TNCs are being "deterritorialized" from their "home" countries into something like a new global system. This is a highly controversial issue in the study of TNC (see Sklair 2001).

4. For example, research on the idea of commodity chains, networks of labor, and the production and marketing of goods has shifted attention away from national economies to global forces to some extent (see Gary Gereffi in Sklair 1994, chap. 11).

5. See Stuart Hall's chapter 6 in Hall, Held, and McGrew. (1992). Also relevant here are Arjun Appadurai's five dimensions of global cultural flows: ethnoscapes, mediascapes, technoscapes, financescapes, and ideoscapes (in Featherstone 1990:295–310).

6. This is quoted in many different places. My source is, significantly, the back page of the 25th Anniversary Issue of *Earthmatters*, the magazine of Friends of the Earth, UK. The quotation is superimposed on a very cloudy map of a rather polluted planet Earth.

7. I take this argument further in the section "Globalization in Everyday Life" in Sklair (2002, chap. 1).

8. For example, Strauss and Falk argue "For a Global People's Assembly" in the *International Herald Tribune* (November 14, 1997), a publication that advertises itself as the newspaper for global elites! For a good survey of the World Social Forum movement and policies (Porto Alegre), see Fisher and Ponniah (2003).

9. Today, more or less every specialism in the social sciences has its "globalization" perspective, for example, globalization of law, social welfare, crime, labor, and politics. Among the most important substantive issues, discussed by globalization researchers inside and outside the four approaches outlined above, are global environ-

mental change, gender and globalization, global cities, and globalization and regionalization, discussed in Sklair (2002).

10. I say in the long run. In the short term, authoritarian regimes can ignore demands for democratization and push forward consumerist market reforms. It is by no
means obvious that everyone in the world prefers "democracy" to "economic prosperity," if that is the choice they are persuaded to accept. This argument is extended in
terms of the globalization of human rights in Sklair (2002, chapt. 11).

References

Albrow, M. 1996. *The Global Age.* Cambridge, UK: Polity Press.

Albrow, M. and King, E., eds. 1990. *Globalization, Knowledge and Society.* London:
Sage.

Alger, C. 1988. "Perceiving, Analysing and Coping with the Local-Global Nexus." *International Social Science Journal* 117 (August): 321–340.

Barker, Chris. 1997. *Global Television.* Oxford: Blackwell.

Barnet, R. and Cavanagh, J. 1994. *Global Dreams.* New York: Simon and Schuster.

Chase-Dunn, C. 1989. *Global Formation.* Oxford: Blackwell.

Dicken, P. 1998. *Global Shift: Transforming the World Economy.* 3d ed. London: Paul
Chapman.

Dowmunt, T., ed. 1993. *Channels of Resistance: Global Television and Local Empowerment.* London: BFI/Channel Four.

Dunning, J. 1993. *Multinational Enterprises and the Global Economy.* Wokingham, UK:
Addison-Wesley.

Durning, A. 1992. *How Much Is Enough?* London: Earthscan.

Ekins, P. 1992. *A New World Order: Grassroots Movements for Global Change.* London:
Routledge.

Featherstone, M., ed. 1990. *Global Culture: Nationalism, Globalization and Identity.*
London: Sage.

Fisher, W. and Ponniah, T., eds. 2003. *Another World Is Possible: Popular Alternatives to
Globalization at the World Social Forum.* London: Zed Books.

Giddens, A. 1991. *The Consequences of Modernity.* Cambridge, UK: Polity Press.

Hall, S., D. Held, and T. McGrew, eds. 1992. *Modernity and Its Futures.* Cambridge, UK:
Polity Press.

Harvey, D. 1989. *The Condition of Postmodernity.* Oxford: Blackwell.

Held, D. 1995. *Democracy and the Global Order.* Cambridge, UK: Polity Press.

Herman, E. and McChesney, R. 1997. *The Global Media: The New Missionaries of Corporate Capitalism,* London: Cassell.

Hirst, P. and G. Thompson. 1996. *Globalization in Question: The International Economy
and the Possibilities of Governance.* Cambridge, UK: Polity Press.

Jameson, F. and M. Miyoshi, eds. 1998. *Cultures of Globalization.* Durham, NC: Duke
University Press.

King, A. D., ed. 1991. *Culture, Globalization and the World-System.* New York: Macmillan.

Mander, Jerry and Edward Goldsmith, eds. 1996. *The Case against the Global Economy.* San Francisco: Sierra Club.

McGrew, T. 1992. "A Global Society?" In *Modernity and Its Futures,* edited by S. Hall, D. Held, and T. McGrew. Cambridge, UK: Polity Press.

McMichael, P. 1996. *Development and Social Change: A Global Perspective.* Thousand Oaks, CA: Pine Forge Press.

Mlinar, Z., ed. 1992. *Globalization and Territorial Identities.* Aldershot, UK: Avebury.

Nordenstreng, K. and H. Schiller, eds. *Beyond National Sovereignty: International Communications in the 1990s.* Norwood, NJ: Ablex.

Ritzer, G. 1995. *The McDonaldization of Society.* 2d ed. Thousand Oaks, CA: Pine Forge.

Robertson, R. 1992. *Globalization: Social Theory and Global Culture.* London: Sage.

Robinson, William. 1996. "Globalisation: Nine Theses on Our Epoch." *Race and Class* 38 (2): 13–31.

Ross, R. and Trachte, K. 1990. *Global Capitalism: The New Leviathan.* Albany, NY: State University of New York Press.

Scott, Alan, ed. 1997. *The Limits of Globalization.* London: Routledge.

Shannon, T. 1989. *An Introduction to the World-System Perspective.* Boulder, CO: Westview.

Sklair, L. 1991. *Sociology of the Global System.* Baltimore, MD: Johns Hopkins University Press.

———, ed. 1994. *Capitalism and Development.* London: Routledge.

———. 1995. *Sociology of the Global System.* 2d ed. Baltimore, MD: Johns Hopkins University Press.

———. 2001. *The Transnational Capitalist Class,* Oxford: Blackwell.

———. 2002. *Globalization: Capitalism and Its Alternatives.* Oxford: Oxford University Press. (Updated and expanded 3d ed. of L. Sklair, *Sociology of the Global System,* Baltimore, MD: Johns Hopkins University Press, 1991; 2d. ed., 1995.)

———. 2004. "Generic Globalization, Capitalist Globalization and Alternative Globalizations." In *Critical Globalization Studies,* edited by W. Robinson and R. Applebaum. New York: Routledge.

Sklair, L. and Robbins, P. 2002. "Global Capitalism and Major Corporations from the Third World." *Third World Quarterly* 23 (1): 81–100.

Smith, J. and H. Johnston, eds. 2002. *Globalization and Resistance.* Lanham, MD: Rowman and Littlefield.

Spybey, T. 1995. *Globalization and World Society.* Cambridge, UK: Polity Press.

Sussman, G. and J. Lent, eds. 1991. *Transnational Communications: Wiring the Third World.* Thousand Oaks, CA: Sage.

United Nations Development Programme. 1993. *Human Development Report 1993.* Oxford: Oxford University Press.

Wallerstein, I. 1979. *The Capitalist World-Economy.* Cambridge, UK: Cambridge University Press.

———. 1991. "The Construction of Peoplehood: Racism, Nationalism, Ethnicity." In *"Race," Nation, Class,* edited by E. Balibar and I. Wallerstein. London: Verso.

Waters, M. 1995. *Globalization.* New York: Routledge.

Yearley, S. 1996. *Sociology, Environmentalism, Globalization: Reinventing the Globe.* London: Sage.

5

Globalization

A World-Systems Perspective

CHRISTOPHER CHASE-DUNN

Using the world-systems perspective, this chapter discusses the trajectories of several types of globalization over the past 100 years and the surge in public cognizance of global processes that has occurred in the past two decades. Different types of globalization have different temporal characteristics. Some are long-term upward trends, while others are waves that display large cyclical oscillations. The factors that explain the recent emergence of the globalization discourse are examined, and this phenomenon is analyzed in terms of the contradictory interests of powerful and less powerful groups. I contend that there is a lag between economic and political-cultural globalization and that the latter needs to catch up if we are to convert the contemporary world-system of "casino capitalism" into a more humane, democratic, balanced, and sustainable world society.

The discourse on globalization flooded, crested, and is yet to subside, though many are growing weary of it. What are the trends and processes that are alleged to constitute globalization? How do they correspond with actual recent and long-term changes in the world economy and the world polity? What are the interests of different groups in the political programs implied by the notions of globalization? And what should be the response of those peoples who have been left out or pauperized by the grand project of world economic deregulation and the free reign of global capital?

These questions are addressed from the world-systems perspective, a historically oriented analysis of cycles, trends, and long-run structural features of the whole single system that has involved all the humans on Earth since the nineteenth century. The recent explosion of awareness of transnational, international, and global processes needs to be understood from a historical view of the 600-year emergence of a capitalist world region in Europe and its incorporation of the whole globe.

Intercontinental economic integration has been a long-term upward spiral since the expansion of the great chartered companies in the seventeenth century. This spiral has included repeated waves of global integration that have been followed by periods of disintegration and deglobalization (Chase-Dunn, Kawano, and Brewer 2000). Political globalization also has a long history that can be seen in the punctuated emergence of governmental and nongovernmental international political organizations over the past 200 years. Much of the globalization discourse focuses on a recent qualitative transformation and emphasizes the unique qualities of the new stage (e.g., Sklair, Chapter 4, this volume), while the longer view sees recent changes as part of a much older process of capitalist development and expansion in which there have been important continuities as well as important new developments.

The trends and cycles reveal important continuities and imply that future struggles for economic justice and democracy should be based on an analysis of how earlier struggles changed the scale and nature of development in the world-system. While some populists have suggested that progressive movements should employ the tools of economic nationalism to counter world market forces (e.g., Moore 1995; Hines and Lang 1996), I agree with those who contend that the political globalization of popular movements will be necessary in order to create a democratic and collectively rational global system.

The World-Systems Perspective

Today the terms "world economy," "world market," and "globalization" are commonplace, appearing in the sound bites of politicians, media commentators, and unemployed workers alike. But few know that the most important source for these phrases lies with work started by sociologists in the early 1970s. At a time when the mainstream assumption of accepted social, political, and economic science held that the "wealth of nations" reflected mainly on the cultural developments within those nations, a growing group of social scientists recognized that national "development" could be best understood as the complex outcome of local interactions with an aggressively expanding Europe-centered "world-system" (Wallerstein 1974; Frank 1978).[1] Not only did these scientists perceive the global nature of economic networks 20 years before they entered popular discourse, but they also saw that many of these networks extend back at least 600 years. Over this time, the peoples of the globe became linked into one integrated unit: the modern world-system.

Now, 30 years later, social scientists working in the area are trying to understand the history and evolution of the whole system, as well as how local, national, and regional entities have been integrated into it. This current research has required broadening our perspective to include deeper temporal and larger spatial frameworks. For example, some recent research has compared the modern Europe-centered world region of the past 600 years with earlier, smaller intersocietal networks that have existed for millennia (Frank and Gills 1993; Chase-Dunn and Hall 1997b; Hall and Chase-Dunn, Chapter 3, this volume). Other work uses the knowledge of cycles and trends that has grown out of world-systems research to anticipate likely future events with a precision impossible before the advent of the theory. This is still a new field, and much remains to be done, but enough has already been achieved to provide a valuable understanding of the phenomenon of globalization.

The discourse about globalization has emerged mainly in the past decade. The term means many different things, and there are many reasons for its emergence as a popular concept. The usage of this term generally implies that a recent change (within the past decade or two) has occurred in technology and in the size of the arena of economic competition. The general idea is that information technology has created a context in which the global market, rather than separate national markets, is the relevant arena for economic competition. It then follows that economic competitiveness needs to be assessed in the global context, rather than in a national or local context. These notions have been used to justify the adoption of new practices by firms and governments all over the world, and these developments have altered the political balances among states, firms, unions, and other interest groups.

The first task is to put this development into historical context. The world-systems perspective has shown that intersocietal geopolitics and geoeconomics have been important arenas of competition for national states, firms, and classes for hundreds of years. The degree of intercontinental connectedness of economic and political-military networks was already important in the fourteenth and fifteenth centuries. The first transnational corporations (TNCs) were the great chartered companies of the seventeenth century. They organized both production and exchange on an intercontinental scale. The rise and fall of hegemonic core powers, which continues today with the relative decline of the United States hegemony, was already in full operation in the seventeenth-century rise and fall of Dutch hegemony (see Arrighi 1994; Modelski and Thompson 1996; Taylor 1996).

The capitalist world-economy has experienced cyclical processes and secular trends for hundreds of years (Chase-Dunn 1998, chap. 2). The cyclical processes include the rise and fall of hegemons, the Kondratieff wave (a 40- to 60-year business cycle),[2] a cycle of warfare among core states (Goldstein

1988), and cycles of colonization and decolonization (Bergesen and Schoen-berg 1980). The world-system has also experienced several secular trends including a long-term proletarianization of the world workforce, growing concentration of capital into larger and larger firms, increasing internation-alization of capital investment and of trade, and accelerating international-ization of political structures.

In this perspective, globalization is a long-term upward trend of political and economic integration that includes strong waves of connectedness that are followed by dramatic periods of deglobalization. The most recent techno-logical changes, and the expansions of international trade and investment, are part of these long-run changes. Exactly how do the most recent changes compare with the long-run trends? And what are the important continuities as well as the qualitative differences that accompany these changes?

Types of Globalization

The term "globalization" as used by social scientists and in popular discourse has many meanings. I contend that it is important to distinguish between globalization as a particular contemporary political ideology and what we call *structural globalization*—the increasing worldwide density of large-scale in-teraction networks relative to the density of smaller networks. Social scien-tific approaches to globalization disagree about how the structure of the world economy has changed over time. Some social scientists, and much of the public, believe that in the recent past national economies were largely in-dependent entities. It is believed that since the 1960s a new transnational economy has emerged in which national societies have become integrated into a global network of trade and an interdependent division of labor. A sec-ond perspective imagines a centuries-long trend toward increasing global in-tegration as transportation and communications costs have declined. And yet a third approach envisions a cyclical process of phases of increased inter-national integration followed by phases in which national economies return toward autarchy.

The term "globalization" often refers to changes in technologies of com-munication and transportation, increasingly internationalized financial flows and commodity trade, and the transition from national to world mar-kets as the main arena for economic competition. The information age and the stage of global capitalism are asserted to constitute a new and qualita-tively different epoch. The term is also sometimes used to refer to what has been called Reaganism-Thatcherism, the "Washington Consensus," or the "globalization project" (McMichael 1996), a neoliberal political ideology that celebrates the victory of capitalism over socialism and proclaims marketization and privatization as solutions to the world's problems. This became the predominant global policy rationale during the 1980s and has only recently been challenged by a new global Keysianism and multiple proposals for global democratization.

It is important to distinguish between the "globalization project" as a hegemonic political ideology and structural globalization—changes in the density of international and global interactions relative to local or national networks. Charles Tilly (1995) proposed a similar definition of structural globalization: "an increase in the geographic range of locally consequential social interactions, especially when that increase stretches a significant proportion of all interactions across international or intercontinental limits" (pp. 1–2). If national-level networks and global networks increased in density at the same rate, there would be no increase in globalization in the sense of connectedness.

I conceptualize structural economic and political globalization as the differential density and power of large versus small interaction networks and organizations. *Economic globalization* means greater integration in the organization of production, distribution, and consumption of commodities in the world economy. It seems that our breakfasts increasingly come from distant lands. But sugar has been an intercontinental commodity since the eighteenth century in the sense that global market forces and the policies of competing states have massively affected its conditions of production and consumption. Fresh grapes, on the other hand, have become a global commodity only since jets started transporting them seasonally between the southern and northern hemispheres. But if we count all the commodities and adjust for the overall growth of production, is the average breakfast more "globalized" now than it was in nineteenth century? This is an important question to ask.

Political globalization is understood as the institutional form of global and interregional formal governmental and nongovernmental political and military organizations (including "economic" ones such as the World Bank and the International Monetary Fund) and their strengths relative to the strengths of national states and other local political organizations in the world-system. This is analogous to the idea defined above of economic globalization as the relative density and importance of large versus small interaction networks.

There are other types of structural globalization as well. Common ecological constraints are an aspect of globalization that involves global threats due to our fragile ecosystem and the globalization of ecological risks. Anthropogenic causes of ecological degradation (resource depletion and pollution) have long operated, and these in turn have affected human social evolution (Chase-Dunn and Hall 1997a). But ecological degradation has only recently begun to operate on a global scale. This fact creates a set of systemic constraints that require global collective action.

Cultural globalization is an aspect of globalization that relates to the widespread diffusion of cultural phenomena and reactions against them: the proliferation of individualized values, originally of Western origin, to ever larger parts of the world population. These values are expressed in social constitutions that recognize individual rights and identities and transnational and international efforts to protect "human rights" and the adoption of originally Western institutional practices. Bureaucratic organization and rationality, belief in a lawlike natural universe, the values of economic efficiency, and political democracy have been spreading throughout the world since they were propagated in the European Enlightenment (Markoff 1996; Meyer 1996).

Whereas some of the discussions of the world polity assume that cultural components have been a central aspect of the modern world-system from the start (e.g., Mann 1986; Meyer 1989), I emphasize the comparatively non-normative nature of the modern world-system (Chase-Dunn 1998, chap. 5). But I acknowledge the growing salience of cultural consensus in the past 100 years. Although the modern world-system has always been, and is still, multicultural, the growing influence of Western values of rationality, individualism, equality, and efficiency began to be an important trend of the twentieth century. The spread of these values has also caused important reactions against Westernization—revitalization movements in which indigenous peoples reassert their traditional cultures, and multiple forms of "fundamentalism" in which the multicultural and secular values of the European Enlightenment and science are challenged by groups that feel marginalized in the processes of economic and political globalization.

Another aspect of globalization, *globalization of communication,* is connected with the new era of information technology. Anthony Giddens (1996) has insisted that social space comes to acquire new qualities with generalized electronic communications, albeit only in the networked parts of the world. In terms of accessibility, cost, and velocity, the hitherto more local political and geographic parameters that structured social relationships are greatly expanded.

One may well argue that time-space compression (Harvey 1989) by new information technologies is simply an extension and acceleration of the very long term trend toward technological development over the past 10 millennia (Chase-Dunn 1994). Yet the rapid decrease in the cost of communications may have qualitatively altered the relationship between states and consciousness, and this may be an important basis for the formation of a much stronger global civil society. Global communication facilities have the power to move things visible and invisible from one part of the globe to another whether any nation-state likes it or not. This applies not only to economic exchange but also to ideas, and these new networks of communication can create new political groups and alignments. How, and to what extent, will this undermine the power of states to structure social relationships?

Political globalization consists of the institutionalization of international political structures. The Europe-centered world-system has been primarily constituted as an interstate system—a system of conflicting and allying states and empires. Earlier world-systems, in which accumulation was mainly accomplished by means of institutionalized coercive power, experienced an oscillation between multicentric interstate systems and corewide world empires in which a single "universal" state conquered all or most of the core states in a region. The Europe-centered system has also experienced a cyclical alternation between political centralization and decentralization, but this has taken the form of the rise and fall of hegemonic core states that do not conquer the other core states. Hence the modern world-system has remained multicentric in the core, and this is due mainly to the shift toward a form of accumulation based more on the production and profitable sale of commodities—capitalism. The hegemons have been the most thoroughly capitalist states, and they have preferred to follow a strategy of controlling trade and access to raw material imports from the periphery rather than conquering other core states to extract tribute or taxes.

Power competition in an interstate system does not require much in the way of cross-state cultural consensus to operate systemically. But since the early nineteenth century the European interstate system has been developing both an increasingly consensual international normative order and a set of international political structures that regulate all sorts of interaction. This phenomenon has been termed "global governance" by Craig Murphy (1994) and others. It refers to the growth of both specialized and general international organizations. The general organizations that have emerged are the

Concert of Europe, the League of Nations, and the United Nations. The sequence of these "proto-world-states" constitutes a process of institution building, but unlike earlier "universal states," this one is slowly emerging by means of condominium among core states rather than conquest. This is the trend of political globalization. It is yet a weak, but persistent, concentration of sovereignty in international institutions. If it continues, it will eventuate in a single global state that could effectively outlaw warfare and enforce its illegality. The important empirical question, analogous to the discussion of economic globalization above, is the relative balance of power between international and global political organizations vis-à-vis national states. I assume this to be an upward trend, but like economic globalization, it probably is also a cycle.

Measuring Economic Globalization

The brief discussion above of economic globalization implies that it is a long-run upward trend. The idea is that international economic competition and geopolitical competition were already important in the fourteenth century and that they became increasingly important as more and more international trade and international investment occurred. In its simplest form this would posit a linear upward trend of economic globalization. An extreme alternative hypothesis about economic globalization would posit a completely unintegrated world composed of autarchic national economies until some point (perhaps in the past few decades) at which a completely global market for commodities and capital suddenly emerged.

Let us examine data that can tell us more about the temporal emergence of economic globalization. There are potentially a large number of different indicators of economic globalization, and they may or may not exhibit similar patterns with respect to change over time. Trade globalization can be operationalized as the proportion of all world production that crosses international boundaries. Investment globalization would be the proportion of all invested capital in the world that is owned by non-nationals (i.e., "foreigners").

It would be ideal to have these measures over several centuries, but comparable figures are not available before the nineteenth century, and indeed even these are sparse and probably unrepresentative of the whole system until well into the twentieth century. Nevertheless, we can learn some important things by examining those comparable data that are available.

Economic globalization is both a long-term trend and a cyclical phenomenon. If we calculate the ratio of international investments to investments within countries, the world economy had nearly as high a level of "investment globalization" in 1910 as it did in 1990 (Bairoch 1996). A recent study of world trade as a proportion of world GDP (Chase-Dunn et al. 2000) also shows that trade integration is both a cycle and a trend (fig. 5.1).

Figure 5.1 shows average openness trade globalization. Trade globalization is the ratio of estimated total world exports (the sum of the value of exports of all countries) divided by an estimate of total world product (the sum of all the national GDPs). The trade globalization figures show the hypothesized upward trend as well as a downturn that occurred between 1929 and 1950.There was a shorter and less well defined wave of trade globalization from 1900 to 1929 (Chase-Dunn et al. 2000).

Another indicator of economic globalization is the correlation of national GDP growth rates (Grimes 1993). This shows the extent to which periods of national economic growth and stagnation have been synchronized across countries. In a fully integrated global economy it would be expected that growth and stagnation periods would be synchronized across countries and so there would be a high correlation of national growth rates. Grimes shows that, contrary to the hypothesis of a secular upward trend toward increasing global integration, the correlation among national growth rates fluctuates cyclically over the past two centuries. In a data series from 1860 to 1988 Grimes found two periods in which national economic growth-decline sequences are highly correlated across countries: 1913–1927; and after 1970. Before and in between these peaks are periods of very low synchronization.

Further research needs to be done to determine the temporal patterns of different sorts of economic globalization. At this point we can say that the step-function version of a sudden recent leap to globalization can be rejected. The evidence we have indicates that there are both long-term secular trends and huge cyclical oscillations. Trade globalization shows a long-term trend with a big dip during the depression of the 1930s. The investment globalization indicates a cycle with at least two peaks, one before World War I and one after 1980. Grimes's indicator of synchronous economic growth indicates a cyclical fluctuation with one peak in the 1920s and another since 1970.

These results, especially those that imply cycles, indicate that change occurs relatively quickly and that the most recent period of globalization shares important features with earlier periods of intense international economic interaction. The question of the similarities and differences between the most recent wave and earlier waves of globalization is clearly an important one.

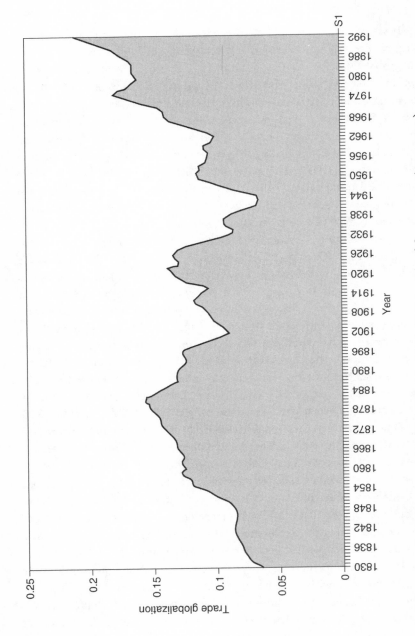

Fig. 5.1. Average Openness Trade Globalization, 1830–1992 (weighted five-year moving average)

Systemic Cycles of Accumulation

Giovanni Arrighi (1994) shows how hegemony in the modern world-system has evolved in a series of "systemic cycles of accumulation" (SCAs) in which finance capital has employed different forms of organization and different relationships with organized state power. These qualitative organizational changes have accompanied the secular increase in the power of money and markets as regulatory forces in the modern world-system. The SCAs have been occurring in the Europe-centered world-system since at least the fourteenth century.

Arrighi's model shows both the similarities and the differences in the relationships that obtain between financial capital and states within the different systemic cycles of accumulation. The British SCA and the American SCA had both similarities and important differences. The main differences that Arrighi emphasizes are the "internalization of transaction costs" (represented by the vertical integration of TNCs) and the extent to which the United States tried to create "organized capitalism" on a global scale. The British SCA had fewer global firms and pushed hard for international free trade. The U.S. SCA is characterized by a much heavier focus on global firms and by a more structured approach to "global governance" possibly intended to produce economic growth in other core regions, especially those that are geopolitically strategic.

Arrighi argues that President Roosevelt used the power of the hegemonic state to try to create a balanced world of capitalist growth. This sometimes meant going against the preferences of finance capital and U.S. corporations. For example, the Japanese miracle was made possible because the U.S. government prevented U.S. corporations from turning Japan (and Korea) into just one more dependent and peripheralized country. This policy of enlightened global Keynesianism was continued in a somewhat constrained form under later presidents, albeit in the guise of domestic "military Keynesianism" justified by the Soviet threat.

In this interpretation the big companies and the finance capitalists returned to power with the decline in competitiveness of the U.S. economy. The rise of the Eurodollar market forced Nixon to abandon the Bretton Woods financial structure, and this was followed by Reaganism-Thatcherism, IMF structural adjustment, streamlining, deregulation, and the delegitimation of anything that constrained the desires of global capital investment. The idea that we are all subject to the forces of a global marketplace, and that any constraint on the freedom to invest will result in a deficit of "competitiveness," is a powerful justification for destroying the institutions of the "Second Wave" (e.g., labor unions, welfare, agricultural subsidies).

Under conditions of increased economic globalization the ability of national states to protect their citizens from world market forces decreases. This results in increasing inequalities within countries and increasing levels of dissatisfaction compared with the relative harmony of national integration achieved under the Keynesian regimes. It is also produces political reactions, especially national-populist movements. Indeed, Philip McMichael (1996) attributes the antigovernment movements that have emerged in the U.S. West, including the bombing of the Federal Building in Oklahoma City, to the frustrations caused by the deregulation of U.S. agriculture.

It would also be useful to investigate the temporal patterns of the other types of globalization: cultural,[3] political, technological, and ecological. Of interest too are the relationships between these and economic globalization. Much empirical work needs to be done to operationalize these concepts and to assemble the relevant information. Here, for now, I will hypothesize that all these types exhibit both long-run secular and cyclical features. I will also surmise that cultural and political globalization are lagged behind the secular upward trend of economic globalization.

The Politics of Globalization

This last hypothesis bears on the question of adjustments of political and social institutions to increases in economic and technological globalization. I would submit that the current period of economic globalization has occurred in part as a result of technological changes that are linked to Kondratieff waves and in part because of the profit squeezes and declining hegemony of the U.S. economy in the larger world market.

The financial aspects of the current period of economic globalization began when President Nixon canceled the Bretton Woods agreement in response to pressures on the value of the U.S. dollar coming from the rapidly growing Eurodollar market (Harvey 1995). This occurred in 1967, and this date is used by many to mark the beginning of a K-wave downturn.

The saturation of the world market demand for the products of the post–World War II upswing, the constraints on capital accumulation posed by business unionism, and the political entitlements of the welfare states in core countries caused a profit squeeze that motivated large firms and investors and their political helpers to try to break out of these constraints. The possibilities for global investment opened up by new communications and information technology created new maneuverability for capital. The demise of the Soviet Union added legitimacy to the revitalized ideology of the free market, and this ideology swept the Earth. Not only Reagan and Thatcher but also Eurocommunists and labor governments in both the core and the periphery adopted the ideology of the "lean state," deregulation, privatization, and the notion that everything must be evaluated in terms of global efficiency and competitiveness.

Cultural globalization has been a very long term upward trend since the emergence of the world religions in which any person, regardless of ethnicity or kinship, could become a member of the moral community by confessing faith in the "universal" god. But moral and political cosmography has usually encompassed a smaller realm than the real dimensions of the objective trade and political-military networks in which people have been involved. What has occurred at the end of the twentieth century is a near convergence between subjective cosmography and objective networks. The main cause of this is probably the practical limitation of human habitation to the planet Earth. But the long-run declining costs of transportation and communications are also an important element. Whatever the causes, the emergent reality is one in which consciousness embraces (or goes beyond) the real systemic networks of interaction. This geographic feature of the global system is one of its unique aspects, and it makes possible for the future a level of normative order that has not existed since human societies were very small and egalitarian (Chase-Dunn and Hall 1997b).

The ideology of globalization has undercut the support and the rationale behind all sorts of so-called Second Wave institutions—labor unions, socialist parties, welfare programs, and communist states. While these institutions have not been destroyed everywhere, the politicians of the Right (e.g., Newt Gingrich in the United States) have explicitly argued for their elimination.

At the same time, the very technologies that made capitalist economic globalization possible also have the potential to allow those who do not benefit from the free reign of capital to organize new forms of resistance or to revitalize old forms. It is now widely agreed by many, even in the financial community, that the honeymoon of neoliberalism will eventually end and that the rough edges of global capitalism will need to be buffed. Patrick Buchanan, a conservative candidate for the U.S. presidency in 1996, tried to capitalize on popular resentment of corporate downsizing. The *Wall Street Journal* has reported that stock analysts worry about the "lean and mean" philosophy becoming a fad that has the potential to delegitimate the business system and to create political backlashes. This was expressed in the context of a discussion of the announcement of huge bonuses for AT&T executives following another round of downsizing.

States are already facing difficulties in controlling communications on the Internet. I do not believe the warnings of those who predict a massive disruption of civilization by hordes of sociopaths waging "cyberwar," but I do think that the new communications technologies provide new opportunities for the less powerful to organize themselves to respond should global capitalism run them over or leave them out.

The important question is, What are the most useful organizational forms for resistance? What we already see are all sorts of nutty localisms, nationalisms, and a proliferation of identity politics. The militias of the U.S. West are ordering large amounts of fertilizer with which to resist the coming of the "Blue Helmets"—a fantasized world state that is going to take away their handguns and assault rifles.

Localisms and specialized identities are the postmodern political forms that are supposedly produced by information technology, flexible specialization, and global capitalism (Harvey 1989). I think that at least some of this trend is a result of desperation and the demise of plausible alternatives in the face of the ideological hegemony of neoliberalism and the much touted triumph of efficiency over justice. Be that as it may, a historical perspective on the latest phase of globalization allows us to see the long-run patterns of interaction between capitalist expansion and the movements of opposition that have tried to protect people from the negative aspects of market forces and exploitation. And this perspective has implications for going beyond the impasse of the present to build a more cooperative and humane global system (Boswell and Chase-Dunn 2000).

The Spiral of Capitalism and Socialism

The interaction between expansive commodification and resistance movements can be denoted as "the spiral of capitalism and socialism." The world-systems perspective provides a view of the long-term interaction between the expansion and deepening of capitalism and the efforts of people to protect themselves from exploitation and domination. The historical development of the communist states is explained as part of a long-run spiraling interaction between expanding capitalism and socialist counterresponses. The history and developmental trajectory of the communist states can be explained as socialist movements in the semiperiphery that attempted to transform the basic logic of capitalism but ended up using socialist ideology to mobilize industrialization for the purpose of catching up with core capitalism.

The spiraling interaction between capitalist development and socialist movements can be seen in the history of labor movements, socialist parties, and communist states over the past 200 years. This long-run comparative perspective enables one to see recent events in China, Russia, and Eastern Europe in a framework that has implications for the future of social democracy. The metaphor of the spiral means this: Both capitalism and socialism affect each other's growth and organizational forms. Capitalism spurs socialist responses by exploiting and dominating peoples, and socialism spurs capitalism to expand its scale of production and market integration and to revolutionize technology.

Defined broadly, socialist movements are those political and organizational means by which people try to protect themselves from market forces, exploitation, and domination and to build more cooperative institutions. The sequence of industrial revolutions, by which capitalism has restructured production and taken control of labor, has stimulated a series of political organizations and institutions created by workers to protect their livelihoods. This happened differently under different political and economic conditions in different parts of the world-system. Skilled workers created guilds and craft unions. Less skilled workers created industrial unions. Sometimes these coalesced into labor parties that played important roles in supporting the development of political democracies, mass education, and welfare states (Rueschemeyer, Stephens, and Stephens 1992). In other regions workers were less politically successful but managed at least to protect access to rural areas or subsistence plots for a fallback or hedge against the insecurities of employment in capitalist enterprises. To some extent the burgeoning contemporary "informal sector" in both core and peripheral societies provides such a fallback.

The mixed success of workers' organizations also had an impact on the further development of capitalism. In some areas workers or communities were successful at raising the wage bill or protecting the environment in ways that raised the costs of production for capital. When this happened, either capitalists displaced workers by automating them out of jobs or capital migrated to places where fewer constraints allowed cheaper production. The process of capital flight is not a new feature of the world-system. It has been an important force behind the uneven development of capitalism and the spreading scale of market integration for centuries. Labor unions and socialist parties were able to obtain some power in certain states, but capitalism became yet more international. Firm size increased. International markets became more and more important to successful capitalist competition. Fordism, the employment of large numbers of easily organizable workers in centralized production locations, has been supplanted by "flexible accumulation" (small firms producing small customized products) and global sourcing (the use of substitutable components from broadly dispersed competing producers), production strategies that make traditional labor-organizing approaches much less viable.

Communist States in the World-System

Socialists were able to gain state power in certain semiperipheral states and use this power to create political mechanisms of protection against competition with core capital. This was not a wholly new phenomenon. As discussed below, capitalist semiperipheral states had done and were doing similar things. But the communist states claimed a fundamentally oppositional ideology in which socialism was allegedly a superior system that would eventually replace capitalism. Ideological opposition is a phenomenon that the capitalist world-economy has seen before. The geopolitical and economic battles of the Thirty Years' War were fought in the name of Protestantism against Catholicism. The content of the ideology may make some difference for the internal organization of states and parties, but every contender must be able to legitimate itself in the eyes and hearts of its cadre. The claim to represent a qualitatively different and superior socioeconomic system is not evidence that the communist states were indeed structurally autonomous from world capitalism.

The communist states severely restricted the access of core capitalist firms to their internal markets and raw materials, and this constraint on the mobility of capital was an important force behind the post–World War II upsurge in the spatial scale of market integration and a new revolution of technology. In certain areas capitalism was driven to further revolutionize technology or to improve living conditions for workers and peasants because of the demonstration effect of propinquity to a communist state. U.S. support for state-led industrialization of Japan and Korea (in contrast to U.S. policy in Latin America) is only understandable as a geopolitical response to the Chinese revolution. The existence of "two superpowers"—one capitalist and one communist—in the period since World War II provided a fertile context for the success of international liberalism within the "capitalist" bloc. This was the political-military basis of the rapid growth of transnational corporations and the latest revolutionary "time-space compression" (Harvey 1989). This technological revolution has once again restructured the international division of labor and created a new regime of labor regulation called "flexible accumulation." The process by which the communist states have become reintegrated into the capitalist world-system has been long, as described below. But the final phase of reintegration was provoked by the inability to be competitive with the new form of capitalist regulation. Thus, capitalism spurs socialism, which spurs capitalism, which spurs socialism again in a wheel that turns and turns while getting larger.

The economic reincorporation of the communist states into the capitalist world-economy did not occur recently and suddenly. It began with the mobilization toward autarchic industrialization using socialist ideology, an effort that was quite successful in terms of standard measures of economic development. Most of the communist states were increasing their percentage of world product and energy consumption up until the 1980s.

The economic reincorporation of the communist states moved to a new stage of integration with the world market and foreign firms in the 1970s. Andre Gunder Frank (1980, chap. 4) documented a trend toward reintegration in which the communist states increased their exports for sale on the world market, increased imports from the avowedly capitalist countries, and made deals with transnational firms for investments within their borders. The economic crisis in Eastern Europe and the Soviet Union was not much worse than the economic crisis in the rest of the world during the global economic downturn that began in the late 1960s (see Boswell and Peters 1990, table 1). Data presented by World Bank analysts indicate that GDP growth rates were positive in most of the "historically planned economies" in Europe until 1989 or 1990 (Marer et al.1991, table 7a).

Put simply, the big transformations that occurred in the Soviet Union and China after 1989 were part of a process that had been under way since the 1970s. The big sociopolitical changes were a matter of the superstructure catching up with the economic base. The democratization of these societies is, of course, a welcome trend, but democratic political forms do not automatically lead to a society without exploitation or domination. The outcomes of current political struggles are rather uncertain in most of the former communist countries. New types of authoritarian regimes seem at least as likely as real democratization.

As trends in the past two decades have shown, austerity regimes, deregulation, and marketization within nearly all the communist states occurred during the same period as similar phenomena in noncommunist states. The synchrony and broad similarities between Reagan/Thatcher deregulation and attacks on the welfare state, austerity socialism in most of the rest of the world, and increasing pressures for marketization in the Soviet Union and China are all related to the B-phase downturn of the Kondratieff wave, as are the current moves toward austerity and privatization in many semiperipheral and peripheral states. The trend toward privatization, deregulation, and market-based solutions among parties of the Left in almost every country is thoroughly documented by Lipset (1991). Nearly all socialists with access to political power have abandoned the idea of doing more than buffing off the rough edges of capitalism. The way in which the pressures of a stagnating world economy affect national policies certainly varies from country to country, but the ability of any single national society to construct collective rationality is limited by its interaction within the larger system. The most recent expansion of capitalist integration, termed "globalization of the economy," has made autarchic national economic planning seem anachronistic. Yet a political reaction against economic globalization is now under way in the form of revived former communist parties, economic nationalism (e.g., Brazil, Venezuela, Bolivia), and a coalition of oppositional forces who are critiquing the ideological hegemony of neoliberalism (e.g., Ralph Nader, environmentalists, populists of the right).

Political Implications of the World-Systems Perspective

The age of U.S. hegemonic decline and the rise of postmodernist philosophy have cast the liberal ideology of the European Enlightenment (science, progress, rationality, liberty, democracy, and equality) into the dustbin of totalizing universalisms. It is alleged that these values have been the basis of imperialism, domination, and exploitation and thus they should be cast out in favor of each group asserting its own set of values. Note that self-determination and a considerable dose of multiculturalism (especially regarding religion) were already central elements in Enlightenment liberalism.

The structuralist and historical materialist world-systems approach poses this problem of values in a different way. The problem with the capitalist world-system has not been with its values. The philosophy of liberalism is fine. It has quite often been an embarrassment to the pragmatics of imperial power and has frequently provided justifications for resistance to domination and exploitation. The philosophy of the Enlightenment has never been a major cause of exploitation and domination. Rather, it was the military and economic power generated by capitalism that made European hegemony possible.

To humanize the world-system we may need to construct a new philosophy of democratic and egalitarian liberation. Of course, many of the principal ideals that have been the core of the Left's critique of capitalism are shared by non-European philosophies. Democracy in the sense of popular control over collective decision-making was not invented in Greece. It was a characteristic of all nonhierarchical human societies on every continent before the emergence of complex chiefdoms and states. My point is that a new egalitarian universalism can usefully incorporate quite a lot from the old universalisms. It is not liberal ideology that caused so much exploitation and domination. It was the failure of real capitalism to live up to its own ideals (liberty and equality) in most of the world. That is the problem that progressives must solve.

A central question for any strategy of transformation is the question of agency. Who are the actors who will most vigorously and effectively resist capitalism and construct democratic socialism? Where is the most favorable terrain, the weak link, where concerted action could bear the most fruit? Samir Amin (1990) contends that the agents of socialism have been most heavily concentrated in the periphery. It is there that the capitalist world-system is most oppressive, and thus peripheral workers and peasants, the vast majority of the world proletariat, have the most to win and the least to lose.

On the other hand, Marx and many contemporary Marxists have argued that socialism will be most effectively built by the action of core proletarians. Since core areas have already attained a high level of technological development, the establishment of socialized production and distribution should be easiest in the core. And organized core workers have had the longest experience with industrial capitalism and the most opportunity to create socialist social relations.

I submit that both "workerist" and "Third Worldist" positions have important elements of truth, but there is another alternative that is suggested by the structural theory of the world-system: the semiperiphery as the weak link.

Core workers may have experience and opportunity, but a sizable segment of the core working classes lack motivation because they have benefited from a nonconfrontational relationship with core capital. The existence of a labor aristocracy has divided the working class in the core and, in combination with a large middle stratum, has undermined political challenges to capitalism. Also, the "long experience" in which business unionism and social democracy have been the outcome of a series of struggles between radical workers and the labor aristocracy has created a residue of trade union practices, party structures, legal and governmental institutions, and ideological heritages that act as barriers to new socialist challenges. These conditions have changed to some extent during the past two decades as hypermobile capital has attacked organized labor, dismantled welfare states, and downsized middle-class workforces. These create new possibilities for popular movements within the core, and we can expect more confrontational popular movements to emerge as workers devise new forms of organization (or revitalize old forms). Economic globalization makes labor internationalism a necessity, and so we can expect to see the old idea take new forms and become more organizationally real. Even small victories in the core have important effects on peripheral and semiperipheral areas because of demonstration effects and the power of core states.

The main problem with "Third Worldism" is not motivation but opportunity. Democratic socialist movements that take state power in the periphery are soon beset by powerful external forces that either overthrow them or force them to abandon most of their socialist program. Popular movements in the periphery are most usually anti-imperialist class alliances that succeed in establishing at least the trappings of national sovereignty, but not socialism. The low level of the development of the productive forces also makes it harder to establish socialist forms of accumulation, although this is not impossible in principle. It is simply harder to share power and wealth when there are very little of either. But the emergence of democratic regimes in the periphery will facilitate new forms of mutual aid, cooperative development, and popular movements once the current ideological hegemony of neoliberalism has broken down.

Semiperipheral Democratic Socialism

In the semiperiphery both motivation and opportunity exist. Semiperipheral areas, especially those in which the territorial state is large, have sufficient resources to be able to stave off core attempts at overthrow and to provide some protection to socialist institutions if the political conditions for their emergence should arise. Semiperipheral regions (e.g., Russia and China) have experienced more militant class-based socialist revolutions and movements because of their intermediate position in the core-periphery hierarchy. While core exploitation of the periphery creates and sustains alliances among classes in both the core and the periphery, in the semiperiphery an interme-

diate world-system position undermines class alliances and provides a fruitful terrain for strong challenges to capitalism. Semiperipheral revolutions
and movements are not always socialist in character, as we have seen in Iran.
But when socialist intentions are strong, there are greater possibilities for
real transformation than in the core or the periphery. Thus, the semiperiphery is the weak link in the capitalist world-system. It is the terrain upon
which the strongest efforts to establish socialism have been made, and this is
likely to be true of the future as well.

On the other hand, the results of the efforts so far, while they have undoubtedly been important experiments with the logic of socialism, have left
much to be desired. The tendency for authoritarian regimes to emerge in the
communist states betrayed Marx's idea of a freely constituted association of
direct producers. And the imperial control of Eastern Europe by the Russians
was an insult to the idea of proletarian internationalism. Democracy within
and between nations must be a constituent element of true socialism.

It does not follow that efforts to build socialism in the semiperiphery will
always be so constrained and thwarted. The revolutions in the Soviet Union
and the People's Republic of China have increased our collective knowledge
about how to build socialism despite their only partial successes and their obvious failures. It is important for all of us who want to build a more humane
and peaceful world-system to understand the lessons of socialist movements
in the semiperiphery and the potential for future, more successful, forms of
socialism there (e.g., Chase-Dunn and Boswell 1998).

Once again the core has developed new lead industries—computers and
biotechnology—and much of large-scale heavy industry, the classical terrain
of strong labor movements and socialist parties, has been moved to the semiperiphery. This means that new socialist bids for state power in the semiperiphery (e.g., South Africa, Brazil, Mexico, perhaps Korea) will be much more
based on an urbanized and organized proletariat in large scale industry than
the earlier semiperipheral socialist revolutions were. This should have happy
consequences for the nature of new socialist states in the semiperiphery because the relationship between the city and the countryside within these
countries should be less antagonistic. Less internal conflict will make more
democratic socialist regimes possible and will lessen the likelihood of core in-
terference. The global expansion of communications has increased the
salience of events in the semiperiphery for audiences in the core, and this
may serve to dampen core state intervention into the affairs of democratic
socialist semiperipheral states.

Some critics of the world-systems perspective have argued that emphasis on the structural importance of global relations leads to political do-nothing-ism while we wait for socialism to emerge at the world level. The world-systems perspective does indeed encourage us to examine global-level constraints (and opportunities) and to allocate our political energies in ways that will be most productive when these structural constraints are taken into account. It does not follow that building socialism at the local or national level is futile, but we must expend resources on transorganizational, trans-national, and international socialist relations. The environmental and feminist movements are now in the lead, and labor needs to follow their example.

A simple domino theory of transformation to democratic socialism is misleading and inadequate. Suppose that all firms or all nation-states adopted socialist relations internally but continued to relate to one another through competitive commodity production and political-military conflict. Such a hypothetical world-system would still be dominated by the logic of capitalism, and that logic would be likely to repenetrate the "socialist" firms and states. This cautionary tale advises us to invest political resources in the construction of multilevel (transorganizational, transnational, and international) socialist relations lest we simply repeat the process of driving capitalism to once again perform an end run by operating on a yet larger scale.

A Democratic Socialist World-System

These considerations lead us to a discussion of socialist relations at the level of the whole world-system. The emergence of democratic collective rationality (socialism) at the world-system level is likely to be a slow process. What might such a world-system look like and how might it emerge? It is obvious that such a system would require a democratically controlled world federation that can effectively adjudicate disputes among nation-states and eliminate warfare (Goldstein 1988). This is a bare minimum. There are many other problems that badly need to be coordinated at the global level: ecologically sustainable development, a more balanced and egalitarian approach to economic growth, and the lowering of population growth rates.

The idea of global democracy is important for this struggle. The movement needs to push toward a kind of popular democracy that goes beyond the election of representatives to include popular participation in decision-making at every level. Global democracy can be real only if it is composed of civil societies and national states that are themselves truly democratic (Robinson 1996). And global democracy is probably the best way to lower the probability of another war among core states. For that reason it is in everyone's interest.

How might such a global social democracy come into existence? The process of the growth of international organizations that has been going on for at least 200 years will eventually result in a world state if we are not blown up first. Even international capitalists have some uses for global regulation, as is attested by the International Monetary Fund and the World Bank. Capitalists do not want the massive economic and political upheavals that would likely accompany collapse of the world monetary system, and so they support efforts to regulate "ruinous" competition and beggar-thy-neighborism. Some of these same capitalists also fear nuclear holocaust, and so they may support a strengthened global government that can effectively adjudicate conflicts among nation-states.

Of course, capitalists know as well as others that effective adjudication means the establishment of a global monopoly of legitimate violence. The process of state formation has a long history, and the king's army needs to be bigger than any combination of private armies that might be brought against him. While the idea of a world state may be a frightening specter to some, I am optimistic about it for several reasons. First, a world state is probably the most direct and stable way to prevent nuclear holocaust, a desideratum that must be at the top of everyone's list. Second, the creation of a global state that can peacefully adjudicate disputes among nations will transform the existing interstate system. The interstate system is the political structure that stands behind the maneuverability of capital and its ability to escape organized workers and other social constraints on profitable accumulation. While a world state may at first be dominated by capitalists, the very existence of such a state will provide a single focus for struggles to socially regulate investment decisions and to create a more balanced, egalitarian, and ecologically sound form of production and distribution.

The progressive response to neoliberalism needs to be organized at national, international, and global levels if it is to succeed. Democratic socialists should be wary of strategies that focus only on economic nationalism and national autarchy as a response to economic globalization. Socialism in one country has never worked in the past, and it certainly will not work in a world that is more interlinked than ever before. The old forms of progressive internationalism were somewhat premature, but internationalism has finally become not only desirable but also necessary. This does not mean that local-, regional-, and national-level struggles are irrelevant. They are just as relevant as they always have been. But they also need to have a global strategy and global-level cooperation lest they be isolated and defeated. Communications technology can certainly be an important tool for the kinds of long-distance interactions that will be required for truly international cooperation and coordination among popular movements. It would be a mistake to pit global strategies against national or local ones. All fronts should be the focus of a coordinated effort.

W. Warren Wagar (1996) has proposed the formation of a "World Party" as an instrument of "mundialization"—the creation of a global socialist commonwealth. His proposal has been critiqued from many angles—as a throwback to the Third International and so on. I suggest that Wagar's idea is a good one and that a party of the sort he is advocating will indeed emerge and that it will contribute a great deal toward bringing about a more humane world-system. Self-doubt and postmodern reticence may make such a direct approach appear Napoleonic. It is certainly necessary to learn from past mistakes, but this should not prevent us debating the pros and cons of positive action.

The international segment of the world capitalist class is indeed moving slowly toward global state formation. The World Trade Organization is only the latest element in this process. Rather than simply oppose this move with a return to nationalism, progressives should make every effort to organize social and political globalization and to democratize the emerging global state. We need to prevent the normal operation of the interstate system and future hegemonic rivalry from causing another war among core powers (e.g., Wagar 1992). And we need to shape the emerging world society into a global democratic commonwealth based on collective rationality, liberty, and equality. This possibility is present in existing and evolving structures. The agents are all those who are tired of wars and hatred and who desire a humane, sustainable, and fair world-system. This is certainly a majority of the people of the Earth.

Notes

This chapter is a revised version of an article that appeared in the *Journal of World-Systems Research* 5 (1999): 165–185. Peter Grimes and Volker Bornschier deserve recognition for their contributions to this essay. Some sentences have been taken from Chase- Dunn and Grimes (1995) and from Bornschier and Chase-Dunn (1999).

1. For a useful introduction see Shannon (1996).

2. It has become conventional to refer to the expansion phase of the K-wave as the "A-phase," while the contraction or stagnation period is called the "B-phase."

3. Linguistic diversity, a distributional measure of the proportions of the world's population that speak the various languages, is a valuable long-term indicator of cultural globalization. Linguistic diversity has decreased greatly over the past centuries, but recent movements to revitalize and legitimate indigenous cultures have slowed the long-term decrease in linguistic diversity, and electronic translation programs will make it easier for small language communities to survive in the future.

References

Amin, Samir. 1990. *Delinking: Towards a Polycentric World.* London: Zed Books.

Arrighi, Giovanni. 1994. *The Long Twentieth Century.* New York: Verso.

Bairoch, Paul. 1996. "Globalization Myths and Realities: One Century of External Trade and Foreign Investment." In *States against Markets: The Limits of Globalization,* edited by Robert Boyer and Daniel Drache. London: Routledge.

Bergesen, Albert and Ronald Schoenberg. 1980. "Long Waves of Colonial Expansion and Contraction, 1415–1969." Pp. 231–278 in *Studies of the Modern World-System,* edited by Albert J. Bergesen. New York: Academic Press.

Bornschier, Volker and Christopher Chase-Dunn. 1999. "Globalization and Change in Technological Style—The Withering Away of the State?" Pp. 285–302 in *The Future of Global Conflict,* edited by V. Bornschier and C. Chase-Dunn. London: Sage.

Boswell, Terry and Christopher Chase-Dunn. 2000. *The Spiral of Capitalism and Socialism: Toward Global Democracy.* Boulder, CO: Lynne Rienner.

Boswell, Terry and Ralph Peters. 1990. "State Socialism and the Industrial Divide in the World-Economy: A Comparative Essay on the Rebellions in Poland and China." *Critical Sociology* 17:3–35.

Chase-Dunn, Christopher. 1994. "Technology and the Changing Logic of World-Systems." Pp. 85–106 in *The State-Global Divide: A Neostructural Agenda in International Relations,* edited by Ronen Palan and Barry Gills. Boulder, CO: Lynne Rienner.

———. 1998. *Global Formation: Structures of the World-Economy.* 2d ed. Lanham, MD: Rowman and Littlefield.

Chase-Dunn, Christopher and Terry Boswell. 1998. "Post-Communism and the Global Commonwealth." *Humboldt Journal of Social Relations* 24:195–220.

Chase-Dunn, Christopher and Peter Grimes. 1995. "World-Systems Analysis." *Annual Review of Sociology* 21:387–417.

Chase-Dunn, Christopher and Thomas D. Hall. 1997a. "Ecological Degradation and the Evolution of World-Systems." *Journal of World-Systems Research* <http://jwsr.ucr.edu/> 3:403–431.

———. 1997b. *Rise and Demise: The Comparative Study of World-Systems.* Boulder, CO: Westview.

Chase-Dunn, Christopher, Yukio Kawano, and Benjamin Brewer. 2000. "Trade Globalization since 1795: Waves of Integration in the World-System." *American Sociological Review* 65:77–95.

Frank, Andre Gunder. 1978. *World Accumulation 1492–1789.* New York: Monthly Review Press.

———. 1980. *Crisis: In the World Economy.* New York: Holmes and Meier.

Frank, Andre Gunder, and Barry Gills, eds. 1993. *The World System: Five Hundred Years or Five Thousand?* London: Routledge.

Giddens, Anthony. 1996. *Introduction to Sociology.* New York: Norton.

Goldstein, Joshua. 1988. *Long Cycles: Prosperity and War in the Modern Age.* New Haven, CT: Yale University Press.

Grimes, Peter. 1993. "Harmonic Convergence? Frequency of Economic Cycles and Global Integration, 1790–1990." Manuscript.

Harvey, David. 1989. *The Condition of Postmodernity.* Cambridge, MA: Blackwell.

———. 1995. "Globalization in Question." *Rethinking Marxism* 8 (4): 1–17.

Hines, Colin and Tim Lang. 1996. "In Favor of a New Protectionism." Pp. 485–493 in *The Case against the Global Economy and for a Turn toward the Local,* edited by Jerry Mander and Edward Goldsmith. San Francisco: Sierra Club Books.

Lipset, Seymour Martin. 1991. "No Third Way: A Comparative Perspective on the Left." Pp. 183–232 in *The Crisis of Leninism and the Decline of the Left: The Revolutions of 1989,* edited by Daniel Chirot. Seattle, WA: University of Washington Press.

Mann, Michael. 1986. *Sources of Social Power.* Vol. 1. Cambridge, UK: Cambridge University Press.

Marer, Paul, Janos Arvay, John O'Connor, and Dan Swenson. 1991. "Historically Planned Economies: A Guide to the Data." *I.B.R.D. (World Bank), Socioeconomic Data Division and Socialist Economies Reform Unit.*

Markoff, John. 1996. *Waves of Democracy: Social Movements and Political Change.* Thousand Oaks, CA: Pine Forge Press.

McMichael, Philip. 1996. *Development and Social Change: A Global Perspective.* Thousand Oaks, CA: Pine Forge Press.

Meyer, John W. 1989. "Conceptions of Christendom: Notes on the Distinctiveness of the West." Pp. 395–413 in *Cross-national Research in Sociology,* edited by Melvin L. Kohn. Newbury Park, CA: Sage.

———. 1996. "The Changing Cultural Content of the Nation-State: A World Society Perspective." In *New Approaches to the State in the Social Sciences,* edited by George Steinmetz. Ithaca, NY: Cornell University Press.

Modelski, George and William R. Thompson. 1996. *Leading Sectors and World Powers: The Coevolution of Global Politics and Economics.* Columbia, SC: University of South Carolina Press.

Moore, Richard K. 1995. "On Saving Democracy." A Contribution to a Conversation about Global Praxis on the World-Systems Network (WSN).

Murphy, Craig. 1994. *International Organization and Industrial Change: Global Governance since 1850*. New York: Oxford University Press.

Robinson, William. 1996. *Promoting Polyarchy*. Cambridge, UK: Cambridge University Press.

Rueschemeyer, Dietrich, Evelyne Huber Stephens, and John Stephens. 1992. *Capitalist Development and Democracy*. Chicago: University of Chicago Press.

Shannon, Thomas R. 1996. *An Introduction to the World-Systems Perspective*. Boulder, CO: Westview.

Taylor, Peter J. 1996. *The Way the Modern World Works: World Hegemony to World Impasse*. New York: John Wiley.

Wagar, W. Warren. 1992. *A Short History of the Future*. Chicago: University of Chicago Press.

———. 1996. "Toward a Praxis of World Integration." *Journal of World-Systems Research* 2 (2): 1–18.

Wallerstein, Immanuel. 1974. *The Modern World-System*. Vol. 1. New York: Academic Press.

II | Global Inequality

6

Global Inequality
An Introduction

JONATHAN H. TURNER AND SALVATORE J. BABONES

The valuable resources of the world—money, education, and quality of life—are distributed unequally within and between societies. At the top of the stratification system are the early industrializing societies of Europe, the United States, and Canada and select Asian societies like Japan, Singapore, and Hong Kong. At the bottom are more than a billion people who live on just a dollar a day. The World Bank (1990) provides several definitions of poverty in order to gauge the level of deprivation that people must endure. *Absolute poverty* is defined as a situation in which people do not have enough money for survival, with two distinct subcategories: *world poverty,* in which people live on less than $365 per year, and *extreme poverty,* in which individuals must live on less than $275 per year. There are more than 600 million people living in such extreme poverty and many hundreds of millions at or just above the world poverty level. For example, the World Bank (2000) estimates that 49 percent of those in sub-Saharan Africa and 44 percent of those in South Asia live below world poverty levels.

The United Nations (2003) formulates a human poverty index that measures several dimensions of life, such as how long one is likely to live, how well off people are economically, how much knowledge people have or can acquire, and how included in the social fabric they are. At one time this was termed the "misery" index because so many people in the world have little income, few opportunities for education, and short life spans. Because standards of living are so different between advanced, postindustrial societies and poor nations, a sliding scale is necessary in this index for industrialized and developing countries, but index of human misery is nonetheless revealing. In some countries such as Ethiopia, well over 50 percent of the people fall into the most deprived categories, but even in some industrial societies, significant numbers exist in poverty. For example, in Russia almost 30 percent are in poverty, and almost 14 percent fall below the standards of the world poverty index and cannot meet minimal standards of subsistence.

An alternative definition of poverty is to consider poverty within the context of a given society. No Americans or Western Europeans live in absolute poverty (as defined by the United Nations), but many people in the developed world live in *relative poverty,* meaning that they lack the resources necessary to survive as full participants in the society in which they live. Thus, according to standards set by the Census Bureau, approximately 12 percent of Americans live in poverty, but poverty in the United States is defined by a national poverty line of around $17,000 income for a family of four, or more than $4,000 per person. This is more than *10 times* the United Nations definition of absolute poverty.

There is also what is sometimes termed *double deprivation* in poverty rates, which refers to the fact that women and children are much more likely to be in poverty than adult males. For example, although the data are somewhat dated, the United Nations Commission on the Status of Women (1996) found that women constitute 60 percent of the world's population but receive just 10 percent of the income and hold only 1 percent of the world's wealth, even though the hours worked by women account for two-thirds of all working hours. These problems are compounded by the fact that, on the whole, the poorest populations are the fastest growing, assuring that most people and particularly women and children will remain at the bottom levels of the global stratification system. In this chapter, our goal is to gain some purchase on the extent of global inequality and on the forces that generate and sustain this inequality.

Assessing the Level of Inequality

Per Capita GNP

One rough measure of global inequality is per capita GNP. This figure is calculated by measuring GNP—the total amount of goods and services produced by the citizens of a country for a society—and then dividing this figure by the total number of people in this society. The resulting number is per capita GNP. This figure tells us very little about inequalities within a society, since these are averaged out, but it can give us a sense for differences in income across societies. This measure is, however, reliable only for societies with a money economy; many poor trade in services and barter goods with the result that the per capita GNP is not very reliable for these societies in which many noncash transactions occur.

Per capita GNP is not the same as per capita income, since there are other components to GNP besides personal income. For example, investments in physical infrastructure such as roads or telecommunications networks are a part of GNP but not a part of personal income. People can't eat phone lines, and those living without telephones cannot even use phone lines. Still, per capita GNP is a good indicator of what a society can afford to buy. Whether through government programs or market systems, high GNP countries are able to allocate far greater resources to health, education, and general welfare than are low GNP countries. For example, per capita GNP in India is only $400 per year, and according to the United Nations, infant mortality in India runs 64 per 1,000 live births, 43 percent of the population is illiterate, and 69 percent of the population lives without sanitary sewerage. In comparison, per capita GNP in Mexico is $4,440 per year, infant mortality is 28 per 1,000, the illiteracy rate is 9 percent, and only 27 percent of the population lives without sanitary sewerage. Although there are scattered exceptions, per capita GNP offers a reasonable measure of how well people can live.

Per capita GNP also serves as a good indicator of whether the barriers to poverty reduction in a country are strictly economic or are, to some degree, political. Clearly, the 31 countries with per capita GNPs under $365 could not conceivably eradicate absolute poverty given their current levels of resources, since even a policy that redirected all economic resources to poverty reduction would leave the entire population living on less than $365 per year. These countries, and most of the other 37 countries with per capita GNPs under $1,000 per year, will require massive foreign aid to achieve the goal of eliminating absolute poverty. On the other hand, the 72 middle-income countries with per capita GNPs falling between $1,000 and $10,000 per year (roughly the Philippines through Slovenia) have more capacity for eliminating absolute poverty from purely domestic resources. Countries with per capita GNPs over $10,000 per year typically exhibit little or no absolute poverty, though they may experience high levels of relative poverty, depending on how income is distributed within their borders. Indeed, some societies such as the United States and United Kingdom with high per capita GNPs evidence considerable poverty because income is distributed very unequally. One way to assess within-society inequalities is by using Gini coefficients.

Gini Coefficients

Figure 6.1 summarizes the logic of a Gini coefficient. The straight line indicates perfect equality in the distribution of income. That is, 10 percent of the population receives 10 percent of the income, 20 percent gets 20 percent of the income, and so on. The curved line is the actual distribution of income in a given society. The distance between the curved and straight lines in figure

6.1 thus denotes the level of inequality in the distribution of income for a society. The farther the Lorenz curve is from the straight line, the greater the inequality is. This distance is captured by the Gini coefficient—the larger the Gini coefficient for a society, the greater the level of inequality in the distribution of income.[1]

Figure 6.2 illustrates the distribution of Gini coefficients by per capita GNP. As the graph shows, inequality generally declines with income (although the trend is weak compared with the total variation in inequality). High inequality in poor and middle-income countries compounds the problem of limited societal resources, represented by the level of per capita GNP. A low level of per capita GNP combined with a high level of inequality is a recipe for widespread poverty. In many moderately poor to very poor societies revealing high levels of internal inequality, much of the population lives at or below the world and extreme poverty levels. These poor have virtually nothing, and they lead lives of chronic desperation.

Population pressures compound the danger of this recipe. A larger proportion of poor countries than of rich countries are experiencing rapid increases in their populations that will burden the resources of the poor nations even more (indeed, rank-order correlation between per capita GNP and population growth is -.585, which is significant at the p.01 level). Thus, if current trends continue, the number of people living in poverty categories will increase in many societies over the coming decades. The expansion of the numbers in poverty at the world level is arrested only by low population growth and strong economic performance in China and, to a lesser extent, in India. However, China's recent economic and demographic success has been accomplished at the cost of a massive increase in domestic inequality, which has kept China's poverty rate relatively higher than it otherwise would be. In much of Africa and parts of Latin America and south Asia, though, high population growth, low economic growth, and high inequality combine to ensure that misery will be the fate of billions of people at the bottom rungs of the stratification system in most societies for decades to come.

Quality of Life among the Rich and Poor

The World Bank (2000) also assembles quality-of-life data in societies of varying levels of per capita GNP. One procedure is to divide the nations of the world into four categories: high-income nations, upper-middle-income nations, lower-middle-income nations, and poorest nations. Then a variety of quality-of-life measures are calculated for each of these four levels. For example, life expectancy, infant mortality, percentage of women enrolled in pri-

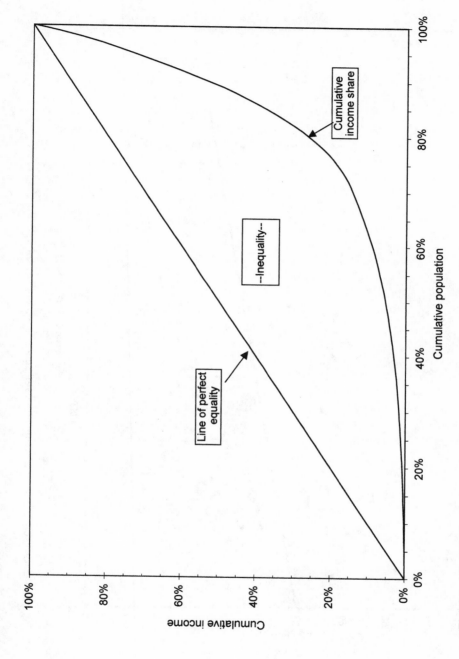

Fig. 6.1. A Lorenz Curve

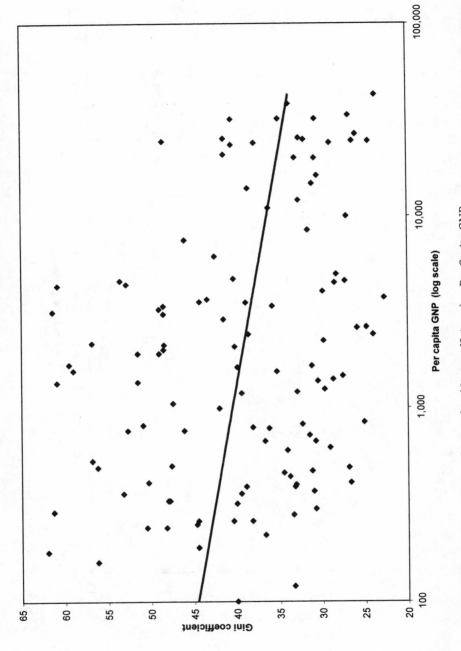

Fig. 6.2. Relationship of National Inequality (Gini coefficients) to Per Capita GNP

mary school, and access to safe water are often examined for each level of national income. Life expectancy—the ultimate quality of life issue—reaches 78 years for high-income nations but only 63 years for poor nations. More dramatic are infant mortality rates per 1,000 live births, reaching almost 58 in poor nations, compared with 5.5 per 1,000 for affluent nations. Women are almost universally enrolled in primary schools in wealthy nations, but this number falls off to about 83 percent in poor nations and continues to fall off through secondary schools. Without education women will have diminished job opportunities, and, hence, they and their children will suffer.

Trends in Global Inequality

Over the past decade, several studies have sought to discover trends in global inequality. Depending on the data set and methods employed as well as the time frame used, results have varied. Let us begin with very long term trends over the past 2,000 years and then focus in on the past four or five decades to see whether the long-term trend for increased inequality has been reversed or leveled off.

Long-Term Trends in Global Inequality

Over the past two millennia, economic inequality between broad regions of the world has increased. The principal reason for this trend is that the world is much more differentiated in terms of the level of development than it was even a few hundred years ago. Most countries were agrarian with similar levels of national income, with the large mass of their populations living at or near subsistence. Within-nation inequality varied somewhat, depending on the capacity of elites to extract economic surplus generated by agrarian labor, but in general, agrarian societies revealed very high levels of internal inequality. Yet across the whole range of agrarian societies, differences were comparatively small, at least by today's standards of inequality, and as a result, between-nation inequality was not dramatic. Industrialization has decreased internal inequality within nations (Lenski 1966) as old elites have been replaced and as new middle classes have emerged, but because nations have developed at different rates and with varying degrees of success, between-nation inequality has increased. Industrialization dramatically accelerates total productive output and per capita income; thus, early industrializing nations inevitably leaped ahead of those that remained agrarian. The end result was for world inequality to increase, at least until capitalism began to be truly global.

Figure 6.3 documents the long-term trend in global (between-region) inequality. The global Gini coefficients at each time period ignore any within-country variation and represent only the differences in average income levels between regions of the world. The coefficients themselves are calculated in the same way as they are for individual people within a society, but with societies within the world as the units of analysis.

As figure 6.3 indicates, even before the beginning of the industrial revolution, differences in average incomes had begun to emerge between broad areas of the world. Between the years 1000 and 1820, incomes in western Europe and Japan grew nearly four times as fast as did incomes in the rest of the world. The nineteenth and twentieth centuries saw a continuation of this already existing trend, with incomes in western Europe, North America, Japan, and Australia rising more than three times faster than in the rest of the world (Maddison 2001, chap. 1). The results are clear: Over the long haul of history, global inequality has increased dramatically. Today, however, the tools of capitalist development have become globally applicable. This suggests at least the possibility that the long-term trend toward increasing inequality might be stopped or even reversed.

Recent Trends in Global Inequality

Currently, there is considerable debate over whether inequality has increased or decreased over the past four decades. Korzeniewicz and Moran (1997) reported rising inequality from 1960 to 1992, whereas Schultz (1998) and Firebaugh (1999) found that inequality had remained relatively stable over this period. Both studies weighted their measures of inequality between countries by the population of each country. The reason behind these contradictory findings probably resides in the respective methodologies of investigators (Firebaugh 1999; Babones 2002). The Korzeniewicz and Moran findings relied on the level of the GNP evaluated at international exchange rates to de-

(Facing page)

Fig. 6.3. Millennial Trends in International Income Inequality (Gini coefficients) Based on Purchasing Power Parity.

Data source: Maddison 2001, tables 1-1 and 1-2, pp. 27–28.

Notes: Gini coefficients are computed based on population and GNP estimates for seven regions of the world: Africa, Asia outside Japan, Eastern Europe, Latin America, the Western "offshoots" (United States, Canada, Australia, and New Zealand), and Western Europe. Time axis not to scale.

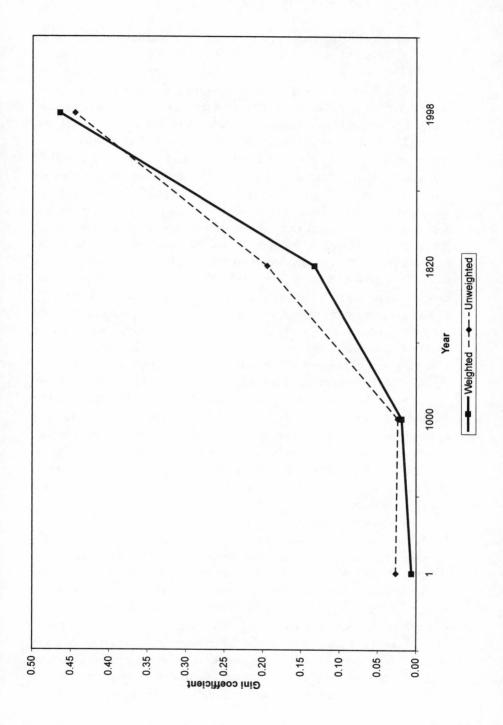

termine national income, whereas Schultz and Firebaugh used the GDP evaluated with respect the actual purchasing power of dollars within a given nation. Differences produced by using GNP or GDP measures are relatively minor because the ratio between the two measures of total economic output tends to remain stable over time. The real difference between the two sets of results hinges mainly on the choice of currency conversion used—that is, on how national GNP figures in local currency units are converted into the common language of U.S. dollars. Firebaugh and Schultz convert national GDP figures into dollars using the relative domestic purchasing power of the currency, which effectively asks the question, "What is the GDP of country X in terms of the loaves of bread, gallons of gasoline, and numbers of shirts that such a quantity of money can buy within the country?" Korzeniewicz and Moran convert national GNP figures into dollars using the international exchange value of the currency, which effectively asks the question, "What is the GNP of country X in terms of the bushels of wheat, barrels of oil, and cases of shirts that such a quantity of money can buy on the world market?"

Firebaugh argues that it is the purchasing power of the currency in the society that matters for issues of poverty and inequality, whereas Korzeniewicz and Moran emphasize the ability of a country to purchase enough food to feed itself on world markets. Firebaugh criticizes the uncertainty and volatility in exchange rate figures; Korzeniewicz and Moran object that the procedures for calculating purchasing power are ridden with estimation problems and heroic assumptions, including difficulties in securing sufficient numbers of benchmark countries and years as well as the inability to account for the quality of goods and services (which exchange rates would capture). In the end, it is difficult to determine conclusively that one methodology is better than the other, and it is perhaps most reasonable to consider the results from both when evaluating trends in global inequality.

Another methodological issue is the weighting of the national Gini coefficients by the size of a population in a country. Unweighted procedures clearly document increasing income inequality on a country-by-country basis. Since the richest countries have increased domestic output and national income while the less developed countries have remained stagnant or declined economically, it is not surprising that overall inequality between nations has increased. Indeed, more than half of all developing countries have had negative growth rates since 1980, with most of the rest having growth rates below the average of all societies. And these figures ignore those nations that have stopped reporting data on productivity and income, presumably because they are doing so poorly in raising productivity and national income. Thus, when countries are the unit of analysis, it is not surprising that inequalities between nations have increased because there are so many poor nations that have not developed in comparison with the smaller number of advanced postindustrial and rapidly developing nations.

When measures of inequality take into account the size of a nation's population, however, the story is different depending on the measures used. Weighting international Gini coefficients by population size is akin to computing a worldwide Gini coefficient using the person (rather than the country) as the unit of analysis, and people are assigned incomes equal to the per capita GNP of their countries of residence. For example, Luxembourg, a nation of 432,000 people, enters into the computation of the international Gini 432,000 times, each time at an income level of $42,930 per year (the per capita GNP for Luxembourg). A Gini coefficient is then calculated for the whole world, with countries' income levels effectively weighted according to their populations.[2]

It is difficult to compare Korzeniewicz and Moran's findings with those of Schultz and Firebaugh because they use not only different measures of real GNP (based on exchange rates and purchasing power, respectively) but also different sets of countries for which they have data available. We have replicated results for both methodologies using a common set of countries, for which data are available for both foreign exchange (FX) and purchasing power parity (PPP) based on real per capita GNP (fig. 6.4). Clearly, the FX and the PPP series report dramatically different levels of inequality, with the FX series consistently higher. This is because high GNP countries, such as the United States, the European Union countries, and Japan, have very high costs of living. A loaf of bread that costs a dollar in the United States costs the equivalent of a few cents in India. Thus, when relative purchasing powers are taken into account, the United States is still richer than India (13 times richer), but not by *as much* as when relative purchasing power is ignored (70 times richer). Because poor countries generally have low costs of living, the PPP-adjusted series shows less overall inequality.

More to the point, there is also a marked difference in trend between the two series. Both series show relatively stable levels of inequality from 1960 through 1980, with a slight drift toward greater inequality. After 1980, however, the two trends diverge. The FX trend is rising through the mid-1990s, while the PPP trend is declining. Since the countries and population data used in the two series are the same, the differences in behavior must be due to the currency conversion method used. The divergence between the two series after 1980 can be interpreted in this light. The global distribution of pur-

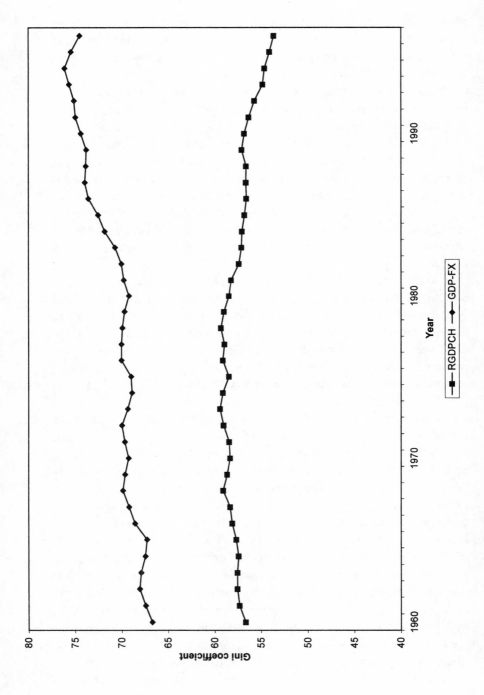

Fig. 6.4. Population-Weighted International Gini Coefficients, 1960–1996

chasing power, in terms of ability to buy goods on the world market (FX series), definitely seems to have diverged in the two decades after 1980. However, at the same time, the gap between the cost of living in richer countries and the cost of living in poorer countries must also have widened, and to an extent that more than compensated for the divergence in (FX-rated) incomes. As a result, the PPP-based inequality series shows a decline in inequality over the same period.

What, then, can we conclude from these findings? Weighting the measures of national income by population size make a difference, and this difference reflects some important substantive dynamics. Some large, lower-income societies have increased their overall levels of production and national income significantly over the past decades; and this fact, along with the continued growth in national income of many advanced societies, accounts for the decrease in inequality, at least as reported by measures using the local purchasing power of the currency as the measure of national income. At the same time, some of the poorest countries have not grown at all or have declined in both national income and overall production, thus creating a widening gap between already developed and rapidly developing societies, on the one side, and stagnant and very poor countries on the other side. This conclusion echoes the findings of Melchior and Telle (2001), who report general population-weighted convergence being driven by growth in large developing countries but punctuated by growth failures in the very poorest countries. Similarly, Jones (1997) reports increasing dichotomization of global incomes levels.

Changing Patterns of Inequality within Nations

Total global inequality, of course, consists not just of inequality between countries but also of inequality within countries themselves. Until recently, we had no standardized international database of Gini coefficients with worldwide coverage. Collating 2,621 observations from more than 100 sources, scholars at the World Bank put together such a database, making truly global international comparisons possible for the first time (Deininger and Squire 1996). Moreover, the Deininger-Squire database contains observations for most countries going back to 1970 and for some countries as far back as the nineteenth century. It has become the foundation database for a United Nations University initiative to extend the data coverage to as many countries and time periods as possible (WIDER 2000).

Collating their national data by region of the world, Deininger and Squire (1996) found that domestic income inequality (measured using the Gini coefficient) is highest in Latin America and sub-Saharan Africa and lowest in Eastern Europe, where income inequality, though now on the rise, is still lower than in the developed countries. Aside from the formerly communist states of Eastern Europe, income inequality is lowest in the developed countries of the world (see Deininger and Squire 1996, table 5).

The publication of the Deininger-Squire database has sparked a flurry of interest in studying changes in domestic inequality over time. Li, Squire, and Zou (1998) show that in general within-country inequality is quite stable over time. They studied trends in the 49 countries in the Deininger-Squire database that had observed Gini coefficients for at least four distinct time points over the period 1947–1994. Carefully adjusting for the differing Gini definitions and methodologies used in the various countries over the course of the study period, they found that 32 of the 49 countries showed no significant trend in income inequality. Seven countries showed declining inequality, while 10 countries showed rising inequality. Even among those countries with significant trends, 10 of the 17 countries had trends that, though statistically significant, were quantitatively negligible. China, however, the world's most populous country, stood out as having by far the strongest increasing trend in income inequality over the study period. Other studies have reached different conclusions, but they have used the Deininger-Squire data indiscriminately, without adjusting for methodological changes over time.

The level of domestic inequality within a country is important not only for what it says about the current structure of society in that country but also for what it implies for the future. In an article following the publication of their database, Deininger and Squire (1998) show that high initial inequality tends to depress subsequent economic growth, especially income growth for the poor. This means that poor, high-inequality countries may find themselves in a poverty trap in which their high levels of inequality not only contribute to the current misery of their populations but also reduce the chances of any improvement in the future. Rather than hope for growth to reduce poverty over time, a better strategy might be to fight inequality in order to foster growth. Desperately poor people do not have the resources to invest in their future and in the future of their countries. Reducing poverty through redistribution may have the fortuitous side effect of increasing rates of economic growth. Economic growth through lower inequality could prove to operate in a virtuous cycle to eliminate poverty.

Problems Posed by Global Inequality

Malthusian Problems

A major consequence of the level of global inequality found in the world to-day is that entire nations and even entire regions of the world are mired in poverty. If domestic inequality retards rates of economic growth, widespread societal poverty may preclude growth altogether. A long history of demographic theories of growth, beginning with Malthus and the classical economists and extending through the midcentury work of Leibenstein (1957), focused on the risk that poverty on a national and societal scale would be self-perpetuating. Leibenstein argued that under conditions in which the fertility rate was positively related to income, any absolute economic expansion would simply feed back into population growth, potentially precluding any increase in per capita incomes. The argument is that, in countries with very low income levels, additional income is used to fund additional children. Such fertility strategies are most likely in environments where children are a family's only safety net against old age and incapacitating disease. In effect, individually adaptive behavior (providing for one's and one's family's future) becomes socially maladaptive, as the increasing number of mouths to feed exacerbates a cycle of poverty, malnutrition, and disease.

Billions of people are now living a life that is below acceptable standards in the more developed world, and at least 1.2 billion live at or below the level of subsistence by any standards. This situation represents a humanitarian problem not only of why so many people must live in such misery but also of whether such poverty is, in fact, self-perpetuating. Symptomatic of a self-perpetuating poverty trap, people are dying from poor nutrition in many parts of the world, and areas in their societies are becoming breeding grounds for new kinds of diseases or variants of older ones. In a world where germs can move across the globe in a matter of hours, these threats pose potential problems for everyone, even those in the developed world. If individuals could live substantially above subsistence, the threat of a pandemic would be greatly reduced.

Disease is not, of course, the only Malthusian pressure. War between populations and, more more significant, between subpopulations within societies will increase when people lack resources. Traditional rivalries, past enemies, members of different ethnic groups, and other lines of division are often aggravated when access to resources—land, jobs, patronage, political power, health care, and the like—is seen in zero-sum terms. What one segment of a population receives is seen by another as depriving them of their due, leading the latter to violence, which in turn breeds counterviolence in potentially escalating spirals. Indeed, the globe is covered with hot zones where inequalities within and between populations have caused warfare and other acts of violence.

These kinds of Malthusian pressures are dramatically compounded by the growth rates of the poorest populations. Understandably, suffering people will pursue their short-term interests in staying alive but will, in the process, commit long-term harm to the ecosystem of their society and, in some cases, the world. For example, deforestation in search of land that can be used for planting is inevitably going to make significant alterations in the world's climate and in other geo-atmospheric processes. Moreover, the simplification of ecosystems stemming from efforts to clear forest for agricultural production and from overuse of single-crop agriculture will increase the vulnerability of the world's ecosystem to new forms of pestilence that are likely to have effects on the ecosystems of the more advanced nations.

Globalization of capitalism is likely to aggravate ecological problems as postindustrial nations export industrial production to poor populations desperate for jobs and income. As a result, environmental controls that have been slowly taking hold in the postindustrial countries will be seen by capitalists as an additional cost that cuts into profits and by poor governments as a drain on limited public funds, with the result that the ecological crisis that has been looming for some time will move to much of the developing world. As the world industrializes, then, world ecological disaster becomes an ever more real threat. Not only will global warming increase, but the emission of effluents into the air, soil, and water will likely disrupt the key flows, cycles, and chains that reproduce those renewable resources on which all life depends. As long as rich nations horde resources and use poor populations as a means to externalize costs, global inequality will increase the likelihood of a Malthusian correction on a world scale, far beyond what Thomas Malthus could have envisioned two centuries ago.

Navigating the Demographic Transition

All the currently developed countries of the world were once, by today's standards, quite poor. All experienced Malthusian pressures in waves of famine and disease as late as the nineteenth century. A common misperception is that the now-developed countries of the world conquered cataclysmic waves of epidemic disease through the advance of medical science. In fact, most epidemic diseases ceased to be major killers in western Europe and North America by the 1930s, well before their cures (or in many cases even their causes) were known. Epidemic disease ceased to function as a Malthusian valve on excess population not because of better medicine but because of rising personal income and the improvements in nutrition and sanitation that this brought (and bought).

Over the course of the nineteenth and early twentieth centuries, the countries of western Europe and North America underwent what is called a "demographic transition" from an initial state of high mortality and fertility rates to today's environment of low mortality and fertility rates. A demographic transition is a three-phase phenomenon, driven largely by increasing incomes. In the first phase, a poor nation exhibits a high rate of mortality, exacerbated by poor nutrition. Many children die in infancy, and for those who survive infancy life expectancy is low (often less than 50 years). Social mores and individual incentives emphasize high fertility rates, since many children never make it to adulthood. Many of the poorest nations of the world fit this description even today.

Improvements in a country's levels of nutrition and sanitation can reduce its death rate, increasing life expectancy. One way to improve nutrition is to reduce inequality; this is often accomplished through rural land reform. Another way to improve nutrition is through overall economic growth while keeping inequality constant. Either way, the resulting increase in life expectancy brings on the second phase of the demographic transition. In this phase, the birth rate is still high, but the death rate drops, with the result that the overall population expands dramatically. Not only does the population expand, but as adults live longer, the ratio of working adults to dependent children also increases. This imparts a further boost to nutrition and general well-being, as there are now more wage-earners per capita in the economy.

In the third phase of the demographic transition, the birth rate adjusts to the new reality of longer lives, lower infant death rates, and greater prosperity. With the lower birth rate comes a further economic boost, as again an increasing proportion of the population is made up of productive adults. Such a three-phase demographic transition from a state of high fertility and mortality to a state of low fertility and mortality has occurred in all countries that have grown from low-income to middle-income or high-income status.

Bloom and Williamson (1998) have documented the effects of the demographic transition on the East Asian "miracle" of the past 30 years, finding that demographic factors accounted for as much as one-third of total East Asian growth and fully half of "excess" East Asian growth (i.e., growth in excess of the worldwide mean of 2 percent). It is difficult now to remember that the East Asian "miracle" economies were, in 1950, among the world's poorest countries, with per capita GNPs below those of sub-Saharan Africa. Now, they are comfortably middle income. Similarly, China has made great strides in reducing poverty through a kind of forced demographic transition. China's one-child policy increased the proportion of working adults in the population by reducing fertility instead of increasing life expectancy. Although not following the "natural" pattern exhibited historically by developing economies, this policy has perhaps allowed China to leapfrog to a higher level of economic well-being without going through the usual intermediate steps. The social cost of this policy, however, has been enormous.

Why is it that many countries do not undergo a demographic transition? Why do some countries seem to be caught in a Leibenstein-style poverty trap, in which any economic growth is simply channeled back into population growth, while other countries are able to parlay initial economic growth into a successful demographic transition? The answer may lie in the nature of the initial boost to income that gets the demographic ball rolling. On the one hand, an increase in job opportunities and economic security will encourage adults to invest in their own future, with the confidence that they will not need children to support them in an early old age. On the other hand, a one-time windfall of the sort represented by clearing a forest preserve for slash-and-burn agriculture, selling mineral rights, or receiving foreign disaster assistance may simply be channeled into the insurance policy of additional children. In the end, it is probably the incentive sets faced by ordinary citizens living in poverty that determine a society's potential growth path.

Geopolitical Problems

Inequalities between nations almost always generate political problems. Strong and wealthy nations tend to exploit weak and poor nations, with the consequence that the latter come to resent the actions of the developed world. Whether through empire-building, colonization, or exploitive practices of multinational corporations of wealthy nations, tensions exist between the developed and underdeveloped world. These tensions manifest themselves in many ways: border conflicts, internal revolts against political leaders who have supported colonial powers or exploitive multinational corporations, renewed rivalries between ethnic groups, and, as is now evident, acts of terrorism against those who are seen to exploit the resources and sovereignty of a nation. These kinds of political problems are aggravated when wealthy nations export the resources of poor nations with the help of elites who skim profits for themselves, exacerbating internal inequalities. The fact that many of the terrorists working against the United States come from Saudi Arabia is not surprising because inequality has been increasing over the past decades in Saudi Arabia during the period when the United States has supported corrupt leaders in order to assure a stable supply of oil. And it is often the frustrated middle classes of these societies rather than the abject poor who become the ideological spokespersons and front-line combatants in conflict with rich powers. For these middle classes, internal inequalities have shut off sources of capital that could provide the career opportunities for which they have been trained and to which they rightly feel entitled. Coupled with mobilization of the poor masses, this kind of threat to the developed world is considerable, especially as the elements of nuclear bombs and biological toxins circulate in underground world-level markets.

As a general rule, then, inequality always creates tensions, not only within a society but between societies. As these tensions lead to mobilizations within societies, they often have consequences outside a society's borders, encouraging military adventurism from hostile neighbors or encouraging leaders to engage in external conflict to deflect attention from internal domestic problems. And if any of these regional conflicts pull in more advanced nations that have interests in, or alliances with, the conflicting parties, then the possibility of wider geopolitical tensions increases. Thus, as long as there is global inequality, geopolitical conflicts will have ample fuel.

Geoeconomic Problems

Global inequality encourages developed nations to export labor and manufacturing costs to poorer nations with cheap pools of labor and unregulated manufacturing sectors. This kind of development causes problems at both ends of this exchange: Wealthy nations continue to lose manufacturing jobs to poorer nations, thus increasing welfare burdens and other problems associated with loss of unskilled jobs; poorer nations develop dependencies on the technology and capital of wealthy nations that, at any time, can pull capital and move it to another poor nation. The end result is that wealthy nations are generating a divide between their high-technology and high-skill sectors, on the one side, and their marginally employed and unskilled poor sectors, on the other, whereas many poor nations are undergoing development dependent on conditions imposed by foreign capitalists.

Another geoeconomic pattern is for residents of poorer nations to migrate, often illegally, to wealthier nations in search of low-skill jobs. These kinds of migratory patterns create a large foreign-born work pool in host countries that typically arouses ethnic tensions and deprives low-skill native workers of potential jobs. At the same time, the country of origin for workers often becomes dependent on the income (sent home) of emigrants, with the result that the economy of the poorer country that is exporting workers does not develop the structural base to employ all its citizens. Of course, this is often a blessing for an underdeveloped economy that exports its unemployment problems while receiving the currency of more developed nations, but while this pattern generates short-term benefits to poorer countries, it stagnates development in the long run because it does not encourage elites to deploy capital to develop the economic structures that can employ all its citizens. Instead, development is uneven and does not address the problems that are causing workers to emigrate.

At times, migrants are the skilled workers or the entrepreneurs of a poorer nation who fill in holes and gaps in the labor markets of the host nation, but in emigrating, they deprive their country of needed human capital. For example, the United States simply cannot produce enough skilled scientists to fill all positions, and thus it must import them from poorer countries like India; and although this exchange appears even—India cannot employ all its skilled workers, and the United States needs them—it works against both countries because U.S. educational policies are not adjusted to fill skilled positions, and India loses the vanguard of human capital for future development. In more recent years, however, countries like India have been able to retain many skilled workers as higher-technology companies have developed in India, on their own or with capital from Western multinationals. This recent trend is part of the reason for India's economic growth and rising national income; it also confirms the need of societies to retain skilled workers and create economic structures that can employ them (rather than letting them emigrate to more developed nations). A further benefit of developing countries creating new, higher-technology economic structures is that it levels exchange relations between developed and developing nations and, in so doing, reduces dependence of poorer nations for foreign capital and technology.

Explaining Global Inequality

There are no universally accepted explanations for world inequality. Indeed, the ebb and flow of historical empires, the early industrialization of the West, the unequal distribution of natural resources, and other unique historical events still help account for some patterns of inequality. Such historical explanations, however, do not capture all the dynamics involved. The problem with all these explanations is that they are loaded with ideological overtones, and as a consequence it is difficult to have a rational debate about the explanatory power of each explanation. There are now three basic modes of explaining world inequality: (1) modernization theories, (2) dependency theories, and (3) world-systems theories. We will examine each of these in terms of what they have to offer an explanation of global inequality.

Modernization Approaches

Modernization theories argue that the values, beliefs, and motives of people must change before a society can develop economically, and so it is not surprising that advocates of this approach emphasize the functions of the educational system in creating people with "modern" attributes. What are these modern attributes? The list varies but includes such changes as the abandonment of traditional beliefs in fate in favor of an active and manipulative stance toward the world; the acquisition of achievement motives and values; the development of acquisitive orientations; and the desire to use and enter markets in preference to traditional patterns of ascription for assigning roles.

Critics of this approach have argued that it blames the victims for their lack of economic progress; while this interpretation is not without merit, it ignores the fact that economic development depends on the skills and orientations of people. Human capital is an important ingredient—along with technology, organizational systems, and physical capital—for development. Moreover, critics of the approach tend to underemphasize that its proponents were well aware that structured changes must occur for new kinds of "modern" individuals to emerge. There must be free and dynamic markets, universal education, rational organizations systems, and capital available for development. If these more macrostructure conditions do not exist, it is difficult to transform people; but conversely, if individuals remain locked into traditional patterns of ascription, they will undermine efforts to alter macrostructural changes in a society. Whatever the merits of the criticisms of modernization theory, it has been rejected by scholars working on globalization questions, but these scholars may have overreacted to the approach as they sought alternative explanations. Even as scholars have rejected the approach, it is still the underpinning of much policy in the World Bank, which has over the years emphasized the need to expand the educational system to create new kinds of citizens; indeed, the bank often makes its loans of capital to governments dependent on significant reforms in the educational system of a society.

Dependency Approaches

This approach emphasizes that the lack of development of some countries is the result of policies of more developed nations. Nations have difficulty developing and moving out of poverty because of their dependency on more powerful countries that, in essence, exploit them. Whether this was done through colonization, whereby a more powerful country took control of a less powerful one in order to extract resources, or through efforts of multinational corporations to secure resources at the cheapest price, the result has been the same: Dominant nations and their corporations gain control over significant segments of the economy and the political system as well and then use this control to extract a nation's resources without reinvesting capital in ways that would encourage broad-based development. As a consequence, a society becomes dependent on more powerful nations or multinational corporations for capital, technology, and employment opportunities that are used not for the development of the dependent country as a whole but for the well-being of the more powerful nation or the profits of multinationals. This dependency is compounded by dominant powers' use of coercion to maintain control or, in more recent times, by co-optation of corrupt political regimes that support the interests of outside nations or multinationals in order to maintain their privilege.

This approach has merit but it does not explain all global inequality. Many poor nations have never been dependent; they simply have been poor for many centuries. Other formerly dependent colonies, such as Singapore, Hong Kong, India, and even many Latin American countries, now enjoy considerable prosperity, perhaps as a result of investment by former colonial powers and multinationals. Dependency theory certainly has an element of truth, and it does correct for the lack of attention by modernization theories to the system of relationships in which a society has been historically implicated.

World-Systems Approaches

Dependency theories are a kind of world-systems approach, but world-systems analysis added certain conceptual elements. The most critical element is the division of societies into core, peripheral, and semiperipheral. Core societies are economically developed and politically dominant, using their power and economic resources to control world-level markets, extracting resources from poor peripheral countries, often through arrangements with semiperipheral nations that stand between poor nations and the core. Core nations seek to extract resources and use cheap labor for their benefit, while semiperipheral countries try to develop and enter the core so that they too can exploit weaker nations. Much of this analysis is historical, and the three-part categorization has many problems; as a consequence, this approach increasingly emphasizes the international division of labor in which various nations stand at somewhat different points in world markets. The core nations still use their political power—but, more significant, their multinationals' capital and technology—to invest in poor countries in order to produce products less expensively. Semiperipheral countries like Korea, Singapore, Brazil, Mexico, and others at this level of development often use the capital and technology of the core but seek to develop their own export-oriented indigenous industries, thereby gaining some control over their economic fate while increasing production and national income. The periphery either stands outside this system, as is the case for countries like Ethiopia and much of sub-Saharan Africa, or is the place where both core and semiperiphery seek cheap raw materials, labor, and manufacturing venues.

As the world-system has evolved over the past 50 years, core nations increasingly export their labor and manufacturing costs to the periphery and semiperiphery. Indeed, in extreme cases such as shoe and clothing manufacturing or low-end computer technologies, the core only designs and markets a product that often goes through steps in the manufacturing that cross the borders of several countries. Those semiperipheral countries that can begin to gain some control over how multinationals invest and that can generate their own industrial base independently from the capital and technology of core nations are likely to experience the greatest amount of economic development and rise in national income. Those that cannot do so, however, remain poor or stagnate, and, of course, those countries that are so peripheral as to be virtually ignored by the core and semiperiphery are not likely to develop at all because they simply do not have access to capital, technology, or organizational systems that can move them out of poverty.

World-systems theories, like dependency theories, have the virtue of emphasizing the connectedness of the nations through market and geopolitical dynamics. Increasingly, it is the fate of a nation in the world's markets that determines its capacity to develop. If it has few indigenous resources that are useful to industrial powers, if its labor pool is too unskilled or isolated, if it has no capacity to develop and use technologies, and if it has no capital to stimulate investment in production, it will remain isolated from world markets, even as a consumer of goods produced elsewhere. If a nation can provide cheap labor and low-cost manufacturing environments, it can experience some development, but if a country is wholly dependent on the capital and technology of multinationals of core and semiperipheral nations, it will be difficult in the short run to develop economically. Over the long run, however, rising national income might spur less dependent indigenous production that can lead to development and some independence, but if multinationals come and then leave, they are likely to throw these developing nations into an economic tailspin. Semiperipheral development is most likely when a society has a favored geopolitical position, as does China, and the capacity to develop export-oriented industries that are not wholly dependent on foreign capital and technology. As production and national income rise, these translate into more internal market demand that stimulates further independent development. It is countries in this situation that have caused the dichotomization of world societies. They have become more affluent, moving in the same direction as the European-origin core and leaving behind those nations that remain outside the dynamic markets of the world-system or that remain dependent on core and semiperipheral nations.

Clearly, enormous inequalities exist between the nations of the world. National income, however, is not the only relevant measure of inequality. There are also enormous disparities between the countries of the world in terms of education, health, and general welfare. In general, the rich countries of the world are able to provide basic services such as schooling, sanitation, and medical care to their entire populations, while poorer countries are not, and thus most facets of global inequality can ultimately be traced to economic inequality. On the other hand, the success of individual poor countries at achieving specific quality-of-life goals, despite the relatively low level of resources at their command, suggests that social welfare measures need not necessarily vary as dramatically across countries as they do. Little formal cross-national research has been done on the determinants of welfare success in the face of economic failure; more is needed.

Ultimately, though, the key to improving welfare in the poorer countries of the world is to improve their economic prospects. Our review of trends in inequality over the course of the past several decades (and centuries) does not give much cause for optimism on this front. While a small subset of the countries of the world grew rapidly in the nineteenth and twentieth centuries to become the "developed" countries of today, most people in most countries live at income levels that are little changed from the year 1800 or even the year 1000. Similarly, the distributions of income within countries seem to be very stable over time, certainly over periods of decades. Although some, especially Asian, countries have achieved spectacular success in promoting economic growth without increasing internal inequality, such successes have been the exception rather than the rule. More common have been cases of rapid economic decline combined with increasing inequality—consider Russia, Eastern Europe, and Central Asia; Congo and central Africa; and so on.

The problems posed by the long-term persistence of high levels of within-nation and between-nation inequality are many and varied. The broad swath of the world's population living at or near biological survival levels is chronically exposed to Malthusian pressures of malnutrition and disease. If the rich countries of the world will not act to alleviate such misery out of humanitarian concern, they may be forced to act simply for self-preservation. Diseases incubated within such weakened human populations do not stop at the boundaries of high-income countries. Moreover, geopolitical and geo-economic problems that originate in poor countries can have a profound impact on rich countries. International refugee flows, wars and civil conflicts, and international terrorism will continue to be high policy priorities for developed nations for the foreseeable future.

Notes

1. In geometric terms, the Gini coefficient can be represented as a function of the area between a population's Lorenz curve and the 45-degree diagonal equal-incomes line. The Gini coefficient is the percentage of the total area under the diagonal that falls into the "inequality" zone in figure 6.1. Since, by construction, the area under the diagonal equals $1/2$ (each axis has length 1), the Gini coefficient equals the area of the "inequality" zone divided by $1/2$, or simply the area times 2. For the computational formula for the Gini coefficient and a more technical discussion of its properties, see Fields (2001, chap. 2).

2. Such weighted international Gini coefficients have two drawbacks. First, they assume that all citizens of a given country share the same level of income, which is equal to the per capita GNP. Clearly, this is not the case. Second, they ignore the fact that the global income distribution is not really a single distribution but is made up of many national and regional distributions. Several scholars are currently working on the problem of properly aggregating the full distribution of incomes across all countries of the world and how this distribution has changed over time. See Babones (2002), Milanovic (2002), and Sala-i-Martin (2002) for more information.

References

Babones, Salvatore J. 2002. "Population and Sample Selection Effects in Measuring International Income Inequality." *Journal of World-Systems Research* 8:1–22.

Miracles in Emerging Asia." *World Bank Economic Review* 12:419–455.

Deininger, Klaus and Lyn Squire. 1996. "A New Data Set Measuring Income Inequality." *World Bank Economic Review* 10:565–591.

———. 1998. "New Ways of Looking at Old Issues: Inequality and Growth." *Journal of Development Economics* 57:259–287.

Fields, Gary S. 2000. *Distribution and Development: A New Look at the Developing World.* New York: Russell Sage.

Firebaugh, Glenn. 1999. "Empirics of World Income Inequality." *American Journal of Sociology* 104:1597–1630.

Jones, Charles I. 1997. "On the Evolution of the World Income Distribution." *Journal of Economic Perspectives* 11:19–36.

Korzeniewicz, Roberto Patricio and Timothy Patrick Moran. 1997. "World-Economic Trends in the Distribution of Income, 1965–1992." *American Journal of Sociology* 102:1000–1039.

Leibenstein, Harvey. 1957. *Economic Backwardness and Economic Growth.* New York: John Wiley.

Lenski, Gerhard. 1966. *Power and Privilege: A Theory of Social Stratification.* New York: McGraw-Hill.

Li, Hongyi, Lyn Squire, and Heng-fu Zou. 1998. "Explaining International and Intertemporal Variations in Income Inequality." *Economic Journal* 108:26–43.

Maddison, Angus. 2001. *The World Economy: A Millennial Perspective.* Paris: OECD.

Melchior, Arne and Kjetil Telle. 2001. "Global Income Distribution 1965–98: Convergence and Marginalisation." *Forum for Development Studies* 28:75–98.

Milanovic, Branko. 2002. "True World Income Distribution, 1988 and 1993: First Calculation Based on Household Surveys Alone." *Economic Journal* 112:51–92.

Sala-i-Martin, Xavier. 2002. "The Disturbing 'Rise' of World Income Inequality." National Bureau of Economic Research, Working Paper 8904.

Schultz, T. Paul. 1998. "Inequality in the Distribution of Personal Income in the World: How It Is Changing and Why." *Journal of Population Economics* 11:307–344.

United Nations. 2003. *Human Development Report.* New York: United Nations.

WIDER. 2000. *World Income Inequality Database, V 1.0.* Tokyo: United Nations University.

World Bank. 1990. *World Development Report.* Washington, DC: World Bank.

———. 2000. *Global Poverty Report (July).* New York: World Bank.

7

Global Energy Inequalities
Exploring the Long-Term Implications

BRUCE PODOBNIK

Mainstream energy studies have paid insufficient attention to the unequal levels of energy consumption that have become embedded in the foundations of the world-system. This inattention is problematic, given that these energy inequalities pose increasingly severe environmental and human challenges. In a world characterized by strikingly unequal rates of energy consumption, for instance, it will be difficult to develop collectively rational responses to global climate threats. Furthermore, energy inequalities increase the potential for resource-based geopolitical conflicts. And they foster unhealthy consumption habits throughout the developed world while preventing entire generations of men, women, and children in the developing world from fully realizing their potential as citizens of the modern world.

In light of these multiple threats, it is not unreasonable to suggest that energy-related difficulties will begin undermining stability in the world community in coming decades. Indeed, an analysis informed by the world-systems approach highlights contradictions that are likely to generate multiple kinds of energy-related crises in the medium to long term.

In recent years, a variety of researchers working within the world-systems tradition have shed important light on the ways in which the expanding capitalist world-economy intensifies processes of environmental degradation.[1] By focusing on the material consequences of capital accumulation and the enduring inequalities fostered by the world-system, these researchers have developed novel analyses of long-term, problematic patterns of evolution in the humanity-nature nexus. In the analysis that follows, I draw on this research tradition in order to bring a greatly underexamined characteristic of the global energy system into sharper focus—and to examine prospects for reforming inequalities in this energy system.

Global Energy Inequalities

Debates have long raged as to whether the world-economy operates as a zero-sum, bounded system in which gains by one country imply losses for another. In the case of the energy foundations of the world-economy the zero-sum, bounded nature of the world-system is quite clear. The fact that 90 percent of the commercial energy consumed in the world derives from nonrenewable resources provides one important boundary.[2] And the fact that global ecological constraints are tightening provides another. Although some elasticity in these boundaries is offered by changing technologies, in fundamental terms the consumption of commercial energy resources by one group implies a future inability to consume for other groups. This zero-sum feature of the world energy system raises particularly severe dilemmas, as highlighted in a global analysis of patterns of energy consumption.

As with most cross-national research, when examining large-scale patterns of energy consumption we are forced to rely on nationally aggregated data. The limited amount of research that has been conducted at local levels reveals that lower-class citizens, rural residents, women, and minority populations are often forced to rely on traditional, highly polluting, and labor-intensive forms of energy to meet their basic needs.[3] As more research is conducted at the within-country level, our understanding of local and regional inequalities will be strengthened. The present analysis, however, is forced to utilize national data that undoubtedly underestimate true levels of inequality in energy consumption. Given this likely distortion, it is quite remarkable how stark the inequalities are that are registered in nationally aggregated data.

Let me start with a couple of observations regarding relatively long historical trends in the global energy system. As shown in figure 7.1, through the end of World War II the developed world was almost totally self-sufficient in energy.[4] Since then, however, nations of the global south have been transferring energy resources to nations in the global north at a steady rate. A number of oil-exporting countries have achieved impressive levels of economic growth on the basis of this trade. However, the main effect has been to intensify long-standing global inequalities in levels of energy consumption. As indicated in figure 7.2, throughout the modern period core states have attained much higher levels of per capita commercial energy consumption than their semiperipheral or peripheral counterparts. While there was a slight closing of the gap between core and semiperipheral regions during the 1970s,[5] by the

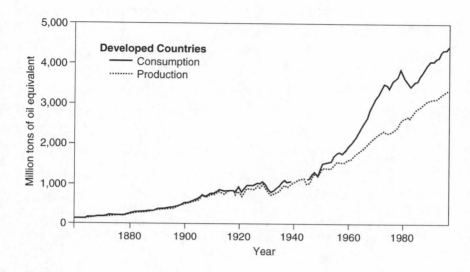

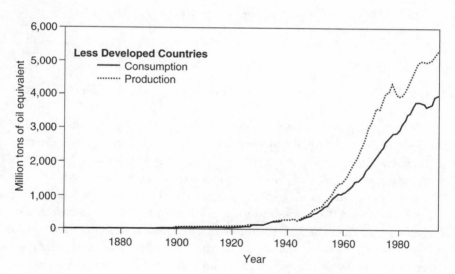

Fig. 7.1. Commercial Energy Production and Consumption, 1860–1998.
Sources: See appendix.

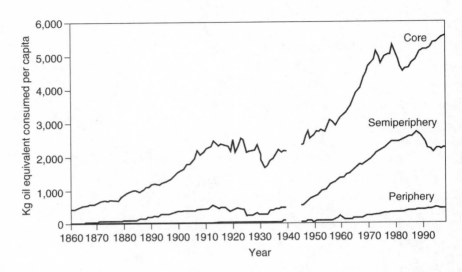

Fig. 7.2. Per Capita Commercial Energy Consumption, 1860–1998.
Sources: See appendix.

mid-1980s long-term patterns of intensifying inequality had reasserted themselves.

If we focus our attention on the post–World War II period and examine world regions in more detail, we again see enduring patterns of inequality. As shown in figure 7.3, North America (the United States and Canada) has persistently outstripped all other regions in terms of commercial energy consumption. After seeing substantial gains in the three and a half decades following World War II, meanwhile, countries in Eastern Europe have undergone a significant decline in consumption. Western Europe, which saw a slight pause following the shocks of the 1970s, has reasserted moderate growth. The Pacific region, which includes Japan, East Asia, and Australia, has seen steady growth. Africa and Asia, meanwhile, have seen little increase in per capita consumption of commercial energy since the 1970s (see table 7.1 for data on the evolution of per capita consumption rates for selected countries over the period 1958-1998).

Turning to a more focused analysis of the present situation, we again find that countries exhibit very divergent patterns of energy consumption. As shown in figure 7.4, the average citizen in the United States consumes 5 times as much as the world average, 10 times as much energy as a typical person in China, and over 30 times more than a resident of India. Even in such major oil-exporting nations as Venezuela and Iran, per capita consumption of commercial energy resources is less than one-half and one-quarter of the U.S. average, respectively. A starker illustration of these inequalities is captured in the estimation that around 40 percent of the world's people—more than 2 billion—still have no regular access to commercial energy products in their homes (World Energy Council 2000).

It must also be observed that these unequal patterns of consumption show little sign of easing. This can be demonstrated through two related techniques: a Gini-style analysis, and a quintile-based analysis.

The advantage of the Gini-style analysis is that it compares the relationship between every individual country's per capita energy consumption and its population size. It therefore makes full use of country-level information. It has one disadvantage, however, in that the scale of the graph used largely determines the image conveyed. Take figure 7.5, for instance. It charts the evolution of the world energy Gini coefficient over the period 1958–1998, focusing in on a very small band on the *y*-axis.[6] As shown at this very focused scale, during the period 1978–1988 the Gini coefficient got slightly smaller —meaning that world commercial energy consumption was becoming slight-

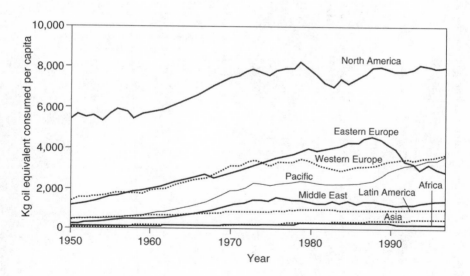

Fig. 7.3. Per Capita Commercial Energy Consumption, 1950–1998.
Sources: See appendix.

Table 7.1. Per Capita Commercial Energy Consumption for Selected Countries

Country	PCAP58	PCAP68	PCAP78	PCAP88	PCAP98	C58_68	C68_78	C78_88	C88_98
United Arab Emirates	352	3,356	16,450	19,314	15,188	852	390	17	-21
Canada	4,110	6,084	8,041	8,445	8,877	48	32	5	5
Singapore	563	3,748	5,735	5,338	8,700	566	53	-7	63
Kuwait	7,085	6,104	4,293	3,525	8,407	-14	-30	-18	139
United States	5,583	7,239	7,970	7,890	7,960	30	10	-1	1
Netherlands	2,511	4,418	7,123	6,081	6,801	76	61	-15	12
Australia	2,599	3,551	4,457	4,607	6,480	37	26	3	41
Belgium	2,653	4,218	5,693	4,855	5,914	59	35	-15	22
Sweden	2,980	4,830	3,919	5,099	5,822	62	-19	30	14
New Zealand	1,174	2,333	2,585	3,605	4,769	99	11	39	32
Saudi Arabia	1,808	6,171	8,503	6,166	4,715	241	38	-27	-24
Russia/USSR	2,001	2,291	3,743	4,740	4,026	15	63	27	-15
France	1,806	2,661	3,474	3,137	3,857	47	31	-10	23
Japan	557	1,721	2,735	2,463	3,821	209	59	-10	55
United Kingdom	3,026	3,499	3,818	3,671	3,753	16	9	-4	2
Taiwan	288	569	1,421	2,035	3,448	97	150	43	69
Denmark	786	2,102	2,404	3,217	3,426	167	14	34	7
South Korea	119	428	847	1,675	3,388	259	98	98	102
Italy	846	2,311	2,702	2,417	3,156	173	17	-11	31
Israel	642	1,071	2,232	1,830	2,890	67	108	-18	58
Venezuela	6,949	5,557	3,504	2,845	2,569	-20	-37	-19	-10
South Africa	1,161	1,283	1,753	2,269	2,279	11	37	29	0
Hong Kong	43	21	583	1,354	2,273	-51	2,670	132	68
Poland	1,622	2,263	3,392	3,447	2,060	40	50	2	-40
Malaysia	236	279	606	1,000	1,846	19	117	65	85
Argentina	630	1,124	1,437	1,593	1,709	78	28	11	7
Iran	1,165	1,724	2,361	1,312	1,642	48	37	-44	25
Chile	534	1,327	1,073	930	1,394	149	-19	-13	50

	PCAP58							C58_68
Mexico	639	796	1,217	1,410	1,366	25	53	16	-3
North Korea	390	1,046	1,416	2,104	1,331	168	35	49	5
Jamaica	93	680	491	912	1,300	632	-28	86	42
Iraq	345	918	1,578	2,049	1,104	166	72	30	-46
Brazil	154	302	628	679	1,080	96	108	8	59
Thailand	40	159	196	296	877	303	23	51	196
Turkey	146	335	481	721	876	130	44	50	22
Cuba	580	473	680	765	857	-18	44	13	12
Colombia	495	571	600	615	706	15	5	3	15
Egypt	165	248	447	614	681	50	80	37	11
China	215	168	430	564	614	-22	156	31	9
Peru	258	366	535	486	485	42	46	-9	-0
Zimbabwe	641	331	329	387	473	-48	-1	18	22
Indonesia	151	127	216	338	402	-16	70	57	19
Bolivia	102	153	298	205	374	50	95	-31	82
El Salvador	105	157	268	244	357	49	71	-9	46
Philippines	109	233	238	281	333	114	2	18	18
India	64	103	126	201	292	61	22	60	45
Honduras	107	142	157	183	266	33	11	17	45
Ivory Coast	36	141	222	318	252	295	57	43	-21
Zambia	58	516	315	168	242	788	-39	-47	44
Guatemala	103	144	127	96	236	41	-12	-25	147
Nigeria	11	53	178	171	183	402	236	-4	7
Ghana	71	117	129	111	142	65	10	-14	28
Kenya	39	184	192	118	121	366	5	-39	3
Zaire	26	48	67	39	12	87	39	-41	-71

Sources: See appendix.

Note: PCAP58 = kg of oil equivalent, commercial energy consumed per capita in 1958; C58_68 = percentage change in per capita consumption over period 1958–1968.

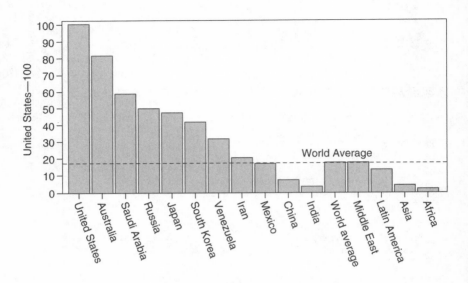

Fig. 7.4. Per Capita Commercial Energy Consumption Relative to the United States, 1998. *Sources:* See appendix.

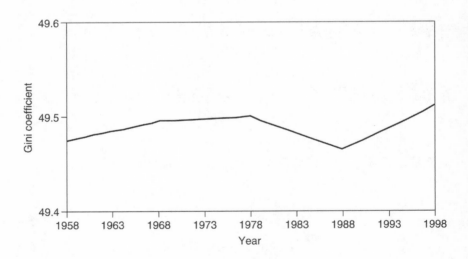

Fig. 7.5. World Energy Gini Coefficient, 1958–1998. *Sources:* See appendix.

ly more equitable. The post-1988 period, however, saw a relatively rapid return to a long-standing pattern of inequality.

While serving the useful purpose of highlighting a modest pause in the overall trend, the Gini analysis has the potential to overemphasize quite minor changes. Changing the y-axis to cover a range from 49.0 to 50.0, for instance, results in a largely horizontal line (which would emphasize an unchanging distribution of energy consumption). It is possible to guard against an overly sensitive Gini analysis by performing a breakdown by quintile groups. This method is based on a five-category aggregation of countries, and so it makes less full use of individual country-level data. Nevertheless, by providing a more structured set of categories to compare over time, it is less sensitive to presentational decisions.

So what does the quintile analysis show us? As shown in figure 7.6, in 1998 the top quintile (containing the wealthiest 20% of the world's population) consumed about 68 percent of the world's commercial energy, while the lowest quintile consumed under 2 percent of these resources. Figure 7.7 shows how these categories have evolved over time. The following patterns can be identified: The proportion of energy consumed by the top quintile fell slightly during the period 1958-1978 and then largely remained steady; the second quintile saw gains up to 1978, then fell slightly; the third quintile has seen some growth in the post-1968 period; and the fourth and fifth quintiles have seen very limited growth in the post-1958 period.

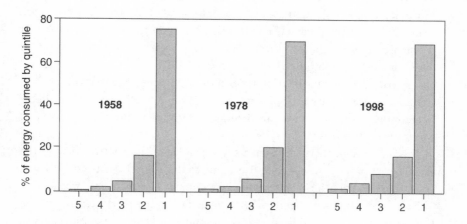

Fig. 7.6. World Commercial Energy Consumption by Quintiles, 1958–1998.
Sources: See appendix.

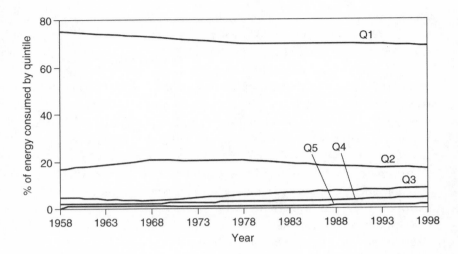

Fig. 7.7. World Commercial Energy Consumption, 1958–1998 (evolution of quintiles over time). *Sources:* See appendix.

There are a couple of noteworthy points to make about this quintile analysis. First, the overall endurance of inequality is again remarkable. Within this overall continuity, however, we can again identify slight modulations. Specifically, the upper middle group (the upper end of the semiperiphery) has seen its share of commercial energy consumption decline since the late 1960s. At the same time, the middle group (the lower end of the semiperiphery) has seen its share increase slowly but steadily. This reflects the fact that part of the semiperiphery (mainly Eastern Europe) has seen its energy consumption rates slip, while another part (East Asia) has increased its proportional energy consumption in the post-1968 period. This suggests that the semiperipheral pattern identified by Chase-Dunn (1989:265) may need to be slightly modified to take into account diverging fortunes within that category of countries in the post-1970 period.

In sum, though there has been a slight change in the relative share of the world's commercial energy resources going to the second and third quintiles, the overall distribution has remained fundamentally unaltered in the post-1958 period. One of the central challenges facing the world community in this century will be to begin to alter these embedded patterns of inequality in the global energy system.

Environmental Implications

While many people in the developing world struggle to gain access to modern energy technologies, citizens and companies in the global north are generally consuming energy resources at an unsustainable rate. The high levels of energy use found in wealthy countries are the source of most of the greenhouse gases emitted into the atmosphere today.[7] In contrast, most citizens in the global south produce relatively modest energy-related greenhouse emissions. Since these gases remain in the atmosphere for long periods of time, it should also be noted that nations of the developed north have emitted most of the total anthropogenic greenhouse gases that have accumulated in the atmosphere over the past two centuries.

Scientific evidence continues to mount that greenhouse gases generated by human activities are having detrimental impacts on local, regional, and global ecosystems. For instance, a recent report of the Intergovernmental Panel on Climate Change (2001) concludes that most of the global warming observed over the past 50 years can be attributed to human activities. The report also provides evidence to suggest that this warming trend is likely to have more severe environmental and human consequences than had been predicted only a few years ago. In short, the ecological boundary surrounding the global energy system is turning out to be much tighter than expected.

With the scientific consensus suggesting that dangerous climatic dynamics are already being triggered, it becomes imperative to contain greenhouse gas emissions on a global scale at the earliest opportunity. Unfortunately, the difficulties inherent in achieving such a policy objective are exacerbated by the inequalities embedded in the world energy system. Let us pause to examine the startlingly unequal emissions rates that derive from these unequal patterns of consumption.

It has been suggested that the most equitable approach to addressing the problem of global climate change would be to define a standard per capita emissions rate and then levy penalties on nations that exceed the standard (Meyerson 1998). Enshrined within the United Nations Framework Convention on Climate Change (UNFCCC) is one such standard that could be applied in this kind of calculation. Specifically, the Framework Convention states that anthropogenic carbon dioxide emissions should be stabilized at slightly less than 1990 levels. This target level is largely symbolic, since it is not assumed to be capable by itself of forestalling significant global warming. Furthermore, it has not been formally ratified by anything approaching a majority of the world's governments. It has nevertheless come to represent the first widely promulgated threshold relating to a major greenhouse gas. As such, it provides one standard on which to compare the behavior of countries across the world.

Table 7.2 carries out an analysis designed to show how actual 1998 carbon emission rates for each country compare with their 1990 target levels. The calculations involved are quite simple. First, note that estimated world anthropogenic carbon emissions totaled 5.832 billion metric tons of carbon dioxide in 1990 (U.S. Energy Information Administration 1999). The world's population, meanwhile, totaled 5.260 billion people in 1990. The UNFCCC target rate, therefore, theoretically allows every person on the planet to emit roughly 1.108 metric tons of carbon per year. Given this per-person theoretical emission allowance, each country's cumulative target rate can be calculated by multiplying its population by 1.108. Carrying these multiplications out for the year 1990 then gives us the population-weighted target levels for each country, consistent with the UNFCCC threshold. In the case of the United States, for example, we multiply 1.108 by 249.8 million (the U.S. population in 1990) to get a 1990 carbon target level of 277 million metric tons. This is the amount of carbon the U.S. population could emit, consistent with the UNFCCC target, on a yearly basis for an interim period.

Of course, few countries emit the amount of carbon dioxide suggested by the 1990 target. Many poor countries emit less than their population-weighted theoretical allowance, while many wealthy countries emit much more than their population-weighted allowance. A ratio can be computed to reflect precisely how far any country is from its UNFCCC theoretical allowance for any given year (remembering that the 1990 level is supposed to be fixed over time). To calculate the ratio we just take the actual carbon emission level of a country for a particular year and divide it by that country's 1990 target rate.[8] The higher the ratio, the more severely a country is exceeding its population-weighted 1990 theoretical allowance. A ratio of 1 (attained only by Argentina in 1998) signifies that a country is emitting at exactly its theoretical allowance. And a ratio of less than 1 signifies that a country is emitting less than its population-weighted 1990 theoretical allowance.

As can be seen in table 7.2, energy consumption inequalities translate into substantially different rates of greenhouse gas emissions across the world. Just as the United States consumes five times the global average, it also emits over five times more carbon than theoretically allowed for by the UNFCCC threshold. Canada and Australia exhibit quite elevated carbon emission rates, while even Japan emits twice its theoretical allowance. Overall, a broad band of Western European countries emit two or three times more carbon than

Table 7.2. Comparison of 1990 Target Carbon Emissions Rates with Actual 1998 Carbon Emissions

Country	1990 Target (million metric tons)	1998 Actual (million metric tons)	Ratio	Country	1990 Target (million metric tons)	1998 Actual (million metric tons)	Ratio
United Arab Emirates	2	31	15.16	Venezuela	21	37	1.73
Bahrain	1	5	8.97	France	63	106	1.69
Singapore	3	25	8.34	Switzerland	7	12	1.61
United States	277	1,494	5.38	Sweden	9	15	1.58
Kuwait	2	12	5.09	Bulgaria	9	14	1.45
Canada	31	138	4.48	Malaysia	20	28	1.41
Australia	19	83	4.39	Hungary	11	15	1.31
Netherlands	17	65	3.92	Iran	62	79	1.28
Saudi Arabia	18	63	3.60	Portugal	11	14	1.28
Belgium	11	38	3.44	Russia	339	405	1.19
Israel	5	15	2.91	Mexico	93	95	1.03
Denmark	5	16	2.81	Argentina*	36	36	1.00
Taiwan	22	58	2.65	Chile*	15	14	0.96
Germany	89	227	2.55	Iraq*	20	19	0.95
South Africa	41	101	2.46	Turkey*	62	47	0.76
Finland	6	13	2.35	Thailand*	62	42	0.68
Norway	5	11	2.34	China*	1,259	740	0.59
United Kingdom	64	147	2.30	Egypt*	58	31	0.53
South Korea	48	107	2.25	Brazil*	164	84	0.51
Greece	11	25	2.22	Colombia*	37	17	0.46
New Zealand	4	8	2.15	Zimbabwe*	11	4	0.37
Japan	137	288	2.10	Indonesia*	198	67	0.34
Hong Kong	6	12	1.90	India*	942	252	0.27
Italy	63	119	1.89	Nigeria*	107	27	0.25
Austria	9	16	1.87	Philippines*	68	17	0.25
Poland	42	77	1.82	Pakistan*	125	26	0.21
Spain	43	75	1.74	Bangladesh*	122	6	0.05

Sources: See appendix.

* Indicates countries equal to or under threshold recommended by the Intergovernmental Panel on Climate Change (IPCC).

suggested by the UNFCCC guidelines. Interestingly, though, a handful of core nations (Italy, Austria, France, Switzerland, and Sweden) come close to attaining their symbolic emissions allotments. Broadly speaking, semiperipheral nations generally approximate the UNFCCC threshold, while peripheral nations (including China and India) emit far below their symbolically allotted rates.

The data presented in table 7.2 suggest how politically difficult it would be to implement an equitable approach to global carbon reduction. In order for most core nations to approach their per capita global emissions norm, they would have to reduce their commercial energy consumption levels by factors of three, four, or five. Moreover, these reductions would have to be achieved in a context in which per capita emissions from peripheral nations were allowed to rise toward the global threshold. In other words, the historically ingrained transfer of resources characteristic of the world energy system would have to be reversed. Nothing short of a fundamental change in the material structures and political culture of the world-system itself would be required to attain an equitably distributed allotment of energy consumption rights.

In the absence of significant reform, the contradictions originating from unequal patterns of energy consumption in this zero-sum, ecologically bounded system promise to heighten tensions in coming years. These tensions are already manifesting themselves in increasingly acrimonious negotiations at global climate conferences. But they will surely manifest themselves as heightened political, commercial, and social competition as well, as discussed in the next section of this analysis.

Long-Term Geopolitical, Commercial, and Social Implications

Though prone to neglect dimensions of inequality, mainstream energy analyses have paid a great deal of attention to the ways in which competition for access to energy resources has influenced dynamics of geopolitical rivalry in the modern era.[9] Additionally, there is a well-developed literature that describes the competitive struggles pursued by private energy corporations in the twentieth century.[10] Even given these extensive bodies of research, however, it is important to note that world-systems researchers have still been able to shed new light on geopolitical and commercial dynamics surrounding extractive industries.

By engaging in comparative historical research, for instance, Stephen Bunker and his colleagues[11] have shown that the tendency of ascendant core states to engage in competitive struggles for access to raw materials has been a central feature of the world-economy since at least the sixteenth century. They have also drawn attention to the fact that attempts to achieve national economic ascent involve the extraction of natural resources in processes that are disrupting fragile ecosystems across the world. Far from reflecting any widespread process of dematerialization, these national development efforts continue to involve the appropriation of tremendous volumes of raw materials by specific social groups—most often to the detriment of other segments of society.

The operation of these extractive dynamics has taken on particularly severe forms in the case of modern energy sectors. For instance, it is widely acknowledged that competition for access to Southeast Asian oil resources was a fundamental cause of warfare between the United States and Japan in World War II. Similarly, the largest military conflict in the post–Cold War era—the Persian Gulf War—was motivated primarily by competition for control over one of the world's key reserves of petroleum. And every indication is that competition for petroleum will generate renewed geopolitical tensions on both regional and global levels in the coming decades, as resource and ecological boundaries draw tighter.[12]

It is important to note that more than 70 percent of the world's proven reserves of petroleum, and more than 75 percent of known natural gas reserves, are located in the Middle East and Central Asia.[13] As petroleum and natural gas reserves in other parts of the world become depleted during the coming decades, developing nations such as China will be forced to turn toward Middle Eastern and Central Asian oil and gas resources to satisfy their growing domestic demand (Ogutcu 1998; Xu 2000). This will bring large nations in the global south, which have historically consumed very small quantities of petroleum, into direct competition with nations of the global north. Though there is uncertainty as to exactly when depletion effects will begin hitting Middle Eastern and Central Asian reserves, it appears likely that, under rising demand pressure from both core and peripheral nations, the pools of low-cost oil and gas located in these regions will themselves begin to run dry sometime during the 2020–2070 period. As resource constraints tighten, the material inequalities embedded in the international petroleum system are then likely to become a potent source of geopolitical tension.

Growing reliance on petroleum and natural gas resources from the Middle East and Central Asia is also likely to expose the world-economy to substantial financial vulnerability. As argued in recent studies,[14] countries in these regions are likely to be convulsed by political and social unrest in the coming decades. This suggests that price volatility will regularly emanate from the world's key sources of conventional energy at a time when depletion effects are likely to begin placing sustained upward pressure on oil and gas prices throughout most of the rest of the world (Pindyck 1999). If deregulation continues to sweep through global electricity markets, another source of market volatility will be added to this already uncertain commercial environment.

Recent experience has revealed that inflationary trends in global energy markets can rapidly undermine conditions for capital accumulation in broad regions of the world-economy. In more than 35 countries energy imports exceed 10 percent of the value of their exports, and so even modestly elevated global energy prices can quickly generate serious trade deficits (International Monetary Fund 2000). Even in core nations such as the United States, spikes in electricity prices have led to substantial commercial and political unease.

It certainly remains the case that, as world-systems researchers have repeatedly pointed out, prices of raw materials such as energy fundamentally impact rates of profit and capital accumulation in virtually all sectors (Barham, Bunker, and O'Hearn 1994:5). In this regard, the "new economy" is not so different from the old economy. Indeed, given their high level of demand for uninterrupted electricity, information-based industries may be more acutely sensitive to the cost and reliability of energy inputs than many traditional industries (Feder 2000). The most advanced sectors of modern economies, in short, are not likely to be able to escape the commercial turbulence generated by tightening constraints emerging in conventional global energy industries.

In addition to the mounting possibility that geopolitical tensions and commercial instability will be generated by global energy inequalities, there are problematic social dynamics that may kick into effect as well. Most important, it is not at all clear that the relatively soft constraints represented by environmental regulations can remain resilient in the face of growing supply difficulties in global energy industries.

While public support for stronger environmental regulations has been widespread in core countries during the economic upturn of the 1990s, it is unclear how strong these environmental commitments will prove to be during periods of crisis in energy sectors. Recall that, following the temporary oil price hikes of 2000–2001, protests against energy taxes swept across Western Europe. Though labor and green political representatives tried to defend the taxes on the basis of their environmental benefits, in most cases these taxes were reduced in the face of consumer anger (Barnard 2000). Similarly, in the context of the current electrical crisis that is assailing California, political and corporate leaders are calling for the suspension of some federal and state regulations in order to allow for increased electricity production in conventional and nuclear-powered stations (Booth 2001).

If public commitment to environmental regulations proves to be soft in core nations during a time of relative affluence, then this has ominous implications for the viability of such regulations in developing countries throughout the world. Wallerstein's (1999) suggestion that reformist environmental regulations will prove ineffective in containing the ecologically destructive tendencies of the capitalist world-system may well end up being correct. What is certain is that a time of significant challenges to environmental achievements will come as the contemporary global economic expansion ends, competition for increasingly scarce conventional fuels intensifies, and the costs of climate change begin to mount.

Prospects for the Future

There are many reasons to be pessimistic about the future evolution of the global energy system. Indeed, analysts from diverse ideological perspectives argue that fundamental changes in contemporary patterns of energy use cannot be made and that catastrophe is inevitable. Still, it is important not to underestimate the ability of capitalist firms to innovate and adapt to new material circumstances. And it is certainly premature to assume that concerted political and social pressures for equitable reforms would be unable to move the global energy system toward a more collectively rational trajectory.

In this last section, one possible scenario of true reform—resulting from a particular conjuncture of systemic dynamics—is described. Whether it will materialize is partly dependent on broad structural forces beyond the control of individual nations and partly dependent on the ability of state planners, corporate leaders, and broad groups from civil society to push for reform. In this respect, we have arrived at the classically ambiguous conclusion found in most world-systems analyses: Though structural processes of evolution are leading in dangerous directions, there is at least some possibility that human agency can have unusually powerful effects precisely because we find ourselves in a crisis period.[15]

As discussed in the previous section, geopolitical rivalries for dwindling conventional energy resources are likely to fuel serious conflicts between ascendant states and long-established core powers (CSIS 2001). It also appears, however, that these same dynamics of geopolitical rivalry are spurring some states to fund new energy technology development programs. State agencies in the United States, Western Europe, and Japan, for instance, have already sponsored joint projects with private corporations to commercialize a variety of new energy systems in this decade. Underlying these efforts is a pressing need to find new ways to utilize the extensive networks of government laboratories that, during the post–World War II era, specialized in the development of nuclear weapons and delivery systems.[16] One unanticipated consequence of contemporary efforts to legitimize continuing public support for military-industrial complexes may therefore be to foster more innovative patterns of state intervention in energy sectors during the coming decades.

Similarly, rising prices in petroleum and natural gas industries will stimulate a renewed wave of capital investments in conventional energy sectors—thereby partially reinforcing business-as-usual commercial dynamics. At the same time, however, rising conventional energy prices will stimulate interest in alternative energy technologies. In this context, it is important to note that a tremendous amount of innovation is occurring in a variety of alternative energy sectors. Indeed, new kinds of business ventures—which link small engineering firms such as Ballard Power with long-established automotive and petroleum corporations—are fostering rapid commercial advances in new wind, solar, and fuel cell technologies.[17] Through such cooperative, multifirm joint efforts, resistance encountered in the marketplace can be more effectively countered. Historical and contemporary trends therefore suggest that competitive dynamics can indeed foster the entrepreneurial and organizational innovations required for the commercialization of a variety of new energy technologies.

There is another factor that is likely to enhance dynamics of innovation in global energy industries. In contrast to the global energy shifts of the nineteenth and twentieth centuries, future energy transitions may be facilitated by the existence of multilateral agencies that can assist in setting common agendas and coordinating policies undertaken by individual governments. Although organizations such as the World Bank and the International Energy Agency have long directed the bulk of their institutional support toward conventional energy systems, there are indications that these organizations are in the process of modifying their priorities. As a result of pressure from nongovernmental organizations, for instance, the World Bank recently committed itself to increasing funding for environmentally sustainable energy projects (World Bank 1999).

Multilateral institutions are also assisting in national efforts to reduce subsidies to conventional energy industries throughout the world. If the field of energy pricing can be leveled through these national and international policy efforts, possibilities for a shift toward greater reliance on new energy technologies will be significantly improved.

What is still missing from contemporary efforts at generating innovative changes in the global energy system, however, is any concerted attempt to reduce enduring energy inequalities by reigning in habits of overconsumption found in many core countries. It is here that groups rooted in civil society, such as consumer and environmental movements, have an important role to play. Such movements have demonstrated in practice that they have the capacity to alter the trajectories of energy sectors by mobilizing against nuclear power and by pushing for tighter environmental regulations on conventional sectors in many regions of the world.[18] Now, not only must they strengthen their defense of existing regulatory controls, but they must also work to transform cultural propensities to overconsume energy resources that are found in such countries as the United States, Canada, and Australia (Nye 1999). Behind these intentional efforts at reform, meanwhile, lies what might be a more powerful source of social pressure for fundamental change in the global energy system. Escalating social tensions in the Middle East and Central Asia may in the end prove to be the key, unintended factor propelling the system in innovative directions in the twenty-first century.

There are clearly inherent uncertainties in the manner in which geopolitical, commercial, and social dynamics will interact in coming decades. What is clear, however, is that the massive inequalities embedded in the global energy system must begin to be reformed if potentially dire trends are to be avoided. Whether this process can be initiated soon will have a tremendous impact on determining whether the world can move in a collectively rational direction regarding energy policy or whether we will become caught in escalating energy-related crises in this century.

Appendix: Energy Data Sources and Methods

The analyses undertaken in this chapter are based on data covering coal, petroleum, natural gas, nuclear, hydro, geothermal, and alternative energy industries for the period 1800–1998. The following sources were drawn on for the production and consumption data: for the period 1800-1949, Etemad and Luciani (1991); for the period 1950–1997, United Nations (1997), provided in the annual volumes published by the United Nations entitled *Energy Statistics Yearbooks* and supplemented by updated computerized files provided by the United Nations Energy Statistics Unit. Some additional consumption data for the years 1925–1949 were taken from United Nations (1952) and from Darmstadter, Teitelbaum, and Polach (1971).

Where missing data has been estimated, the method of linear interpolations between specific data points has been used. This method is judged to be reasonable, given the fact that national patterns in energy production and consumption generally follow smooth trajectories. The method of linear interpolation is widely used in the construction of other energy data sets. Because of severe missing data problems during the years 1940–1945, the series on consumption were left as missing during this period.

Reliability checks were carried out on the energy data files. Specifically, the United Nations data has been cross-checked with information provided in International Energy Agency energy publications, the U.S. Energy Information Administration's Annual Energy Review, and the British Petroleum Survey of Energy Resources. These comparisons reveal a very high level of reliability.

In calculating the world energy Gini coefficient, each year was calculated separately. First, for each country a variable (perpop) was calculated—equal to the percentage of the world's population represented by that country in that year. Second, for each country a variable (perenc) was calculated—equal to the percentage of world commercial energy consumption represented by that country in that year. The Gini coefficient for each year was then calculated using this formula:

Gini = 0.5*(sum of absolute values of (perpop-perenc) for all countries in that year).

In notational form:

Gini = 0.5*(|perpop 1 − perenc 1| + |perpop 2 − perenc 2| . . .
+ |perpopN − perencN|)

where perpop 1 is percentage of world population in country 1 and

perencN is percentage of world energy consumed in country N.

Contact the author at podobnik@lclark.edu for a more detailed discussion of data sources and methods, as well as descriptions of exactly which countries are included in global regional categories used.

Notes

1. Of particular note are Bunker (1985), Burns et al. (1994), and the studies presented in the volume edited by Goldfrank, Goodman, and Szasz (1999).

2. The nonrenewable energy resources of coal, petroleum, and natural gas currently provide around 90 percent of the world's commercial energy, while nuclear and hydroelectricity provide most of the rest. It should be noted that the data analyzed in this chapter relate exclusively to commercial forms of energy and do not include traditional resources such as wood (which are estimated to provide under 5% of the

world's energy). Consult the appendix for further information on data sources and methods.

3. See Alam, Sathaye, and Barnes (1998) and Komives, Whittington, and Wu (2000) for examples of these within-country studies.

4. Consult the appendix for information on data sources and methods.

5. Chase-Dunn (1989:265–266) correctly highlighted the growing share of energy that flowed to certain semiperipheral states in the pre-1980 period. This pattern reversed itself in the post-1980 period, however, as Eastern Europe declined and core states once again expanded their consumption.

6. That is to say, the Gini coefficient range from 49.4 to 49.6 is extremely small. See the appendix for a description of exactly how the world energy Gini coefficient was calculated.

7. Greenhouse gases primarily include carbon dioxide, methane, and nitrous oxide—all of which are by-products of fossil-fuel consumption (though there are other sources of these gases as well). See Intergovernmental Panel on Climate Change (2001) for a recent summary on greenhouse gases and global climate change.

8. In table 7.2, the numbers in the "1990 Target" and "1998 Actual" columns have been rounded. However, the ratio numbers were calculated on unrounded numbers.

9. For particularly useful studies on the geopolitical dimensions of energy issues, see Vernon (1983), Bromley (1991), and Yergin (1991).

10. See Penrose (1968) and Moran (1987), for instance.

11. Bunker and Ciccantell (1999) contains a list of additional studies completed by this group of researchers.

12. See Podobnik (2000, chap. 3) for a more detailed examination of the ways in which competition for access to energy resources has influenced dynamics of geopolitical rivalry in the modern era.

13. These estimates of proven petroleum and natural gas reserves come from British Petroleum Company (1998) and World Energy Council (1999).

14. See studies conducted by the National Intelligence Council (2000) and the Center for Strategic and International Studies (CSIS 2001) for discussion of this point.

15. See Wallerstein (1999) and Boswell and Chase-Dunn (2000, chap. 6) for particularly useful descriptions of the complexities inherent in these bifurcation points in world history.

16. See Nakaoka (1994), Sissine (1999), and U.S. General Accounting Office (1999) for surveys of government-supported efforts to commercialize new energy technologies.

17. See Srinivasan et al. (1999), Podobnik (2000:254), and Worrell et al. (2001) for discussions of private-sector investments in new energy systems.

18. See Rudig (1990), Nilsson and Johansson (1994), and Podobnik (2000, chap. 5) for discussions of the impact of social movements on global energy industries.

References

Alam, Manzoor, Jayant Sathaye, and Doug Barnes. 1998. "Urban Household Energy Use in India: Efficiency and Policy Implications." *Energy Policy* 26:885–891.

Barham, Bradford, Stephen Bunker, and Denis O'Hearn. 1994. "Raw Material Industries in Resource-Rich Regions." Pp. 3–38 in *States, Firms, and Raw Materials: The World Economy and Ecology of Aluminum*, edited by Bradford Barham, Stephen Bunker, and Denis O'Hearn. Madison, WI: University of Wisconsin Press.

Barnard, Bruce. 2000. "Trucking Battle Over, but War Goes On." *Journal of Commerce*, September 18.

Booth, William. 2001. "California Pollution Laws Blamed in Crisis." *Washington Post*, February 10.

Boswell, Terry and Christopher Chase-Dunn. 2000. *The Spiral of Capitalism and Socialism: Toward Global Democracy*. Boulder, CO: Lynne Rienner Publishers.

British Petroleum Company. 1998. *BP Statistical Review of World Energy*. London: British Petroleum Co.

Bromley, Simon. 1991. *American Hegemony and World Oil*. University Park, PA: Pennsylvania State University Press.

Bunker, Stephen. 1985. *Underdeveloping the Amazon: Extraction, Unequal Exchange, and the Failure of the Modern State*. Urbana, IL: University of Illinois Press.

Bunker, Stephen and Paul Ciccantell. 1999. "Economic Ascent and the Global Environment: World-Systems Theory and the New Historical Materialism." Pp.107–122 in *Ecology and the World-System*, edited by Walter Goldfrank, David Goodman and Andrew Szasz. Westport, CT: Greenwood Press.

Burns, Thomas, Edward Kick, David Murray, and Dixie Murray. 1994. "Demography, Development and Deforestation in a World-System Perspective." *International Journal of Comparative Sociology* 35:221–239.

Chase-Dunn, Christopher. 1989. *Global Formation: Structures of the World-Economy*. Cambridge, MA: Basil Blackwell.

CSIS (Center for Strategic and International Studies). 2001. *The Geopolitics of Energy into the 21st Century*. Washington, DC: CSIS.

Darmstadter, Joel, Perry Teitelbaum, and Jaroslav Polach. 1971. *Energy in the World Economy: A Statistical Review of Trends in Output, Trade, and Consumption since 1925*. Baltimore, MD: Johns Hopkins Press.

Etemad, Bouda and Jean Luciani. 1991. *World Energy Production, 1800–1985*. Geneva: Libraire DROZ.

Feder, Barnaby. 2000. "Digital Economy's Demand for Steady Power Strains Utilities." *New York Times*, July 3.

Goldfrank, Walter, David Goodman, and Andrew Szasz, eds. 1999. *Ecology and the World-System*. Westport, CT: Greenwood Press.

Intergovernmental Panel on Climage Change. 2001. *Third Assessment Report of Working Group I*. Shanghai: UN IPCC.

International Monetary Fund. 2000. *The Impact of Higher Oil Prices on the Global Economy.* Washington, DC: IMF.

Komives, Kristin, Dale Whittington, and Xun Wu. 2000. "Energy Use around the World—Evidence from Household Surveys." Pp. 14–24 in *Energy and Development Report 2000,* edited by Penelope J. Brook and Suzanne Smith. Washington, DC: World Bank.

Meyerson, Frederick. 1998. "Population, Carbon Emissions, and Global Warming: The Forgotten Relationship at Kyoto." *Population and Develoment Review* 24: 115–130.

Moran, Theodore. 1987. "Managing an Oligopoly of Would-Be Sovereigns: The Dynamics of Joint Control and Self-Control in the International Oil Industry Past, Present, and Future." *International Organization* 41:575–607.

Nakaoka, Akira. 1994. "Current Status of NEDO's Fuel Cell Power Generation Technology R&D." *Japan 21st* 39 (11): 24–26.

National Intelligence Council. 2000. *Global Trends 2015: A Dialogue about the Future with Nongovernment Experts.* Washington, DC: National Intelligence Council.

Nilsson, Lars and Thomas Johansson. 1994. "Environmental Challenges to the Energy Industries." Pp. 47–79 in *Sustainable Development and the Energy Industries: Implementation and Impacts of Environmental Legislation,* edited by Nicola Steen. London: Earthscan Publications.

Nye, David. 1999. "Path Insistence: Comparing European and American Attitudes toward Energy." *Journal of International Affairs* 53:129–148.

Ogutcu, Mehmet. 1998. "China and the World Energy System: New Links." *Journal of Energy and Development* 23:281–318.

Penrose, Edith. 1968. *The Large International Firms in Developing Countries: The International Petroleum Industry.* London: Allen and Unwin.

Pindyck, Robert. 1999. "The Long-Run Evolution of Energy Prices." *Energy Journal* 20:1–27.

Podobnik, Bruce. 2000. *Global Energy Shifts: Future Possibilities in Historical Perspective.* Ann Arbor, MI: UMI Dissertation Services.

Rudig, Wolfgang. 1990. *Anti-Nuclear Movements: A World Survey of Opposition to Nuclear Energy.* London: Longman Group.

Sissine, Fred. 1999. *Renewable Energy: Key to Sustainable Energy Supply.* Washington, DC: Congressional Research Service.

Srinivasan, Supramaniam, Renaut Mosdale, Philippe Stevens, and Christopher Yang. 1999. "Fuel Cells: Reaching the Era of Clean and Efficient Power Generation in the Twenty-First Century." *Annual Review of Energy and the Environment* 24:281–328.

United Nations. 1952. *World Energy Supplies in Selected Years, 1929–1950.* New York: United Nations.

———. 1997. *The United Nations Energy Statistics Database.* New York: United Nations.

U.S. Energy Information Administration. 1999. *International Carbon Dioxide Emissions from the Consumption and Flaring of Fossil Fuels.* Washington, DC: US EIA.

U.S. General Accounting Office. 1999. *Renewable Energy: DOE's Funding and Markets for Wind Energy and Solar Cell Technologies.* Washington, DC: GAO.

Vernon, Raymond. 1983. *Two Hungry Giants: The United States and Japan in the Quest for Oil and Ores.* Cambridge, MA: Harvard University Press.

Wallerstein, Immanuel. 1999. "Ecology and Capitalist Costs of Production: No Exit." Pp. 3–11 in *Ecology and the World-System,* edited by Walter Goldfrank, David Goodman, and Andrew Szasz. Westport, CT: Greenwood Press.

World Bank. 1999. *Fuel for Thought: Environmental Strategy for the Energy Sector.* Washington, DC: World Bank.

World Energy Council. 1999. *Survey of Energy Resources 1998.* London: World Energy Council.

———. 2000. *Energy for Tomorrow's World.* London: World Energy Council.

Worrell, Ernst, Rene Van Berkel, Zhou Fengqi, Christoph Menke, Roberto Schaeffer, and Robert Williams. 2001. "Technology Transfer of Energy Efficient Technologies in Industry: A Review of Trends and Policy Issues" *Energy Policy* 29:29–43.

Xu, Xiaojie. 2000. "China and the Middle East: Cross-Investment in the Energy Sector." *Middle East Policy* 7 (3): 122–136.

Yergin, Daniel. 1991. *The Prize: The Epic Quest for Oil, Money, and Power.* New York: Simon and Schuster.

III | Globalization and the Environment

8

Ecosystems and World-Systems

Accumulation as an Ecological Process

ALF HORNBORG

Perhaps the most fundamental aspect of a world-systems perspective is the conclusion that global society in some respects resembles a zero-sum game. Most world-systems analysts would acknowledge that the economic and technological accomplishments of the core to a significant extent rely on a systematic appropriation of resources from the periphery. To expose "growth" or "development" as accumulation, however, is not as self-congratulatory as the neoliberal discourse to which most powerful actors today subscribe. In order to stand a chance of persuading a significant number of people, advocates of the zero-sum perspective thus need to argue along two academically quite separate lines.

First, they would need to show how, underneath the veil of market reciprocity, there is a continuous net transfer of productive resources from peripheral to core regions, within as well as between nations. To do this, they need to develop measures of "productive potential" that are independent of monetary measures, which tell us only at which rates different commodities are exchanged on the market. There has long been an interest, in the context of such arguments, in the unequal exchange of energy between different sectors of global society (Bunker 1985; Odum and Arding 1991; Hornborg 1998). Important work in this direction is also being carried out, for instance, by proponents of "ecological footprints" (Wackernagel and Rees 1996) and material flow analysis (Fischer-Kowalski and Haberl 1997). In this part of the argument, it is crucial to be able to maintain an analytical distinction between physical, productive potential (whether measured in energy, labor time, hectares, or weight), on one hand, and economic "value," on the other. In fact, the logic of market institutions implies that these two kinds of measures will tend to be inversely related to each other, as physical potential dissipates while economic value is being created, which in effect means that dissipation of resources is continuously rewarded by the market with ever greater quantities of resources to dissipate. On the other hand, it is also crucial to be able to show that the net transfer of productive potential (for instance, the energy in fossil fuels) to core regions is essential to the growth of industrial infrastructure, the products of which are ultimately convertible into money and thus more purchasing power vis-à-vis resources in the periphery.

Second, proponents of a zero-sum perspective need to be able to explain by which cognitive mechanisms the above-mentioned relations between technology and world trade tend to be hidden from our view. Like Karl Marx, they need to ask by which means unequal exchange tends to be masked by a hegemonic ideology or "false consciousness" representing the glaring inequalities as natural or in some sense justifiable. It is obvious that the mainstream economists' exclusive obsession with monetary measures and national statistics contributes to such mystification. At a deeper and epistemologically more complex level, we may also need to revive the Marxian concept of "fetishism." Marx observed how some material objects (particularly money) are attributed with an autonomous capacity to generate more of their own kind and how such illusions (as in the notion of "interest") tend to mask the social relations of unequal exchange that in reality are the basis of capital accumulation. I have argued (Hornborg 2001) that this important observation should be extended from the fetishism of money and commodities to the fetishism of machines. Machines, too, are material objects attributed with autonomous, generative powers masking their derivation from global relations of unequal exchange. In being conceptually divorced from the unequal flows of labor and natural resources, the productive potential of which it manifests, the entire phenomenon of industrial technology tends to present itself to our consciousness as morally and politically neutral. Perhaps it is only in combination with the argument in the preceding paragraph that the deceptiveness of this stance can be made to emerge.

Ecosystems and World-Systems in Historical Perspective

World-systemic processes of capital accumulation are inextricably intermeshed with ecology. Not only do they have obvious repercussions on landscapes and ecosystems (e.g., erosion, deforestation), but they are also fundamentally dependent on ecological assets such as topsoil, forests, or minerals. The disjunction of ecology and economics is a persistent feature of modern science. The minority of researchers who have seriously tried to integrate them in a common theoretical framework (see Martinez-Alier 1987) have run into major, conceptual difficulties. This chapter addresses some of the analytical issues raised in an attempt to ground the notion of capital accumulation in the physical realities of ecology and thermodynamics.

There are two bodies of data that would need to be brought together if we are to get a fuller picture of the past few centuries of global environmental change. On the one hand, there is the tangible evidence from paleobotany, geology, and other natural sciences of long-term changes in vegetation, soil quality, and other parameters. On the other hand, there is the record of economic history, plotting the expansion and decline of centers of accumulation founded on various regimes of production and trade. Both types of data are easily and regularly represented in the form of maps. It would be most useful if maps could be developed that highlight the very connections between economic history and changes in land cover (Hornborg et al. forthcoming).

Making such connections clearer would be an important corrective to the illusion of a "disembodied" economy that seems to underlie mainstream economic thought. A "greening" of world-systems theory could thus serve as an empirical complement to the emerging field of "ecological economics" (Martinez-Alier 1987). It would also provide a deeper understanding of the complex relationship between issues of ecological sustainability, on the one hand, and issues relating to the global distribution of resources, on the other. Although the connection between these two threats to human survival have been at the center of attention since the United Nations Conference on Environment and Development in Rio de Janeiro in 1992, its fundamental logic continues to escape us as we reiterate the conventional rhetoric on "sustainable development."

In several articles and a recent book (Hornborg 2001), I have argued that the capacity of technological systems and other social institutions to shift resource extraction to less empowered social categories renders ecological and distributional issues inseparable. To restrict attention to either type of issues is to miss the complete picture. Ecological conditions are implicated in all processes of accumulation, and such processes of accumulation in turn tend to transform ecosystems. It would be impossible to understand the global polarization of rich and poor without reference to ecological factors (such as net energy transfer to core regions), just as it would be impossible to understand the expansion of unsustainable technological systems without reference to the unequal, global exchange of energy. Yet the hegemonic doctrines of economics remain impervious to both these issues, that is, the material and the moral correlates of capital flows, the first by ignoring the laws of physics (Georgescu-Roegen 1971), the second by assuming, as an implicit axiom, that (noncoerced) market prices by definition are just and fair. It is no coincidence that these two seemingly unrelated aspects have been repressed by mainstream economics, for it is only by closing our eyes to the material dimensions of exchange that we can circumambulate its moral aspects and only in opening them that a moral perspective becomes unavoidable.

Challenging these dominant doctrines, I would advocate an ecologized version of dependency theory that recognizes the world market and modern technology as more of a zero-sum game than a cornucopia. What we have long perceived as "development" is basically a manifestation of capital accumulation, and capital accumulation has always been an uneven and inequitable process, generating an increasing polarization between "developed" centers and "underdeveloped" peripheries. Against this background, the faith of the Brundtland report in global economic growth as a road to equity and sustainability is not very persuasive. We need only recall Wackernagel's (Wackernagel et al. 1997) observation that global equity along Western standards of living would require three additional Earths.

How do we conceptualize the interface between ecosystems and worldsystems? It could be argued that all the major issues of global survival (environmental destruction, resource depletion, world poverty, armament) can ultimately be traced to capital accumulation. The concept of "capital," however, continues to elude stringent analysis. To many authors (Marx included) it has an aspect that leads us to think of a material infrastructure of some kind. On the other hand, it suggests abstract wealth, or purchasing power. This is the dimension of capital emphasized, for instance, by Max Weber. It is also the perspective that has achieved hegemony both in standard economics and in world-systems theory (see Wallerstein 1974-1989; Frank 1978; Braudel 1979), suggesting a disembodied, immaterial force moving about the planet in pursuit of rewarding investment opportunities. In advocating a revival of Aristotle's distinction between *oikonomia* and "chrematistics" (Martinez-Alier 1987; Daly and Cobb 1989), the proponents of "ecological economics" in a sense join forces with Marx in trying to show how the symbolic and the material interact. There are a lot of obstacles on the way, however. For instance, most "ecological economists" are as ignorant of world-systems theory as Marx was of thermodynamics.

The absence of a common definition of "capital" has made it difficult for historians to date the origins of "capitalism." The orthodox, Marxist definition (involving industrial machinery and the commoditization of labor) would date capitalism no earlier than eighteenth-century England (see Wolf 1982). If the focus is shifted from industrial to merchant capital, and to production for the world market as the basic criterion, "capitalism" recedes backward in history. Wallerstein (1974–1989) traces it to the sixteenth century, Braudel (1979) to the thirteenth, and finally Frank (1995) collapses the concept entirely by identifying capital accumulation and a world-system as far back as 3000 BC.

"Industrial capitalism" and "merchant capitalism" should be seen not as different historical stages but as strategies for accumulation practiced by different agents in the same system. Industrial capitalism could thus be viewed as the latest in a series of local "modes of production" anchored in material infrastructures of different kinds, whereas supralocal strategies of merchant capitalism have always integrated such local production processes in larger reproductive totalities. It is the complex interdependency of local and supralocal strategies that tends to obscure this analytical distinction.

Modes of Accumulation

Let us systematically consider the various strategies possible. We may speak of them as modes of accumulation, or simply ways of increasing one's access to resources. The strategies can be grouped into five main categories.

1. Plunder. There are good reasons to believe that it is as old as the human species. To this category belong, for instance, the practice of bride capture, horse raids, slave raids, and colonial wars of conquest.

2. Merchant Capitalism. This is also known as the exploitation of cultural differences in how goods are evaluated ("buying cheap and selling dear"). This strategy certainly can be traced back thousands of years—for example, to the ancient tin-silver trade between Assyria and Anatolia in the second millennium BC (Yoffee 1988). Merchant capitalism does not in itself imply any form of material (infrastructural) "capital," but historically it generally has required some form of transport apparatus—for example, ships, wagons, horses, donkeys, camels, or llamas—as well as a military apparatus to protect its interests.

3. Financial Capitalism. This is also referred to as the servicing of debts. Demanding interest on credit can be traced back to ancient Sumer in 3000 BC. It was controversial in Europe prior to its explicit legitimization in the Reformation. Today it is one of the major institutional means by which resources from the "underdeveloped" south are transferred to the affluent north (Körner et al. 1984; Altvater et al. 1987). Financial capitalism does not in itself imply material capital but tends to require a voluminous financial bureaucracy, judicial apparatus, and police force, both nationally and internationally.

4. Undercompensation of Labor. I would specify "undercompensation" as

referring to the relation between what the laborer produces and what he or she gets in return, in terms of either labor time, energy, resources, or money. Various cultural strategies are applied: (a) The most obvious form is coercion (i.e., slavery), known at least from the time of the earliest urban civilizations and particularly essential to the economies of ancient Greece and Rome. (b) The second, most ancient form is that which may occur in conjunction with gift exchange or barter transactions conforming to the principle that Karl Polanyi (1944) called reciprocity. It has been shown that even the direct exchange of simple, manufactured items between tribal groups can entail an asymmetric transfer of labor time (Godelier 1969). (c) The third and classic form is associated with the principle that Polanyi called redistribution. It has been characteristic of chiefdoms, states, and empires, where it is usually quite easy to show that the grassroots producers deliver more tribute, taxes, and so forth to the centers of power than is returned to them, or those centers would not survive. (d) The fourth and most subtle form is wage labor, which belongs to Polanyi's third principle, the market. Marx showed that capitalist accumulation can be based on the difference between the value of what a laborer produces and the wages that he or she is paid, that is, the difference between the output and the cost of labor.

The first of these forms of the fourth type, coercion (4a), like those in the first category, differs from all the rest in not involving some form of cultural persuasion, that is, in not requiring that the exploited party subscribes to some particular form of ideology that represents the exchange as reciprocal or at least legitimate. In all the other cases listed in this typology, there are fundamental, cultural concepts—vernacular representations of "tribute" or "corvée," "price," "interest," "wage," and so on—that have to be shared by both parties in order for the mode of accumulation to operate.

5. Underpayment for Resources. In this category, resources include raw materials and forms of energy other than labor. Again, by "underpayment" I refer to the relation between the quantity of finished goods or services that these resources can be converted into (their productive potential, so to speak) and the fraction of that quantity (or equivalent of it) that is obtained in exchange for them. In parallel with the previous mode (see particularly 4d above), this could also be expressed in terms of the difference between the productive output and the cost of fuels and raw materials. The nature of the resources involved is geared to the technological mode of production and the kind of material infrastructure that needs to be reproduced: (a) For preindustrial, urban manufacturing centers, mines, or specialized slave plantations, a major source of energy is the foodstuffs imported to maintain the labor

force. (b) For the maintenance of draft animals, caravans, or cavalry, the major source of energy is fodder. (c) For most workshops or industries, finally, the primary energy resource is fuels. As mentioned, specific kinds of raw materials (e.g., ores or fibers) may also be required and underpaid for in the process.

We could define "undercompensation" and "underpayment" as a condition in which the exchange rates allow the manufacturer to increase his or her relative share of the system's total purchasing power at the expense of the groups delivering labor power, energy, or raw materials. By "purchasing power" I here mean something more general than money, namely, the symbolic capacity to make claims on other people's resources. If the total purchasing power were constant, it would not be hard to conclude that any increase is unilateral and that the system is a zero-sum game. However, the total purchasing power in a system obviously can expand (e.g., by striking gold or printing more money), which gives the illusion of global "growth" and tends to obscure its zero-sum properties. Economists would object that the resource base can also be expanded, but to a very large extent this must be recognized as an illusion. First, in transforming ecosystems to our immediate purposes, we may gain a specific kind of resource, but only at the expense of others (e.g., farmland at the expense of wetlands or forests), the value of which may not become apparent until later (see Jansson et al. 1994). Second, many resources are simply physically impossible to expand (e.g., fossil fuels, phosphates, or metal ores). Third and finally, what locally appears as an expansion of resources may conceal an asymmetric social transfer implying a loss of resources elsewhere.

The point I wish to make, here, however, is that any increment in one party's relative share of the total purchasing power will alter the exchange rates, or terms of trade. Such relative increments tend to be self-reinforcing because the altered terms of trade in material goods and resources may increase the aggrandized party's technology-mediated capacity to accumulate an even greater share of the purchasing power, and so on. In other words, even if the system as a whole gives the appearance of "growing," any increase in the relative share of total purchasing power will be at the long-run expense of another party because it will aggravate unequal exchange and systematically drain the latter's labor (Emmanuel 1972) or other resources (Bunker 1985).

Let us now apply these perspectives to a classic example of accumulation, the triangle trade between Europe, West Africa, and America, in order to consider how different modes of accumulation can be combined in the same system. Merchants carried manufactured goods such as rifles and textiles from England to Africa, where they were exchanged for slaves. The slaves were then transported to America and sold in exchange for cotton and other plantation produce. Finally, the cotton was brought back to England and exchanged for manufactured goods. The completed cycle involved several points of accumulation, enriching merchants, African chiefs, American plantation owners, and British industrialists. With reference to the typology offered above, we can detect, within this trading system, the occurrence of all the modes of accumulation mentioned: (1) European and African slave raiders pursuing their victims; (2) European merchants exploiting cultural differences between three continents; (3) merchants, cotton growers, and industrialists servicing their debts to European bankers; (4a) American slave owners thrashing their African labor; (4b) African chiefs bartering slaves for rifles; (4c) African commoners paying tribute to their chiefs; (4d) British textile workers collecting their wages; (5a) slave owners bargaining for cheap corn and wheat to feed their slaves; (5b) American grain merchants buying fodder for their horse-drawn transports to the eastern slave plantations; and (5c) British industrialists haggling over the price of cotton and coal.

All in all, this combination of strategies within a larger, reproductive totality provided the conditions for the Industrial Revolution. Marx's theoretical edifice on "capitalism" was built on the observation that the local mode of production in England combined strategies 4d and 5c—wage labor and mechanization. But rather than a historical stage, industrial capitalism should be understood as a functional specialization within a larger field of accumulative strategies. Rosa Luxemburg (1913) was probably the first to see the full implications of this. Still today, industrial capitalism is very far from the universal condition of humankind; it is rather a privileged activity, the existence of which would be unthinkable without various other modes of transferring surpluses of labor and resources from peripheral sectors to centers of accumulation at different spatial scales.

"Greening" the Concept of Capital

The debate about whether to define "capitalism" in terms of merchant or industrial capital can thus be solved only by recognizing that circulation and production are mutually interdependent. In relying on fossil fuels and combustion engines, industrialization was certainly revolutionary, but the growth of a material infrastructure through unequal exchange was not an innovation of eighteenth-century England. In order to trace such processes further back in history, as would Wallerstein (1974–1989), Chase-Dunn and Hall (1991), and Frank (1995), we would need to widen Marx's concept of "capital" so as to make it more abstract and inclusive, in both its symbolic and its material aspects. I have elsewhere (Hornborg 1998, 2000) argued that such an extended concept of "capital" could be defined as a recursive (positive feedback) relationship between some kind of technological infrastructure and some kind of symbolic capacity to make claims on other people's resources and that such a definition would be as applicable to the agricultural terraces of the Inca emperor in ancient Peru as to the textile factories of eighteenth-century England. What the two examples have in common is the recursivity between the symbolic and the material. In both cases, the material infrastructure is used to produce an output that is culturally transformed (i.e., through the mediation of symbolic constructs) into more infrastructure. Industrial machinery is only the latest version of infrastructure, and wage labor only the latest version of cultural persuasion.

Marx was probably too focused on the exploitation of labor to see that unequal exchange could also take the form of draining another society's natural resources. Nor could he see Luxemburg's (1913) crucial deduction that capitalism could never constitute its own, self-contained market. Like his contemporaries, he was thus able to put his faith in the global, emancipatory potential of the industrial machine. As the twentieth century drew to a close, however, mounting global inequities gave us reason to reexamine the promise of the machine. Could the industrial infrastructures of Europe, North America, and Japan exist without the abysmal gap between rich and poor? Or are they one and the same, inextricably linked, as the material and the social dimensions of a single, global phenomenon?

The global gap is deepening (see Adams 1993). It has been calculated that the 225 wealthiest individuals in the world own assets equal to the purchasing power of the poorest 47 percent of the planet's population (Hart 1999 based on United Nations data). Yet, ironically, dependency theory has been on the wane. A major problem for its opponents seems to be the difficulties they are having in visualizing "metropolis-satellite" (Frank 1966) or "core-periphery" (Wallerstein 1974–1989) relations, and "surplus exploitation," as spatial, material realities (see Brewer 1990:168–169). There is often a tenuous congruity between the different spatial parameters that one can think of. Where are the investments made? Where do the capitalists live? Where are their bank accounts? Where is the infrastructure being accumulated? Where are the products consumed? These difficulties can be alleviated, I believe, by thinking less in terms of national trade statistics and more in terms of net flows of energy and materials, irrespective of political boundaries. Nightly satellite images of luminescent technomass in urbanized areas of Europe, Japan, and eastern North America are convincing evidence of the material reality of center-periphery relations. But a major handicap in our struggles to expose such polarities is that trade statistics by and large continue to ignore flows of energy and materials between central and peripheral areas within nations, the omission of which tends to distort the total, physical geography of core-periphery relations by forcing us to couch them in the idiom of political geography.

A "greening" of world-systems theory essentially means supplementing the labor-oriented, Marxist concept of exploitation (focused on category 4 above) with a resource-oriented one (category 5). A lot of analytical work remains to be done, however (Bunker 1985; Martinez-Alier 1987; Hornborg 2001). An important step is to see that human economies rely on two types of resources, labor time and natural space. These correspond to the two factors of production known as "labor" and "land." They can be variously combined and transformed into material infrastructure ("capital"), generally for purposes of saving time or space (or both) for somebody. This is the essence of human technology: the use of time and space to save time or space (or both) for some social category. Technology or capital thus amounts to a way of redistributing temporal and spatial resources in global society. The time saved by nineteenth-century train passengers (relative to travel by stagecoach) should be weighed against the time spent by steel and railway workers to make these train rides possible.

Similarly, the space (land) saved by more "efficient" (intensive) forms of industrial agriculture in nineteenth-century England should be weighed against the space elsewhere devoted to making this local mode of production possible, either by supplying the requisite resources for industrial technology or by alleviating pressure on England's limited land resources—for example, cotton plantations in America, sheep pastures in Australia, and mines and forests in Sweden (see Wilkinson 1973, 1988). More recently, we could add the global acreages devoted to provisioning industrial farmers with fossil fuels, chemical fertilizers, pesticides, machinery, biotechnology, and so forth. In becoming interfused with each other in "capital," moreover, the economies of time and space are rendered indistinguishable, so that time saved can represent space lost, and vice versa. Perhaps it is in the very nature of advanced technology that one party's gain of time or space is some other party's loss.

The same kind of logic applies to the intensified use of space that we know as urbanization. High-rise buildings can be visualized as gigantic machines for accommodating a maximum volume of marketable services per unit of urban space but elsewhere demanding vast spaces of natural resources. Rather than fulfilling the economists' visions of "dematerialization" and environmental load reduction in an absolute sense (i.e., not merely relative to GNP), "development" generally continues to imply increasingly sophisticated patterns of environmental load displacement (Muradian and Martinez-Alier 2001; Martinez-Alier 2002).

A second major handicap in our pursuit of a clearer understanding of these relationships is the fact that most trade statistics are in monetary units, rather than invested labor time, energy, or hectares. Let me give an example of how this can lead us astray. Opponents of Emmanuel's (1972) argument that low-salary countries were victims of unequal exchange suggested that the import into developed countries of produce from the developing countries was too marginal (2.5% in 1965) to be of any significance to the condition of either category. Emmanuel replied, however, that if salaries had been the same as in the advanced countries, the cost of that import would have been 10 times as high, or equivalent to 25 percent (Brewer 1990: 208). Brewer (1990:208) writes that one can "doubt whether anything like the same volume of trade would take place at these prices," but this, of course, is precisely the point. The entire rationale of the trade is the asymmetric transfer of labor time. Statistics in dollars obscure the real transfers in hours of labor. Similarly, if invested energy (Odum and Arding 1991) or hectares (Wackernagel and Rees 1996) were counted instead of dollars, the significance of imports from the south would be recognized as much greater than that suggested by monetary measures. Still, even the dollar-based GATT statistics reflect a fundamental feature of global, center-periphery relationships: In 1984, fuels accounted for 46.8 percent of exports from "developing areas" but only 7.8 percent of those from developed countries (see Chisholm 1990:96).

Methodologically, the perspective on economic growth outlined here could perhaps best be tested by systematically translating a given set of exchanges between two nations—say between England and one of its colonies around 1800—into hours of labor and hectare yields that were invested in the commodities, on one hand, and that were "saved" (i.e., substituted for) by the buyers, on the other. Such analyses would probably become more difficult and complex to carry out the closer in time we get to our contemporary, more thoroughly globalized economy.

One of the benefits of the suggested framework is that it would help us to analytically distinguish between different kinds of "environmental problems" in world-systems history. In view of the twin problems of importing available energy ("negative entropy") and exporting entropy (see Georgescu-Roegen 1971), different historical and contemporary cases of environmental crisis require different analytical tools. There are cases, such as the Classic Maya or Easter Island, in which ecological overshoot is not so much a consequence of long-distance resource extraction as of locally generated overexploitation of resources. There are clearly also a great number of cases, such as Roman North Africa, British North America, or the Sahel region of Africa, in which environmental degradation was or is the result of the systematic appropriation of local resources by distant centers. A third type of environmental problems would be represented by nineteenth-century London or twentieth-century Moscow, in which the accumulation of distantly derived resources is not sufficiently balanced by an export of entropy (pollution, waste) generated in the process. Finally, the recent north-to-south export of the most polluting industries, as well as waste itself, suggests a fourth version of ecological crisis, in which world-system peripheries are converted into dumping grounds for entropy generated by affluent core areas. With reference to the last two versions, problems of "environmental justice" and environmental load displacement can thus be shown to have two distinct aspects, since peripheral areas can be exploited both as sources of "negative entropy" and as sinks for entropy.

If, in these analytical considerations, I have been preoccupied more with the dynamic of world-systems than with the transformations of ecosystems, it is because we are so much better acquainted with the latter. I need here only hint at the connections between the two types of systems. Let us return to the trans-Atlantic trade and briefly consider some of its ecological repercussions. Without this particular constellation of accumulative strategies, England would not have industrialized in the eighteenth century, and the environmental history of the past few centuries would have taken a different course (Worster 1988). The soils of the American South would not have been cultivated in such an unsustainable manner (see Earle 1988). The American wheat belt would not have been pushed as far into areas vulnerable to erosion. Australia and Argentina would not have been converted in such a wholesale fashion into pasture, nor the West Indies into sugar plantations. The deforestation of India would probably not have been as severe (Tucker 1988). The list can be extended indefinitely. These global, environmental changes are tangible imprints of the world-system of capital accumulation. The industrial infrastructure of eighteenth- and nineteenth-century Lancashire grew not only from the sweat of the British proletariat and of African slaves but also from American soils, Australian pastures, and Swedish forests. Vast quantities of human time and natural space were exploited and intertwined in the process. After 200 years, such concentrations of technomass in Europe, North America, and Japan are still expanding at the expense of their peripheries and of global life-support systems. Capital accumulation is a blind, self-reinforcing process. Instead of just continuing to monitor its ecological effects, we urgently need to grasp its fundamental dynamics. Recent concepts such as "political ecology" (Johnston 1994; Martinez-Alier 2002) and "environmental justice" (Harvey 1996) recognize that such an understanding can emerge only from a consideration of how ecological issues and distributional issues are interfused.

References

Adams, N. A. 1993. *Worlds Apart: The North-South Divide and the International System.* London: Zed Books.

Altvater, E., K. Hübner, J. Lorentzen, and R. Rojas, eds. 1987. *The Poverty of Nations: A Guide to the Debt Crisis from Argentina to Zaire.* London: Zed Books.

Braudel, F. 1979. *Le Temps du Monde.* Paris: Librarie Armand Colin.

Brewer, A. 1990. *Marxist Theories of Imperialism: A Critical Survey.* 2d ed. New York: Routledge.

Bunker, S. G. 1985. *Underdeveloping the Amazon: Extraction, Unequal Exchange and the Failure of the Modern State.* Chicago: University of Chicago Press.

Chase-Dunn, C. and T. Hall. 1991. *Core/Periphery Relations in Precapitalist Worlds.* Boulder, CO: Westview Press.

Chisholm, M. 1990. "The Increasing Separation of Production and Consumption." Pp. 87–101 in *The Earth as Transformed by Human Action: Global and Regional Changes in the Biosphere over the Past 300 Years.* edited by B. L. Turner II et al. Cambridge, UK: Cambridge University Press.

Daly, H. E. and J. B. Cobb Jr. 1989. *For the Common Good: Redirecting the Economy towards Community, the Environment and a Sustainable Future.* Boston: Beacon Press.

Earle, C. 1988. "The Myth of the Southern Soil Miner: Macrohistory, Agricultural Innovation, and Environmental Change." Pp. 175–210 in *The Ends of the Earth: Perspectives on Modern Environmental History,* edited by D. Worster. Cambridge, UK: Cambridge University Press.

Emmanuel, A. 1972. *Unequal Exchange: A Study of the Imperialism of Trade.* New York: Monthly Review Press.

Fischer-Kowalski, M. and H. Haberl. 1997. "Tons, Joules and Money: Modes of Production and Their Sustainability Problems." *Society and Natural Resources* 10 (1): 61–68.

Frank, A. G. 1966. "The Development of Underdevelopment." *Monthly Review* 18: 17–31.

———. 1978. *World Accumulation, 1492–1789.* New York: Monthly Review Press.

———. 1995. "The Modern World System Revisited." Pp.163–194 in *Civilizations and World Systems: Studying World-Historical Change,* edited by S. K. Sanderson. Lanham, MD: AltaMira.

Georgescu-Roegen, N. 1971. *The Entropy Law and the Economic Process.* Cambridge, MA: Harvard University Press.

Godelier, M. 1969. "La monnaie de sel des Baruya de Nouvelle-Guinée." *L'Homme* 9 (2): 5–37.

Hart, K. 1999. "An Unequal World: Money as the Problem and the Solution." Manuscript.

Harvey, D. 1996. *Justice, Nature and the Geography of Difference.* London: Blackwell.

Hornborg, A. 1998. "Towards an Ecological Theory of Unequal Exchange: Articulating World System Theory and Ecological Economics." *Ecological Economics* 25 (1): 127–136.

———. 2000. "Accumulation Based on Symbolic versus Intrinsic 'Productivity': Conceptualizing Unequal Exchange from Spondylus Shells to Fossil Fuels." Pp. 235–252 in *World Systems History: The Social Science of Long-Term Change,* edited by R. Denemark et al. New York: Routledge.

———. 2001. *The Power of the Machine: Global Inequalities of Economy, Technology, and Environment.* Lanham, MD: AltaMira.

Hornborg, A. et al., eds. Forthcoming. *World System History and Global Environmental Change.* New York: Columbia University Press.

Jansson, A. M., M. Hammer, C. Folke, and R. Costanza, eds. 1994. *Investing in Natural Capital: The Ecological Economics Approach to Sustainability.* Washington, DC: Island Press.

Johnston, B. R., ed. 1994. *Who Pays the Price? The Sociocultural Context of Environmental Crisis.* Washington, DC: Island Press.

Körner, P., G. Maass, T. Siebold, and R. Tetzlaff. 1984. *The IMF and the Debt Crisis: A Guide to the Third World's Dilemmas.* London: Zed Books.

Luxemburg, R. 1913. *The Accumulation of Capital.* New York: Routledge.

Martinez-Alier, J. 1987. *Ecological Economics: Energy, Environment and Society.* London: Blackwell.

———. 2002. *The Environmentalism of the Poor: A Study of Ecological Conflicts and Valuation.* Cheltenham, UK: Edward Elgar.

Muradian, R. and J. Martinez-Alier. 2001. "South-North Materials Flow: History and Environmental Repercussions." *Innovation* 14 (2): 171–187.

Odum, H. T. and J. E. Arding. 1991. *Energy Analysis of Shrimp Mariculture in Ecuador.* Narragansett, RI: University of Rhode Island.

Polanyi, K. 1944. *The Great Transformation.* Austin, TX: Holt, Rinehart and Winston.

Tucker, R. P. 1988. "The Depletion of India's Forests under British Imperialism:

Planters, Foresters, and Peasants in Assam and Kerala." Pp. 118–140 in *The Ends of the Earth: Perspectives on Modern Environmental History,* edited by D. Worster. Cambridge, UK: Cambridge University Press.

Wackernagel, M. et al. 1997. *Ecological Footprints of Nations.* Centre for Sustainability Studies, Universidad Anáhuac de Xalapa, Mexico.

Wackernagel, M. and W. E. Rees 1996. *Our Ecological Footprint: Reducing Human Impact on the Earth.* Gabriola Island, BC: New Society Publishers.

Wallerstein, I. M. 1974–1989. *The Modern World-System.* Vols. 1–3. Burlington, MA: Academic Press.

Wilkinson, R. G. 1973. *Poverty and Progress: An Ecological Model of Economic Development.* London: Methuen.

———. 1988. "The English Industrial Revolution." Pp. 80–99 in *The Ends of the Earth: Perspectives on Modern Environmental History,* edited by D. Worster. Cambridge, UK: Cambridge University Press.

Wolf, E. R. 1982. *Europe and the People without History.* Berkeley, CA: University of California Press.

Worster, D. 1988. "The Vulnerable Earth: Toward a Planetary History." Pp. 3–20 in *The Ends of the Earth: Perspectives on Modern Environmental History,* edited by D. Worster. Cambridge, UK: Cambridge University Press.

Yoffee, N. 1988. "The Collapse of Ancient Mesopotamian States and Civilization." Pp. 44–68 in *The Collapse of Ancient States and Civilizations,* edited by N. Yoffee and G. L. Cowgill. Tucson, AZ: University of Arizona Press.

9

Global Social Change, Natural Resource Consumption, and Environmental Degradation

ANDREW K. JORGENSON

Human societies have long experienced the rapid expansion of the modern world-system, a system that has existed since at least the middle 1400s, meeting crisis after crisis in accumulation. Rapid technological growth has been part and parcel of this expansion that tightened the global division of labor and importance of distant events for all humans. This division of labor permits further expansion in rationalized production and reaches everywhere to enlarge markets and offer up cheap labor and material resources to increase surplus value. Overall, these processes of global social change have significantly impacted regional ecological systems and the global biosphere, and these effects in turn worsen the quality of life for human populations, particularly in less developed, peripheral countries of the world-system.

Generally lacking in the social science literature on the environment, as well as in the globalization literature, is a mature historical approach that explains the emergence of such dynamics. This is beginning to be provided by the world-systems approach. Indeed, the past two decades have witnessed a burgeoning area of inquiry in the social sciences that blends environmental sociology and political economy with a world-systems perspective.[1] There is a consensus in this blossoming, multidisciplinary literature that the capitalist world-economy is now in crisis because it cannot find solutions to key dilemmas including the inability to contain ecological destruction. Global modes of production, accumulation, and consumption are intimately linked to environmental degradation. Furthermore, the core-periphery model of exploitation provides historically grounded explanations of focal environmental and ecological outcomes, and degradation can be seen as both a cause and a consequence of underdevelopment in noncore regions.

Social scientists commonly consider processes of social change in the modern world-economy as falling under the rubric of "globalization." Moreover, globalization continues to be a buzzword in political discourses that employ ideas about global integration, technology, and competition to justify certain conservative policies. Social scientists working in the world-systems tradition have empirically charted structural globalization as understood to be different kinds of broadening and intensifying interaction networks.

In this chapter I discuss the relationships between global social change, natural resource consumption, and unevenly dispersed forms of environmental degradation.

Intersocietal Evolution and the Environment

World-systems are fundamentally social structures that include different cultural groups and polities within them (Chase-Dunn and Hall 1997b; Chase-Dunn and Jorgenson 2003). World-systems, or systems of societies, began when groups of people first developed sedentism. Sedentary villages of diversified foragers interacted with nomadic neighbors, which led to the invention of territoriality—the claim that one group possessed certain rights to use and control local natural resources. This form of fixed boundaries and collective property was an institutional invention for regulating access to natural resources and was often motivated by a desire to mitigate the overexploitation of these resources. Overall, human-caused ecological degradation was a critical process in the origin of institutions that control the uses of natural resources (Chase-Dunn and Hall 1997a).

Chase-Dunn and Hall (1997a, 1997b) offer an iteration model that explains the primary factors involved in the evolution of systems of societies. Ecological factors are a central component of this model. Historically, ecological degradation, population growth, and population pressure are driving forces leading to economic intensification and hierarchy formation between societies. Population growth increases the decline in natural resources, leading to greater ecological degradation. The form and scale of ecological degradation vary with the scale of the exploitation of natural resources and the nature of production technology. Population pressure often results when resource depletion causes people to increase their individual and collective efforts necessary to meet their material wants and needs. Moreover, population pressure leads to emigration to new regions where natural resources might be less pressured. However, environmental circumscription occurs when suitable new locations do not exist geographically in contiguous areas. Social circumscription occurs when existing regions are already inhabited by other populations that resist immigration. Hence, population pressure causes competition between societies for land and other resources. This competition over scarce resources often increases intersocietal conflict and warfare.

In some earlier systems of societies warfare acted as a "demographic regulator" by reducing populations and temporarily alleviating population pressure on the environment. In other cases larger polities and new hierarchies emerged to regulate the use and consumption of natural resources. Through these processes new technologies of production developed that enabled larger groups of people to live within a given region. Groups and individuals toward the top of newly formed hierarchies often controlled the dissemination and use of these new technologies, but technological advances generally offer only a temporary fix to population pressure, compounded by the unequal distribution of natural resources with more powerful groups consuming resources at levels higher than can be supported by the environment (Chase-Dunn and Hall 1997a; York and Rosa 2003).

The spatial scale of environmental degradation increases as world-systems become larger and more complex. Forms of degradation are also caused by side effects of natural resource consumption, which I address in later sections of this chapter. Once systems of societies evolved into a global world-system, the possibilities of escaping ecological degradation and resource depletion became greatly reduced. More modern forms of global industrial production and development degrade the environment on a global, yet uneven, scale, whereas earlier intensification, population pressures, and hierarchically enforced uneven consumption damaged the environment on a more local scale (Chase-Dunn and Hall 1997a; Chew 2001; Broswimmer 2002).

Population Dynamics, Uneven Accumulation, Development, and the Environment

At the end of the fifteenth century, the world began to experience a "demographic takeover" by Europeans that was largely facilitated by a population explosion resulting from a sharp decline in death rates. This decline was a function of the beneficial effects of improved nutrition and sanitation and the expansion of peripheral capitalism and extraction into eastern Europe and colonized regions on other continents (Wallerstein 1974; Chase-Dunn 1998; Broswimmer 2002). The European population explosion tapered off in the early twentieth century. By this period most of Europe and its settler colonies had reached relatively advanced stages of economic development and further imposition of peripheral exploitation of land and labor. Birth rates began to fall in the final phase of this demographic transition. This was largely in response to higher levels of affluence (Foster 1999:15).

During demographic transitions, populations experience a gradual change from a demographic equilibrium of high death rates and high birth rates to a demographic equilibrium of low death rates and low birth rates. In the first phase of the transition, such as during early European industrialization, there is a decline in the death rate that is not matched by a corresponding decline in the birth rate, which leads to a population explosion. In the second phase, economic development, stimulated by peripheral exploitation, leads to a drop in the birth rate as well, which slows down the rate of population growth (e.g., Foster 1999; Broswimmer 2002). Thus in Europe relative power and affluence eventually resulted in lower population growth rates, which then tended to reinforce and reproduce relative power and affluence. With population explosions, additional natural resources are required to sustain the larger populations. Through peripheral exploitation, additional resources were expropriated and consumed (Moore 2003). Yet as the population growth rate diminished, relative power enabled overall resource consumption to remain high, which increased levels of resource consumption in core regions of Europe and its settler colonies at the expense of resource consumption of populations in other colonized regions (Chase-Dunn and Hall 1997a; Foster 1999; Chew 2001).

Owing to structural conditions and relative levels of inequality between core and peripheral areas, colonized regions and countries in the periphery of the world were unable to experience a similar path of industrialization followed by the completion of the demographic transition. Rather, these areas experienced a legacy of colonialism and the "development of underdevelopment" (Frank 1966; Foster 1999) in which there was a continual outflow of surplus natural resources from peripheral areas to core regions, rather than the internal development of the peripheral areas themselves (O'Connor 1998; Foster 1999; Moore 2003). This also contributed to the growing gap in per capita income between core and peripheral regions (e.g., Jorgenson 2003b). Many underdeveloped peripheral societies were and continue to be caught in a demographic trap between an industrial death rate and an agricultural birth rate (Foster 1999). Overall, their populations have continued to grow while their rates of economic development are retarded by their subordinate position in the world-economy. Barry Commoner (1992) and John Bellamy Foster (1999) characterize this as "demographic parasitism," in which the second population-balancing phase of the demographic transition in more powerful countries was and is fed by the suppression of the same phase in impoverished, less developed countries.

Historically, urbanization, the process of increasing percentages of populations living in cities, occurred as part of the accumulation of surplus and wealth and the structuring of the global core-periphery hierarchy. By its very nature, urbanization is highly resource consumptive (Cronon 1991; Chew 2001; Jorgenson 2003a). As the modern world-system emerged, urbanization in core regions increased at rapid rates. Great amounts of natural resources were transported to urban areas, where accumulation of populations and manufacturing processes emerged. Forested areas were often cut for agricultural production in which grown foodstuffs were transported to densely populated urban regions. Energy inputs for the transportation of natural resources to urbanizing regions depleted resource stocks, and additional materials were required to build and maintain urban infrastructures for the local movement and transportation of food products and other natural resources (Chew 2001). Moreover, urbanizing areas required vast amounts of materials for the construction of housing for intensifying populations. Thus, urbanization is a resource-dependent and resource-intensive process, which casts a disruptive shadow on the peripheral areas of core urban regions (Cronon 1991).

The shifting structure of the emerging modern world-system often led to various pressures to feed and provide goods to the growing populations of urbanizing regions in societies and nation-states. A primary mode of transportation for these goods was shipping, which required vast amounts of wood for the construction and maintenance of maritime fleets. With increasing levels of trade in the nineteenth century, maritime shipping continued to increase, resulting in further wood consumption (Chase-Dunn, Kawano, and Brewer 2000; Chew 2001). Land transportation of people and goods became largely dependent on railway systems. Railroads engendered deforestation. Crossties were replaced every decade or so, and for every kilometer of track, approximately 1,500 crossties were utilized (Chew 2001). Core countries in the nineteenth century, the dominant colonizers of the era, built and maintained railway systems that extended deeply into the peripheralized colonies. This provided resources for consumption, largely in urbanized areas of western Europe (Davis 2001). Thus, train transportation in the nineteenth and early twentieth centuries impacted regional environments through a combination of wood consumption for the construction and maintenance of the railway systems and the expansion of peripheral resource extraction by core European colonizers. We now turn to a discussion of global resource consumption and uneven environmental impacts in the contemporary world-economy.

Natural Resource Consumption, Global Commodity Chains, and Trade Globalization

Some social scientists have argued that ever increasing consumption in the contemporary world—a by-product of the logic of capitalism and its need for continual growth and interrelated social and ecological contradictions—is ultimately destructive and self-defeating (e.g., Schnaiberg and Gould 1994; O'-Connor 1998; Foster 1999; Grimes 1999; Wallerstein 1999; Princen, Maniates, and Conca 2002; Roberts and Grimes 2002; Jorgenson 2003a, 2004a, 2004b, 2004c; Moore 2003; York and Rosa 2003). Recently, a new series of analytical and conceptual frameworks were developed that address consumption from a more structural political-economic perspective. These include attention to the social structural embeddedness of consumption, the linkages between commodity chains of resource use that shape consumption-oriented decisions, and stress on the hidden forms of consuming embedded in all stages of global economic activity (e.g., Maniates 2002; Manno 2002; White 2002).

The social embeddedness of consumption is part and parcel of the institutionalization of material consumption in all contemporary societies. At every stage in the production process, material resources are consumed while commodities are being produced. Paradoxically, there is an inverse relationship between exchange value and the productive potential of commodified goods (e.g., Bunker 1985; Hornborg 2001). In accordance with the second law of thermodynamics, the productive potential of a given set of resources diminishes as it is being converted into a product, that is, as its exchange value or utility increases (Hornborg 2001). A significant aspect of this conversion process is the consumption via fuels, waste, and manipulation of potentially productive materials and energy. Many forms of consumption during production are unintended consequences of "inefficiency" in production processes that negatively impact the biosphere (e.g., Princen et al. 2002). Ironically, these forms of inefficiency contradict the material interests of producers.

The commodity-chain approach asserts that consumption decisions are heavily influenced by, constrained by, and shaped through a chain of linked choices about profits being made by relatively powerful forces as commodities are being designed, produced, distributed, used, and disposed of into the ecological sinks of the natural environment (e.g., O'Connor 1998; Foster 2002; Princen et al. 2002). Two critical underlying processes are revealed through a commodity-chain perspective: distancing and downstreaming.

Distancing refers to the severing of ecological and social feedback as decision points along the chain are increasingly separated by geography, culture, and power (e.g., core-periphery distancing). This concept also points out the isolated character of consumption choices as decision makers at individual nodes in the commodity chain are cut off from a more contextualized understanding of the ramification of their choices, both upstream and downstream (Princen 2002). *Downstreaming*—in this context—refers to the increasingly disproportionate exercise of power and authority at certain critical nodes in the chain (Conca 2002).

Schnaiberg (1980) and Schnaiberag and Gould (1994) apply the analytical concept "the treadmill of production" to represent the forces underlying economic growth, production, and consumption in modern capitalist industrial societies. The treadmill represents the relentless expansion of production, accumulation, and consumption, which are all critical to the logic of capitalism as a continual process. The heart of the treadmill is the increasingly dominant role of monopoly capitalism headquartered in the most powerful countries of the world-economy—especially in terms of the consequences of investments in production and monopoly capitalism's influence on political institutions and decision-making.

The treadmill also creates conditions in which the first and second contradictions of capitalism occur (O'Connor 1998). These contradictions suggest that capitalism is inherently its own gravedigger—in the long run. The first contradiction is central to Marxist analyses of the relations of production to labor. Technologies introduced to deskill workers and to decrease wages constantly generate crises of overproduction. Yet such changes in the modes of production are in contradiction with the social relations of production because overproduction can lead to large-scale layoffs and declining rates of profit (Harvey 1999; Dickens 2002). Similarly, Marx and later O'Connor have argued that there is a contradiction between capitalist growth, the environment, and labor power (Marx 1906; O'Connor 1998). In modern agriculture, much like urban industry, the relative increase in the productivity and mobility of labor is purchased at the cost of emitting waste and debilitating labor power. Furthermore, "progress" in capitalist agriculture usually involves the destruction of the longer-lasting productive potential of the soil (Marx 1906; Dickens 2002). This describes what O'Connor (1998) calls the "second contradiction of capitalism," which characterizes the inherent tendency of capitalism to create further barriers for capital accumulation by ruining the natural material conditions needed for its continual expansion (York and Rosa 2003). In the modern world-economy, like earlier periods, this largely involves environmental degradation displacement by more powerful societies to less powerful ones, much like the peripheral exploitation of formal colonies by their colonizers (e.g., Chase-Dunn 1998; Chew 2001; Jorgenson and Kick 2003).

Ecological modernization theory has emerged as one of the more prominent neoliberal theories in macroenvironmental sociology. The theory's general argument is that continued industrial development offers the best solution to escaping the ecological problems faced in the contemporary world-economy (Mol 1995; Mol and Sonnenfeld 2000; Mol and Spaargaren 2000). Specifically, "the only possible way out of the ecological crisis is by going further into the process of modernization" (Mol 1995:42). Moreover, ecological modernization theory asserts that inherent in the process of societal modernization are self-referential mechanisms. These self-referential mechanisms include the need to internalize environmental impacts in order to ensure future resources available for commodity production and consumption, which should lead to ecological sustainability. Contrary to the other theoretical perspectives reviewed in preceding sections, ecological modernization theory argues for the potential of attaining ecological sustainability from within a capitalist system by the greening of production rather than significant structural changes (York and Rosa 2003). However, other environmental social scientists have raised several important criticisms of this perspective and its empirical validity (e.g., York and Rosa 2003; Jorgenson 2004a). For example, proponents of ecological modernization theory have failed to provide adequate evidence that the change in the structure of institutions has reduced the overall environmental impacts of capitalist-based production (Buttel 2000; York and Rosa 2003). Most studies that provide support for ecological modernization theory are organizational-level case studies (e.g., Mol 1995; Sonnenfeld 1998). As York and Rosa (2003:277) assert, "these studies are certainly valuable for detailing processes that may occur in specific industries, but they cannot yet speak to the general premises of ecological modernization theory regarding the presumed effects of modernization (political, economic, or otherwise) on environmental sustainability." Moreover, cross-national studies described in the following paragraphs provide robust evidence indicating that the most modern and developed countries with greater levels of institutional environmental commitment via nation-state responsibility have the most severe negative impacts on the global ecological system (Jorgenson 2003a, 2004c; York, Rosa, and Dietz 2003; Jorgenson and Burns 2004).

A growing body of empirical work in the social sciences specifically addresses structural and relational factors that explain variation in cross-national levels of total and per capita consumption of all natural resources in the contemporary world-economy. This comprehensive approach to material consumption and its environmental impacts focuses on the ecological footprints of given populations (e.g., Jorgenson 2003a, 2004c; York, Rosa, and Dietz 2003; Jorgenson and Burns 2004). Mathis Wackernagel and associates (2000) have calculated national-level ecological footprints (both total and per capita) for the majority of nations in the world. These footprints consist of the area of cropland required to produce the crops consumed, the area of grazing land required to produce the animal products, the area of forest required to produce the wood and paper, the area of sea required to produce the marine fish and seafood, the area of land required to accommodate housing and infrastructure, and the area of forest that would be required to absorb the carbon dioxide emissions resulting from the unit's energy consumption (Wackernagel et al. 2000). Footprints are measured in area units whereby one footprint equals one hectare.[2] The footprint method captures indirect effects of consumption that are difficult to measure. This approach does not require knowing specifically what each consumed resource is used for.

Social scientists have modeled and tested the effects of population, affluence, and other factors on *total national-level ecological footprints* (York, Rosa, and Dietz 2003). The results indicate that population and affluence by themselves account for 95 percent of the variance in total national footprints. The explanation set forth is a mix of neo-Malthusian and political-economic perspectives whereby total consumption is a function of population size and growth but the impact of population is greater in more developed countries. The analysis of York et al. (2003) provides robust evidence of the impacts of total population and economic development (i.e., affluence) on total consumption of natural resources. Moreover, countries with relatively larger percentages of domestic populations between the ages of 15 and 65 and higher percentages of urban populations possess larger total footprints.

Utilizing a world-systems perspective, Jorgenson (2003a, 2004c) analyzed the structural causes of *per capita ecological footprints* and found that a country's level of per capita consumption is largely a function of its relative position in the international stratification system. Overall, core countries consume at the highest levels, followed by semiperipheral and peripheral countries. Furthermore, countries with relatively higher levels of urbanization and literacy rates consume resources at much higher per capita levels, and most countries with relatively lower levels of domestic income inequality experience elevated levels of per capita consumption (Jorgenson 2003a). The impact of urbanization on natural resource consumption is more pronounced in the core, followed by the semiperiphery, high periphery, and low periphery. Moreover, the effect of domestic income inequality on natural resource consumption is positive in the core and negative in all other zones of the world-economy (Jorgenson 2004c). This positive effect in the core is largely a function of heightened conspicuous consumption by all socioeconomic groups in the United States (Manning 2000).

On average, core countries contain more productive economies and articulated markets while peripheral regions generally contain more extractive-oriented economies and disarticulated markets (Bunker 1985; Boswell and Chase-Dunn 2000).[3] Unprocessed natural resources are generally exported from more extractive peripheral economies to productive semiperipheral and core economies, where they are either consumed in their natural form or transformed through industrial material production into commodities. These commodities generally remain in the same regions that contain articulated markets or are transported to other core regions where—owing to domestic levels of development and relative position in the world-economy—consumption levels are relatively high as well. On average, noncore countries with extractive economies are rather highly dependent on a small number of primary exports, most notably agricultural products and other natural resources (e.g., Burns, Kentor, and Jorgenson 2003; Jorgenson 2004b). The complicated processes of underdevelopment, emerging dependent industrialization,[4] and economic stagnation limit the domestic levels of natural resource consumption in nations dependent on foreign capital. This is further exacerbated by the classically dependent, extractive characteristics of many noncore countries (Bunker 1985; Jorgenson 2003a).

Populations in core nations have relative economic advantages when compared with populations in noncore countries, which enable them to acquire and consume natural resources and produce commodities at higher levels (Burns et al. 2001; Jorgenson 2003a). Moreover, core nations possess relatively greater military size, strength, and international political dominance, which increase their abilities to maintain and reproduce unequal trade relations with less powerful countries, and overall military size as well as continual research and development elevate both total and per capita consumption levels (Chase-Dunn 1998; Kentor 2000).

Within countries possessing higher levels of income inequality, a relatively higher proportion of a nation's annual income is accounted for by the top 10 or 20 percent of the domestic population (Beer 1999; Beer and Boswell 2002). Noncore countries with higher levels of intra-inequality also tend to possess characteristics of disarticulated extractive economies. Thus, these regions possess relatively lower per capita consumption levels, since on average (1) the majority of the population has substantially lower income levels and (2) the domestic market focuses on the exportation of raw materials and commodities produced by means of dependent industrialization (Jorgenson 2003a).

Many core nations with higher levels of urbanization contain productive economies of scale that favor large and integrated economic enterprises and a spatial concentration of economic and industrial activities (Bornschier and Chase-Dunn 1985). Biospheric resources are consumed at higher levels in core urban regions through (1) modern industrial processes of commodity production and (2) corresponding domestic articulated consumer markets (Jorgenson 2003a). These areas, some of which fit the criteria of global cities, are key markets for material goods that require bioproductive elements in their production (Sassen 1991). Moreover, major urban regions require vast amounts of natural resources in their development and continual maintenance.

Most urban areas possess relatively higher literacy rates than agrarian regions. On average, educational institutions are more developed and accessible in urban areas, and higher literacy rates are a characteristic of the managerial sectors and specialized labor populations nested within urban regions of core countries in the world-economy (Bornschier and Chase-Dunn 1985). Generally, higher levels of literacy correspond with higher incomes, which increase the opportunities for greater material consumption. More literate populations are also subjected to increased consumerist ideologies and contextual images of "the good life" (Princen et al. 2002) through mass media, primarily advertising, which corresponds with what many social scientists label the "cultural ideology of consumerism/consumption" (Sklair 2001; Clapp 2002).

Urbanization processes in less developed countries vary substantially from urban regions in more developed core nations. Foreign capital dependence accelerates rates of urbanization in many peripheral nations, but only certain sectors of the domestic urban economy experience relative growth: the informal and tertiary sectors (e.g., Kentor 1981; Smith 1996). Moreover, this effect of investment dependence is accompanied by its inhibition of growth in the industrial labor sector and often results in overurbanization (Kentor 1981; Timberlake and Kentor 1983).[5] Often, overurbanization leads to out-migration, also referred to as rural encroachment, which generally leads to growing pressures on domestic forested areas and water sources because of increases in slash-and-burn and slash-and-mulch activities accompanied by agricultural production (Burns et al. 1994; Burns, Kick, and Davis 2003; Jorgenson 2004a; Jorgenson and Burns 2004).

Many urbanized regions in less developed peripheral countries are largely characterized by their relative increases in outdated manufacturing sectors that are exported from more developed cities of core nations (Grimes and Kentor 2003). This is coupled with their increased roles as nodes in the exportation of natural resources from regional extractive economies (Bunker 1985; Smith 1996). These urbanized areas generally do not experience significant increases in the size of labor pools for manufacturing relative to the tertiary and informal sectors. Manufacturing employment may increase, but it remains inadequate to absorb the burgeoning urban populations (Burns et al. 1994; Kick et al. 1996; Smith 1996).

Various major cities in less developed peripheral countries experienced domestic changes resulting from regional economic crises and the restructuring of the world-economy in the 1980s (Smith 1996; Portes, Dore-Cabral, and Landolt 1997). Furthermore, this led to a major shift in the roles many of these cities play in the global economy. Specifically, this shift is largely a function of the movement from import substitution industrialization (ISI) to export-oriented development (EOD) and reduced government intervention (Portes et al. 1997). These structural changes dramatically impacted levels of urban inequality, poverty, the structure of informal sectors, and spatial/residential polarization (Smith 1996).

Overall, slowed rates of economic development and increased levels of domestic inequality in overurbanized regions of less developed countries limits relative levels of domestic per capita consumption of natural resources. This is further exacerbated by the common shift to export-oriented development coupled with the continual role as nodes for the exportation of natural resources from regional extractive economies to core nations in the world-economy (Jorgenson 2004c).

Core Consumption and the Externalization of Environmental Impacts

Material consumption in core nations is a significant cause of environmental degradation in less developed countries of the contemporary world-economy. This becomes increasingly pronounced over time as less developed countries increase domestic production of manufactured goods and agricultural products and extract natural resources for consumption in other parts of the world, particularly the core (e.g.. Bunker 1985; Grimes 1999; Hornborg 2001;

Burns, Kentor, and Jorgenson 2003; Frey 2003; Jorgenson 2003a, 2004c; Jorgenson and Burns 2004). Countries with the lowest levels of per capita resource consumption experience the highest rates of deforestation and organic water pollution and the greatest increases in levels of carbon dioxide emissions per capita (e.g., Burns, Kick, and Davis 2003; Grimes and Kentor 2003; Jorgenson 2003a; Roberts, Grimes, and Manale 2003; Jorgenson and Burns 2004). As Bunker (1985) and Hornborg (2001) poignantly assert, such dynamics in extractive peripheral nations are underdevelopmental in the extreme, yet paradoxically they foster further developmental processes in developed core countries.

Less developed countries are more likely to be dependent on certain exports that end up in core markets with higher rates of consumption. Quite often these exports are different sorts of agricultural products. Export dependence often involves extraction of precious resources, thereby making the country less able to meet basic human needs, including adequate health care (Bornschier and Chase-Dunn 1985; Boswell and Dixon 1990). In some areas, this dependence has also led to the widespread use of pesticides in nonurbanized agricultural regions and placement of toxic waste dumps in locations close to aquifers—practices that in turn affect groundwater and other critical sources of human livelihood (Frey 1995, 1998; Burns, Kentor, and Jorgenson 2003). Not surprisingly, there is a relationship between the quality of a country's water supply and its levels of infant survivability (Jorgenson 2004b; Jorgenson and Burns 2004). Residues of fat-soluble organic pollutants, such as organochlorine from pesticides, which themselves are more likely to be used in massive quantities with monocrop agricultural practices, tend to put women and infants at particular risk because the biomagnification of organic pollutants tends to occur in fatty tissue, such as women's breasts. Many of these toxins are passed in concentrated form from mother to child, both in utero and, after birth, through breast milk, which in turn increases infant mortality levels (Burns, Kentor, and Jorgenson 2003; Jorgenson and Burns 2004). Moreover, many of the pesticides used in less developed countries are exported by core-based transnational corporations searching for markets where governmental regulations do not impinge on their abilities to distribute their harmful products to local monocrop collectives as well as large-scale transnational agribusiness operations that take advantage of the relaxed environmental regulations of host countries (Frey 1995, 1998).

Peripheral countries with higher rates of dependence on export partnerships with more economically developed and militarily powerful countries experience heightened levels of deforestation (Lofdahl 2002; Jorgenson 2004a). Simply, more powerful and developed nations externalize their ecological costs associated with high resource consumption levels to less developed countries dependent on export relationships with them. The pernicious environmental impacts of export partner dependence have increased over the last three decades of the twentieth century (Jorgenson 2004a). The relative emphasis on extractive export-oriented economic practices in less developed countries fuels domestic wood harvesting and other extractive practices that increase domestic rates of deforestation and other forms of environmental degradation (e.g., Burns et al. 1994; Kick et al. 1996). Moreover, food shortages in less developed countries are not entirely the result of overpopulation (e.g., Davis 2001). Rather, they are also a function of domestic situations in which forested land is cleared by relatively affluent livestock owners for grazing but, paradoxically, the meat produced by these practices is more often than not exported to developed countries for consumption (Burns, Kick, and Davis 2003; Donohoe 2003). For example, in addition to a growing dependence on monoagricultural exports, particularly coffee, El Salvador has experienced an expansionary trend in the export-oriented beef industry. In fact, the extensive nature of the domestic cattle industry meant that by the early 1980s cattle ranches occupied more land area than coffee plantations and other large-scale agricultural operations in El Salvador (Koope and Tole 1997).

The volume of energy production and concomitant carbon dioxide emissions is largely a function of a country's relative position in the international stratification system (Burns, Davis, and Kick 1997; Grimes and Kentor 2003). However, since the mid-1970s, production efficiency, measured as the ratio CO_2/GDP, has grown in core countries while decreasing in semiperipheral countries. The latter is largely a function of the relocation of dirty manufacturing to areas with politically repressed wages and environmental regulations (Grimes and Kentor 2003; Roberts et al. 2003). Paradoxically, commodities produced under these conditions are primarily exported to developed countries for domestic consumption (Jorgenson 2003a, 2004c). With the increasing globalization of production, it has become more and more cost effective to distribute the production of individual components of a given product across multiple socially and geographically distant locations, assemble parts in a different location, and distribute assembled goods to developed countries with articulated markets for sale (Grimes and Kentor 2003). A sizable proportion of this activity, prior to the selling of produced commodities, takes place in less developed regions of the world-economy. As

Grimes and Kentor (2003:265) observe, "While this globalization of production may increase the profits of transnational corporations, it also increases the amount of international transportation, which accelerates the consumption of fossil fuels."

Less developed countries also serve as sinks for the wastes generated by material consumption in core countries (e.g., Frey 1998, 2002). For example, many forms of hazardous materials are exported for storage in noncore regions where governmental regulations are relatively weak and local elites act in partnership with transnational corporations. This has become even more pronounced over time as a result of the constant reduction in price of container transport of goods. Furthermore, in various localities of East Asia, junked computer equipment is brought for recycling to places where mainly female and child labor is used to strip the components into either recyclable or unsalvageable piles. Aside from the exploitation of female and child labor via wages, the components contain hazardous levels of lead and other potential contaminants that are absorbed through the skin of the workers as well as into the local water tables (Frey 2002).

An additional relevant case is the transfer of hazardous industries to the maquiladora centers located on the Mexican side of the Mexico-U.S. border (Frey 2003). With the emergence of maquiladoras, degradation of both the built and natural environments has escalated. This has taken several forms, including inadequate drinking water, poor sewage services, insufficient housing, improper garbage disposal, and air and water pollution. In fact, children are often more likely to drink soda beverages than clean water because the latter in bottled form is generally more expensive and less accessible than the former in these areas (Shiva 2002). Maquila plants produce hazardous wastes and other substances that are not managed effectively and contaminate the air, water, and soil, as well as put workers and others at risk of death, disease, and injury (e.g., Clapp 2002; Frey 2003). These facilities produce commodities for consumption in core markets. Furthermore, the maquiladoras are not unique to northern Mexico. Similar production areas exist in other semiperipheral and peripheral regions of the world-economy.

Uneven levels of natural resource consumption and concomitant environmental degradation are largely grounded in sociohistorical processes of global social change. Throughout human history, more powerful societies and nation-states have utilized their geopolitical-economic power to create and maintain ecologically unequal exchanges with less powerful and less developed societies and countries. Peripheral regions, such as less developed countries in the contemporary world-economy, are treated as both the environmental taps and sinks for developed countries and transnational corporations headquartered within them. At every stage of the commodity production process natural resources are consumed and wastes generated, and the productive potential of a given set of resources diminishes as it is being converted into a produced commodity. With the continual globalization of trade, finance, and production of goods for core consumption comes the broadening and intensification of environmental destruction, a form of ecological polarization in which the former colonies of the core absorb the environmental costs of natural resource extraction and consumption, many of which are spatially fixed. This ecological polarization corresponds with the increasing economic polarization between the core and periphery. As evidenced by the preceding discussion, these environmental and economic outcomes have pernicious impacts for the well-being of human populations, particularly those living in less developed countries.

In order to build an understanding of the global interconnections between the capitalist economy and ecology, we must first treat the world as a system of stratified countries in which the affluence and material consumption of one country usually come at the social and environmental expenses of other countries. The more powerful and affluent nations in the core consume resources at higher levels than the Earth can sustain ecologically, and environmental degradation and contemporaneous human suffering are global problems that require a global solution. Ultimately, the solution involves a structural transformation of the capitalist world-economy in which a form of global governance emerges that represents the collective interests of all people, nonhuman species, and the natural resources of the planet. Global decisions and action concerning alternative renewable forms of energy need to be institutionalized; large-scale beef production and consumption need to be reduced;monoagricultural production needs to be replaced with organic farming practices; and the conspicuous consumption habits of more affluent groups in core regions need to be scrutinized and reduced to levels at or below the global biocapacity per capita (Wackernagel et al. 2000). What's more, to reduce the growing gap between the core and periphery, material consumption levels of the people living in less developed countries need to increase to sustainable levels parallel with reduced levels of the core, and cleaner forms of manufacturing and production need to replace the environmentally pernicious facilities and practices in less developed countries that are largely controlled by core-based transnational corporations.

Recent transnational coalition-building among different segments of the global justice movement (e.g., labor movement, antiwar movement, environmental movement) illustrates the growing awareness of such global problems and the need for a systemic solution. A prime example of this coalition-building is Environmentalists Against War, a global network of social movement organizations that opposes the unevenly dispersed environmental impacts of war, militarism, and the capitalist world-economy (www.envirosagainstwar .org). Given the geopolitical-economic climate of the contemporary world and the increasing destruction of the global ecological system, it is likely that these coalitions will continue to develop and gain institutional legitimacy, which will eventually foster the emergence of an effective global form of democratic governance that can institute systematic structural changes to reduce human-caused environmental degradation and create a more egalitarian world community. Without these large-scale structural changes, the world will eventually experience a global ecological catastrophe that cannot be remedied by technological solutions. The ramifications of such a calamity could include global warfare and the ultimate demise of all living species.

Notes

1. A current example of this growing area of inquiry is a special issue of the *Journal of World-Systems Research* (vol. 9, no. 2; www.jwsr.ucr.edu) titled "Globalization and the Environment."

2. One hectare is the equivalent of approximately 2.47 acres.

3. Disarticulated economies depend on external markets, whereas articulated economies are able to focus on internal, domestic markets.

4. *Dependent industrialization* refers to industrial development that results from dependence on foreign capital in less developed countries and that focuses on the production of goods via cheap labor and less efficient, dirty production practices for the exportation to more developed core countries.

5. *Overurbanization* usually refers to an excessive growth of a region's urban population relative to its economic growth, usually represented by the size of the industrial labor force

References

Beer, Linda. 1999. "Income Inequality and Transnational Corporate Penetration." *Journal of World-Systems Research* 5:1–25.

Beer, Linda and Terry Boswell. 2002. "The Resilience of Dependency Effects in Explaining Income Inequality in the Global Economy: A Cross-National Analysis, 1975–1995." *Journal of World-Systems Research* 8:30–59.

Bornschier, Volker and Christopher Chase-Dunn. 1985. *Transnational Corporations and Underdevelopment.* New York: Praeger.

Boswell, Terry and Christopher Chase-Dunn. 2000. *The Spiral of Capitalism and Socialism: Toward Global Democracy.* Boulder, CO: Lynne Rienner Publishers.

Boswell, Terry and William J. Dixon. 1990. "Dependency and Rebellion: A Cross-National Analysis." *American Sociological Review* 55:540–559.

Broswimmer, Franz J. 2002. *Ecocide: A Short History of the Mass Extinction of Species.* London: Pluto Press.

Bunker, Stephen G. 1985. *Underdeveloping the Amazon: Extraction, Unequal Exchange, and the Failure of the Modern State.* Urbana, IL: University of Illinois Press.

Burns, Thomas J., Byron L. Davis, Andrew K. Jorgenson, and Edward L. Kick. 2001. "Assessing the Short- and Long-Term Impacts of Environmental Degradation on Social and Economic Outcomes." Paper presented at the annual meetings of the American Sociological Association, Anaheim, California, August 2001.

Burns, Thomas J., Byron L. Davis, and Edward L. Kick. 1997. "Position in the World-System and National Emissions of Greenhouse Gases." *Journal of World-Systems Research* 3:432–466.

Burns, Thomas J., Jeffrey Kentor, and Andrew K. Jorgenson. 2003. "Trade Dependence, Pollution, and Infant Mortality in Less Developed Countries." Pp. 14–28 in *Crises and Resistance in the 21st Century World-System,* edited by Wilma A. Dunaway. Westport, CT: Praeger.

Burns, Thomas J., Edward L. Kick, and Byron L. Davis. 2003. "Theorizing and Rethinking Linkages between the Natural Environment and the Modern World-System: Deforestation in the Late 20th Century." *Journal of World-Systems Research* 9:357–392.

Burns, Thomas J., Edward L. Kick, David A. Murray, and Dixie A. Murray. 1994. "Demography, Development, and Deforestation in a World-System Perspective." *International Journal of Comparative Sociology* 35 (3–4): 221–239.

Buttel, Fred. 2000. "World Society, the Nation-State, and Environmental Protection: Comment on Frank, Hironaka, and Schofer." *American Sociological Review* 65:117–121.

Chase-Dunn, Christopher. 1998. *Global Formation: Structures of the World-Economy.* Lanham, MD: Rowman and Littlefield.

Chase-Dunn, Christopher and Thomas D. Hall. 1997a. "Ecological Degradation and the Evolution of World-Systems." *Journal of World-Systems Research* 3:403–431.

————. 1997b. *Rise and Demise: Comparing World-Systems.* Boulder, CO: Westview.

Chase-Dunn, Christopher, and Andrew K. Jorgenson. 2003. "Regions and Interaction Networks: An Institutional-Materialist Approach." *International Journal of Comparative Sociology* 44:433–450.

Chase-Dunn, Christopher, Y. Kawano, and B. Brewer. 2000. "Trade Globalization since 1795: Waves of Integration in the World-System." *American Sociological Review* 65:77–95.

Chew, Sing C. 2001. *World Ecological Degradation: Accumulation, Urbanization, and Deforestation 3000 B.C.–A.D. 2000.* Walnut Creek, CA: AltaMira Press.

Clapp, Jennifer. 2002. "The Distancing of Waste: Overconsumption in a Global Economy." Pp. 155–176 in *Confronting Consumption,* edited by Thomas Princen, Michael Maniates, and Ken Conca. Cambridge, MA: MIT Press.

Commoner, Barry. 1992. *Making Peace with the Planet.* New York: Free Press.

Conca, Ken. 2002. "Consumption and Environment in a Global Economy." Pp. 133–154 in *Confronting Consumption,* edited by Thomas Princen, Michael Maniates, and Ken Conca. Cambridge, MA: MIT Press.

Cronon, William. 1991. *Nature's Metropolis: Chicago and the Great West.* New York: Norton.

Davis, Mike. 2001. *Late Victorian Holocausts.* London: Verso.

Dickens, Peter. 2002. "A Green Marxism? Labor Processes, Alienation, and the Division of Labor." Pp. 51–72 in *Sociological Theory and the Environment: Classical Foundations, Contemporary Insights,* edited by Riley Dunlap, Fredrick Buttel, Peter Dickens, and August Gijswijt. Boulder, CO: Rowman and Littlefield.

Donohoe, Martin. 2003. "Causes and Health Consequences of Environmental Degradation and Social Injustice." *Social Science and Medicine* 56:573–587.

Foster, John Bellamy. 1999. *The Vulnerable Planet.* New York: Monthly Review Press.

———. 2002. *Ecology against Capitalism.* New York: Monthly Review Press.

Frank, Andre Gunder. 1966. "The Development of Underdevelopment." *Monthly Review* 18:17–31.

Frey, R. Scott. 1995. "The International Traffic in Pesticides." *Technological Forecasting and Social Change* 50:151–169.

———. 1998. "The Hazardous Waste Stream in the World-System." In *Space and Transport in the Modern World-System,* edited by Paul Ciccantell and Stephen Bunker. Westport, CT: Greenwood Press.

———. 2002. "The International Traffic in Heavy Metals." Paper presented at the annual meeting of the American Sociological Association, Chicago.

———. 2003. "The Transfer of Core-Based Hazardous Production Processes to the Export Processing Zones of the Periphery: The Maquiladora Centers of Northern Mexico." *Journal of World-Systems Research* 9:317–356.

Grimes, Peter. 1999. "The Horsemen and the Killing Fields: The Final Contradiction of Capitalism." Pp. 13–43 in *Ecology and the World-System,* edited by Walter Goldfrank, David Goodman, and Andrew Szasz. Westport, CT: Greenwood Press.

Grimes, Peter and Jeffrey Kentor. 2003. "Exporting the Greenhouse: Foreign Capital Penetration and CO2 Emissions 1980–1996." *Journal of World-Systems Research* 9:261–276.

Harvey, David. 1999. *The Limits to Capital.* London: Verso.

Hornborg, Alf. 2001. *The Power of the Machine: Global Inequalities of Economy, Technology, and Environment.* Walnut Creek, CA: AltaMira Press.

Jorgenson, Andrew K. 2003a. "Consumption and Environmental Degradation: A Cross-National Analysis of the Ecological Footprint." *Social Problems* 50:374–394.

———. 2003b. "International Economic Inequality 1500–2000: A Quantitative Analysis." Manuscript, Department of Sociology, University of California, Riverside.

———. 2004a. "Export Partner Dependence and Environmental Degradation 1965–2000: A Cross-National Study." Ph.D. dissertation, Department of Sociology, University of California, Riverside.

———. 2004b. "Global Inequality, Water Pollution, and Infant Mortality." *Social Science Journal* 41:279–288.

———. 2004c. "Uneven Processes and Environmental Degradation in the World-Economy." *Human Ecology Review* 11 (2): 103–117.

Jorgenson, Andrew K. and Tom Burns. 2004. "Globalization, the Environment, and Infant Mortality: A Cross-National Study." *Humboldt Journal of Social Relations* 28:7–52.

Jorgenson, Andrew K. and Edward Kick. 2003. "Globalization and the Environment." *Journal of World-Systems Research* 9:195–204.

Kentor, Jeffrey. 1981. "Structural Determinants of Peripheral Urbanization: The Effects of International Dependence." *American Sociological Review* 46:201–211.

———. 2000. *Capital and Coercion: The Economic and Military Processes That Have Shaped the World-Economy 1800–1990.* New York: Garland Press.

Kick, Edward L., Thomas J. Burns, Byron L. Davis, David A. Murray, and Dixie A. Murray. 1996. "Impacts of Domestic Population Dynamics and Foreign Wood Trade on Deforestation: A World-System Perspective." *Journal of Developing Societies* 12: 68–87.

Koop, Gary and Lise Tole. 1997. "Measuring Differential Forest Outcomes: A Tale of Two Countries." *World Development* 25:2043–2056.

Lofdahl, Corey. 2002. *Environmental Impacts of Globalization and Trade.* Cambridge, MA: MIT Press.

Maniates, Michael. 2002. "Individualization: Plant a Tree, Buy a Bike, Save the World?" Pp. 43–66 in *Confronting Consumption,* edited by Thomas Princen, Michael Maniates, and Ken Conca. Cambridge, MA: MIT Press.

Manning, Robert. 2000. *Credit Card Nation: The Consequences of America's Addiction to Credit.* New York: Basic Books.

Manno, Jack. 2002. "Commoditization: Consumption Efficiency and an Economy of Care and Connection." Pp. 67–100 in *Confronting Consumption,* edited by Thomas Princen, Michael Maniates, and Ken Conca. Cambridge, MA: MIT Press.

Marx, Karl. 1906. *Capital: A Critique of Political Economy.* New York: Modern Library.

Mol, Arthur. 1995. *The Refinement of Production: Ecological Modernization Theory and the Chemical Industry.* Utrecht, Netherlands: Van Arkel.

Mol, Arthur and David Sonnenfeld, eds. 2000. *Ecological Modernisation around the World: Perspectives and Critical Debates.* London: Frank Cass.

Mol, Arthur and Gert Spaargaren. 2000. "Ecological Modernization Theory in Debate: A Review." Pp. 17–49 in *Ecological Modernisation around the World: Perspectives and Critical Debates,* edited by Arthur Mol and David Sonnenfeld. London: Frank Cass.

Moore, Jason. 2003. "The Modern World-System as Environmental History? Ecology and the Rise of Capitalism." *Theory and Society* 32:307–377.

O'Connor, James. 1998. *Natural Causes: Essays in Ecological Marxism.* New York: Guilford Publishing.

Portes, Alejandro, Carlos Dore-Cabral, and Patricia Landolt, eds. 1997. *The Urban Caribbean: Transition to the New Global Economy.* Baltimore, MD: Johns Hopkins University Press.

Princen, Thomas. 2002. "Consumption and Externalities: Where Economy Meets Ecology." Pp. 23–42 in *Confronting Consumption,* edited by Thomas Princen, Michael Maniates, and Ken Conca. Cambridge, MA: MIT Press.

Princen, Thomas, Michael Maniates, and Ken Conca. 2002. "Confronting Consumption." Pp. 1–20 in *Confronting Consumption,* edited by Thomas Princen, Michael Maniates, and Ken Conca. Cambridge, MA: MIT Press.

Roberts, Timmons and Peter E Grimes. 2002. "World-System Theory and the Environment: Toward a New Synthesis." Pp. 167–196 in *Sociological Theory and the Environment: Classical Foundations, Contemporary Insights,* edited by Riley Dunlap, Frederick Buttel, Peter Dickens, and August Gijswijt. Lanham, MD: Rowman and Littlefield,

Roberts, Timmons, Peter Grimes, and Jodie Manale. 2003. "Social Roots of Global Environmental Change: A World-Systems Analysis of Carbon Dioxide Emissions." *Journal of World-Systems Research* 9:277–316.

Sassen, Saskia. 1991. *The Global City: New York, London, and Tokyo.* Princeton, NJ: Princeton University Press.

Schnaiberg, Allan. 1980. *The Environment.* New York: Oxford University Press.

Schnaiberg, Allan and Kenneth Gould. 1994. *Environment and Society: The Enduring Conflict.* New York: St Martin's Press.

Shiva, Vandanna. 2002. *Water Wars: Privatization, Pollution, and Profit.* Cambridge, MA: South End Press.

Sklair, Leslie. 2001. *The Transnational Capitalist Class.* Oxford: Blackwell Press.

Smith, David A. 1996. *Third World Cities in a Global Perspective: The Political Economy of Uneven Urbanization.* Boulder, CO: Westview.

Sonnenfeld, David. 1998. "From Brown to Green? Late Industrialization, Social Conflict, and the Adoption of Environmental Technologies in Thailand's Pulp Industry." *Organization and Environment* 11:59–87.

Timberlake, Michael and Jeffrey Kentor. 1983. "Economic Dependence, Overurbanization and Economic Growth: A Study of Less Developed Countries." *Sociological Quarterly* 24:489–507.

Wackernagel, Mathis, Alejandro C. Linares, Diana Deumling, Maria A. V. Sanchez, Ina S. L. Falfan, and Jonathan Loh. 2000. *Ecological Footprints and Ecological Capacities of 152 Nations: The 1996 Update.* San Francisco, CA: Redefining Progress.

Wallerstein, Immanuel. 1974. *The Modern World-System.* New York: Academic Press.

————. 1999. "Ecology and Capitalist Costs of Production: No Exit." Pp. 3–12 in *Ecology and the World-System,* edited by Walter Goldfrank, David Goodman, and Andrew Szasz. Westport, CT: Greenwood Press.

White, Rob. 2002. "Environmental Harm and the Political Economy of Consumption." *Social Justice* 29:82–102.

York, Richard and Eugene Rosa. 2003. "Key Challenges to Ecological Modernization Theory." *Organization and Environment* 16:273–288.

York, Richard, Eugene Rosa, and Thomas Dietz. 2003. "Footprints on the Earth: The Environmental Consequences of Modernity." *American Sociological Review* 68:279–300.

IV | Globalization, Hegemony, and Global Governance

10

Spatial and Other "Fixes" of Historical Capitalism

GIOVANNI ARRIGHI

Capitalism is the first and only historical social system that has become truly global in scale and scope. Mapping this transformation over time is a particularly challenging task. The purpose of this chapter is to propose a conceptual map focused specifically on the processes associated with the globalization of historical capitalism. This is a first necessary step in the identification of the kind of geographical and historical information that is needed in order to represent graphically the spatial-temporal dynamic of historical capitalism.

The chapter begins with a brief discussion of David Harvey's (2003) concepts of "spatio-temporal fix," "switching crises," and "accumulation by dispossession." It goes on to show that these concepts find a close correspondence in the evolutionary pattern of world capitalism identified in *The Long Twentieth Century* (Arrighi 1994) and developed further in *Chaos and Governance in the Modern World System* (Arrighi and Silver 1999).

Spatial Fixes, Switching Crises, and Accumulation by Dispossession

In seeking a connection between processes of capital accumulation and expansionist political-military projects—such as the Project for the New American Century, which has inspired the U.S. War on Terrorism and the invasion of Iraq—Harvey has deployed a complex conceptual apparatus, the centerpiece of which is the notion of "spatio-temporal" fix. In his argument, the term "fix" has a double meaning.

> A certain portion of the total capital is literally fixed in and on the land in some physical form for a relatively long period of time (depending on its economic and physical lifetime). Some social expenditures (such as public education or a health-care system) also become territorialized and rendered geographically immobile through state commitments. The spatio-temporal "fix," on the other hand, is a metaphor for a particular kind of solution to capitalist crises through temporal deferral and geographical expansion. (2003:115)

Temporal deferral and geographical expansion "fix" the overaccumulation crises that arise from the chronic tendency of capital to accumulate over and above what can be reinvested profitably in the production and exchange of commodities. As a result of this tendency, surpluses of capital and labor are left unutilized or underutilized. The incorporation of new space into the system of accumulation absorbs these surpluses in two ways. At first, it promotes their utilization in the activities involved in opening up the new space and endowing it with the necessary infrastructure, both physical and social. And then, once the new space has been adequately "produced," the surpluses of labor and capital can be absorbed in the new productive combinations that have been made profitable by the spatial enlargement of the system of accumulation (Harvey 2003:109–112).

As Harvey notes, this metaphorical meaning of spatial-temporal fix as solution to capitalist crises can and recurrently does enter into contradiction with the material meaning of the expression, for the geographical expansion, reorganization, and reconstruction that absorb surplus capital and labor "threaten . . . the values already fixed in place (embedded in the land) but not yet realized." Hence

> the vast quantities of capital fixed in place act as a drag upon the capacity to realize a spatial fix elsewhere. . . . If capital does move out, then it leaves behind a trail of devastation and devaluation; the deindustrializations experienced in the heartlands of capitalism . . . in the 1970s and 1980s are cases in point. If capital does not or cannot move . . . then overaccumulated capital stands to be devalued directly through the onset of a deflationary recession or depression. (Harvey 2003:116)

Either way, spatial fixes can be expected to be associated with interregional volatility and the redirection of capital flows from one space to another. The redirection may occur smoothly, or it may involve what Harvey calls "switching crises" (2003:121–123; 1982:428–429). Switching crises are volatile interregional relocations of capital that disrupt local accumulation but smooth accumulation in the system as a whole. Harvey does not spell out the relationship between overaccumulation crises, spatial-temporal fixes, and switching crises. But the drift of his argument seems to be that, while overaccumulation crises are the cause, switching crises are a possible effect of the spatial-temporal fixes that recurrently revolutionize the historical geography of capitalism. They stem from resistance to the relocations involved in spatial fixes—a resistance that at least in part originates from the contradictory logic of capital accumulation itself. Indeed, "the more capitalism devel-

ops, the more it tends to succumb to the forces making for geographical inertia," argues Harvey.

> The circulation of capital is increasingly imprisoned within immobile physical
> and social infrastructures which are crafted to support certain kinds of pro-
> duction . . . labor processes, distributional arrangements, consumption pat-
> terns, and so on. Increasing quantities of fixed capital . . . check uninhibited
> mobility. . . . Territorial alliances, which often become increasingly powerful
> and more deeply entrenched, arise. . . . to conserve privileges already won, to
> sustain investments already made, to keep a local compromise intact, and to
> protect itself from the chill winds of spatial competition. . . . New spatial con-
> figurations cannot be achieved because regional devaluations are not allowed
> to run their course. The uneven geographical development of capitalism then
> assumes a form that is totally inconsistent with sustained accumulation ei-
> ther within the region or on a global scale. (1982:428–429)

In discussing the spatial fix that in his view is most prominent in the present conjuncture (the emergence of China as the main absorber of surplus
capital), Harvey adds a new element to the forces of geographical inertia that
may prevent new spatial configurations from being achieved: resistance to
hegemonic change. This "remarkable version" of spatial-temporal fix "has
global implications not only for absorbing overaccumulated capital, but also
for shifting the balance of economic and political power to China as the regional hegemon and perhaps placing the Asian region, under Chinese leadership, in a much more competitive position vis-à-vis the United States." This
possibility makes U.S. resistance to a smooth spatial fix all the more likely,
even though such a fix holds out the best prospect for a solution of the underlying overaccumulation crisis (Harvey 2003:123–124).

The association between spatial fixes and hegemonic shifts thus strength-
ens the catch-22 that always confronts previously leading centers of capitalist development. The unconstrained development of capitalism in new regions brings devaluation to these centers through intensified international
competition. Constrained development abroad limits international competition but blocks off opportunities for the profitable investment of surplus
capital and so sparks internally generated devaluations (Harvey 1982:435). If
the competitively challenged center is also a hegemonic center, either outcome threatens to deflate not just its assets but its power as well.

Harvey envisages two possible ways out of this catch-22. One is the use of
financial means "to rid the system of overaccumulation by the visitation of
crises of devaluation upon vulnerable territories" (2003:134). And the other

is the use of political and military means to turn international competition to the advantage of the more powerful states. The deployment of these means constitutes the "sinister and destructive side of spatial-temporal fixes to the overaccumulation problem." He explains,

> Like war in relation to diplomacy, finance capital intervention backed by state power frequently amounts to accumulation by other means. An unholy alliance between state powers and the predatory aspects of finance capital forms the cutting edge of a "vulture capitalism" that is as much about cannibalistic practices and forced devaluations as it is about achieving harmonious global development. (2003:135–136)

Harvey goes on to note that these "other means" are what Karl Marx, following Adam Smith, referred to as the means of "primitive" or "original" accumulation. He quotes approvingly Hannah Arendt's observation that "the emergence of 'superfluous' money . . . which could no longer find productive investment within the national borders" created a situation in the late nineteenth and early twentieth centuries whereby Marx's "original sin of simple robbery . . . had eventually to be repeated lest the motor of accumulation suddenly die down" (Harvey 2003:142). Since a similar situation appears to have emerged again in the late twentieth and early twenty-first centuries, Harvey advocates a "general reevaluation of the continuous role and persistence of the predatory practices of 'primitive' or 'original' accumulation within the long historical geography of capital accumulation." And since he finds it peculiar to call an ongoing process "primitive" or "original," he proposes to replace these terms with the concept of "accumulation by dispossession."

Historically, accumulation by dispossession has taken many different forms, including the conversion of various forms of property rights (common, collective, state, etc.) into exclusive property rights; colonial, semicolonial, neocolonial, and imperial appropriations of assets and natural resources; and the suppression of alternatives to the capitalistic use of human and natural resources. Although much has been contingent and haphazard in the modus operandi of these processes, finance capital and the credit system have been major levers of dispossession, while the states, with their monopolies of violence and definitions of legality, have been crucial protagonists (Harvey 2003:145–149). But whatever its manifestations, agencies, and instruments, "what accumulation by dispossession does is to release a set of assets (including labor power) at very low (and in some instances zero) cost. Overaccumulated capital can seize hold of such assets and immediately turn them to profitable use" (Harvey 2003:149).

Accumulation by dispossession can take place both at home and abroad. The more developed capitalistically a state is, however, the greater the difficulties involved in practicing it at home and the greater the incentives and the capabilities to practice it abroad. It follows that accumulation by dispossession is only in part a substitute for spatial fixes to overaccumulation crises. To an extent that increases with the development of capitalism in the states or regions facing overaccumulation problems, it involves a spatial fix of its own—a spatial fix, that is, that expands the geographical scope of the system of accumulation through the forcible or fraudulent appropriation of something for nothing, rather than through the exchange of nominally equivalent values.

A Conceptual Map of Historical Capitalism

The concepts reviewed in the preceding section can be used, as Harvey does, to interpret current U.S. dispositions to remake the map of the world to suit U.S interests and values, in comparison with the dispositions that drove the territorial expansion of capitalist states in the late nineteenth century and early twentieth. But they can also be used to interpret the peculiar expansionary tendencies of historical capitalism over a much longer time horizon than that encompassed by Harvey's observations. This much longer horizon stretches as far back in time as we can detect overaccumulation crises that are in key respects comparable to the present one.

As I have argued in *The Long Twentieth Century*, persistent systemwide overaccumulation crises have characterized historical capitalism long before it became a mode of production in the late eighteenth and early nineteenth centuries. Taking long periods of "financialization" across political jurisdictions as the most valid and reliable indicator of an underlying overaccumulation crisis, I identified four partly overlapping "systemic cycles of accumulation" of increasing scale and decreasing duration, each consisting of a phase of material expansion—in the course of which capital accumulates primarily through investment in trade and production—and a phase of financial expansion, in the course of which capital accumulates primarily through investment in property titles and other claims on future incomes. Contrary to the reading of some critics, the identification of these cycles does not portray the history of capitalism as "the eternal return of the same," as Michael Hardt and Antonio Negri put it (2000:239). Rather, they show that, precisely when the "same" (in the form of recurrent systemwide financial expansions) appears to return, new spatial-temporal fixes, major switching crises, and long periods of accumulation by dispossession have revolutionized the historical geography of capitalism. Integral to these "revolutions" was the emergence of a new leading agency and a new organization of the system of accumulation.

A comparison of these distinct agencies and organizations reveals not only that they are different but also that the sequence of these differences describes an evolutionary pattern toward regimes of increasing size, scope, and complexity. This evolutionary pattern is summed up in figure 10.1 (the figure and much of what follows in this section are taken from Arrighi and Silver 2001:264–268). The first column of the figure focuses on the "containers of power"—as Anthony Giddens (1987) has aptly characterized states—that have housed the "headquarters" of the leading capitalist agencies of the successive regimes: the Republic of Genoa, the United Provinces, the United Kingdom, and the United States.

At the time of the rise and full expansion of the Genoese regime, the Republic of Genoa was a city-state small in size and simple in organization,

Leading Governmental Organization	Regime type/cycle		Costs internalized			
	Extensive	Intensive	Protection	Production	Transaction	Reproduction
World-state						
		U.S.	Yes	Yes	Yes	No
	British		Yes	Yes	No	No
Nation-state						
		Dutch	Yes	No	No	No
	Genoese		No	No	No	No
City-state						

Fig. 10.1. Evolutionary Pattern of World Capitalism

which contained very little power indeed. Yet, thanks to its far-flung commercial and financial networks, the Genoese capitalist class, organized in a cosmopolitan diaspora, could deal on a par with the most powerful territorialist rulers of Europe and turn the relentless competition for mobile capital among these rulers into a powerful engine for the self-expansion of its own capital. At the time of the rise and full expansion of the Dutch regime of accumulation, the United Provinces was a hybrid kind of organization that combined some of the features of the disappearing city-states with some of the features of the rising nation-states. The greater power of the Dutch state relative to the Genoese enabled the Dutch capitalist class to do what the Genoese had already been doing—turn interstate competition for mobile capital into an engine for the self-expansion of its own capital—but without having to "buy" protection from territorialist states, as the Genoese had done through a relationship of political exchange with Iberian rulers. The Dutch regime, in other words, "internalized" the protection costs that the Genoese had "externalized" (see fig. 10.1, col. 4).

At the time of the rise and full expansion of the British regime of accumulation, the United Kingdom was not only a fully developed nation-state. It was also in the process of conquering a world-encompassing commercial and territorial empire that gave its ruling groups and its capitalist class a command over the world's human and natural resources without parallel or precedent. This command enabled the British capitalist class to do what the Dutch had already been able to do—turn to its own advantage interstate competition for mobile capital and "produce" all the protection required by the self-expansion of its capital—but without having to rely on foreign and often hostile territorialist organizations for most of the agro-industrial production on which the profitability of its commercial activities rested. If the Dutch regime relative to the Genoese had internalized protection costs, the British regime relative to the Dutch internalized production costs as well (see fig. 10.1, col. 5). As a consequence of this internalization, world capitalism continued to be a mode of accumulation and rule but became also a mode of production.

Finally, at the time of the rise and full expansion of the U.S. regime of accumulation, the United States was already something more than a fully developed nation-state. It was a continental military-industrial complex with sufficient power to provide a wide range of subordinate and allied governments with effective protection and to make credible threats of economic strangulation or military annihilation toward unfriendly governments anywhere in the world. Combined with the size, insularity, and natural wealth of its domestic territory, this power enabled the U.S. capitalist class to internalize not just protection and production costs—as the British capitalist class had already done—but transaction costs as well, that is to say, the markets on which the self-expansion of its capital depended (see fig. 10.1, col. 6).

This steady increase in the geographical size and functional scope of successive regimes of capital accumulation on a world scale is somewhat obscured by another feature of the temporal sequence of such regimes. This feature is a double movement, forward and backward at the same time. Each step forward in the process of internalization of costs by a new regime of accumulation has involved a revival of governmental and business strategies and structures that had been superseded by the preceding regime. Thus, the internalization of protection costs by the Dutch regime in comparison with the Genoese regime occurred through a revival of the strategies and structures of Venetian state monopoly capitalism that the Genoese regime had superseded. Similarly, the internalization of production costs by the British regime in comparison with the Dutch regime occurred through a revival in new and more complex forms of the strategies and structures of Genoese cosmopolitan capitalism and Iberian global territorialism. And the same pattern occurred once again with the rise and full expansion of the U.S. regime, which internalized transaction costs by reviving in new and more complex forms the strategies and structures of Dutch corporate capitalism (see fig. 10.1, cols. 1 and 2).

This recurrent revival of previously superseded strategies and structures of accumulation generates a pendulum-like movement between "cosmopolitan-imperial" and "corporate-national" organizational structures. The first is typical of "extensive" regimes, as the Genoese-Iberian and the British were, and the second is typical of "intensive" regimes, as the Dutch and the United States were. The Genoese-Iberian and British "cosmopolitan-imperial" regimes were extensive in the sense that they have been responsible for most of the geographical expansion of world capitalism. Under the Genoese regime, the world was "discovered," and under the British it was "conquered." The Dutch and the U.S. "corporate-national" regimes, in contrast, were intensive in the sense that they have been responsible for the geographical consolidation, rather than the expansion, of historical capitalism. Under the Dutch regime, the "discovery" of the world realized primarily by the Iberian partners of the Genoese was consolidated into an Amsterdam-centered system of commercial entrepôts and joint-stock chartered companies. And under the U.S. regime, the "conquest" of the world realized primarily by the British themselves was consolidated into a U.S.-centered system of national states and transnational corporations.

This alternation of extensive and intensive regimes blurs our perception of the underlying, truly long-term tendency toward the formation of regimes of increasing geographical scope. When the pendulum swings in the direction of extensive regimes, the underlying trend is magnified, and when it swings in the direction of intensive regimes, the underlying trend appears to have been less significant than it really was. Nevertheless, once we control for these swings by comparing the two intensive and the two extensive regimes with one another—the Genoese-Iberian with the British, and the Dutch with the U.S.—the underlying trend becomes unmistakable.

The globalization of historical capitalism has thus been based on the formation of ever more powerful cosmopolitan-imperial (or corporate-national) blocs of governmental and business organizations endowed with the capacity to widen (or deepen) the functional and spatial scope of the system of accumulation. And yet the more powerful these blocs have become, the shorter the life cycle of the regimes of accumulation that they have brought into being—the shorter, that is, the time that it has taken for these regimes to emerge out of the overaccumulation crisis of the preceding dominant regime, to become themselves dominant, and to attain their limits as signaled by the beginning of a new overaccumulation crisis. Relying on Braudel's dating of the beginning of financial expansions, I have calculated that this time was less than half both in the case of the British regime relative to the Genoese and in the case of the U.S. regime relative to the Dutch (Arrighi 1994:216–217).

This pattern of capitalist development whereby an increase in the power of regimes of accumulation is associated with a decrease in their duration calls to mind Marx's contention that "the real barrier of capitalist production is capital itself" and that capitalist production continually overcomes its immanent barriers "only by means which again place these barriers in its way on a more formidable scale" (1962:244–245). But the contradiction between the self-expansion of capital, on the one side, and the development of the material forces of production and of an appropriate world market, on the other, can in fact be reformulated in even more general terms than those used by Marx, for capitalism as a historical social system became a "mode of production"—that is, it internalized production costs—only in its third (British) stage of development. And yet the principle remained unchanged that the real barrier of capitalist development is capital itself, that the self-expansion of existing capital is in constant tension, and recurrently enters into open contradiction, with the expansion of world trade and production and the creation of an appropriate world market. All this was clearly at work already in the Genoese and Dutch stages of development, notwithstanding the continuing externalization of agro-industrial production by their leading agencies. In all instances the contradiction is that the expansion of trade and production was mere means in endeavors aimed primarily at increasing the value of capital. And yet over time it tended to generate more capital than could be absorbed profitably within the confines of the extant spatial-temporal fix (in the material meaning of the expression), thereby threatening to drive down overall returns to capital and thus deflate its value.

The resolution of the ensuing overaccumulation crises through a new spatial-temporal fix (in both meanings of the expression) has taken relatively long periods of time—as a rule more than half a century. In all instances, the resolutions have been punctuated by major switching crises and have involved processes typical of accumulation by dispossession. Although much in the modus operandi of these processes has indeed been contingent and haphazard, as Harvey suggests, in *Chaos and Governance* my coauthors and I have detected some regularities, three of which are especially germane to our present concerns.

First, one kind or another of financialization has always been the predominant response to the overaccumulation problem of the established organizing centers of the system of accumulation. Thanks to their continuing centrality in networks of high finance, these centers have been best positioned to turn the intensifying competition for mobile capital to their advantage and thereby reflate their profits and power at the expense of the rest of the system. Over time, however, financial expansions have promoted the geographical relocation of the centers of capital accumulation by rerouting surplus capital to states and regions capable of ensuring a more secure and profitable spatial-temporal fix to the overaccumulation crisis. Previously dominant centers have thus been faced with the Sisyphean task of containing forces that keep rolling forth with ever renewed strength. Sooner or later, even a small disturbance can tilt (and small disturbances historically have invariably tilted) the balance in favor of the forces that wittingly or unwittingly are undermining the already precarious stability of existing structures, thereby provoking a breakdown of the system of accumulation (Arrighi and Silver 1999:258–264).

Second, the states have been key protagonists of the struggles through which old spatial-temporal fixes are destroyed and fixes of greater geographical scope are attained. In the past, switches to fixes of greater geographical scope were premised on the interstitial emergence of governmental-business complexes that were (or could plausibly become) more powerful both militarily and financially than the still dominant governmental-business complex— as the U.S. complex was relative to the British in the early twentieth century, the British complex relative to the Dutch in the early eighteenth century, and the Dutch relative to the Genoese in the late sixteenth century. In the present transition, it is not yet clear whether and how a governmental-business complex more powerful than the U.S. complex can emerge and eventually provide a solution to the ongoing overaccumulation crisis. But insofar as the past dynamic of historical capitalism is concerned, this tendency toward the formation of ever more powerful governmental-business complexes is one of its most important features (Arrighi and Silver 1999:88–96, 263–270, 275–278, 286–289).

Finally, in each transition accumulation by dispossession has provoked movements of resistance and rebellion by subordinate groups and strata whose established ways of life were coming under attack. Interacting with the interstate power struggle, these movements eventually forced the dominant groups to form new hegemonic social blocs that selectively included previously excluded groups and strata. This increasing "democratization" of historical capitalism has been accompanied by a speedup in the impact of social conflict on overaccumulation crises. Thus, while the overaccumulation crisis of the Dutch regime of accumulation was a long-drawn-out process in which systemwide social conflict came much later than the systemwide financial expansion, in the overaccumulation crisis of the British regime the systemwide financial expansion gave rise almost immediately to systemwide social conflict. This speedup in the social history of capitalism has culminated in the explosion of social conflict of the late 1960s and early 1970s, which preceded and thoroughly shaped the crisis of the U.S. regime of accumulation (Arrighi and Silver 1999:153–216, 282–286; Silver 2003).

References

Arrighi, Giovanni. 1994. *The Long Twentieth Century: Money, Power, and the Origins of Our Time*. London: Verso.

Arrighi, Giovanni and Beverly J. Silver. 1999. *Chaos and Governance in the Modern World System*. Minneapolis, MN: University of Minnesota Press.

———. 2001. "Capitalism and World (Dis)order." *Review of International Studies* 27:257–279.

Giddens, Anthony. 1987. *The Nation-State and Violence*. Berkeley, CA: University of California Press.

Hardt, Michael and Antonio Negri. 2000. *Empire*. Cambridge, MA: Harvard University Press.

Harvey, David. 1982. *The Limits to Capital*. Chicago: University of Chicago Press.

———. 2003. *The New Imperialism*. Oxford: Oxford University Press

Marx, Karl. 1962. *Capital*. Vol. 3. Moscow: Foreign Languages Publishing House.

Silver, Beverly J. 2003. *Forces of Labor: Workers' Movements and Globalization since 1870*. Cambridge, UK: Cambridge University Press.

11

Contemporary Intracore Relations and World-Systems Theory

PETER GOWAN

This chapter focuses on one small area of world-systems theory (WST) but one that is important for analysis of the contemporary world: the dynamics of intracore relations. I address three questions:

1. Does WST's theory of the historically cyclical patterns of intracore relations provide us with a persuasive framework for understanding contemporary core dynamics?

2. Specifically, can the reach and depth of the power of the United States within the contemporary core be captured by WST's theory of capitalist hegemons and their rise and decline?

3. Is WST's insistence that its concept of corewide world empires cannot be established in the modern world-system valid?

In addressing these issues, I begin by outlining WST's general approach to the analysis of intracore relations, focusing in particular on WST's concept of core hegemons and their rise and fall. I then look at WST's arguments as to why a capitalist world empire is impossible, explore how we might conceive of the victory of a world empire, and examine the situation today and the current character of U.S. power.

The Theory of Hegemony and Contemporary Conditions

One of the great strengths of WST is that it insists on the need to analyze contemporary dynamics within a long historical perspective. It argues that we can make sense of historical continuity and change through its concepts of core-periphery relations reproducing themselves across time. And it also identifies a recurrent pattern—or series of patterns—in intracore relations in the modern world-system since the sixteenth century involving a plurality of core powers both competing and cooperating with one another. Unlike, say, liberal international relations theory, WST sees intracore relations as being marked by recurrent structural conflict as core powers compete with one another. But unlike realist international relations theory, WST does not derive its theory of structural conflict between core powers from purely political drives for power maximization on the part of states. Instead, WST identifies the sources of conflict in the compulsions of capitalism as a socioeconomic as well as an interstate system.

In this chapter, we will accept WST's theory of the sources of structural conflict between core powers within what Wallerstein calls the modern world-system. Our critique will be directed toward WST's theorization of resulting conflicts as a recurrent pattern of hegemonic cycles.

Mainstream WST's Theory of Intracore Relations and Hegemonic Cycles

All the main trends in WST agree on the idea that within the modern world-system there have been recurrent cyclical patterns in intracore relationships. The cycles can be thought of as beginning when one core power rises to a dominant position within the hierarchy, becoming a "hegemon" and establishing some order in and stability to the core as other states adapt to the new hegemon's regime. This phase is followed by attempts on the part of other core powers to innovate and challenge the hegemon. As this challenge mounts, the core enters a phase of instability and conflict, typically resolved by intracore wars that eventually lead to the emergence of a new hegemon while the previous hegemon declines.[1]

Within the broad field of WST we can distinguish two contrasting emphases in the ways in which these cycles are theorized. One emphasis is close to realist theories of international relations, stressing the determinant as being the military-political capacities of core states. Writers like Modelski and Thompson along with Gilpin see the economic dimension as being subordinated to and structured by this issue of military-political capacity. But what might be called the mainstream of WST represented by Wallerstein, Chase-Dunn and Arrighi emphasizes capitalist economic systems as the determinant element in the competition, understanding these economic systems in a Marxist sense as production systems generating streams of surplus value. They by no means ignore the role of military-political power, but they view its role as an indispensable *support* for the struggle for dominance at the level of production. Thus we can summarize their theory of the hegemonic cycles as having two main components:

1. A constant search by a plurality of core powers to gain dominance in the most sophisticated and desirable capital-intensive products. Hegemons are

those capitalist powers that achieve dominance in this production field, thus positioning themselves at the top of the international division of labor, penetrating the markets of other core states, gaining the largest streams of surplus value, and being able to set the framework for other core states in the economic field.

2. Military-political action is viewed mainly as a *buttress* or support for this economic dominance, protecting the core economy from external attack or internal challenge and removing obstacles to the flow of its products across the system.

It is this very specific definition of hegemony that results in the WST mainstream's identification of the three hegemonic powers as Holland, Britain, and the United States. The military-political perspective of Modelski and Thompson focuses on sea power rather than dominance in capital-intensive commodities as the key to hegemony, and this gives Portugal a place on the list before Holland. But with either version we should note that the idea of hegemonic cycles in the core derives from the identification of hegemons and their fates.

This mainstream WST conception is perfectly coherent internally. But it is important to note that it employs a highly restricted concept of hegemony and one anchored in production systems. It is on the basis of that specific and restricted concept of hegemony that WST can derive its historical chain of hegemons and the cyclical patterns of their rise and decline. But WST also, as an inevitable consequence of its specific theory of hegemonic cycles, downplays other aspects of intracore relations and is predisposed toward certain expectations of the contemporary dynamics rather than others. Three specific consequences of these kinds are important:

1. The equation sign between the three powers designated as successive hegemons tends toward downplaying some *radical differences* between the three hegemonies in terms of the type of capitalism, the nature of the core context in which the hegemons operate, and the distinctive political capacities of the successive hegemons.

2. It tends to downplay the possibility that a hegemon with great political capacities may be able to exploit interstate system–productive system feedback mechanisms other than the traditional feedback mechanisms of intracore war.

3. It predisposes Wallerstein, Chase-Dunn, and Arrighi in their analysis of contemporary developments in the 1980s and 1990s to view the United

States as having entered a phase of hegemonic decline after its dominance in capital-intensive production for core markets was challenged by German and Japanese capitalism in the 1970s.

The United States as a Sui Generis Hegemon: Is It a Cycle Breaker?

Wallerstein, Chase-Dunn, and especially Arrighi do, of course, note various differences between the successive hegemonies in terms of both their own attributes and the contexts in which they have operated. But they have underestimated the qualitative differences between the United States and Britain either by overplaying British power in the nineteenth century or by underplaying U.S. power in the second half of the twentieth century or both. They have thereby tended to ignore the possibility that the peculiarities of U.S. hegemonic capacities could disrupt the cyclical pattern by which WST has characterized core dynamics. We identify four central peculiarities of U.S. hegemony since 1945: its unipolar core, the structural character of U.S. political subordination of the core, the regime-making capacities of the United States, and U.S. feedback mechanisms for cycle breaking.

The Unipolar Core

Since 1945 U.S. dominance within the core has been *qualitatively* different from that of Britain in the nineteenth century, not to speak of Holland in the seventeenth century. The political dimension of the Britain-core relationship in the nineteenth century and the United States–core relationship in the second half of the twentieth century has been radically different. The British relationship was marked by balance-of-power mechanisms—political multipolarity; the American relationship since 1945 has been marked by political unipolarity.

The Structural Character of U.S. Political Subordination of the Core

U.S. political dominance over the core does not simply derive from the United States' quantitatively greater military power resources. It derives from how those military resources are deployed to politically shape the foreign and security policy context facing other core states. By shaping this context the United States has indirectly shaped the actual substance of the foreign policies of other core states. Some key features of this shaping activity are discussed in the following paragraphs.

1. The United States has the ability to shape and control the regional strategic environment of the Western European powers and Japan. In the case of Western Europe this has been achieved through making Western Eu-

rope strategically dependent on the U.S.-Soviet and now U.S.-Russia relationship; in the case of Japan, through making it dependent first on the U.S.-Soviet relationship in the Cold War but now also on the U.S.-China relationship.

2. The United States has the ability to control, through its military-political reach, the regional peripheries of its major allies. In the Western European case, the United States has long controlled the Mediterranean area, and it now also has extended its military-political predominance across southeastern and Eastern Europe through both NATO enlargement and the Partnership for Peace as well as through bilateral agreements. On the Pacific Rim it has important military-political bridgeheads in South Korea and Southeast Asia and privileged security relationships with Australia and New Zealand. As a result of this U.S. military-political predominance in the hinterlands of the other core centers, the United States can steer events in those hinterlands to the benefit or detriment of those core regions. And it can do so either to the benefit or to the detriment of these other core states.

3. The United States has the ability to control the sources of and transport routes for crucial energy and other strategic material supplies needed by its allies, through its positions in the Middle East and its sea and air dominance in the Mediterranean, the Indian Ocean, the Pacific, and the Atlantic (it has also, of course, been seeking to extend its control into the Caspian area in the recent past). Interruptions of supplies can have very grave consequences for the other core states, but they are dependent on the United States to assure these supplies.

4. Importantly, the United States has also had the capacity to homogenize the political cultures of its allies around sets of political values articulated to serve U.S. interests, symbolic structures rooted in the U.S. victory over Japan and Germany in World War II embodying such highly sensitive symbols as "Munich," "Hitler," ethnicist nationalism and exterminism, totalitarianism, democracy, and individual rights. It is a structure of political values that throws the main allied powers (Germany and Japan) into a very vulnerable international position, and it has also repeatedly demonstrated the United States' capacity to trump the rival potential center of internationalist liberal and democratic universalism, France.

Taken together, these four capacities have reduced the foreign policy and power projection autonomy of the United States' allies to near zero. This marks, at the very least, a profound structural modification in the interstate system in comparison with earlier epochs. Behind unipolarity lies a series of structural dependencies of other core states on the United States for their political security.

The Regime-Making Capacities of the United States

WST argues that each hegemon establishes an international regime of accumulation suited to its dominance in a particular set of capital-intensive commodities and the other core powers adapt to that regime and then launch a competitive challenge within it. The regime then is eventually reshaped through intracore wars. But there have been striking differences between the regime-making capacities of the United States and of Britain.

Trade Regimes. Unlike Britain, the United States was never a unilateral free trader. It has adopted the ideology of free trade in the postwar period but it has restricted its implementation in very important ways and has continually demonstrated its readiness, if necessary, to flout free trade principles and pursue a policy of reciprocity rather than most favored nation (MFN) status in trade relations. At the start of the 1990s the GATT was the embodiment of free trade principles, but it was far from being the organizer of actual trade relations as a whole—on some estimates it embraced no more than about 5 percent of all international trade.

The United States has presided over a (partial) free trade regime for the rest of the world and simultaneously given itself the right both to control the scope of that regime and to flout its own regime, when necessary, to suit its own interests. And this refusal to be bound by global economic law has been combined with vigorous attempts in some fields to extend the jurisdictional reach of U.S domestic economic laws internationally, applying it to non-American corporations operating outside the United States. Regarding actions in this field, Kahler (1995:46) reports that "the list was long."

International Monetary Relations. The contrast is equally striking and structurally similar in international monetary relations. The international monetary system established at Bretton Woods was always conditionally and partially implemented, and although it did begin with the United States accepting a discipline on its dollar policy through the gold link, when that discipline was perceived by the U.S. government in the 1970s to be detrimental to U.S. interests, it was simply scrapped through unilateral action by the United States against opposition from all other core states. From then on the international monetary system became a pure dollar standard, thus manipulable by the U.S. government as it wished.

This dollar-standard international monetary system has enabled the United States to escape from the usual balance-of-payments constraints on a state's economic management and also to escape the consequences of large swings in dollar exchange rates with other currencies, such as the deutsche mark and the yen. It has thus been able to swing the dollar up or down against other currencies in line with purely U.S. economic or political objectives.

International Financial Regimes. The same pattern has applied to the international financial regime: When the U.S. government decided that the Bretton Woods system of state control of international financial flows was detrimental to U.S. interests, it had the capacity in the 1970s to transform the regime, placing international financial flows in the hands of private financial operators and markets and making New York the international financial center from the early 1980s. Since the 1970s this transformation has also involved effectively dismantling the financial regimes of its allies (ending capital controls).

Product and Asset Market Regimes. U.S. regime-shaping capacities have extended also to all other areas of international economic flows and international markets. Markets are often treated as if they were spheres of exchange autonomous from state policy, but in the modern world they are highly complex mechanisms grounded in intricate networks of public and private law, institutions, and conventions. The state executives and big businesses of the core states work together to seek to shape markets in their own interests. And in this field the United States has demonstrated great and continuing influence. These so-called behind-the-border international regimes are another distinctive feature of the phase of U.S. hegemony.

Giovanni Arrighi, who, more than other WST authors, has understood some crucial distinctive features of U.S. global power, provides us with an interesting perspective on this. He calls American capitalism "autocentric" in its relation to the international political economy, while British capitalism was, in an important sense, shaped by the distinctive relationship of each of its parts with the world economy. The "autocentric" character of U.S. capitalism—made possible not only by its internal characteristics but also by its extraordinary power vis-à-vis the rest of the world, as explained above—has involved an ambitious agenda of reorganizing the world economy along the lines of American capitalism. Arrighi (1994) stresses internalization within the organizational domains of U.S. multinational corporations, but U.S. restructuring of the social relations of production abroad has been far more extensive than that. We do not wish to suggest that these capacities to restructure the internal regimes of its allies have been absolute—absolutely not. And we will not, at this stage, consider how extensive they have been.

U.S. Feedback Mechanisms for Cycle Breaking

WST's focus on a definition of hegemony centered on production systems has thus been combined with an inadequate stress on the mechanisms available to the United States but not to earlier hegemons for responding to challenges from core competitors in the sphere of production and striking back. We can think of these mechanisms as a kind of feedback from outside the productive sector onto the course of events within the productive sector. The most important of these mechanisms has been the United States' extraordinary military-political reach, but also of great importance has been its power of the monetary-financial system. Both these mechanisms have given the United States the ability to change repeatedly the rules of the game in the sphere of production and commodity exchange in order to create the conditions for rebuilding U.S. hegemony in the narrow sense in which it has been used by WST.

A very important indirect effect of the United States' military-political capacity has been its control over energy and strategic mineral sources and transport routes, the most dramatic example of which is its use of the oil price rises in the early 1970s.

The potency of the monetary-financial levers has been equally striking, with the U.S. government demonstrating repeatedly that, through the threat or actual use of U.S. control over the international monetary and financial regime, it can profoundly negatively affect the economic outcomes of allied economies, disrupting their macroeconomic strategies—what I have described elsewhere as the Dollar–Wall Street Regime constructed in the 1970s and early 1980s (Gowan 1999). Examples of such strategies would include monetary pressure on the French economy to defeat the Keynesian growth strategy of the early 1980s and the manipulation of the dollar-yen exchange rate to exert intense pressure on Japan's trade position in order to gain an opening of Japanese finance for U.S. financial operators in the 1980s and to gain various kinds of managed trade agreements with Japan in the 1990s. On top of the security pact tactic of earlier years, in the 1980s and 1990s the United States began using economic statecraft in the monetary and financial field to encourage states to "deal" with it on restructuring its approaches to economic policy and organization.

Taken together, these levers have enabled the United States to "internalize" the international political economy, as Arrighi puts it, to a considerable extent—or, to express the same idea in another way, to make significant inroads into the capacity of its allies to manage their own internal affairs autonomously.

The Mistake about U.S. Hegemonic Decline

Aggregating all these distinctive features of U.S. hegemony, we can see how, when faced with serious challenges to its dominance in capital-intensive sectors in the 1970s, the United States developed a very wide range of instruments, essentially derived from its structural power over the interstate system of the core, with which to strike back at competitors. These instruments have been largely ignored or downplayed by mainstream WST. And even Arrighi, who stresses them more than others, still remains wedded to the thesis of precipitate U.S. hegemonic decline.

Arrighi's account (1994) of the supposed decline focuses on financialization. He provides a brilliant description of the way in which earlier hegemonic powers, when faced with defeat in product markets, switched to financialization and to gaining profits from the competitive success of their rivals. This pattern fits Genoa, Holland, and Britain. Chase-Dunn (1999) provides a supporting theorization with his strong emphasis on capital mobility across the interstate system. He adds to Arrighi's argument by saying that the declining hegemon's domestic capitals are not prepared to foot the bill for the mobilization of state resources to resubordinate rivals by military means.

Arrighi then suggests that the international financialization that we have witnessed since the 1970s has essentially been a repeat of this earlier cyclical pattern of financialization. But this has not been the case: quite the opposite. First, the financialization process was initiated as much by the U.S. state as by U.S. capitals. Second, it should be understood as part and parcel of the U.S. state's drive to construct the Dollar–Wall Street Regime as a weapon for the U.S. fight-back. Third, U.S. leadership of international monetary and financial relations has been a double lever for this fight-back: both an instrument of pressure on other core states, as we have suggested above, and an instrument for providing the U.S. state with the financial resources for massively strengthening its state military-political capacity in the 1980s. With all these instruments the United States has thus been able to "hold the line" against its allied competitors, and during the 1990s it was able to pressure its allies into accepting its own, internally generated new leading sectors of capital-intensive industries as the "hegemonic" industrial driving forces of the new phase of the world economy: the "information" and telecommunication industries.

WST and the Possibility of Capitalist World Empires

Our critique of WST analysis of contemporary intracore relations suggests that the scheme of hegemonic cycles in a politically pluralistic core may need structural modification in the light of the characteristics of U.S. hegemony. Some writers, particularly American realists, go much further and insist that the advanced capitalist core today is organized as an American world empire.

Zbigniew Brzezinski has forcefully advanced this argument that today we have imperial dominance of the United States over its European and East Asian allies. He underlines the fact that "the scope and pervasiveness of American global power today are unique. . . . Its military legions are firmly perched on the western and eastern extremities of Eurasia, and they also control the Persian Gulf. American vassals and tributaries, some yearning to be embraced by even more formal ties to Washington, dot the entire Eurasian continent, as the map on page 22 shows" (Brzezinski 1997:23). What the map in question shows is areas of U.S. "geopolitical preponderance" and other areas of U.S. "political influence." The whole of Western Europe, Japan, South Korea, and Australia and New Zealand, as well as some parts of the Middle East and Canada, fall into the category of U.S. geopolitical preponderance, not just influence.

Kenneth Waltz and Paul Wolfowitz claimed that the George H. W. Bush and Clinton administrations were guided precisely by the goal of establishing political dominance over the rest of the core. The famous 1992 Bush administration document on American Grand Strategy for the post–Cold War world order frankly placed at the very center of U.S. strategic priorities the subordination of the rest of the core, in the version of the text leaked to the *New York Times* early in 1992.[2] This advocated as a central goal "discouraging the advanced industrialized nations from . . . even aspiring to a larger global or regional role." Waltz (2000) points out that despite protests at the time that the document was only a draft, its tenets guideed American policy. The chair of the interagency committee that produced the 1992 Grand Strategy, Paul Wolfowitz (2000), agrees with Waltz both that the 1992 strategy guidelines have guided U.S. policy and that they have been centered on creating a Pax Americana in the sense of maintaining the subordination of the allies.

The concept of world empires also plays a prominent role in WST. When Wallerstein first launched WST on the world in 1974, he argued that historically world-systems have taken two forms: world economies and world empires. At the start of volume 1 of Wallerstein's (1974) *The Modern World-System*, he draws this distinction very sharply. A world economy, he explains, is an "economic" unit, while a world empire is a "political" unit in which one political center dominates the entire world-system.

Chase-Dunn and Hall (1997) have modified Wallerstein's original conception, arguing that the concept of a world empire should be defined as one power dominating the core rather than the entire international division of labor involving the whole periphery as well. As they put it: "There have not been true 'world-empires' in the sense that a single state encompassed an entire trade network. . . . Rather, so-called world-empires have a relatively high degree of control over a relatively large proportion of a world system. The term we prefer because it is more precise, is core-wide empire" (p. 210).

They also acknowledge that there have been a series of attempts by capitalist powers precisely to achieve, through war, a capitalist world empire. They mention in particular the Napoleonic attempt and the German attempt in the first part of the twentieth century.

Furthermore, Chase-Dunn, in his book *Global Formation,* gives an even clearer and more analytically operational concept of a capitalist world empire: He says it is "the formation of a core state large enough to end the operation of the balance of power system" (1999:147). This is precisely the condition that has applied in the core since 1945. Thus, Chase-Dunn's reformulation sharply raises the question whether what we have today is precisely just such a world empire dominating the core.

Yet a consistent and distinctive feature of WST since 1974 has been the insistence of Wallerstein and Chase-Dunn on the theoretical impossibility of a capitalist world empire. Thus, even while Chase-Dunn defines a world empire as a condition in which a single core state suppresses the balance-of-power mechanism within the core—a very weak definition of a world empire—he does not acknowledge that the United States has effectively achieved this since 1945. And like Wallerstein and other mainstream WST authors, he resolutely argues that in the modern, capitalist world-system a corewide empire is theoretically impossible. We will therefore examine in some detail the arguments of WST authors as to why a capitalist world empire should be ruled out in the contemporary world.

WST authors reach this conclusion by various significantly different, though overlapping, routes. Wallerstein acknowledges that both world economies and world empires seek the extraction of economic surplus. But he says that they employ different modes of extraction—world empires use a statist tributary mode, while world economies use market exchange mechanisms. And since, for Wallerstein, market mechanisms are integral to capitalism, capitalist world empires are contradictions in terms. His conclusions as to the impossibility of a world empire are thus contained in his premises. He excludes ab initio the possibility that world empires could be other than tributary states. As he explains: "Political empires are a primitive means of economic domination. It is the social achievement of the modern world, if you will, to have invented the technology that makes it possible to increase the flow of the surplus from the lower strata to the upper strata, from the periphery to the center, from the majority to the minority, by eliminating the 'waste' of too cumbersome a political superstructure" (Wallerstein 1974:15–16).

In *Rise and Demise* Chase-Dunn and Hall make a similar point. They state: "Capitalists prefer a multicentric international political system. Hence the most powerful states in the modern inter-state system do not try to create a core-wide empire but seek rather to sustain the interstate system. This is because their main method of accumulation is commodity production, which contrasts with precapitalist systems, in which state power itself was the main basis of accumulation, through taxes or tribute. Phrased differently, capitalist states are qualitatively different from tributary states" (1997:33) This argument is reiterated in slightly different terms toward the end of their book, when they say that in the modern world-system, unlike earlier ones, a hegemonic power "never takes over the other core states. This is not merely a systematic difference in the degree of peak political concentration. The whole nature of the process of rise and fall is different in the modern world-system. The structural difference is primarily due to the relatively much greater importance that capital accumulation has in the modern world-system" (p. 210).

There is, indeed, a slightly different stress here than in Wallerstein, particularly in the implicit idea of Chase-Dunn and Hall that core capitalists will display solidarity against a world empire being established by a hegemon because it would restrict their freedom of movement as capitals and block their scope for exploiting interstate arbitrage, a point to which we will return.

But in Chase-Dunn's earlier book, *Global Formation,* he provides a much more specified and testable series of arguments as to why the modern capitalist core will successfully resist the establishment of a world empire. His argumentative route passes from an initial acceptance that a capitalist core-wide empire involving capitalist market exchange is possible in principle to deploying a series of arguments to the effect that overwhelmingly powerful forces are built into the structure of the modern world-system preventing this theoretical possibility from occurring. Some of these arguments derive resistances to world empire from structural characteristics of the interstate system in the modern world. Others focus on structural features of capitalism as an economic and social power system of production and on the derived interest perceptions of capitalists.

While Chase-Dunn presents his argumentation as a set of reasons why a corewide empire is impossible, we can reangle his claims to present them as the necessary preconditions for achieving a corewide empire. Some of these are preconditions in the interstate system; others are preconditions concerning capitalist impulses and interests. We can summarize these as follows:

A. Interstate system preconditions:

1. An empire-state would have to be strong enough to suppress the balance-of-power system and establish a unipolar organization of core politics.

2. It would have to find ways of preventing the diffusion of military technologies to other core states, to prevent them mounting a military challenge to the empire-state.

3. It would have to be able to suppress the possibility of other core states using their sovereignty to experiment and innovate to challenge the hegemon in the productive field.

4. It would have to be able to prevent countertendencies and movements toward world government from other core capitalists and states, perhaps in alliance with other, subordinate social groups.

B. Capitalist interest/incentive preconditions:

5. It would have to prevent international capitalists from ganging up to weaken its control over the international political economy in order to protect their own freedom of movement and of operations from its predatory demands.

6. It would have to convince international capitalists that the world empire would avoid undermining the basis of capitalist social domination within other core and periphery states, avoiding, for example, the possibility of transnational antisystemic movements challenging both the empire and capitalism.

Chase-Dunn's arguments are important. We can agree that many of them do indeed offer us a theory of the preconditions for a secure, long-term, corewide empire highlighting important internal tensions in any such project. But after examining each in turn, we will question some of the premises underlying Chase-Dunn's theorization.

Interstate Preconditions

The maintenance of unipolarity in the core, preventing other core states from allying against the world-empire project, is clearly a fundamental precondition. But Chase-Dunn's argument that the empire-state would have to prevent the diffusion of military technological knowledge across the core—something that Chase-Dunn considers impossible in the modern world—is surely one-sided. The empire-state would simply have to maintain at any one time a decisive technological lead sufficient to deter any challenge at any given time. This would indeed be a precondition but one linked as much to relative resources for military research and development as to capacities to block information flows in this area.

The third point in this area—suppression of effective competitive challenges in the productive sector from other sovereign core nation-states—is clearly fundamental. We can express this as the ability of the empire-state effectively to control socioeconomic developments and outcomes *within* juridically sovereign core states. Many would regard such a task as a contradiction in terms and thus a decisive basis for ruling out a world empire in which juridically sovereign states are retained in the core. We shall return to this subject later.

The fourth point—the world-state's ability to prevent the other core states from transforming the world dominated by a single empire-state into a world-state—is also, of course, fundamental.

Capitalist Interest/Incentive Preconditions

This set of arguments essentially rest on the idea that the interests/incentives of core capitals, including those of the incipient empire-state, would be radically opposed to any such world-empire project because of the systemic needs of capitalism as such. As Chase-Dunn and Hall put it in the quotation above, "capitalists *prefer* a multicentric international political system" (emphasis added). They do so for both economic and political reasons.

Freedom of international movement of capital is important both to exploit unevenness and as a decisive source of structural power over geographically immobile labor. Both depend on real competition between core states in the international political economy. This competition offers capital the chance for regime arbitrage across states; checks the ability of any state, not least the empire-state, to impose restrictions and extra fiscal and other burdens on capital; and drives labor constantly to accept restructuring of production within any state for fear of capital migration. Thus the maintenance of interstate competition is necessary for the preservation of the social domination of capital.

But the interstate system is not only a lever for negatively disciplining the working class and other subordinate groups in the economic system. It also provides a basis for subordination through providing strong "vertical" political identities connecting different social groups within a given state: identities based on the supposed priority of racial/ethnic, cultural, or religious bonds between social classes within the state overriding other social divisions. The resulting "state-worship" based on the state's supposed embodiment of the values of the ethnic, cultural, or religious community is a further source of social subordination to the rule of capitalism and one that depends on the maintenance of the authority and capacity of nation-states and thus of the interstate system. Insofar as a set of core nation-states seemed to be subordinated to an empire-state, there could be the risk of movements by subordinate classes across core states to mount challenges to the empire-state with potentially anticapitalist dynamics.

These arguments carry great force. But they rest quite strongly on two premises. The first is that world empires and sovereign states are necessarily mutually exclusive, polar opposites. And the second is that there is a structural tension between capitalists and states that a fortiori must be particularly strong as between capitalists and an empire-state. Both these premises are weak in the contemporary world.

A World Empire of Juridically Sovereign States?

The liberal tradition tends to place juridical relations on a higher plane than political relations. It thus assumes that a world empire in a political sense presupposes juridically imperial relations. The European empires of the first half of the twentieth century were indeed juridically anchored, and liberalism typically assumes that their replacement with a new juridical order of sovereign states encompassing the globe ended the possibility of an era of empires of any kind.

But this concept of an empire presupposes that an imperial relation is one of hierarchical command-compliance: a center gives an order, and the subordinates follow it. According to this concept, a juridical empire is simply the most formalized form of such a hierarchical command empire.

However, a systems approach to the organization of politics and political economies can offer us a very different, more indirect but also more robust and effective form of imperial control, one in which the empire-state has sufficient capacity to design the core as a system of interactions that systematically tends to produce outcomes reenforcing the power and interests of the empire-state.

Joseph Nye (1990) discusses this variant in his book *Bound to Lead.* One central consequence of Nye's concept is that it suggests the possibility that a world empire can be an interstate system and international political economy shaped and structured in ways that *generate empire-state-reinforcing agendas and outcomes.* We can call this an empire-system.

Let us take some simple examples of how an empire-system could work. If the empire-state can shape the geopolitical environment of other core states in such a way that their security is threatened in ways that require the military resources of the empire-state, these other core states will want what the empire-state wants. Or if the other core states' financial sectors' stability is bound up with the safety of their loans to empire-state companies and individuals whose prosperity in turn hinges on rising prices on the empire-state's securities markets, those other core states will want what the government of the empire-state wants: a priority for stability on the empire-state's financial markets. Or if other core states' capitals view their continuing expansion as dependent on further opening of "emerging markets" in the semiperiphery and if the most potent instrument for such opening is the empire-state's manipulation of the international monetary and financial regime, the other core states will want what the empire-state wants.

Of course, in reality, a corewide empire in contemporary conditions would not be exclusively an empire-system of this sort. It would also possess various instruments of command power and indeed of covert action and surveillance within the core to assure its dominance. But the main form of its dominance would be indirect, of the empire-system type, even if the empire-system rested on foundations of extraordinary military-political capacity and reach.

The Empire-State as Friend or Foe of Capital?

The idea that there is a deep antagonism between private business and the state runs deep in Anglo-American liberalism, and it has been radicalized in the neoliberal ideologies of the contemporary period. This preconception can lead one to think that capital would be especially hostile to an imperial superstate.

One referent for this supposed antagonism lies, of course, in the counterposition between private-property-market mechanisms of supplying goods and services and state provision of goods and services. But to define the capitalist state as first and foremost a provider of goods and services is, to say the least, somewhat one-sided. Another referent is the trade-off between state revenue and retained private income. But this can scarcely be seen as a radical opposition between state and capital given that the bulk of such taxation is spent on infrastructures necessary for the reproduction of the private sector itself.

There are, of course, very strong grounds for arguing the opposite case, namely, that in the contemporary core there is a symbiotic relationship between capitalist states and capitalist classes. Arrighi has stressed the closeness of this relationship, pointing out that markets are simply a mediating level in capitalist reproduction rather than an autonomous governing framework for capital accumulation. He emphasizes this with some striking formulations by Braudel on the relationships between capitalism and markets.

Braudel argues that the market should be seen as the "middle layer" of the modern economy; beneath it is the layer of production and subsistence, and above it is the layer that Braudel calls capitalism-or as he expresses it, the "anti-market." Braudel says of this: "Above [the lowest layer], comes the favoured terrain of the market economy, with its many horizontal communications between different markets: here a degree of automatic co-ordination usually links supply, demand and prices. Then alongside, or rather above this layer, comes the zone of the anti-market, where the great predators roam and the law of the jungle operates. This—today as in the past, before and after the industrial revolution—is the real home of capitalism" (Braudel 1982: 229–230). Elsewhere Braudel adds: "Capitalism only triumphs when it becomes identified with the state, when it is the state" (Braudel 1977:64–65)

In this context, it is perfectly possible to envisage bases for strong cooperation between the capitals of the core and an emergent empire-state:

1. If the empire-state presents itself as the champion of the most unrestricted rights of capital over labor within all the states of the core, this empire-state should expect a warm reception from capitals across the core.

2. If the empire-state offers itself as an instrument for expanding the reach of all core capitals into the semiperiphery and periphery, it should also expect a warm reception from capitals across the core.

3. If the empire-state offers a new model of capitalist organization that brings very large additional pecuniary rewards to leading social groups within other core states, it can hope to create a broad constituency of social support in the business classes across the core.

4. If the empire-state offers a mechanism for managing the world economy and world politics that is sufficiently cognizant of transcore business interests, the empire-state may be strongly preferred to the risks of institutionalized world government by core business and political elites.

In conclusion, insofar as Chase-Dunn is arguing that a precondition for a capitalist world empire is that the empire-state must be perceived by strategic sectors of corewide capital as its champion, we could agree with him. But insofar as he argues that this is a theoretical impossibility, we would disagree.

WST authors do not seem to have adequately explored the possibility that within the modern world-system a corewide empire is, under certain conditions, very much a theoretical possibility. Any state seeking to become an empire-state in contemporary conditions must have two key attributes:

1. It must have the resources to organize its empire as a system-empire, not just as a command (or juridical) empire.

2. It must have the capacity to rally strategic constituencies of corewide capital to its empire project.

Of course, the long-term sustainability of the world empire would require many other preconditions: The empire-state would have to use its extraordinary dominance to ensure the continued ascendancy of its capitals in key production sectors. It would have to assure its capacity to extract sufficient resources from the reproduction process to sustain its military-political reach and ascendancy, and it would be faced by the constant danger that its own public policy blunders could drag it down to defeat.

We will now turn to consideration of whether such an empire actually exists.

Current Intracore Dynamics: The United States as a New World Empire?

One of the most striking areas of weakness in Western social science analysis in the past quarter of a century has been its inability to reach anything like a stable, minimal agreement on the role and capacity of the United States in international relations. Within a decade opinion has swung wildly from images of the United States as being in terminal hegemonic decline to images of it as a colossus dominating the planet. And there has generally been no minimal agreement, even within each of the various intellectual paradigms, on the criteria for making analytical judgments on this topic.

Mainstream WST at least has had the merit of maintaining over decades a fairly clear and stable set of theoretical and analytical criteria for approaching this topic. It has ruled out the theoretical possibility of a world empire, it has provided clear criteria for identifying hegemonic status, and it has judged, on the basis of its criteria, that since the 1970s the United States has been in hegemonic decline.

The performance of American capitalism in the 1990s would also seem to provide WST with evidence that the United States is bouncing back and has entered a phase of hegemonic revival—something not excluded as a possibility in WST. In the capital-intensive information and telecommunication industries, which seem to be revolutionizing international economics, the United States seems to possess a substantial competitive advantage. And more than ever it seems to possess the military-political capacity to ensure the diffusion of its products in these fields on a global scale.

But our analysis in this chapter suggests that the United States occupies a place within the contemporary core qualitatively different from the place suggested by the concept of hegemon that mainstream WST advances. It possesses strong elements of what we have called a capitalist world empire.

We will focus here on some critical issues on which a judgment of the nature of U.S. dominance would depend.

International Social Coalition-Building

In pursuing its world-empire project over the past twenty years, the United States' business and political elites have sought to rally support as the champions not just of American business interests but of business interests and the strengthening of capitalism as a social system on a worldwide scale. This, we have argued, is a necessary condition for any capitalist world-empire project.

On the face of it, this task might seem a daunting one. After all, every European or Asian businessperson knows very well that the U.S. government aggressively supports its own businesses against the international competition wherever it can, a feature that has been particularly pronounced in the Clinton administration. Yet the United States has shown that it has very great capacities to present itself as the leader of global capitalist interests in four ways:

1. Being the champion of the rights of capital over labor

2. Strengthening core capital's expansion into the semiperiphery and periphery

3. Having bargaining power with the strongest non-American core businesses

4. Being able to resist pressures from other parts of the core for collegial, institutionalized forms of global government by offering core capitals sufficient scope for their own expansion within an empire-state framework of global governance

This last item has been perhaps the most sensitive area in the efforts of the United States to consolidate its global social coalition in the 1990s. Its operations in monetary, financial, and trade and investment policy at an international level have frequently aroused suspicion on the part of the capitals as well as the governments of other parts of the core that U.S. power is being used narrowly to favor its own capitals and clients. Rather than opting for a capitalist world empire, capitalists are, in the view of Chase-Dunn and Hall, more likely to accept moves toward world government, despite the risks these steps could involve of generating social movements challenging the capitalist market. Thus, in *Rise and Demise,* speaking of the weak forms of global governance supplied by the Concert of Europe, the League of Nations, and the United Nations, Chase-Dunn and Hall continue: "Though these weak forms of global governance did not much alter the pattern of hegemonic rise and fall in the cycle of world wars over the past 200 years, the spiralling strengthening of global governance might, if it continues, eventually lead to a world state that can effectively prevent warfare among core states" (1997: 240). But they underestimate the extent to which the world-empire project can remain an attractive alternative even for the capitalists of competitive core states. One of the reasons for that attractiveness is precisely given by Chase Dunn and Hall when they point out that a "world state would likely be dominated by the hegemony of global capital for a time. However, if the fascist alternative were avoided, it might undergo a reform process that would lead to global democratic socialism" (p. 241).

At a more immediate level, a powerful compensating factor mitigating resentments among other core capitals against U.S. economic nationalism has been the boom in the American economy itself, which has offered wide profitable opportunities for capitals across the core and which has thus eased international business tensions.

All these factors have enabled the United States to gain very broad social support from the business classes of the rest of the core for its world-empire project in the 1990s. No clearer demonstration of that is needed than the fact that the media empires of the core have been prepared to thematize the

American project not as a Pax Americana but as an agentless process of "globalization" that we must all accept and live within.

Progress toward an Empire-System

We have argued that in the contemporary world a corewide empire cannot be sustainable simply as a command empire, whereby the empire-state is reliant on carrots and sticks to maintain its dominance over the rest of the core. These command capacities should be confined largely to crisis situations while the normal functioning of the order leaves them in the background and can rely on the shaping of the power-relevant environments of other core powers to make them "want what the United States wants," in the phrase of Joseph Nye. We will now investigate the extent to which the United States has been able to advance and consolidate this empire-system in the 1990s.

Preventing Other Core Powers from Gaining Regional Geostrategic Autonomy

The Bush administration's 1992 Grand Strategy document was surely right to prioritize the risk of the Western European and Japanese parts of the core acquiring regional political autonomy. One very important dimension of this is geostrategic autonomy. This could be achieved through Germany leading Western Europe into a strategic security partnership with Russia and through Japan entering a strategic security partnership with China. Such partnerships would not, of course, be directed against the United States. They would simply give priority to the formation of a security community of the states involved. In the event of achieving this, the relevant core states would lose their geostrategic dependence on the U.S. relationships respectively with Russia and China.

Preventing European Political Unity

A very important and too little recognized feature of U.S. political dominance in Europe during the Cold War was the fact that NATO states of Western Europe was actually politically fragmented with each fragment having its main political link with the United States rather than with other Western European fragments. The European Community (EC) created the illusion that this was not so. This political fragmentation of Western Europe continued through the 1990s, but significant countertendencies are emerging, focused on a much more political Franco-German axis. The driving forces behind these tendencies lie, first, in the common commitment to the Euro and to give it an adequate political anchorage and, second, in the common concern about the vulnerability of Western European states to events in east central, southeastern, and Eastern Europe that they do not control (and which the United States exerts increasing influence over). These pressures are leading to efforts to build an inner core within the EU and to give that core (with or without Britain) some collective military capacity. These efforts show the Western European states to be a cohesive political group uniting around the Euro, turn the group toward being a Western European caucus within NATO, and and give it, through its collective military instruments, the potential to wield greater influence around Western Europe's immediate hinterland. A secure world empire would need to contain such pressures.

Preventing Pacific Regional Political-Economy Integration

The greatest challenge to a consolidated world empire in the Pacific region would come from the capacity of Japan and China and the ASEAN states to form a stable regional political-economy bloc, whether involving monetary and financial integration or a so-called free trade area (i.e., a zone of relatively protected investment and trade linkages). The United States, whose economic penetration of the region has been weak, has worked hard to prevent such a development. It succeeded triumphantly (with Western European support) in preventing Japan from establishing a regional financial and monetary shield in the autumn of 1997 and in subsequently greatly strengthening U.S. economic penetration of the region as a result of the financial crisis of 1997–1998 and the IMF (i.e., U.S. Treasury) policies in that crisis. But Japanese efforts to build such a financial and perhaps monetary shield have been relaunched in 2000, with support from China and with some initial success. Nevertheless, access to the U.S. market remains critical enough for so many of these economies that the United States retains substantial leverage at a political-economy as well as a military-political level.

Maintaining International Monetary and Financial Leverage

A U.S. world-empire project would have to combine the military-political dimension with continued dominance over international monetary and financial relations. Both Japan and Western Europe have taken steps, in different ways, to protect themselves from the U.S. use of economic statecraft in this field to exert pressure on the rest of the core. In the West European case, this has been attempted through the European Monetary System and its successor, the Euro. The final implementation of the Euro in July 2002 supplied a very substantial shield for Western Europe, which will be even more effective when it is combined with an integrated deep and liquid EU financial system. The strength of this shield is all the greater in that, despite all the talk of economic globalization, the European economy is becoming an increasingly closed one, less and less reliant on transatlantic trade. As far as Japan is concerned, it has not made any serious attempt to turn the yen into a significant international reserve currency or to construct a yen bloc as a shield against U.S. economic statecraft.

Gaining Strategic Control over the International Division of Labor

A fully fledged world-empire project would give the United States the capacity not just to use the market mechanism to assure its ascendancy in product and services markets but to acquire a more structured ascendancy in the markets of the rest of the core. Yet there is continued resistance to efforts in this direction from both Japan and Western Europe. One striking symptom of this is the instability and tension surrounding the functioning of the World Trade Organization. Another is the series of battles raging over biotechnology industries. A third is the very important conflicts over corporate governance issues and the capacity of foreign capitals to engage in hostile takeovers of important domestic companies. A fourth is the constant efforts of the United States to enlarge the reach of U.S. domestic jurisdiction over the political economies of the rest of the core.

Assuring U.S. Ascendancy in the Field of Production

The extraordinary advances made by the United States during the 1990s have received great impetus both from the macroeconomic dynamism of the U.S. economy in the context of continuing stagnation in Japan and Western Europe and from the perceived emergence of a new wave of growth-generating capital-intensive industries within the United States. These two factors have dazzled the capitalists of the rest of the core. But they may not be as solidly based as they seem.

First, there is now widespread agreement that the U.S. boom has been fed by some features that are not only unsustainable but potentially very dangerous: a strongly speculative boom on the stock market that itself has become an ever more central mechanism in the American economy; a huge growth in private indebtedness, with much of the debt tied to stock market speculation; and very large levels of U.S. international debt and U.S. trade deficits. A sudden shock could therefore swiftly transform the boom into a very savage financial crisis and deep recession with multiple consequences for the world economy.

Second, the supposed new growth motors of information industries and telecommunications may not have the long-term effects of sustained productivity gains necessary for what WST authors call the A-phase of a new K-wave, in other words, a new long boom anchored in a new U.S. hegemony in the key productive sectors. Studies of the impact of information technology on productivity do not indicate unequivocally its capacity to be the necessary growth motor for a new long boom.

Third, there are very real doubts about the new American business system of shareholder value. While this system is extremely attractive at a pecuniary level to business classes throughout the core and while it offers great opportunities for U.S. money capital to extend its sway over productive assets in other countries, there must be serious doubts as to whether it is an effective business system for generating long-term large investments in fixed capital, geared to sustaining U.S. innovation and productive ascendancy. If German and Japanese capitalisms can resist the seductions of dramatic short-term financial gains and maintain business systems more geared to long-term investment in innovations, they may well be able to remount a challenge to the United States in the productive sector quite rapidly.

Coping with Future Antisystemic Movements

Too often overlooked in assessments of American resurgence in the 1990s has been one absolutely central feature of the period: the collapse of communism. This has not simply led to a scramble for gain in the former Soviet bloc; it has given a unique accent to transnational class relations because it has resulted in the disorientation and disorganization of labor on an international scale. This has been a fundamental social basis for the extraordinary advance of the new Pax Americana or empire project.

That project's advance has required that the states and capitalist classes of the rest of the core find it relatively risk free to accent their efforts toward bandwagoning with the U.S. program of unfettered capitalism, American style. The weakness of labor has made that emphasis relatively easy to achieve. But in the event of a restabilization of labor and renewed pressure from that quarter, core and semiperiphery capitalist states will face a trade-off between making further adaptations toward the regime goals of the United States and making adaptations to the domestic pressures from labor, even if at the cost of disrupting U.S. regimes. A process can occur somewhat similar to the processes leading to the disintegration of the gold standard and free trade in the interwar period as states in Europe had to cope with the rise of labor then. And, of course, core and semiperiphery states can also use the risk of a challenge from labor as a way of resisting U.S. pressures to accept imperial regimes.

While a revival of the strength of labor may seem to many a fanciful prospect at this moment of postmodernist play and senses of endings, both strong sociological and economic bases for such a resurgence remain. In addition, very substantial resources of the most subversive strands of the modernist project are still available for challenging the narrow strip of liberal individualist universalism through which the current imperial project is ideologically legitimated. Such a revival of the challenge from labor could also be used by core powers to advance a program of more collegial and institutionalized world government against the unipolar, U.S.-governance instruments that have been unchallenged in the 1990s.

WST's historical theorization of intracore relations has been a very great scientific achievement. It provides us with a comprehensive research agenda on this topic, even if it underplays the radical differences between the hegemony of Britain and that of the United States, downgrades some central features of U.S. hegemonic capacities, and rules out too glibly the possibility of a contemporary capitalist world empire. Furthermore, the work of Arrighi contains many insights and leads on which to draw for developing a more adequate analysis of contemporary dynamics. And Chase-Dunn's and Hall's work has helped to transform WST's study of these issues from being a brilliant schema outlined by Wallerstein into a very serious scholarly research program.

Notes

1. WST authors have also noted and explored other cyclical patterns and regularities such as regularities of quantitative economic cycles—Kondratieff waves, with their A-phase of growth and their B-phase of depression. They link these K-waves with theories of cooperation/tension within the core and quantitative regularities in the cycles of core warfare. But we will not consider these issues here.

2. This was the 1992 Draft of the Pentagon Defense Planning Guidance.

References

Arrighi, Giovanni. 1994. *The Long Twentieth Century: Money, Power, and the Origins of Our Times.* London: Verso.

Braudel, Fernand. 1977. *Afterthoughts on Material Civilization and Capitalism*. Baltimore, MD: Johns Hopkins University Press.

———. 1982. *The Perspective of the World: Civilization and Capitalism, 15th–18th Century*. Berkeley, CA: University of California Press.

Brzezinski, Zbigniew. 1997. *The Grand Chessboard: American Primacy and Its Geostrategic Imperatives*. New York: Basic Books.

Chase-Dunn, C. 1999. *Global Formation: Structures of the World-Economy*. New York: Rowan and Littlefield.

Chase-Dunn, C. and T. Hall. 1997. *Rise and Demise: Comparing World-Systems*. Boulder, CO: Westview.

Gowan, P. 1999. *The Global Gamble*. London: Verso.

Kahler, M. 1995. *Regional Futures and Transatlantic Economic Relations*. New York: Council on Foreign Relations Press.

Nye, Joseph. 1990. *Bound to Lead: The Changing Nature of American Power*. New York: Basic Books.

Wallerstein, I. 1974. *The Modern World-System*. Vol. 1: *Capitalist Agriculture and the Origins of the European World-Economy in the 16th Century*. New York: Academic Press.

———. 1984. "The Three Instances of Hegemony in the History of the Capitalist World Economy." In *Current Issues and Research in Macrosociology*, edited by G. Lenski, International Studies in Sociology and Social Anthropology, vol. 37. Leiden, Netherlands: Brill.

Waltz, Kenneth N. 2000. "Globalization and American Power." *National Interest* 59:46–57.

Wolfowitz, Paul. 2000. "Remembering the Future." *National Interest* 59:35–45.

V | Global Social Movements

12

Gender and Globalization
Female Labor and Women's Mobilization

VALENTINE M. MOGHADAM

This chapter casts a gender perspective on globalization to illuminate its contradictory effects on women workers and on women's activism. Its scope is
global. The sources of data are UN publications, country-based data, publications of women's organizations, and the author's fieldwork. The chapter begins by examining the various dimensions of globalization—economic, political, and cultural—with a focus on their contradictory social-gender effects.
These include inequalities in the global economy and the continued hegemony of the core, the feminization of labor, the withering away of the welfarist, developmentalist state, the rise of identity politics and other forms of
particularism, the spread of concepts of human rights and women's rights,
and the proliferation of women's organizations and transnational feminist
networks. I argue that although globalization has had dire economic effects,
the process has created a new constituency—working women and organizing
women—that may herald a potent antisystemic movement. I also show that
the women's movement is not necessarily a heterogeneous and localized
amalgam of groups formed around noneconomic, identity, and personal issues. Rather, the global women's movement has emerged from and addresses
the contradictions of capitalist development and globalization. Globalization
studies should take account of female labor and of oppositional transnational
feminist networks.[1]

Defining Globalization

Globalization is a complex economic, political, cultural, and geographic process in which the mobility of capital, organizations, ideas, discourses, and peoples has taken on an increasingly global or transnational form. There is now
a prodigious literature on the subject from various disciplinary perspectives
(e.g., Sassen 1998; Gilpin 1999), but debates continue to rage on its origins,
dimensions, and consequences. The approach taken in this chapter is that

241

globalization is the latest stage of capitalism, that it is best understood in terms of various dimensions, and that its social-gender effects are variable. Economic globalization pertains to deeper integration and more rapid interaction of economies through production, trade, and (unregulated) financial transactions by banks and multinational corporations, with an increased role for the World Bank and the International Monetary Fund, as well as the more recent World Trade Organization. "Globalizers" include the international financial institutions, the U.S. Treasury, the major capitalist states, multinational corporations, and the transnational capitalist class (Sklair 2001; Steger 2002). Although the capitalist world-system has always been globalizing and there have been various waves of globalization (e.g., the 1870–1914 period, which is well documented), it is said that the trade, capital flows, and technological advances and transfers since the 1970s are more intensive and extensive than in earlier periods. In this respect the world-systems perspective is especially useful in identifying cycles and secular trends in the internationalization of capital. The cyclical processes include the rise and fall of hegemons, the Kondratieff waves, a cycle of warfare among core states, and cycles of colonization and decolonization. Secular trends include the long-term proletarianization of the world's workforce, growing concentration of capital in ever larger firms, and the increasing internationalization of investment and of trade (Chase-Dunn 1998:50–53). To this we can add the internationalization of political structures and the globalization of social movements (see, e.g., Smith, Chatfield, and Pagnucco 1997; Keck and Sikkink, 1998; Moghadam 2000, 2005).

Political globalization refers in part to an increasing trend toward multilateralism, in which the UN plays a key role, national nongovernmental organizations (NGOs) act as watchdogs over governments, and international NGOs increase their activities and influence. Some have called this the making of a global civil society (Boli and Thomas 1997; Anheier, Glasius, and Kaldor 2001). Political scientists and sociologists have pondered the prospects of the nation-state and national sovereignty in a context of regionalization and globalization in which international financial institutions have increasing power over national economies and state decision-making. There is, however, disagreement about the relative power of national states and multinational corporations (e.g., Doremus et al. 1998).

Cultural globalization refers to worldwide cultural standardization—as in "Coca Colonization" and "McDonaldization"—but also to postcolonial cultures, cultural pluralism, and "hybridization." The various aspects of globalization have promoted growing contacts between different cultures, leading partly to greater understanding and cooperation and partly to the emergence of transnational communities and hybrid identities (Pieterse 1992). But globalization also has hardened the opposition of different identities. This has taken the form of, inter alia, reactive movements such as fundamentalisms, which seek to recuperate traditional patterns, including patriarchal gender relations, in reaction to the "Westernizing" trends of globalization. Various forms of identity politics are the paradoxical outgrowth of globalization.

Consistent with the contradictory nature of globalization, the impact on women has been mixed. One feature of economic globalization has been the generation of jobs for women in export processing, free trade zones, and world market factories. This has enabled women in many developing countries to earn and control income and to break away from the hold of patriarchal structures, including traditional household and familial relations. However, much of the work available to women is badly paid, demeaning, or insecure; moreover, women's unemployment rates are higher than men's almost everywhere (Moghadam 1995). The feminization of poverty is another unwelcome feature of economic globalization. Worse still is the apparent growth in trafficking in women or the migration of prostituted women.

The weakening of the nation-state and the national economy similarly has contradictory effects. On the one hand, the withering away of the welfarist, developmentalist state as a result of the neoliberal economic policy has led to the withdrawal or deterioration of state-run social services. Along with the contraction of the public-sector wage bill and limited employment opportunities, this has had adverse effects on women in core but especially semiperipheral regions. On the other hand, state withdrawal from many economic and social activities, in tandem with the new global discourse of democratization, has opened up possibilities for women's enhanced participation in civil society, NGOs, and the business sector. While this may be seen in some respects as entirely consistent with the neoliberal agenda, an unintended consequence is the raising of women's gender and social consciousness and their capacity for self-organization and mobilization.

Indeed, the globalization of concepts and discourses of human rights and of women's rights, and the activities of international NGOs, are emboldening women and creating space for women's organizations to grow at both national and global levels. In turn, this represents a countertrend to the particularisms and the identity politics of contemporary globalization. Thus, at least one positive aspect of globalization may be identified—the proliferation of women's movements at the local level, the emergence of transnational feminist networks working at the global level, and the adoption of international conventions such as the Convention on the Elimination of All Forms of Discrimination Against Women and the Beijing Declaration and Platform for Action of the Fourth World Conference on Women.

In world-systems terms, the secular trends of proletarianization and of the globalization of social movements have gender dynamics. One is the process of female proletarianization and the growing importance of female productive and reproductive activity in capital accumulation processes since the 1970s; another is the globalization of the women's movement and the proliferation of transnational women's organizations. Female proletarianization and women's political mobilization are linked. Just as the labor movement historically emerged from the involvement of workers in social production and the exploitation they experienced, so the feminist movement has emerged from women's involvement in the labor force and from the exploitation and inequality they experience at the workplace and in society more broadly. Historically, trade unions and communist and socialist parties were the organizational expressions of the labor movement. The social movement of women has produced women's organizations; moreover, in a reflection of their growing incorporation in the paid labor force, women are also becoming increasingly involved in unions. If the emergence of the workers' movement represented the contradictions of early capitalism, the emergence of the global women's movement and of transnational women's organizations is indicative of the contradictions of late capitalism in an era of globalization.

Economic Globalization and Female Labor

In this section we consider the broad socioeconomic context in which women have been entering the labor force. This sets the stage for the subsequent discussion of women's involvement in unions and in feminist organizations—both of which are organized responses to women's socioeconomic and political conditions.

The trade, capital flows, and technological advances that characterize economic globalization entail new economic policies and production systems with important implications for national economies, such as skill requirements, labor market regulations, education policy, and employment. The new "flexible" or "post-Fordist" production systems are guided by the current neoliberal economic orthodoxy that also entails "structural adjustment policies" for peripheral countries as the only solution to economic crisis and the only path to economic growth. Structural adjustment policies, which aim to

balance budgets and increase competitiveness through trade and price liberalization, include reduction of the public-sector wage bill and growth of
the private sector, privatization of social services, encouragement of foreign
investment, and the production of goods and services for export ("trad-
ables") through "flexible" labor processes. The international financial institutions, especially the World Bank and the International Monetary Fund, have
been the chief instigators of this free-market policy shift. Structural adjustment policies were first implemented in some African and Latin American
countries as a result of the debt crisis of the early 1980s. They were extended
to other countries in the mid-1980s and were adopted in a number of Middle
Eastern countries, such as Jordan and Egypt, in the 1990s (Moghadam
1998).

Structural adjustment has been a very controversial topic in the development studies literature; some development economists find that it has
worked in some places but not in others, while other economists have regarded the entire turn to be a disaster for national sovereignty and for people's well-being. The now classic UNICEF study *Adjustment with a Human Face*
(Cornia, Jolly, and Stewart 1987) highlighted the social costs of adjustment
and provided empirical evidence of the deterioration of social conditions in
10 countries undergoing adjustment. Subsequent studies found that there
have been differential effects on the various categories of the poor, including
the "chronic" poor, "borderline" poor, and the "new" or "working poor." The
feminist development literature has been especially critical, charging structural adjustment with carrying out its objectives on the backs of the poor and
especially on poor women. Women have had to assume extra productive and
reproductive activities in order to survive the austerities of adjustment and
stabilization policies, including higher prices, and to compensate for the
withdrawal or reduction of government subsidies of food and services (Elson
1991; Sparr 1994; Peterson 2003).

The adverse effects of economic globalization have been felt within all regions and especially by their respective labor forces. With increased trade,
the prices of imported goods often compete with the prices of domestic products, forcing domestic capitalists to attempt to cut labor costs. In the developed countries, as plants relocate to sites elsewhere in search of cheaper
costs of labor and production, jobs disappear and wages erode in the declining industrial sectors. As the developed countries shift from manufacturing
to high-tech services, blue-collar unemployment grows, along with the expansion of part-time and temporary jobs. This has come at the expense of
the kind of stable employment that men came to expect during "the golden

age of capitalism" (Marglin and Schor 1990), or the A-phase of the postwar capitalist expansion, when world real GDP grew by 4.6 percent during 1964–1973. During the more recent B-phase, developing countries saw a shift from internally oriented to externally oriented growth strategies and the shrinkage of large public sectors and nationalized industries. The result has been an expansion of informal sectors, self-employment, and temporary employment. In most of the former socialist world, restructuring has led to loss of output, the creation of unemployment, and increased poverty. In both developing and developed regions, the stable, organized, and mostly male labor force has become increasingly "flexible" and "feminized." Keeping the cost of labor low has encouraged the growth of demand for female labor, while declining household budgets have led to an increase in the supply of job-seeking women.

Through institutions such as the transnational corporation and the state, the world-economy generates capital largely through the exploitation of labor, but it is not indifferent to the gender and ethnicity of that labor. Gender and racial ideologies have been deployed to favor white male workers and exclude others, but they have also been used to integrate and exploit the labor power of women and of members of disadvantaged racial and ethnic groups in the interest of profit-making. In the current global environment of open economies, new trade regimes, and competitive export industries, global accumulation relies heavily on the work of women, both waged and unwaged, in formal sectors and in the home, in manufacturing, and in public and private services. This phenomenon has been termed the "feminization of labor." Guy Standing (1989, 1999) has hypothesized that the increasing globalization of production and the pursuit of flexible forms of labor to retain or increase competitiveness, as well as changing job structures in industrial enterprises, favor the "feminization of employment" in the dual sense of an increase in the numbers of women in the labor force and a deterioration of work conditions (labor standards, income, and employment status). Women have been gaining an increasing share of many kinds of jobs, but this has occurred in the context of a decline in the social power of labor and growing unemployment. Moreover, women's labor market participation has not been accompanied by a redistribution of domestic, household, and child care responsibilities. Women have been disadvantaged in the new labor markets, in terms of wages, training, and occupational segregation. They are also disproportionately involved in forms of employment increasingly used to maximize profits: temporary, part-time, casual, and home-based work. Generally speaking, the situation is better or worse for women depending on the type of state and the strength of the economy. Women workers in the welfare states of northern Europe fare best, followed by women in other core economies. In Eastern Europe and the former Soviet Union, the economic status of working women changed dramatically for the worse following the collapse of communism. In much of the developing world, a class of women professionals and workers employed in the public sector and in private services has certainly emerged due to rising educational attainment, changing aspirations, economic need, and the demand for relatively cheap labor. However, vast numbers of economically active women in the developing world lack formal training, work in the informal sector, have no access to social security, and live in poverty.

Proletarianization and Professionalization: Industry and Services

Let us begin this section on a definitional note. In my usage, *proletarianization* is a reference to the formation of a female working class (as distinct from a relationship to male workers). I distinguish this from the entry of women into the professions, which is characteristic of the middle class. Proletarianization and professionalization coincide with the involvement of working women in trade unions and feminist organizations, including transnational feminist networks.

As world markets have expanded, a process of female proletarianization has taken place. In developing countries—especially in Southeast and East Asia, parts of Latin America and the Caribbean, and Tunisia and Morocco—vast numbers of women have been drawn into the labor-intensive and low-wage industries of textiles, garments, sportswear, electronics, and pharmaceuticals that produce for the home market and for export. The surge in women's waged employment in developing countries began in the 1970s, following an earlier period of capitalist development and economic growth that was characterized by the displacement of labor and craft work, commercialization of agriculture, and rural-urban migration (see Boserup 1970). Some have called the marginalization of women "housewife-ization" (Mies 1986); others have described it as the "U pattern" of female labor force participation in early modernization.[2]

During the 1970s, it was observed that export-processing zones along the U.S.-Mexican border and in Southeast Asia, established by transnational corporations to take advantage of low labor costs in developing countries, were hiring mainly women (Elson and Pearson 1981; Nash and Fernandez-Kelly 1983; Lim 1985). By the early 1980s, it was clear that the new industrialization in what was then called the Third World was drawing heavily on women workers. Many studies by women-in-development specialists and socialist feminists centered on the role played by the available pool of relatively cheap female labor. Gender ideologies emphasizing the "nimble fingers" of young women workers and their capacity for hard work, especially in the Southeast Asian economies, facilitated the recruitment of women for unskilled and semiskilled work in labor-intensive industries at wages lower than men would accept, and in conditions that unions would not permit. In Latin America, women entered the labor force at a time when average wages were falling dramatically. Around the world, women's share of total industrial labor rarely exceeds 30–40 percent, but "the percentage of women workers in export-processing factories producing textiles, electronics components and garments is much higher, with figures as high as 90% in some cases" (Pearson 1992:231). One study concluded that "exports of manufactures from developing countries have been made up in the main of the kinds of goods normally produced by female labor: industrialization in the post-war period has been as much *female* led as *export* led" (Joekes/INSTRAW 1987:81). This was certainly true of East and Southeast Asia, and the geographic scope of female proletarianization subsequently expanded. The feminization of labor continued throughout the recessionary 1980s and into the 1990s, encompassing countries like Bangladesh, which had one of the largest increases in the share of women participating in the labor force—from 5 percent in 1965 to 42 percent in 1995 (UNDP 1999). In 1978 the country had 4 garment factories; by 1995 it had 2,400. These factories employed 1.2 million workers, 90 percent of whom were women under the age of 25 (United Nations 1999).

Feminization occurred also in public services, where throughout the world women's share has grown to 30–50 percent—at a time when public-sector wages, like industrial wages, have been declining. In Iran, Egypt, and Turkey, women's share of public-service employment (including jobs as teachers and university professors in public schools and state universities, nurses and doctors in state hospitals, and workers and administrators across the ministries) has increased. This has occurred at a time when salaries have eroded tremendously and more men are gravitating toward the more lucrative and expanding private sector (Moghadam 1998).

As world trade in services grew and global firms engaged in outsourcing, more women became involved in various occupations and professions of the services sector. Women around the world have made impressive inroads into professional services such as law, banking, accounting, computing, and architecture; tourism-related occupations; and the information services, including offshore airline booking, mail order, credit cards, word processing for publishers, telephone operators, and all manner of data entry and teleservices. The world trade in services also favors women's labor migration, in contrast to the demand for male manufacturing workers during the earlier periods of industrialization in Europe and the United States. Mexican, Central American, and Caribbean women have migrated to the United States to work as nurses, nannies, or domestics; Filipinas and Sri Lankans have gone to neighboring countries as well as to the Middle East to work as waitresses, nurses, nannies, or domestics; Argentine women have gone to Italy to work as nurses; and an increasing number of Moroccan, Tunisian, and Algerian women have migrated alone to work in various occupations in France, Italy, and Spain.

The proletarianization and professionalization of women have cultural repercussions and sometimes entail backlashes and gender conflicts. In some core countries, working women have often encountered serious forms of sexual harassment. In the semiperipheral countries of the Middle East, the increasing participation of women in the labor force was accompanied in the 1980s by subtle and overt pressures on them to conform to religious dictates concerning dress. Hence in Egypt many professional women came to don modest dress and to cover their head. In the earlier stage of the Islamist movement, the influx of women in the work force raised fears of competition with men, leading to calls for the redomestication of women, as occurred immediately after the 1979 Iranian revolution. In the current stage, with the labor force participation of women now a fait accompli, Islamists in Turkey, Iran, Egypt, Sudan, and Yemen are not calling on women to withdraw from the labor force—indeed, among their female adherents are educated and employed women from the lower middle class—but they do insist on veiling, on spatial and functional segregation, and on the concentration of women in "appropriate" occupations only, such as providing education and health services for women and girls. Only the most determined and secular women resist these pressures as they seek employment in various types of public and private services.

The surge in women's employment is characteristic not only of semiperipheral countries. In 16 European countries, the increase in the number of women in the labor force over the period 1983–1991 was quite dramatic, whereas it was relatively modest for men. In six countries the number of employed men actually fell over the period, most significantly by 3.4 percent in Belgium (*Employment Observatory* 1994:11–14). During the 1990s, the Nordic countries, including Finland, had the highest rate of employment among women, with North America following close behind. Moreover, the feminization of labor denotes not only the influx of women into relatively low paying jobs but the growth of part-time and temporary work among *men*, especially in New Zealand, the United Kingdom, and the Netherlands, mainly in retail trade, hotels and catering, banking, and insurance (United Nations 1991:190). Indeed, in the Netherlands, men's part-time work in 1992 was as high as 13.4 percent of total male employment, up from 5.5 percent in 1979.

The Informal Sector, the Income Gap, Unemployment

At the same time that women have been entering the formal labor force in record numbers in the core countries, much of the observed increase in female labor force participation in semiperipheral countries has occurred in the informal sectors of the economy.[3] In much of sub-Saharan Africa, more than one-third of women in nonagricultural activities work in the urban informal sector. Rates are as high as 65-80 percent in Senegal, Benin, Zambia, and Gambia (United Nations 1999). Rates of urban informal activity among women are also very high in parts of Peru, Indonesia, and Iran. Unregistered and small-scale urban enterprises, home-based work, and self-employment fall into this category, and they include an array of commercial and productive activities. In the urban areas of developing countries, many formal jobs have become "informalized" as employers seek to increase "flexibility" and lower labor and production costs through subcontracting, as Beneria and Roldan (1987) showed in their study of Mexico City. Drawing on existing gender ideologies regarding women's roles, their attachment to family, and the perceived lower value of their work, subcontracting arrangements encourage the persistence of home-based work (Cinar 1994; Boris and Prügl 1996; Peterson 2003). Many women accept this kind of work—with its insecurity, low wages, and absence of benefits—as a convenient form of income generation that allows them to carry out domestic responsibilities and care for children. As Fernandez-Kelly (1994) has noted, employers seeking competitive edges in domestic and international markets tap not only into cheap labor, which is both female and male, but also into a substratum of labor, predominately female, that is outside the formal sector.

The social relations of gender account for the pervasive income gap between men and women workers, a gap that is detrimental to women but lucrative to employers. On average women earn 75 percent of men's wages (UNDP 1995:36), with Sweden, Sri Lanka, and Vietnam at the upper and more egalitarian end (90 percent) and Bangladesh, Chile, China, Cyprus, South Korea, the Philippines, and Syria at the lower and more unequal end (42–61 percent). The gender-based income gap is found mainly in the private sector, whereas the public sector tends to reward women more equitably. Explanations for the gender gap are varied. Some point out that the gender difference in the income gap is based on lower education and intermittent employment among women workers. Others emphasize the role of gender bias. For example, in Ecuador, Jamaica, and the Philippines, women earn less than men despite higher qualifications, a problem that is especially acute in the private sector (World Bank 1995:45). Labor market segmentation along gender lines perpetuates the income gap. For example, in the computing and information-processing sectors, the majority of high-skilled jobs go to male workers, while women are concentrated in the low-skilled ones (Pearson and Mitter 1993:50). In fact, all these explanations are true and are consistent. If "the uneven distribution of rewards has been the necessary pendant of capital accumulation" (Hopkins and Wallerstein 1996:4), then it is the deployment of female labor along the commodity chains that guarantees a supply of relatively cheap labor, along with the desired higher profit margins.

Considering the social relations of gender and the function of gender ideologies, it should come as no surprise that despite women's key role in the global economy unemployment rates for women are very high. Global unemployment is partly a function of the nature of global economic restructuring itself, which has entailed massive retrenchment of labor in many semiperipheral countries, the former socialist countries now undergoing marketization, and the core countries. Unemployment rates are especially high in Algeria, Jamaica, Jordan, Egypt, Morocco, Nicaragua, Poland, the Slovak Republic, and Turkey (World Bank 1995:29)—but they are often higher for women than for men (Moghadam 1995, 2001). In many developing countries unemployed women are new entrants to the labor force who are seeking but not finding jobs (as in Egypt, Iran, Turkey, and Chile, where women's unemployment was as high as 30 percent in the 1990s, compared with 10 percent for men). In certain countries where restructuring has occurred in enterprises employing large numbers of women, or in export sectors that have lost markets, the unemployment rates of women may also reflect job losses by previously employed women. This was the case in Malaysia in the mid-1980s, Vietnam in the late 1980s, Poland, Bulgaria, and Russia in the early 1990s, and Morocco, Tunisia, and Turkey in the late 1990s. The Asian financial crisis of the late 1990s entailed further job and income losses for women workers, especially in South Korea, Thailand, and Indonesia. In South Korea, women lost jobs at twice the rate of men, even though before the crisis, they had been the preferred labor supply with an unemployment rate half that of men (United Nations 1999).

In some cases, women experience job loss as a result of technological advances in the workplace. As has been noted above, many enterprises producing textiles and electronics, especially those for export, rely heavily on women workers. And yet as more sophisticated technology is used to produce these goods, women workers tend to be replaced by men or recruited at a slower pace, as appears to have been the case in the Mexican maquiladoras (Sklair 2002) and in the textiles industries of Spain and Italy. In all regions, high unemployment represents the downside of economic globalization, especially for women workers, who must contend with not only the class biases but also the gender biases of free-market economics. The feminization of unemployment, therefore, is as much a characteristic of the global economy as is the feminization of labor.

The analysis thus far may raise questions about the contingency versus permanence of the female labor force and the possibility that female labor remains a reserve army of labor. Because the mass incorporation of women as proletarians and professionals is a relatively recent phenomenon, it is perhaps too soon to tell definitively.[4] However, I would argue that the incorporation of female labor is indeed a secular trend, due to the structural requirements of the capitalist world-system in the era of globalization and due also to women's own aspirations. The analysis also raises question about whether what I have been describing can be regarded as proletarianization. To what extent is informalization a part of the secular trend of proletarianization, and to what extent is it a countertrend? The answer depends in part on how one defines proletarianization—in its strict, classic sense or in a broader sense. Still, although informalization is certainly a characteristic of the world labor force, there has been a definite decline in the share of agricultural labor as a proportion of the total labor force. Moreover, there has been a movement of women out of agriculture and into industry and services, in tandem with urbanization.

Structural Adjustment and Women

In the early 1980s, critical voices argued that adjustment and stabilization programs in developing countries were having particularly adverse effects on women. Da Gama Santos (1985) recognized that the gender division of labor and the differential positions of women and men in the spheres of production and reproduction would mean that the new policy shifts would lead to very different outcomes for women and men, although these gender differences would differ further by social class and by economic sector. Others have found that the burden of adjustment falls on the urban poor, the working class, and women (Elson 1991; Sparr 1994).

In many ways, the women of the working class and urban poor have been the "shock absorbers" of neoliberal economic policies. Structural adjustment policies—with their attendant price increases, elimination of subsidies, social service decreases, and introduction or increase of "user fees" for "cost recovery" in the provision of schooling and health care—heighten the risk and vulnerability of women and children in households in which the distribution of consumption and the provision of health care and education favor men or income-earning adults. Structural adjustment has caused women to bear most of the responsibility of coping with increased prices and shrinking incomes, since in most instances they are responsible for household budgeting and maintenance. Rising unemployment and reduced wages for men in households have led to increased economic activity on the part of women and children. This has occurred also in households headed by women, an increasing proportion of all households in most regions. As discussed in the previous section, household survival strategies have included increases in the unpaid as well as paid labor of women. In the Philippines, mean household size increased as relatives pooled their resources (Chant 1995). One study found that the combined effects of economic crisis and structural adjustment in Peru led to a significant increase in poverty, with worse outcomes for households headed by women (Tanski 1994). Structural adjustment policies and other forms of neoliberalism are said to be a major factor behind the "feminization of poverty" (see Moghadam 1997).

Summary

My argument may be summarized as follows. Women have been incorporated into the global economy as a source of relatively cheap labor, and the social-gender effects of economic globalization have been mixed. The simultaneous emergence and expansion of formal and informal employment among women should be understood in terms of the cyclical processes and secular trends in capitalist development and expansion and the necessary unevenness of those processes. At a mesolevel of analysis, we can understand trends in female employment and unemployment in terms of labor market stratification, various management strategies to extract surplus value or increase profitability, and (during the 1980s and 1990s) the depressed status of unions. At the macrolevel of analysis, the capitalist world-economy is maintained by *gendered* labor, with definitions of skill, allocation of resources, occupational distribution, and modes of remuneration shaped by asymmetrical gender relations. Moreover, gender ideologies define the roles and rights of men and women and the relative value of their labor. But the effects of this incorporation have not been uniformly negative, for there have been unintended consequences of women's economic participation. Tiano (1994) and Kim (1997) provide detailed accounts of how women workers in the Mexican maquilas and in a South Korean free export zone, respectively, accommodate and resist the dominating forces of global capitalism and patriarchy. Others have shown that the entry of women into the labor force in such large numbers has important implications for changes in gender relations and ideologies within the household and the larger society and for women's gender consciousness and activism (Safa 1996). The emergence of working-class consciousness and collective action during the nineteenth and early twentieth centuries has its parallel in the emergence of gender consciousness and collective action in the late twentieth century and into the twenty-first.

The Women's Movement and Globalization

It should come as no surprise, then, that the massive entry of women into the workforce around the world, whether as professionals or as proletarians, has coincided with the political mobilization of women and the expansion of women's organizations of all types. In this section I discuss what are perhaps the two most significant types of women's mobilization: as workers (in unions) and as critics of neoliberalism and inequality in transnational feminist networks.

Women and Unionization

In a number of advanced industrialized countries (the United States, Australia, the Nordic countries) women are the largest growing union constituency. In Japan, the Asian Women Workers' Center studies and promotes the rights of women workers throughout East and Southeast Asia and publishes a newsletter called *Resource Materials on Women's Labor in Japan*. In Taiwan the Grassroots Women Workers Centre, established in 1988, engages in various activities, including defense of the rights of immigrant women workers, and publishes a newsletter called *Female Workers in Taiwan*. Its Spring 1994 newsletter stated that the center intended "to provide opportunities for factory women and family subcontractors to reform the male-dominated workers' union, and to develop women workers' unions and workers' movements through the promotion of feminism." Similar activities and goals are shared by the Committee for Asian Women in Hong Kong. In Morocco, feminist groups came to the assistance of factory women who went on strike over sexual harassment and faced expulsion. In Guatemala, women workers at an export shirt-making factory won a union contract, the first in a Guatemala maquiladora.[5] In India, the Self-Employed Women's Association operates as a trade union and a consciousness-raising feminist organization. In Israel, Arab women workers ignored by the Histadrut formed the Arab Women Workers Project.

In the Middle East and North Africa, the involvement of women in paid employment has resulted in the politicization of women and of gender issues, but women have also responded by joining unions, forming their own organizations, and engaging in collective action. In Tunisia, the National Commission on Working Women was created in July 1991 within the Tunisian General Federation of Workers. The commission has 27 branches throughout Tunisia and carries out surveys and studies pertaining to women and the workplace. In Morocco, a Roundtable on the Rights of Workers was organized in 1995 by the Democratic League of Women's Rights, and a committee structure was subsequently formed, consisting of 12 participating organizations. The group sought to revise the labor code to take into account women's conditions, to include domestic workers in the definition of wage workers and the delineation of their rights and benefits, to set the minimum work age at 15, and to provide workers on maternity leave with full salary and a job-back guarantee. In November 1995, some 500 women textile workers employed by the Manufacture du Maroc factory outside Rabat went on strike for two weeks to protest "repeated violence" against several women employees. This included the arbitrary dismissal of the general secretary of the factory's union of women workers, her subsequent rape by a foreman, and the firing of 17 women workers who protested the union leader's dismissal and rape. Morocco's Association of Democratic Women then set out to "mobilize human rights organizations and all the women's organizations" in defense of the women workers. The incident shows not only the vulnerability of women at the workplace but also the capacity of women workers to fight in defense of their rights and the ability of the feminist organizations to mobilize support for women workers. Moroccan feminist organizations also spearheaded a petition drive to seek the reform of the country's Islamic family law, which they saw as inhibiting women's social participation, and the implementation of the Beijing Platform for Action. Their 10-year-long campaign succeeded in late 2003.

Various transnational advocacy networks have emerged to support women workers. One is Women Working Worldwide, based in Manchester, England, which has links with women worker groups in Central America and in South and Southeast Asia. Another is IRENE (International Restructuring Education Network Europe), based in Tilburg, Holland, which organizes educational seminars for unions from around the world and disseminates a newsletter. The Women's International Committee for Economic Justice is a network of feminist organizations and networks that monitors the status of women workers in light of neoliberal economic policies; it advocates for the reform of global governance and calls on governments to implement the labor standards and social rights enshrined in international conventions.

Historically, the labor movement has been constituted largely by men, and the culture of the labor movement and of unions has been rather masculine. In many countries, particularly in northern Europe, Italy, Australia, and North America, union membership is taking on a female face (Eaton 1992; Hastings and Coleman 1992). In recent years, women have made their way into positions of power in Australian trade unions at a time when overall union membership began to decline. The numbers of women on the national peak council, the Australian Council of Trade Unions, rose from zero to one-third; in the State of South Australia the three major white-collar unions (teachers, nurses, public servants) are all currently led by women. All these gains have been made since the mid-1980s (Franzway 1994). In Canada, where 31 percent of women workers (and 38% of men workers) were unionized in 1992 (Briskin 1999), women's committees have succeeded not only in bringing benefits to women workers but in bringing "increased energy" to unions such as the Ontario Public Service Employees Union (Briskin 1998: 24). According to Briskin, "Canada has a strong movement of union women, and a vibrant autonomous women's movement," which have "successfully pressured the unions to take up the issues of childcare, abortion, sexual harassment, pay equity, affirmative action and employment equity, etc.— as women's issues and as union issues" (Briskin 1999:7). At least one union, the Federation of Women Teachers' Associations of Ontario, is a women-only organization (Brisken 1993). Denmark can also boast the Danish Women Workers' Union, KAD.

In global terms, the highest union density is found in northern Europe— Denmark, Finland, Norway, and Sweden—where women's participation as workers and as union officials is the greatest. In those countries, union density is very high in community, social, and personal services (68–87%), in trade, restaurants, and hotels (47-49%), and in manufacturing (80-100%), in both the public and private sectors. Women are making up an increasing share of union membership, especially in services, with the most impressive figures found in Denmark. Danish women represent 42 and 62 percent of the two main union federations; they account for 30 and 39 percent of the delegates to the union congress and 13 and 41 percent of members of leading committees, as well as 10 and 30 percent of leaders of individual unions (see Hastings and Coleman 1992; Klausen 1997). On at least one occasion that I know of during the 1990s, the Danish labor movement sent an all-women delegation to the annual Congress of the International Labour Organization in Geneva. In Finland during the 1990s women constituted 45 percent of the membership of one of the two labor confederations (SAK); they also made up about 37.5 percent of delegates to the SAK congress and 40 percent of the union council. The proportions of women in union leadership positions also increased in Germany, Portugal, Italy, the Netherlands, France, and England.

The growth of women's involvement in paid employment and in national-level unions has resulted in greater interest in women workers by the international trade unions. The International Confederation of Free Trade Unions (ICFTU) and the Public Services International (PSI) have active women's departments—and now, so does the AFL-CIO of the United States. Both the PSI and the ICFTU attend the annual meetings of the UN's Commission on the Status of Women. Their statements usually describe the exploitative work conditions that many women face, the dangers of "free trade," and the need for implementation of International Labor Organization labor standards and other conventions on worker rights, human rights, and women's rights. The PSI has a comprehensive Web site called WomeNet, which contains news and data about working women around the world. The theme of the ICFTU's Women's Conference, held in May 1999 in Rio de Janeiro, was "Working Women in the 21st Century: Demanding our Space, Taking our Place." In national unions, international unions, and feminist organizations (see below), women respond to the opportunities and the constraints of the globalization process, making demands on employers, states, and the international financial and trade institutions.

Transnational Feminist Networks

Contemporary women's movements constitute one of the most prodigious areas of feminist research in the disciplines of sociology and political science. Jaquette (1994) shows how the women's movement in Latin America was centrally involved in the democratic transitions. India's dynamic women's movement and myriad women's organizations have long been the subject of scholarly and political inquiry, with valuable studies published by Indian scholars and by Western scholars. I have researched the emergence of women's organizations in the Middle East and North Africa (Moghadam 1998, chap. 9). Many studies have sought to explain the rise of the women's movement and of women's organizations in terms of growing female educational attainment and participation in the paid labor force, as well as in terms of the contours of political cultures. Few have examined the rise of transnational feminist networks in an era of globalization (but see Stienstra 1994; Moghadam 1996, 2000). In my view, the emergence of transnational feminism —notwithstanding cultural, class, and ideological differences among the women of the world—is the logical result of the existence of a capitalist world-economy in an era of globalization and the universal fact of gender inequality.

International feminism has existed for more than 100 years. International women's organizations have been in existence for decades, and links were established among women's movements in various countries in the early part of this century. Examples are the Women's International League for Peace and Freedom, the International Women's Council, the Women's International Democratic Federation, and the International Federation of Business and Professional Women. However, *international* is not the same as *transnational*, which suggests a conscious crossing of national boundaries and a superseding of nationalist orientations. The phase of feminist organizing that began in the 1960s was, like many other social movements, initially nationally based and nationally oriented. In the 1970s clashes occurred among nationally or regionally framed feminisms, mainly as a result of disagreements between Western feminists, who emphasized women's need for legal equality and for sex autonomy, and Third World feminists, who emphasized imperialism and underdevelopment as obstacles to women's advancement. In the 1980s, and in the sociodemographic context of a worldwide growth in the population of educated, employed, mobile, and politically aware women, feminist discourses and networking began to spread and to take on not only an international but a transnational form. The new information technologies, along with the changing and increasingly harsh economic realities, broadened the horizons of women's organizations, resulting in considerable international networking and many joint initiatives.

In this regard, women's organizations have been assisted in important ways by the UN, which has facilitated interaction and cooperation among feminist organizations. Key events have been the various world conferences, including the world conferences on women, as well as numerous regional preparatory meetings. The four world conferences on women (Mexico City in

1975, Copenhagen in 1980, Nairobi in 1985, and Beijing in 1995) were perhaps the most important form of UN-assisted networking. Equally important were the women's caucuses that formed in connection with other UN conferences, such as the United Nations Conference on Environment and Development (held in Rio de Janeiro in 1992), the World Conference on Human Rights (held in Vienna in June 1993), the International Conference on Population and Development (held in Cairo in September 1994), and the World Summit on Social Development (held in Copenhagen in March 1995). The result of these meetings and caucuses has been the emergence of "global feminism" and of transnational feminist networks. Today there is a growing number of feminist networks that engage in research, advocacy, solidarity, and lobbying.

Feminist groups and women's organizations remain rooted in national or local issues, but their vocabularies, strategies, and objectives have much in common with one another and have taken on an increasingly supranational form. Transnational feminist networks engage in information exchange, mutual support, and a combination of lobbying, advocacy, and direct action toward the realization of their goals of equality and empowerment for women and social justice and societal democratization. As Sen and Grown (1987:22) put it in a now classic publication: "We know now from our own research that the subordination of women has a long history and is deeply ingrained in economic, political, and cultural processes. What we have managed to do in the last few years is to forge grassroots women's movements and world-wide networks such as never existed before, to begin to transform that subordination and in the process to break down other oppressive structures as well."

Similarly, the network Women in Development Europe is cognizant of the growing political power of women and the importance of their perspectives:

> In the decade since 1985, women have moved a long way in terms of the agenda we are taking on. We have recognized that while pursuing women's rights, we must also take on the context: the political, economic, and social structures. Women are taking the lead and making a huge contribution to defining the international agenda in terms of human rights, macroeconomics, conflict/peace, and sustainable development. We have a valuable and unique perspective on these issues as women and as human beings. We recognize that feminism in one country is not sustainable—we need feminism on a global scale. (WIDE 1995:3)

At the seventh session of the United Nations Commission on Sustainable Development in 1999, the Women's Caucus organized by the Women's Environment and Development Organization (WEDO) issued a statement that condemned ethnic cleansing, the bombing of Yugoslavia, child labor, sex tourism, and market reforms. There were lessons to be learned, they declared:

> Women who have not created the problem are the first to commit to its reso-lution. There is no magic in the market, save and except for the owners—and women do not own the market. We wish to recall Principle 5 of the Rio Decla-ration: "All states and all people shall cooperate in the essential task of eradi-cating poverty as an indispensable requirement for sustainable development, in order to decrease the disparities in standards of living and better meet the needs of the majority of the people of the world."
>
> But Rio was about hope and women have proved that despite our meager resources, with our deep commitment . . . we . . . successfully challenge the brutal reality. We call on this body to take the last opportunity in this century to take a bold step to redress the disparities between nations and within na-tions, between women and men. Gender cannot be mainstreamed in the ab-sence of justice, life, and hope. (WEDO 1999:5, 13)

Transnational feminist networks include Network Women in Develop-ment Europe (WIDE), based in Brussels and consisting of 12 national branches; Development Alternatives with Women for a New Era (DAWN), based in Fiji (previously in the Caribbean) and with active branches in Latin America, Africa, and South Asia; Women Working Worldwide, a coordinating group based in London; the International Association for Feminist Econom-ics and the International Women's Tribune Center, both based in the United States; the Asia-Pacific Research and Resource Organization for Women (AR-ROW), based in Kuala Lumpur; Women Living Under Muslim Laws, first based in Montpelier, France, and now in London and with an active branch, Shirkat Gah, in Lahore, Pakistan; ISIS International Women's Information and Communication Service, with one center in Quezon City, Philippines, and another in Santiago, Chile; and the Association of Women of the Mediterranean Region, based in Malta and Cyprus, bringing together pro-gressive women from all parts of the region, including conflict areas. What is most significant about these networks is their focus on economic and politi-cal issues—along with issues such as violence against women, women's re-productive health and rights, and legal equality for women. Transnational feminist networks make demands on states, cooperate regionally, advocate for women's rights, and agitate for global changes. Inasmuch as their dis-course targets corporate capitalism and advocates for social and gender equality, it appears to be socialist-feminist. Below are summary characteristics of five transnational feminist networks.

DAWN. Development Alternatives with Women for a New Era, formed in 1985, consists of individuals and groups in Latin America, the Caribbean, South Asia, and Southeast Asia. Leading figures are from Barbados, India, and Brazil. Two of the founding members of DAWN now have senior positions in the UN system: Noeleen Heyzer of Malaysia is the head of UNIFEM, and Lourdez Arizpe of Mexico is an assistant director-general at UNESCO. DAWN has focused much of its activity on two issues: economic policy (especially its well-known critiques of structural adjustment and the international financial institutions) and reproductive rights and population policy, and it has published a number of books on those issues. Members of DAWN (e.g., Gita Sen, Peggy Antrobus) are very active in international development circles and in groups such as Women's Eyes on the World Bank, where they monitor and critique economic decision-making and offer alternative visions.

WIDE. Network Women in Development Europe was established in 1985. Its members are women's groups in the European countries, and its secretariat is in Brussels. Its focus is on development assistance and the global economy, with a feminist critique of economic theory and of European trade and foreign aid policies. It holds an annual meeting and conference and has produced many briefing papers, position papers, and other publications on economic policy from a gender perspective. In 1995 its president was accredited to the official conference in Beijing and presented a statement during the General Exchange of Views. WIDE sent a representative to the NGO Forum during the attempted Millennium Round of the World Trade Organization (WTO) in Seattle in late 1999. Its May 2000 annual meeting in Brussels was devoted to an elaboration of globalization and macroeconomics and a critique of current trade policies and rules. Since then it has consistently called for democratization of the WTO and the insertion of human rights, women's rights, and labor rights clauses in all trade agreements.

WEDO. The Women's Environment and Development Organization was cofounded by the late Bella Abzug in the period before the Earth Summit in Rio de Janeiro. Its goal is "to make women more visible as equal participants, experts and leaders in policy-making from the community to the international level, and in formulating alternative, healthy, and peaceful solutions to world problems." Though based in New York, WEDO has a governing body of women in Brazil, Guyana, Norway, Egypt, Kenya, Nigeria, Costa Rica, India, and New Zealand. WEDO has joined feminist critiques of environmental degradation, in particular the link between environmental pollutants and breast cancer. It is also engaged in a critique of the WTO, including the commercialization of food and seeds and the private appropriation of indigenous knowledge and production processes by corporations.

AWMR. The Association of Women of the Mediterranean Region, formed in 1992, unites women of 18 countries bordering the Mediterranean Sea. Its aims are to work toward just and peaceful resolution of regional conflicts; regional demilitarization and global disarmament; elimination of discrimination, poverty, and violence against women; human rights, real democracy, and sustainable development; the welfare and rights of children; education for peace through the family, schools, and media; and common action to end environmental degradation of the Mediterranean Region. AWMR holds annual conferences and forwards its resolutions to parliamentary committees and to the UN secretariat in New York. In addition to its critique of global capitalism and regional conflicts, it has taken strong positions against the NATO bombing of Yugoslavia, the sanctions against Iraq, the continuing Israeli-Palestinian conflict, and the war in Iraq.

WLUML. Women Living Under Muslim Laws, formed in 1985, is an international network of individuals and groups that monitors the legal status and human rights of women in Muslim countries, as well as Muslim women living elsewhere. A secular, antifundamentalist organization, it calls for changes in national states and international organizations to prioritize and advance women's rights. WLUML disseminates action alerts from France and London and a *News Sheet* from Pakistan, along with other publications. Its leading figures, including Marie-Aimée Hélie-Lucas (born in Algeria) and Farida Shaheed (Pakistani) are often invited to expert-group meetings held by the UN or by European governments. In 2003 it collaborated with the Association for Women's Rights in Development (AWID) to form *Fundamentalisms: A Web Resource for Women's Human Rights* (www.whrnet.org/fundamentalisms).

The proliferation of transnational feminist networks may be regarded both as a reflection of the multifaceted process of globalization and as a response to and criticism of its (economic) vagaries. What began in the early part of the 1980s as the formation of a handful of small feminist networks composed of individuals in a few neighboring countries has been transformed into large, sometimes professionalized organizations with officers, publications, annual meetings, Web sites, ties to national and international NGOs (such as human rights groups), consultative status with the UN, and so on. Transnational feminist networks have thus joined other transnational social movement organizations in a broad movement to change the global political landscape. Moreover, contrary to the assertions of certain analysts of "new social movements" (e.g., Kriesi 1996), women's movements and organizations are not necessarily noneconomic and identity-focused. The transnational feminist networks described above organize around issues pertaining to states, legal frameworks, the global economy, and global governance, as well as reproductive rights and violence against women. One reason for the focus on economic issues may be the left-wing and socialist-feminist background of some of the leading figures in the networks; another reason may because these networks link developing and developed countries alike. Transnational feminist networks have arisen in the context of economic, political, and cultural globalization—and they are tackling both the particularistic and the hegemonic trends of globalization. They are advancing criticisms of social inequalities and forms of gender oppression, unsustainable economic growth and consumption, and neoliberal economic policies. In a word, transnational feminist networks are the organizational expression of the transnational women's movement, or global feminism.

Theoretical and Political Implications

This chapter has shown that female labor and women's organizations are integral elements of globalization in its economic, cultural, and political dimensions. The capitalist world-economy functions by means of the deployment of labor that is waged and nonwaged, formal and informal, male and female. In recent decades, the involvement of women in various kinds of labor arrangements has been striking. Capitalist accumulation is achieved through the surplus extraction of labor, and this includes the paid and unpaid economic activities of women, whether in male-headed or female-headed households. The various forms of the deployment of female labor reflect asymmetrical gender relations and gender ideologies. Global accumulation as the driving force of the world-system hinges on class and regional differences across economic zones and is also a gendered process, predicated on gender differences in the spheres of production and reproduction. In an era of economic globalization, the pressure for greater competitiveness through lower labor and production costs encourages the demand for and supply of female labor.

However, in a reflection of the contradictions of capitalism and of exploitation, the incorporation of women in the global economy and in national labor forces also has served to interrogate and modify gender relations and ideologies. Women have been organizing and mobilizing against the particularistic and hegemonic aspects of globalization. Organized and mobilized women—both nationally and transnationally—are raising questions about social and gender arrangements and making demands on employers, governments, and international financial institutions. Many feminist organizations have been middle class and elite, but class lines are increasingly blurred as women professionals and women proletarians find common cause around personal, economic, and social issues, including violence against women, poverty, job security, land rights, the redistribution and socialization of domestic work, reproductive health and rights, and women's roles in decision-making. Indeed, during the 1990s, when the labor movement and left parties alike were in retreat, it was the global women's movement, and specifically a number of transnational feminist networks, that were most vocal about the vagaries of economic globalization.

Moreover, the global women's movement, and in particular transnational feminist networks, may offer lessons to other social movements and their organizations, not least the labor movement. According to one commentary, "[N]o major American institution changed less than the labor movement. At the end of the twentieth century, American unions are as poorly adapted to the economy and society of their time as were the craft unions of iron puddlers and cordwainers to the mass production industries of seventy years ago" (Brecher and Costello 1998:25). This can hardly be said of transnational feminist networks. At the dawn of the new millennium, transnational feminist networks evince the organizational form and supranational solidarities that socialists had expected of the labor movement in the early twentieth century. It remains to be seen whether the labor movement will follow the lead of the women's movement in its approach to globalization and collective action.

Notes

1. Parts of this chapter draw on a previously published paper of mine (see Moghadam 1999). An earlier version of the chapter was also published in 2000 in the online *Journal of World-Systems Research* (vol. 5, no. 2, pp. 301–314). An extension of the argument may be found in Moghadam 2005.

2. Women's employment patterns in other regions of the world-economy were based on somewhat different logics. For example, the communist bloc encouraged high rates of female labor force participation partly for ideological reasons (to achieve social equality) and partly to achieve economic development more rapidly. Some core

countries also began to encourage female employment, in part to expand their labor force and tax base and in part because of the pressures of the second-wave feminist movement.

3. The extent of the urban informal sector and its links to the formal sector are matters of dispute, and women's involvement in it is rarely captured in the official statistics.

4. On the other hand, the proletarianization of women was an integral part of early industrialization in England, France, and parts of the United States (e.g., the textile mills of Lowell, Massachusetts).

5. The union contract had been won at the Camisas Modernas Phillips–Van Heusen plant in 1996. Early in 1999 Phillips–Van Heusen closed the factory.

References

Anheier, Helmut, Marlies Glasius, and Mary Kaldor, eds. 2001. *Global Civil Society.* Oxford: Oxford University Press.

Beneria, Lourdes and Martha Roldan. 1987. *The Crossroads of Class and Gender: Industrial Homework, Subcontracting, and Household Dynamics in Mexico City.* Chicago: University of Chicago Press.

Boli, John and George M. Thomas. 1997. "World Culture in the World Polity." *American Sociological Review* 62 (2): 171–190.

Boris, Eileen and Elisabeth Prügl, eds. 1996. *Homeworkers in Global Perspective.* New York: Routledge.

Boserup, Ester. 1970. *Women and Economic Development.* New York: St. Martin's Press.

Brecher, Jeremy and Tim Costello. 1998. "A 'New Labor Movement' in the Shell of the Old?" Pp. 24–43 in *A New Labor Movement for the New Century,* edited by Gregory Mantsios. New York: Monthly Review Press.

Briskin, Linda. 1993. "Union Women and Separate Organizing." Pp. 89–108 in *Women Challenging Unions: Feminism, Democracy, and Militancy,* edited by Linda Briskin and Patricia McDermott. Toronto: University of Toronto Press.

———. 1998. "Autonomy, Diversity and Integration: Union Women's Separate Organizing in North America and Western Europe in the Context of Restructuring and Globalization." Paper presented at the World Congress of Sociology, Montreal, July 26–August 1.

———. 1999. "Unions and Women's Organizing in Canada and Sweden." Paper presented at the World Congress of Sociology, Montreal, July 26–August 1, 1998. Published in *Women's Organizing, Public Policy and Social Change in Canada and Sweden,* edited by Linda Briskin and Mona Eliasson. Montreal: McGill-Queen's University Press.

Chant, Sylvia. 1995. "Women's Roles in Recession and Economic Restructuring in Mexico and the Philippines." In *Poverty and Global Adjustment: The Urban Experience,* edited by Alan Gilbert. Oxford: Blackwell.

Chase-Dunn, Christopher. 1998. *Global Formation: Structures of the World-Economy.* Lanham, MD: Rowman and Littlefield.

Cinar, Mine. 1994. "Unskilled Urban Migrant Women and Disguised Employment: Homeworking Women in Istanbul, Turkey." *World Development* 22 (3): 369–380.

Cornia, Giovanni A., Richard Jolly, and Frances Stewart, eds. 1987. *Adjustment with a Human Face.* Oxford: Clarendon Press.

da Gama Santos, Margarida. 1985. "The Impact of Adjustment Programmes on Women in Developing Countries." *Public Enterprise* (International Center for Public Enterprises in Developing Countries, Ljubljana, Slovenia) 5 (3): 287–297.

Doremus, Paul N., William W. Kelley, Louis W. Pauley, and Simon Reich. 1998. *The Myth of the Global Corporation.* Princeton, NJ: Princeton University Press.

Eaton, Susan C. 1992. "Women Workers, Unions and Industrial Sectors in North America." IDP Women/Working Paper 1, International Labour Organization, Geneva.

Elson, Diane, ed. 1991. *Male Bias in the Development Process.* London: Macmillan.

Elson, Diane and Ruth Pearson. 1981. "Nimble Fingers Make Cheap Workers: An Analysis of Women's Employment in Third World Export Manufacturing." *Feminist Review* (Spring): 87–107.

Employment Observatory: Trends. 1994. Bulletin of the European System of Documentation on Employment, no. 19.

Fernandez-Kelly, Patricia. 1994. "Broadening the Scope: Gender and the Study of International Development." In *Comparative National Development,* edited by A. Douglas Kincaid and Alejandro Portes. Chapel Hill: University of North Carolina Press.

Franzway, Suzanne. 1994. "Women Working in Australian Unions." Paper prepared for the International Sociological Association, RC44, Bielefeld, Germany, July 18–23.

Gilpin, Robert. 1999. *The Challenge of Global Capitalism: The World Economy in the 21st Century.* Princeton, NJ: Princeton University Press.

Hastings, Sue and Martha Coleman. 1992. "Women Workers and Unions in Europe: An Analysis by Industrial Sector." IDP Women/Working Paper 4, International Labour Organization, Geneva.

Hopkins, Terence K. and Immanuel Wallerstein. 1996. "The World System: Is There a Crisis?" Pp. 1–10 in *The Age of Transition: Trajectory of the World-System 1945–2025,* edited by Immanuel Wallerstein et al. London: Zed.

Jaquette, Jane, ed. 1994. *The Women's Movement in Latin America: Participation and Democracy.* 2nd ed. Boulder, CO: Westview.

Joekes, Susan/INSTRAW. 1987. *Women in the Global Economy: An INSTRAW Study.* New York: Oxford University Press.

Keck, Margaret and Katheryn Sikkink. 1998. *Activists beyond Borders: Advocacy Networks in International Politics.* Ithaca, NY: Cornell University Press.

Kim, Seung-Kyung. 1997. *Class Struggle or Family Struggle? The Lives of Women Factory Workers in South Korea.* Cambridge, UK: Cambridge University Press.

Klausen, Jytte. 1997. "The Declining Significance of Male Workers: Trade Unions Responses to Changing Labor Markets." In *Crisis and Conflict in Contemporary Capitalism*, edited by Peter Lange et al. Cambridge, UK: Cambridge University Press.

Kriesi, Hanspeter. 1996. "The Organizational Structure of New Social Movements in a Political Context." In *Comparative Perspectives on Social Movements: Political Opportunities, Mobilizing Structures, and Cultural Frames*, edited by Doug McAdam, John McCarthy, and Mayer Zald. Cambridge, UK: Cambridge University Press.

Lim, Linda. 1985. *Women Workers in Multinational Enterprises in Developing Countries.* Geneva: ILO.

Marglin, Stephen and Juliet Schor, eds. 1990. *The Golden Age of Capitalism.* Oxford: Clarendon Press.

Mies, Maria. 1986. *Patriarchy and Accumulation on a World Scale.* London: Zed Books.

Moghadam, Valentine M. 1995. "Gender Aspects of Employment and Unemployment in a Global Perspective." In *Global Employment: An Investigation into the Future of Work*, edited by Mihaly Simai. London: Zed Books and United Nations University Press.

———. 1996. "Feminist Networks North and South: DAWN, WIDE and WLUML." *Journal of International Communication* 3 (1): 111–121.

———. 1997. "The Feminization of Poverty? Notes on a Concept and Trends." Illinois State University Women's Studies Program, Occasional Paper No. 2 (August).

———. 1998. *Women, Work and Economic Reform in the Middle East and North Africa.* Boulder, CO: Lynne Rienner Publishers.

———. 1999. "Gender and the Global Economy." Pp. 128–160 in *Revisioning Gender*, edited by Myra Marx Ferree, Judith Lorber, and Beth B. Hess. Thousand Oaks, CA: Sage.

———. 2000. "Transnational Feminist Networks: Collective Action in an Era of Globalization." *International Sociology* 15 (1): 57–85.

———. 2001. "Globalization and Women's Employment in the Arab Region." Background paper prepared for the CAWTAR report "Globalization and Gender: Arab Women's Economic Participation."

———. 2005. *Globalizing Women: Transnational Feminist Networks.* Baltimore, MD: Johns Hopkins University Press.

Nash, June and Maria Fernandez-Kelly, eds. 1983. *Women, Men, and the International Division of Labor.* Albany, NY: State University of New York Press.

Pearson, Ruth. 1992. "Gender Issues in Industrialization." In *Industrialization and Development*, edited by Tom Hewitt, Hazel Johnson, and David Wield. Oxford: Oxford University Press.

Pearson, Ruth and Swasti Mitter. 1993. "Employment and Working Conditions of Low-Skilled Information–Processing Workers in Less-Developed Countries." *International Labour Review* 132 (1): 49–64.

Peterson, V. Spike. 2003. *A Critical Rewriting of Global Political Economy: Integrating Reproductive, Productive, and Virtual Economies.* New York: Routledge.

Pieterse, Jan Nederveen. 1992. "Globalization as Hybridization." Paper prepared for the 10th anniversary conference of *Theory, Culture, and Society,* Champion, Pennsylvania. (August).

Safa, Helen. 1996. "Gender Inequality and Women's Wage Labor: A Theoretical and Empirical Analysis." In *Patriarchy and Development,* edited by V. M. Moghadam. Oxford: Clarendon Press.

Sassen, Saskia. 1998. *Globalization and Its Discontents.* London: New Press.

Sen, Gita and Caren Grown. 1987. *Development, Crises, and Alternative Visions: Third World Women's Perspectives.* New York: Monthly Review Press.

Sklair, Leslie. 2001. *The Transnational Capitalist Class.* London: Blackwell.

———. 2002. *Globalization: Capitalism and Its Alternatives.* 3rd ed. Oxford: Oxford University Press.

Smith, Jackie, Charles Chatfield, and Ron Pagnucco, eds. 1997. *Transnational Social Movements and Global Politics.* Syracuse, NY: Syracuse University Press.

Sparr, Pamela, ed. 1994. *Mortgaging Women's Lives: Feminist Critiques of Structural Adjustment.* London: Zed.

Standing, Guy. 1989. "Global Feminization through Flexible Labor." *World Development* 17 (7): 1077–1095.

———. 1999. "Global Feminization through Flexible Labor: A Theme Revisited." *World Development* 27 (3): 583–602.

Steger, Manfred. 2002. *Globalism: The New Market Ideology.* Lanham, MD: Rowman and Littlefield.

Stienstra, Deborah. 1994. *Women's Movements and International Organizations.* New York: St. Martin's Press.

Tanski, Janet M. 1994. "The Impact of Crisis, Stabilization and Structural Adjustment on Women in Lima, Peru." *World Development* 22 (11): 1627–1642.

Tiano, Susan. 1994. *Patriarchy on the Line: Labor, Gender, and Ideology in the Mexican Maquila Industry.* Philadelphia: Temple University Press.

UNDP. 1995. *The Human Development Report 1995.* New York: Oxford University Press.

———. 1999. *Human Development Report 1999: Globalization with a Human Face.* New York: Oxford University Press.

United Nations. 1991. *World Economic Survey 1991.* New York: UN/DIESA.

———. 1999. *The 1999 World Survey on the Role of Women in Development: Globalization, Gender, and Work.* New York: UN.

WEDO. 1999. "At CDS, Women Say 'No' to War." *WEDO News and Views* 12 (1).

WIDE. 1995. *WIDE Bulletin: From Copenhagen to Beijing.* Brussels: WIDE.

World Bank. 1995. *World Development Report 1995: Workers in an Integrating World.* New York: Oxford University Press.

13

Environmentalism and the Trajectory of the Anti–Corporate Globalization Movement

FREDERICK H. BUTTEL AND KENNETH A. GOULD

In the twenty-first century, many of globalization's key features are challenged directly by a global-scale social movement, the anti–corporate globalization movement (ACGM). Many social scientists believe that in the current era of globalization social movements must *necessarily* be global in their vision and scope if they are to be successful (O'Brien et al. 2000). The power of transnational actors, particularly transnational corporations and trade liberalization institutions such as the World Trade Organization (WTO), regional trade institutions, the World Bank, the International Monetary Fund (IMF), and the G-8, implies that the only possibility of effective challenge to these actors must involve organizations and movements that can counter these globalizing institutions at the scale at which they operate. Indeed, many argue that the ACGM is the most significant left movement of the new millennium (Brecher, Costello, and Smith 2000).

In this chapter we begin by discussing the major structural characteristics of the ACGM, which we define in a broad manner to include not only the participants in protests and in the confederations that have coordinated these protests but also other nongovernmental organizations (NGOs) and groupings that consider themselves to be part of the movement. We then comment on the recent history of the ACGM, focusing on two particular aspects of this movement: the relationships between the ACGM and another important global social movement, the international environmental movement, and the effects that the ACGM might have on various actors and institutions of globalization and on particular nation-states. In this regard we suggest that despite the potential of this movement to produce important social changes, the movement also faces a number of major crossroads in terms of ideology, discursive approach, and strategy. One implication of our analysis is the hypothesis that while the current vitality of the ACGM can be gauged by its having adopted an increasingly coherent and radical ideological stance in which international—especially north-south—economic inequality is targeted, to be successful the movement will need to more fully integrate social justice goals with environmental protection and sustainability agendas.

The Structure of the Movement

The ACGM draws many of its adherents from the groups and networks associated with other social movements. The ACGM is a broad coalition of smaller (antisweatshop, debt relief, fair trade, etc.) and larger (human rights, organized labor, international hunger, etc.) movements and draws participants and participating organizations from a diversity of ideologies (autonomists, socialists, liberal reformists, etc.). What gives cohesion to this "movement of movements" is a common critique of neoliberal economic policies, the antidemocratic nature of international financial institutions (the World Trade Organization, International Monetary Fund, and World Bank in particular), and the increasing power of transnational corporations. Participants and coalition member organizations coordinate activities primarily through electronic media, allowing for intercontinental simultaneous discussion and mobilization. The movement is therefore able to organize globally and maintain communication between very different groups in very different locations. The ACGM organizational structure is based on a commitment to nonhierarchical and consensus-based decision-making. Such an organizational structure ensures that all groups are able to participate in decision-making, thus preventing schisms from developing into obstacles to coordinated action.

There are a number of structural bases for the rise of the ACGM other than the premise that the growing power of transnational actors "requires" global-scale movements to successfully contest new power relations. First, while there is a consensus among economists and state officials in most countries of the north that there are mutual gains to be realized through "freer" world trade, many citizens in the north and south argue that such gains accrue only to domestic and transnational elites. Increased dependence on trade can create social benefits, but it also creates social losses such as an increased risk of unemployment and the loss of worker protections. Second, trade liberalization institutions such as the WTO and the North American Free Trade Agreement (NAFTA) have essentially been established to permit offshore veto of "protectionist" environmental regulations and the traditional measures for enhancing social security such as the welfare state "safety net." Anti–corporate globalization discourses stress the role of the WTO, the World Bank, the the IMF, NAFTA, the emerging Free Trade Area of the Americas (FTAA), and the G-8 as enforcers of the rules of globalization that privilege transnational corporations. Movement discourses refer to the prerogative of offshore corporate veto as creating a powerful "race to the bottom" as nation-states face competitive pressures to "water down" regulations in order to remain attractive for capital investment. Third, there is also a sizable share of cultural revulsion against homogenization, "McDonaldization" (Ritzer 1993), and Americanization, which are associated with globalization. The rise of the ACGM is also related to the advent of a unipolar, U.S.-dominated world order following the collapse of the Soviet Union, the general demise of state socialism, increased U.S. military dominance, and the relative absence of a countervailing world power.

Although there is much debate about the socioeconomic and cultural impacts of globalization, there is a surprising consensus on the growing role of global antisystemic social movements such as the anti–corporate globalization movement. ACGM proponents and many social scientists see much promise in the development of "global civil society." In addition to recognizing that global social movements are intrinsically better positioned than national movements to advance causes such as environmental protection and protective labor legislation, movement proponents and a number of social scientific analysts agree that global social movements (GSMs) have been adept at creating coalitional movement structures across (and within) national borders and new discourses. Generally, these observers of GSMs view these movements as a logical response to global processes such as the establishment of new regional and international "free trade" agreements, the expansion of markets, the establishment of international governmental organizations and regimes, and the growing role of transnational corporations. GSM theorists (e.g., Cohen and Rai 2000; O'Brien et al. 2000) believe these movements can be quite influential because dominant global actors can be vulnerable to negative public opinion and to the scrutiny by governments that is generated by public sentiments. Some observers of GSMs have tended to see the global environmental movement as the key umbrella movement, while the more recent tendency has been to assign that role to the ACGM.

Despite its coalitional character, the ACGM has an identity and organizational structure that serve to distinguish it from other GSMs, such as the hierarchically organized environmental GSM, which has its own distinct identity rooted primarily in the international conservation wing of environmentalism. We focus on the interrelations of these two GSMs by noting that in recent years there have been trends toward both the "environmentalization" and "deenvironmentalization" of the ACGM. We suggest that the role that environmental claims and strategies play in the ACGM's "repertoire of contention" (Tilly 1978, 1986) will be critical to the movement's future.

There are several focal structural properties of the ACGM. First, while those in the north often presume that the essence of the movement is that of periodic protests against institutions and corporations in the north, the majority of protests have actually occurred in the global south. Protests against the Bretton Woods institutions, and IMF structural adjustment policies in particular, have been a regular feature of political conflict in the global South for well over 25 years (Walton and Seddon 1994).[1] While we acknowledge this central point (see Podobnik 2001 for an impressive elaboration), anti-corporate globalization protests in the south are most often confined (by intention or practicalities) to getting the attention of heads of state and finance ministers in the south. The ACGM in the north is in some respects the more strategically significant segment of the movement in that it has the geographical capacity to attack transnational institutions more directly as well as to gain the attention of the heads of state of the countries that have the dominant voices within these institutions.

The vitality of the ACGM is largely due to the actions of the protesters who now contest the annual meetings of essentially all globalization institutions. But another critically important component of the movement is its active NGO supporters and affiliates. The ACGM's cast of NGO supporters and affiliates encompasses the "Seattle coalition," the unprecedentedly broad coalition that formed during the lead-up to and in wake of the protest at the 1999 Third WTO Ministerial Conference in Seattle. The ACGM is now endorsed by a vast array of NGOs and related movements, and these groups are integral components of the ACGM. Much of the ACGM's education, publication, and public outreach work is undertaken by these NGOs. Such NGOs also generate much of the movement's policy analyses and proposals.[2]

Third, the movement is intentionally acephalous. Delegates from various "affinity groups" representing the NGOs, movements, and less formally organized groups of participants form "spokes councils" in which strategic and tactical decisions are made, allowing the movement to operate without formal leaders or a clear organizational hierarchy. Much of the protest organizing occurs through the Internet without the need for a central source of command, greatly reducing resource and bureaucratic needs. Months prior to a protest, groups form to organize teach-ins throughout the host country. The "spokes council" structure and Internet modality of protest organization have facilitated the accommodation of considerable diversity within the movement. Such models minimize infighting but also require acceptance of an inability to generate strong ideological and tactical consensus.

Finally, the ACGM finds itself being defined both advantageously and destructively by the mainstream press, which is itself often the focus of negative movement attention as a corporate vehicle for the dissemination of neoliberal ideology. But since the Seattle protest, which received some positive press coverage for having raised issues of concern to many citizens, the mainstream media's treatment of the ACGM has tended to cast the movement in a distinctly unfavorable light—portraying its members as angry, antagonistic protesters or youthful participants who would rather demonstrate than negotiate; suggesting the presence of violent anarchist groups; portraying the movement's message as incoherent; and so on. Negative and poorly informed mainstream press coverage has led the movement to facilitate the expansion of more sophisticated independent media, primarily through "Indymedia" Web sites.

The Emergence of the "Seattle Coalition"

In the years following the unsuccessful mobilization against NAFTA, there were a number of critical events and phenomena that produced a U.S. expansion of the ACGM coalition, leading up to the "Battle in Seattle." First, in the early 1990s Mexico filed a complaint against the United States under GATT. This resulted in a bilateral negotiation that led to removing the component of the Marine Mammal Protection Act that prohibited import of tuna produced under conditions that result in widespread death of dolphins. Then, in one of the WTO's first rulings, it acted in support of a complaint by Venezuela and Brazil alleging that the United States' ban on imported gasoline that exacerbates air quality problems was an impermissible trade barrier. A similar ruling, against a 1998 U.S. law banning shrimp imports from countries whose shrimp-harvesting methods kill sea turtles, was handed down by the WTO in 1999. Also in late 1999, the Canadian Methanex Corporation filed suit under NAFTA against the State of California for its proposed ban on the gasoline additive MTBE.

The impact of these antienvironmental rulings cannot be overestimated. Until these trade liberalization rulings and suits, groups such as the World Wildlife Fund, the National Wildlife Federation, Audubon, the Natural Resources Defense Council, and the Environmental Defense Fund had supported NAFTA and WTO, while the Defenders of Wildlife and the Nature

Conservancy had been at least nominally neutral toward trade liberalization. The WTO rulings shook most mainstream environmental groups to their foundations. It became apparent to the large mainstream environmental organizations that a domestic environmental regulation may not be very effective unless its scope can be extended to pertain to the conditions of production of imported goods. Further, it became apparent that the WTO might give foreign governments and corporations leverage to overturn domestic environmental legislation. As the end of the 1990s approached, it was becoming apparent to U.S. environmental organizations that the environmental side agreements to NAFTA were largely ineffective. As a result of these revelations there was a fundamental shift in mainstream environmental NGO opinion about globalization in general and trade liberalization in particular. By early 1999 these moderate environmental groups had joined Friends of the Earth, the Sierra Club, and Greenpeace in taking a generally negative stance toward corporate globalization.[3] The willingness to initiate participation in ACGM actions, most notably the Seattle protest of November 1999, is a clear indicator of the political shift.

Second, the Kathie Lee Gifford revelation on live television in 1996 that her clothing line was manufactured by child labor in Honduran sweatshops brought the labor abuses of globalized production to U.S. public attention. That same year, the AFL-CIO, under the leadership of John Sweeney, initiated the Union Summer campaign to bring student activists into the labor movement (Clawson 2003). Union Summer, combined with the efforts of Jobs With Justice (a labor rights NGO) and UNITE! (the garment workers union), generated important revelations about the social and environmental conditions of production of Nike and other apparel manufacturers. These organizing and consciousness-raising efforts were manifested in an aggressive and highly visible student-labor antisweatshop movement. The press attention brought to Nike in particular dramatized the social impacts, in both north and south, of footloose corporate capital shifting its production facilities to low-wage countries in the south.

Finally, the explosion of public sentiments against genetically modified (GM) foods in Europe and East Asia created a crisis of legitimacy for the WTO. WTO rules suggested that the European Union (EU) would have little legal basis for excluding GM agricultural input products and GM foods, while European public sentiments against these technologies were so strong that the EU was forced to act in conflict with WTO rules and with U.S. corporate and federal government views. The GM controversy galvanized the anti-WTO sentiments of many farm groups, such as the United States' National

Farmers Union and sustainable agriculture organizations. These precipitating events and processes combined to help forge the 1999 Seattle coalition.

The Seattle coalition was impressive in its breadth. The coalition included anti–corporate globalization groups; organized labor; environmental organizations; religious organizations; farm, sustainable agriculture, anti-GM, consumer, development/world hunger, and animal rights groups; and the governments (as well as NGOs and activists) of many countries of the south. Perhaps the most telling symbol of the Seattle coalition was the poster that read "Teamsters and Turtles—Together At Last."[4] What made the Seattle WTO protest so pathbreaking was the apparent environmentalization of the ACGM and the prominent role played by mainstream environmental groups in a coalition involving anti-WTO and labor activists. The strong environmental overtone of the Seattle protest was among the major factors that conferred on it a certain legitimacy among the U.S. public and contributed to the partially favorable press coverage of the protest. Since Seattle, there has been a continuous stream of anti–corporate globalization protests across the world disrupting the meetings of globalizing institutions. These protests, ranging in size from tens to hundreds of thousands of participants, have been met with escalating levels of state security and police repression.[5]

Following the terrorist attacks on the World Trade Center and Pentagon on September 11, 2001, protests in the United States were smaller and more subdued. A decision was made on the part of U.S. anti–corporate globalization activists to take a less aggressive approach in order to distance themselves from the violent attacks on the World Trade Center (which at least one member of Congress had initially blamed on the movement). The movement also decreased its protest activity because of an increase in state repression stemming from the curtailment of civil liberties through mechanisms such as the USA PATRIOT Act. The detention of anti–corporate globalization activists at the U.S.-Canadian border and the denial of flying rights to some activists further disrupted movement organizing. However, with organized labor taking the lead in demonstrations at the November 2003 FTAA summit in Miami, the U.S. movement began to recover some lost momentum. But the unprecedented militarization of a U.S. city and widespread civil rights violations by state and federal "law enforcement" agents in Miami clearly illustrated a shift in the U.S. political environment after September 11.

The emergence of an enormous global antiwar movement in the lead-up to the U.S. invasion of Iraq drew heavily on the mobilization infrastructure of the ACGM (Njehu 2004). This anti-imperialist-oriented movement has simultaneously drained resources and attention from the ACGM's primary focus and brought new activists and organizations into the ACGM coalition. Ideologically, the global movement against U.S. (and British) military aggression has served to deepen the ACGM's analysis of the central role of militarism and coercive force in forging and defending the neoliberal world order. However, a notable schism remains between core elements of the antiwar movement, which have a rather narrow focus, and the ACGM, which views the war on Iraq as deeply embedded in other global political-economic forces and agendas.

Movement Dilemmas

In a relatively brief period, the ACGM has produced some major successes. It has led to concessions from various quarters of the "big three," particularly the World Bank (Stiglitz 2003). Anti–corporate globalization protests and related movement activity have largely disabled the machinery for negotiating the Millennial Round of the WTO. The ACGM has also forced a shift in the rhetoric of international financial institutions (IFIs), which are now on the defensive, especially in regard to poverty alleviation, ecological sustainability, and structural adjustment.[6] The World Bank and IMF have expanded their policies on debt relief and increased their focus on the mitigation of poverty (Väryrnen 2000). The World Bank devoted its *World Development Report* for 2000/2001 to poverty alleviation, giving substantial attention to health, environmental, and educational mechanisms for reducing poverty and increasing quality of life in the South. But despite the movement's successes, it faces some significant dilemmas.

Many of the dilemmas faced by the ACGM are issues of discourse and strategy typical of mass movements. Should the movement seek to transform or terminate the main institutions of globalization?[7] On the one hand, the dominant institutions of globalization are deeply entrenched. Thus, a possible shift toward a more conventional "advocacy network" approach, involving formal organization, a decision-making hierarchy, and greater ability to mobilize resources, could exact more concessions from the dominant institutions and generate more favorable media coverage. On the other hand, these institutions are firmly committed to a neoliberal agenda that cannot respond meaningfully to the demands of a diverse array of NGOs, social movements, and nation-states. Some propose that the United Nations offers an institutional alternative to the IFIs through which transnational economic relations may be mediated (Bello 2000; Korten 2001).

Second, the nature of social movements is substantially shaped by their ability to extract resources of time and money from major social institutions as well as from adherents and sympathizers (McCarthy and Zald 1977). Political process theorists (McAdam 1982) have suggested that successful social movements are those that are best able to extract funds from philanthropic foundations or government agencies and that what radical social movements can accomplish is limited by what foundations are willing to fund. Thus, from a political process perspective, we can recognize that capital has latent veto with respect to anti-capital-oriented movements.

The protest components of the ACGM have required relatively few resources, and the most active protest groupings appear to have received essentially no direct funding from major foundations. However, there is a vast NGO network of movement supporters that are critical to the movement's legitimacy. And it is in the NGO affiliate wing of the movement where foundation support has been critical. Foundations have funded numerous NGOs, particularly environmental NGOs, to weigh in on issues of trade, globalization, and the environment.[8] Foundation support of the NGO affiliates has been sufficient to attract the attention of the Capital Research Center.[9] The Capital Research Center is a well-funded right-wing foundation watchdog NGO that aims to pressure the families and firms whose names are affixed to foundations into withholding funding from left-leaning social movement organizations. The ACGM is now one of the center's main targets. The Capital Research Center may not succeed in defunding the NGO affiliate wing of the ACGM, but the foundations may not need to be pressured to do so. Foundations see themselves as agents of innovative thinking and tend not to give long-term funding to a group to undertake the same project. The cult of newness among foundations may lead to foundation defunding of the NGO affiliate branch of the movement. The defunding of this component of the movement will not deter protests, but it will detract from the legitimacy of protests owing to a reduction in more mainstream NGO support.

A third dilemma common to global movements concerns the matter of whether international strategies can succeed in a unipolar, U.S.-dominated global political economy. This concern is even more immediate now that the Bush administration has proved willing to resist any international agreements that institutionalize agendas that conflict with the prerogatives of international capital. Dismissal of the United Nations as "irrelevant" by key Bush administration members and advisers serves to highlight the extent of an increasingly self-confident U.S. unilateralism. Global activist attention to the war on Iraq (and anti–United States sentiment in general) has shifted focus from systemic analyses to "peace" agendas, indicating that U.S. unilateralism poses ideological as well as strategic challenges for the ACGM.

Although some of the dilemmas the movement faces are characteristic of related social movements, the ACGM faces others that are specific to its sphere. One dilemma concerns the nature of the movement's coalition and ideology. Since the Seattle protest, the movement has exhibited a significant shift in its discourses. While the defection of many mainstream environmental groups from the "Washington Consensus" and the resulting environmentalization of the trade and globalization issue were critical to the Seattle mobilization, there has been a decline in the movement's embrace of environmental claims and discourses and an increase in its use of social justice and inequality discourses. The lead role played by organized labor in the Seattle protest helped to skew movement discourse toward issues of sweatshops, child labor, and international labor standards, ironically rhetorically deprioritizing environmental claims just at the moment when many previously reluctant mainstream environmental organizations were joining the ACGM coalition.

There are some rationales for the movement having undergone a progressive "deenvironmentalization" and having undertaken a shift toward north-south inequality claims. One involves increased communication between northern and southern wings of the ACGM following the 1999 Seattle protest. The first World Social Forum (WSF), organized to facilitate dialogue between the globally diverse movements making up the ACGM coalition, was held in Porto Alegre, Brazil, in 2001. That and subsequent WSFs have served to better integrate northern ACGM activists into the global movement and to expose northern groups to southern movement goals and ideologies (Fisher and Ponniah 2003). Increased contact with southern movements and southern NGOs revealed a schism between northern ACGM prioritization of labor and environmental protections and southern focus on equitable and sustainable development (Mertes 2004). Increased ideological synthesis between northern and southern wings of the ACGM required some movement of northern ACGM claims away from the formal environmental regulatory approaches championed by most of the large northern environmental NGOs. Southern ACGM coalition partner movements (such as MST[10] and the Zapatistas) have had conflicts of interest with northern conservation NGOs over the efficacy of preservation versus working landscape and sustainable development approaches to ecological integrity (Weinberg 2003; Stedile 2004).[11] Such conflicts between the development aspirations of southern movements and the agendas of northern environmental NGOs have not been uncommon (Gould 2003). As the northern and southern wings of the ACGM became more fully integrated, both ideologically and strategically, many mainstream environmental organizations' approaches became more marginalized.

Another cause of ACGM "deenvironmentalization" is that while there are good reasons to predict that trade liberalization agreements will lead to pressures toward an environmental "race to the bottom," there is limited evidence of such an impact. Williams (2001:47) has suggested that WTO dispute resolution system officials now appear to be bending over backward to avoid making more controversial antienvironmental rulings. This may stem, in part, from the dominance of "Third Wave" environmental ideology among mainstream environmental movement organizations, whose boards of directors often include a number of executives of transnational corporations (Dowie 1995) and which often rely on financial support from corporations that rank among the worst environmental offenders (Foster 1999).[12] With a foot in both neoliberal and anti–corporate globalization camps (Brulle 2000; Gonzalez 2001), some large mainstream environmental groups are well positioned to leverage traditional northern environmental concerns against the social justice issues that are gaining increased prominence in ACGM discourse.

In contrast to the limited evidence that "free trade" regimes lead to the demise of national and transnational environmental regulations, there is ample evidence of the ecological damage wrought by IMF-imposed structural adjustment policies (SAPs). SAPs structurally coerce heavily indebted southern nations to greatly increase agricultural and natural resource exports in order to meet transnational interest payment obligations (Athanasiou 1996; Roberts and Thanos 2003). IFI-supported increases in the export orientation of southern nations result in widespread land degradation, habitat loss, and the liquidation of the natural capital of southern nations (Gedicks 2001; Korten 2001). SAPs, by reducing public revenues and staffing of public regulatory agencies, also reduce the capacity of states to monitor and enforce compliance with environmental regulations (Kim et al. 2000). Therefore, an increased movement focus on the ecological impacts of structural adjustment policies—rather than on the formal rollback of domestic and international environmental regulations—would help to recover the ecological dimensions of ACGM ideology, while also illustrating the integration of environmental and social justice concerns, since SAPs also increase domestic inequality and reduce access of the poor to health care and education (Kim et al. 2000). Such a focus is consistent with southern environmental movement approaches (Taylor 1995).

While WTO actions that overrule existing national environmental regulations may be slowed for strategic reasons, transnational trade liberalization does reduce the likelihood that southern (and northern) nations will establish stricter environmental regulations as competitive pressures to attract and retain corporate investment have a dampening effect on state willingness to constrain private capital (Gould, Schnaiberg, and Weinberg 1996). The political problems that these processes generate for the ACGM are twofold. First, it is more difficult to make claims about the failure of environmental regulation to emerge (Crenson 1971) than it is to call attention to the elimination of existing regulations. Second, the environmental GSMs' focus on formal regulatory mechanisms rather than on structural processes in identifying the causes of and solutions to environmental problems (Gould et al. 1996; Gould 2003) makes it more difficult to recruit these movements' support in opposition to the IFIs and trade liberalization organizations (such as the FTAA).

In contrast to limited evidence of negative impacts on formal environmental policy, there is ample evidence that since the establishment of WTO there has been an exacerbation of global economic inequality, with roughly three to four dozen countries in the south having exhibited persistent declines in per capita incomes since the mid-1990s while most industrial nations exhibited considerable growth. Even the prominent neoliberal proponent Jeffrey Sachs noted in the *Economist* that the IMF essentially functions as the debt collection enforcer of private banks and that the IMF has sacrificed the economic recovery of most of South and Southeast Asia and elsewhere in the South. Former World Bank chief economist Joseph Stiglitz (2003) concurs. The establishment journal *Foreign Affairs* published a paper documenting the exacerbation of north-south inequality in the 1990s (Scott 2001). The deepening economic marginalization of sub-Saharan Africa is a glaring example of the unevenness of globalization processes and the expansion of international inequalities that result. Thus, there is an empirical underpinning to the shift of movement discourses away from threats to formal environmental regulation and toward issues of socioeconomic inequality and structurally generated environmental disorganization.

The deenvironmentalization of movement discourses and the predominance of claims-making about international inequality involve a major dilemma, however. In most of the north, which is ultimately the most critical audience for the ACGM, the north-south inequality issue is not likely to attract wide support. Environmental claims-making, and discourses stressing environmental and domestic social policy "races to the bottom" in the north, are more likely to generate public support. It seems apparent that the U.S. ACGM will need to be a broad coalition—involving, at a minimum, organized labor, environmental, and minority groups—to achieve its goals (Epstein 2001). Such a coalition requires a focus on neoliberal policy impacts on *domestic* inequality and environmental concerns, in addition to a focus on north-south equity issues (depending on the extent to which such issues can be directly linked to northern job losses and high-profile environmental concerns such as rainforest destruction). The focus on neoliberalism provides the ideological glue that fuses the concerns of diverse coalition participants in a common systemic critique. The ACGM needs to articulate the connectedness of transnational processes and structures to domestic concerns to broaden the domestic support bases of the movement in order to increase its political leverage at the national level, within the G-8 countries that exert the most influence over IFIs.

Further, the shift of the movement toward speaking primarily on behalf of the poor in the global south poses some potential problems. One is that increased emphasis on the IMF and World Bank may tend to threaten the coalition with organized labor, which has tended to be more actively supportive of protests targeting the WTO and FTAA than the IMF and World Bank (Gould, Lewis, and Roberts 2004).[13] Perhaps most fundamental, the northern wing of the ACGM has stressed agendas such as adding labor and environmental standards to the WTO, which state officials from most countries of the south (and some southern movements within the ACGM) are ambivalent about at best. A good indicator of this is that the WTO dispute resolution panel rulings that overrode U.S. environmental laws were the result of complaints filed by southern governments (Williams 2001).[14] Forging and sustaining meaningful north-south coalitions within the ACGM may require deemphasizing formal environmental policy and regulatory standards. The extent of the movement's losses in terms of its northern environmentalist constituency would then hinge on its ability to effectively articulate the structural causes of transnational ecological degradation to mainstream environmentalists who emphasize regulatory policy and market-based environmental protection mechanisms over structural change.

Regardless of whether the ACGM maintains its emphasis on north-south economic inequality or returns to the issues likely to sustain the more diversified coalitional emphasis of the Seattle protest, the political success of the movement will depend on whether it can continue to help induce two potential blocs of nation-states to resist a "deepening" of the WTO during its Millennial Round negotiations (which largely collapsed in Cancun in 2003). In a

sense, the most likely bloc to be enabled and induced by anti–corporate globalization protests to support major reform (or elimination) of the WTO is
that of nation-states of the south. In the Uruguay Round, developing countries essentially signed away their rights to use trade policy as a means of industrialization and development (a strategy that was effectively employed by
the "Asian Tigers" during the 1970s through the early 1990s). Governments
of the south also agreed in the Uruguay Round to open up their markets for
agricultural imports from the agribusiness superpowers, while receiving few
benefits of liberalized markets in the north (Madley 2000, chap. 1). In addition, liberalization of agricultural markets in the south has unleashed a tide
of depeasantization that will have lasting negative effects (e.g., unemployment, mass migration, hyperurbanization) decades hence (Araghi 2000).

Most southern states welcome the movement's efforts to press for debt
relief. But southern governments tend to be more interested in enforcing the
Uruguay Round WTO agreement than they are in achieving a decisive rollback of the WTO. Such southern state orientations may be an indicator of
the gap between the interests of states and those of their domestic citizen-
ries,and of an elite consensus on trade liberalization in both north and south.
While these processes have recently led to grassroots backlash and major political shifts away from overtly neoliberal regimes throughout Latin America,
poor countries have few options other than participating in the world trading
system on the most favorable terms possible. Thus, although one reason the
WTO is now paralyzed has to do with north-south disagreements, the ultimate negotiating position of most southern governments may not be in
sharp conflict with the U.S. position of further market liberalization, deregulation, and more effective enforcement of WTO rules.

The other bloc of nation-states with a potential interest in significant
WTO reform is that of the EU. Hirst and Thompson (1999:228) have noted
that "the role of the European Union is central because it is at one and the
same time the most developed and the most completely structured of the
major trade blocs. The evolution of the EU's capacities for coordinated common action by its member states will determine to a considerable degree
whether the governance of the world economy is strong or minimalist."

The EU's sympathies could well lie toward the minimalist pole. Public support for the ACGM's agenda is significantly stronger in the EU than in the
United States. WTO rebukes of a number of European environmental, trade,
and social policies prompted by U.S. complaints have created a growing
Continent-wide view that the EU must stand up for the preservation of its
worker and environmental protections. This, combined with increasingly ag-

gressive U.S. unilateralism, has hardened and expanded anti-United States sentiment throughout Europe. Thus, while the movement drifts toward north-south inequality discourses, it may find that its most amiable constituencies with significant power to promote policy changes are the EU and Japan, rather than the governments of the global south. The positions ultimately taken by the more anti-neoliberal governments of Latin America in regard to the FTAA may prove crucial to the ACGM's ideological and tactical trajectories.[15]

The Global Road Ahead

The ACGM has already achieved some significant successes. International institutions now must meet in remote locations or behind immense fortifications. These institutions, which already have public relations problems because of their inaccessibility and lack of transparency, are forced to insulate themselves from the public to an even greater degree. There is enough public support for the movement's agendas that several of these international regimes have been compelled to make changes in their discourses and practices (Stiglitz 2003). The Millennial Round of the WTO has been stalled for nearly four years, and the initial U.S. plan for a strong FTAA has been largely abandoned.

Despite these gains, the movement faces important dilemmas of organizational structure, ideological coherency, multiple competing discourses, and strategic choices. But since the movement will continue to be acephalous because of its deeply coalitional character and its organizational structure, it will not "make decisions" in the same manner that most social movements do. The choices that will be made are not choices within a leadership and organization hierarchy but choices made by many different groups of actors who consider themselves to be part of the movement. Some of the most difficult choices concern the discursive emphasis of the movement. Among the critical choices will be whether to emphasize to groups in the north the employment and environmental benefits of restructuring or disabling the institutions of globalization or to emphasize a global social justice agenda of reducing north-south economic inequalities. This is not to suggest that it is impossible to imagine ACGM agendas that have benefits for both groups in the north as well as those in the global south. But those agendas will have to be carefully crafted and clearly articulated, albeit within a highly decentralized structure.

Perhaps greater integration of both northern and southern environmental justice groups and frames offers a potential alternative to attempts to sustain the coalition with the most conservative mainstream environmental NGOs, which in terms of both ideology and constituency will have a tendency to return to their initial alliance with the neoliberal "free trade" agenda (Dowie 1995; Taylor 1995; Athanasiou 1996; Pellow 2002). Such environmental justice and anti–corporate globalization coalitions could facilitate a continued focus on north-south inequality, while constructing a greater focus on intranorth (and intrasouth) inequality. Attention to domestic inequality could help sustain an alliance with organized labor, while simultaneously reaching out to communities of color in the United States whose participation in the ACGM has been minimal. Environmental justice discourse might also allow the movement to retain an environmental agenda that sidesteps the environmental versus social justice trade-off that is deeply entrenched in "Third Wave" environmental ideology and practice. In the post–September 11 political climate, mainstream environmental organizations are likely to return to their traditional resistance to confrontational discourse and direct action tactics (Schnaiberg and Gould 2000), seeking accommodation with the institutions that the ACGM intends to disempower.

Finding an ideological and discursive vehicle through which to link domestic socioeconomic and environmental inequality and unemployment in the north with structurally generated ecological degradation in the south, while still maintaining some emphasis on international inequality, may be necessary to sustain the major components of the ACGM coalition. Although a shift to an environmental justice frame and focus on structurally generated environmental destruction may allow the movement to retain and synthesize north-south inequality and environmental concerns in its discourse, that does not remedy the loss of resources, legitimacy, and constituency that comes with a retreat of (or from) the major environmental NGOs. Environmental justice groups are small in membership, are decentralized, and have limited financial resources that they can bring to the ACGM relative to those of the mainstream environmental GSM organizations. In the end, perhaps the fate of both major GSMs lies not so much with the ideological and discursive decisions of the ACGM but rather with those of the international environmental NGOs. The extent to which the environmental GSM is willing and able to move itself and its broad constituency away from regulatory and "Third Wave" approaches to environmental problems and toward a structural critique of the ecological implications of neoliberalism may ultimately determine the long-term effectiveness of both GSMs.

Notes

An earlier and extended version of this chapter was published in 2004 as "Global Social Movement(s) at the Crossroads: Some Observations on the Trajectory of the Anti-Corporate Globalization Movement" in *Journal of World-Systems Research* (vol. 10, no. 1). This research was supported by the Center for World Affairs and the Global Economy, University of Wisconsin, Madison. Jonathan London and Patrick Jobes provided helpful comments on an earlier version of this chapter. The authors also wish to acknowledge the incisive comments and editorial assistance offered by Andrew D. Van Alstyne, which helped us produce a stronger argument and deeper analysis.

1. Protests have been particularly common in Bolivia, Argentina, Thailand, Ecuador, India, Brazil, and Indonesia, and southern activists are generally more confrontational than their counterparts in the north (Smith 2002).

2. A wide variety of environmental, agricultural, labor, consumer, human rights, women's rights, and related groups now have "trade" or "globalization analyst" staffers. The AFL-CIO has been an effective organizer and has a strong presence at North American anti–corporate globalization protests. Much of the ideological coherence of the movement is provided by a small group of prominent intellectual figures (e.g., Walden Bello, José Bové, Vandana Shiva, Robert Weissman, Naomi Klein, Kevin Danaher, and Lori Wallach), all of whom are associated with NGOs whose work is primarily geared toward publications and education.

3. Both Greenpeace and Friends of the Earth have been actively opposing World Bank projects since the 1980s. Both groups were founding members of 50 Years Is Enough in 1994, an ACGM group focused on debt relief and opposing structural adjustment policies. Greenpeace, Friends of the Earth, and the Sierra Club also have atypical records in supporting domestic environmental justice struggles.

4. The reference to turtles was the 1999 shrimp-turtle ruling by the WTO.

5. Major protests occurred at the April 2000 World Bank/IMF meeting in Washington, DC; the September 2000 World Bank/IMF meeting in Prague; the April 2001 Quebec City Summit of the Americas; the G-8 Summit at Genoa in July 2001; the Tenth Assembly of the UN Conference on Trade and Development in Bangkok (February 2000); the World Economic Forum in Melbourne (September 2000); the EU summit in Gothenburg (June 2001); the EU summit in Barcelona (March 2002); the WTO Ministerial meeting in Cancun (September 2003); and the FTAA summit in Miami (November 2003).

6. The economic collapse of the IMF's structural adjustment poster child, Argentina, significantly reduced the legitimacy of their policy prescriptions.

7. A dilemma often referred to within movement circles as the "fix it or nix it" question

8. These foundations include Pew, MacArthur, Ford, Rockefeller, Kellogg, Mott, McKnight, and other smaller ones.

9. The NGO affiliates emcompass groups as disparate as the Hemispheric Social Alliance, Alliance for Responsible Trade, Institute for Policy Studies, and Development Group for Alternative Policies.

10. The Sem Terra Movement of landless workers in Brazil.

11. More "radical" environmental NGOs such as Greenpeace have been helpful to southern movements because of a deeper appreciation of the complexities of southern development issues.

12. Responding to Ronald Reagan's deregulatory agenda, the Washington, DC–based mainstream environmental organizations moved toward the adoption of "Third Wave" environmentalism in the 1980s, emphasizing (a) cooperation with transnational corporate environmental offenders rather than confrontation, (b) compromise agreements that allowed them to claim victories for their mail-in member constituencies, and (c) increasing acceptance of corporate executives on their boards of directors (Dowie 1995). Third Wave doctrine exacerbated the mainstream environmental movement's historical resistance to incorporation of social justice concerns within its political agendas and reflected a growing alignment with neoliberal agendas emphasizing market-based mechanisms to control pollution and voluntary monitoring and regulation of corporate environmental impacts.

Dowie (1995) contrasts "Third Wave" environmentalism with first-wave environmentalism, which emerged in the United States in the early twentieth century and focused primarily on land and wildlife conservation, and with second-wave environmentalism, which emerged in the United States in the 1960s with a focus on state regulatory approaches to pollution control.

13. This further indicates a need on the part of the ACGM to more clearly articulate linkages between the impacts of SAPs in the south and northern job losses. Labor has shown far greater interest in trade liberalization agreements (United States–Canada FTA 1988, NAFTA 1994, FTAA) and the WTO than in the Bretton Woods institutions, as a result of the more direct threats to northern employment (Gould et al. 2004).

14. Including Mexico, Venezuala, Thailand, Pakistan, Malaysia, and India.

15. The surprisingly neoliberal policies of President Lula in Brazil are not encouraging.

References

Araghi, F. 2000. "The Great Global Enclosure of Our Times: Peasants and the Agrarian Question at the End of the Twentieth Century." Pp. 145–160 in *Hungry for Profit,* edited by F. Magdoff et al. New York: Monthly Review Press.

Athanasiou, T. 1996. *Divided Planet: The Ecology of Rich and Poor.* Boston: Little, Brown and Co.

Bello, Walden. 2000. "UNCTAD: Time to Lead, Time to Challenge the WTO." Pp. 163–174 in *Globalize This! The Battle against the World Trade Organization and Cor-*

porate Rule, edited by K. Danaher and R Burbach. Monroe, ME: Common Courage Press.

Brecher, J., T. Costello, and B. Smith. 2000. *Globalization from Below: The Power of Solidarity.* Boston: South End Press.

Brulle, R. 2000. *Agency, Democracy, and Nature: The U.S. Environmental Movement from a Critical Theory Perspective.* Cambridge, MA: MIT Press.

Clawson, D. 2003. *The Next Upsurge: Labor and the New Social Movements.* Ithaca, NY: Cornell University Press.

Cohen, R. and S. M. Rai, eds. 2000. *Global Social Movements.* London: Athlone Press.

Crenson, M. 1971. *The Un-Politics of Air Pollution: A Study of Non-Decisionmaking in the Cities.* Baltimore, MD: Johns Hopkins Press.

Dowie, M. 1995. *Losing Ground: American Environmentalism at the Close of the Twentieth Century.* Cambridge, MA: MIT Press.

Epstein, B. 2001. "Anarchism and the Anti-corporate globalization Movement." *Monthly Review* 53 (September).

Fisher, W. F. and T. Ponniah. 2003. *Another World Is Possible: Popular Alternatives to Globalization at the World Social Forum.* New York: Zed Books.

Foster, J. 1999. *The Vulnerable Planet: A Short Economic History of the Environment.* New York: Monthly Review Press.

Gedicks, A. 2001. *Resource Rebels: Native Challenges to Mining and Oil Corporations.* Cambridge, MA: South End Press.

Gonzalez, G. 2001. *Corporate Power and the Environment.* New York: Rowman and Littlefield.

Gould, K. 2003. "Transnational Environmentalism, Power and Development in Belize." *Belizean Studies* 25 (2).

Gould, K., T. Lewis, and J. T. Roberts. 2004. "Blue-Green Coalitions: Constraints and Possibilities in the Post 9-11 Political Environment." *Journal of World-Systems Research* 10 (1).

Gould, K., A. Schnaiberg, and A. Weinberg. 1996. *Local Environmental Struggles: Citizen Activism in the Treadmill of Production.* New York: Cambridge University Press.

Hirst, P. and G. Thompson. 1999. *Globalization in Question.* Oxford: Polity.

Kim, J., J. Millen, A. Irwin, and J. Gershman, eds. 2000. *Dying for Growth: Global Inequality and the Health of the Poor.* Monroe, ME: Common Courage Press.

Korten, D. 2001. *When Corporations Rule the World.* Bloomfield, CT: Kumarian Press.

Madley, J. 2000. *Hungry for Trade.* London: Zed Books.

McAdam, D. 1982. *Political Process and the Development of Black Insurgency, 1930–1970.* Chicago: University of Chicago Press.

McCarthy, J. D. and M. N. Zald. 1977. "Resource Mobilization and Social Movements: A Partial Theory." *American Journal of Sociology* 82 (6): 1212–1241.

Mertes, T., ed. 2004. *A Movement of Movements: Is Another World Really Possible?* New York: Verso.

Njehu, N. 2004. "Cancel the Debt." Pp. 94–110 in *A Movement of Movements: Is Another World Really Possible?*, edited by T. Mertes. New York: Verso.

O'Brien, R., A. M. Goetz, J. A. Scholte, and M. Williams. 2000. *Contesting Global Governance: Multilateral Economic Institutions and Global Social Movements*. London: Cambridge University Press.

Pellow, D. 2002. *Garbage Wars: The Struggle for Environmental Justice in Chicago*. Cambridge, MA: MIT Press.

Podobnik, B. 2001. "Globalization Protests in World-Historical Perspective." Paper presented at the annual meeting of the American Sociological Association, Anaheim, California, August.

Ritzer, G. 1993. *The McDonaldization of Society*. Thousand Oaks, CA: Pine Forge Press.

Roberts, J. T. and N. D. Thanos. 2003. *Trouble in Paradise: Globalization and Environmental Crises in Latin America*. New York: Routledge.

Schnaiberg, A. and K. A. Gould. 2000. *Environment and Society: The Enduring Conflict*. Caldwell, NJ: Blackburn Press.

Scott, B. R. 2001. "The Great Divide in the Global Village." *Foreign Affairs* (January–February). <63.236.1.211/articles/scott0102.html>.

Smith, J. 2002. "Bridging Global Divides? Strategic Framing and Solidarity in Transnational Social Movement Organizations." *International Sociology* 17:505–528.

Stedile, J. P. 2004. "Brazil's Landless Battalions." Pp. 17–48 in *A Movement of Movements: Is Another World Really Possible?*, edited by T. Mertes. New York: Verso.

Stiglitz, J. E. 2003. *Globalization and Its Discontents*. New York: Norton.

Taylor, B., ed. 1995. *Ecological Resistance Movements: The Global Emergence of Radical and Popular Environmentalism*. Albany, NY: State University of New York Press.

Tilly, C. 1978. *From Mobilization to Revolution*. Reading, MA: Addison-Wesley.

———. 1986. *The Contentious French*. Cambridge, MA: Harvard University Press.

Väryrnen, R. 2000. "Anti-corporate Globalization Movements at the Cross-roads." Policy Briefs No. 4. Joan B. Kroc Institute for International Peace Studies, University of Notre Dame, South Bend, Indiana.

Walton, J. and D. Seddon. 1994. *Free Markets and Food Riots: The Politics of Global Adjustment*. Cambridge, MA: Blackwell.

Weinberg, B. 2003. "Mexico: Lacandon Selva Conflict Grows." *NACLA Report on the Americas* 6 (6).

Williams, M. 2001. "In Search of Global Standards: The Political Economy of Trade and the Environment." Pp. 39–61 in *The International Political Economy of the Environment*, edited by D. Stevis and A. J. Asetto. Boulder, CO: Lynne Rienner.

14

National and Global Foundations of Global Civil Society

JACKIE SMITH AND DAWN WIEST

We have witnessed in recent years an explosion in transnational citizen activism, and more analysts and scholars acknowledge the expansion of what they call "global civil society." But participation in this global civil society varies widely around the globe. We ask what factors influence who participates in transnational civil society. Contrary to assumptions in popular discourse, the state remains important while global economic integration has little role in determining which countries' citizens participate in transnational associations. But although ties to the global economy do not significantly affect participation, a country's links to global institutions strengthen opportunities for transnational activism. Rich countries' citizens are more active transnationally, but low-income countries with strong ties to the global polity are also more tied to global activist networks. This suggests that transnational social movement organizations (TSMOs) do not simply reproduce world-system stratification but—aided by a supportive institutional environment—help sow the seeds for its transformation.

Globalization, or the expansion of all types of social interactions across national boundaries, has led governments to turn increasingly to global institutions like the World Trade Organization (WTO) and the United Nations to resolve transnational problems. As this happens, social movement actors seeking to change local and national circumstances find that they must look beyond their national boundaries to do so. The global political context both expands and complicates the strategic choices available to those advocating political and social change. Activists increasingly need information and expertise relevant to transnational political arenas in order to pursue their social change goals. Therefore, it is not surprising that the growth of international agreements and organizations among governments has been accompanied by a corresponding proliferation of transnational civil society associations of all types.

The dramatic growth in cross-border interactions among nonstate actors has led scholars of transnational relations to call for an expansion of our traditional, state-bounded notions of civil society to account for a transnational public sphere (see Guidry, Kennedy, and Zald 2000). Many speak of a "global civil society" (see, e.g., Wapner 1996; Clark, Friedman, and Hochstetler 1998; Warkentin and Mingst 2000; Anheier, Glasius, and Kaldor 2001), which we, along with Paul Wapner, define as "that dimension of transnational collective life in which citizens organize themselves—outside their identity with a particular state or their role as a producer or consumer—to advance shared agendas and coordinate political activities throughout the world" (Wapner 2002:204). But there are strong reasons to be skeptical that this "global civil society" is "global" in the sense that it is broadly representative of and accessible to all the world's citizens. Some analysts (e.g., Tarrow 2001b; Rootes 2002) question the very presence of a global civil society by pointing to the limits of its globalness and the weakness of the actual transnational interactions it incorporates. They emphasize that national-level processes and ideologies still dominate much of the discourse and strategic thinking of activists, who continue to organize around nationally or locally defined aims (e.g., Imig and Tarrow 2001).

Global Politics and Civil Society

Globalization's effect on social movement mobilization can be seen as parallel to the transformation of contentious politics during the rise of national states (see Tilly 1984; Markoff 2003). In a global institutional setting, movement efforts to shape the practices of a particular government require international legal or scientific expertise, understandings of the rivalries and practices of interstate political bargaining, and/or capacities for mobilizing protests and otherwise bringing simultaneous pressure against multiple national governments.[1] Activists thus need organizations that can facilitate cross-cultural communication and manage diversity in order to articulate and advance a shared agenda.[2] It should not be surprising, therefore, to find that social movement organizations devoted especially to transnational-level organizing and political action play key roles in global-level contentious politics.

Data from the *Yearbook of International Associations*[3] show that the number of active transnationally organized citizens' groups (international nongovernmental organizations [INGOs]) grew from fewer than 1,000 in the 1950s to nearly 20,000 in 1999 (Union of International Associations 2004).[4] Within this population of transnational voluntary associations we find a subset of groups that are explicitly founded to promote some social or political change. Because such groups are more likely to be involved in processes surrounding social change, we focus our analysis on this smaller set of INGOs, which we call transnational social movement organizations.[5] The population of TSMOs has also expanded at a tremendous rate over recent decades from fewer than 100 organizations in the 1950s to more than 1,000 today. At the same time, we see some expansion in the global reach of these organizations as more groups are based in the global south and as the sector expands to include other groups in society.[6]

However, a closer look reveals that participation in both INGOs and TSMOs varies dramatically across countries, and this is particularly true of countries outside the traditional core of the global economy. Data from the 2000 edition of the *Yearbook* indicate that core countries of the world-system remain the most integrated, while later-industrializing regions are far less active in the international nongovnernmental and transnational social movement sectors. With regard to the broader population of INGOs, citizens in countries of the global north participate in an average of 2,600 organizations, compared with an average of 613 for citizens in the global south. Moreover, there is far less variation in INGO participation across core countries than there is in peripheral and semiperipheral countries.[7] While the difference between core and noncore countries for TSMO participation is not as dramatic, citizens in core countries participate on average in nearly three times as many TSMOs as citizens in noncore countries. The average core country has members in 408 TSMOs, while the average outside the core is just 138 organizations.

Citizens of France are most active in these groups, with 553 TSMOs and 3,551 INGOs reporting members in that country. At the other end of the scale of INGO participation are Afghanistan, North Korea, and Oman, with an average of just 159 INGOs reporting members in those countries. Turkmenistan has the lowest involvement in TSMOs, with 15 organizations listing its citizens among their members. Of the 25 countries with the most active participation in INGOs and TSMOs, 19 are among the traditional core states. But also included here are Brazil, India, Argentina, Russia, Hungary, the Czech Republic, and Poland.

Western Europeans are active in more than 80 percent of all TSMOs, and citizens of the United States and Canada participate in nearly 70 percent of all TSMOs. On the other hand, much of the developing world is less integrated into the transnational social movement sector, even if its participation has grown during the 1980s and 1990s. People from Africa and Asia are active in only about 60 percent of all groups, the former Soviet region is active in about half of all TSMOs, while Middle Eastern countries participate in about 40 percent of TSMOs. This chapter seeks to identify the factors that help explain these differing rates of transnational participation.

Factors Driving Participation in TSMOs

Building transnational alliances is not an easy process. Even when transnational social movement actors consciously work to incorporate more diverse peoples and issues, actually doing so can require exceptional costs and risks, and localized organizing is clearly cheaper and easier in many ways (Liebowitz 2000; Smith 2000; Tarrow 2001a, 2001b). But the observed growth in transnational association suggests that various forces are working both to reduce the costs and risks of transnational organizing and to increase demand for it. We would thus expect that the distribution of participation in global civil society is not random but rather is shaped by these social, political, and economic factors that affect the costs and benefits of transnational association. Both state- and global-level factors shape the character and scope of transnational alliances. Global political and economic dynamics lead some regions and nations to be more or less oriented toward a global polity, and state-level political processes allow variable levels of political participation by citizens (see, e.g., Kitchelt 1986; Jenkins and Schock 1992; Joppke 1992; della Porta and Kriesi 1999; Koopmans 1999). Below we outline the major theoretical orientations that guide our attempt to explain participation in global civil society.

National Opportunities and Resources

A major theme in theories of globalization is that the rise of supranational institutions and transnational problems is reducing the power and autonomy of the state. Nevertheless, it is clear that the state remains crucial to both defining major political opportunities for challengers and shaping the forms and character of political association:

> [S]tates remain dominant in most areas of policy—for example in maintaining domestic security—even if they have become weaker in their ability to control capital flows. . . . [C]itizens . . . still live in states and, in democratic ones at least, they have the opportunities, the networks, and the well-known repertoires of national politics. Those are incentives to operate on native ground that the hypothetical attractions of "global civil society" cannot easily match. (Tarrow 2001b:2–3)

However, it is also important to remember that states vary tremendously in the extent to which they are able to affect conditions within or outside their borders. The governments of the United States and France might be considered fairly autonomous and consequential domestic and international actors, while Bolivia and Somalia are much more limited in their abilities to affect global policy decisions or even to determine their own domestic policies. Similarly, citizens in global north countries tend to enjoy greater access to the resources and skills needed for global activism than do their southern counterparts, and more important, they also have greater political access to states with the largest influence over global policies (see, e.g., Bob, 2001, 2005). Despite such differences, many analyses of political mobilization tend to treat the state as a comparable unit of analysis.[8] We will explore this assumption further in our analysis, which asks whether the factors shaping participation in TSMOs vary among different countries. Below we discuss how national contexts shape the possibilities for political participation and alter the costs and benefits of such participation.

Political Openness and Repression

Studies of national political opportunity emphasize the role of the national state in determining opportunities for citizens to engage in political discourse and action. Because participation in transnational social movements is one measure of an available infrastructure for coordinated protest activity, factors associated with the emergence of domestic protest are useful for our analysis. Among the domestic factors at work are the availability of resources for association, legislative and judicial systems that protect individual rights to free association and public speech, electoral rules that govern possibilities for political competition, alliances and conflicts between elites, and capacities for state action, including repression (see, e.g., Tarrow 1988).

In her analysis of transnational conservation mobilization, Lewis (2002) found that the states that were most likely to be selected for transnational conservation projects were those that were both politically open and that had strong civil societies, reflected by the presence of large numbers of NGOs. She suggests that this pattern might be different from that found in the human rights issue area, where there is evidence that the least open and most repressive societies would attract more transnational human rights activism (e.g., those trying to engage what Keck and Sikkink [1998] call the "boomerang effect"). Political regimes that discourage popular engagement in politics are not likely to be associated with high levels of civic engagement. On the other hand, we would expect that politically open states with vigorous and active civil societies would be the most involved in TSMOs.[9]

Patricia Chilton tested the assumption that strong national civil societies would be required for effective transnational cooperation in the context of Eastern Europe during the Cold War era. She found, however, that while this was true for some cases, in East Germany and Czechoslovakia, where national civil societies were comparatively weak, there were strong connections to transnational coalitions (Chilton 1995:206). A capacity to form transnational coalitions in these cases was not dependent on previous levels of (national) civil society development (Chilton 1995). Commonalities of language, symbolic references, and the larger political context that affected all countries of Eastern and Western Europe served to condition the possibility of transnational coalition-building despite the absence of liberal societal institutions in some of the countries. This finding leads to the question we investigate later of how supranational conditions might facilitate transnationalism between less geographically or culturally proximate peoples in cases in which there are few domestic opportunities for organizing political challenges.

State repression also affects participation in transnational associations, but in some cases it can serve to counter the intentions of repressive states. High levels of repression may stifle citizen participation in associations, or it might encourage the formation of ties to transnational associations that can serve as a source of protection against government repression (see, e.g., Sikkink 1993; Coy 1997). Also, countries with longer histories of democratic governance should have more of the human capital necessary for active civil societies both nationally and transnationally. For instance, in his study of the formation of human rights associations, Patrick Ball (2000) found that countries with longer democratic traditions were more fruitful sites for organizing. In short, state policies that affect the costs of participation in politics and public associations should have strong influences on the levels of participation in TSMOs.

Resources

Economic and social resources are also crucial to the emergence and strength of social movements (McCarthy and Zald 1977; McAdam, McCarthy and Zald 1996; McCarthy 1996). We would expect, therefore, that participation in TSMOs will vary with the availability of resources for mobilization across countries. Thus, we expect that countries with a relatively large and educated middle class would have greater participation rates in TSMOs than poorer countries. Levels of economic development will also have a strong influence on citizens' access to important communications infrastructures that assist participation in global civil society groups.

Participation in transnational associations is also likely to be determined by the character of the national voluntary sector (see, e.g., Curtis, Baer, and Grabb 2001; Schofer and Fourcade-Gournchas 2001). Associational networks, or mobilizing structures, provide the foundation for movement organizing, structuring spaces for information sharing, building solidarity, and cultivating shared identities. Where there are opportunities for citizens to freely engage in a variety of voluntary associations, there is a greater propensity toward involvement in diverse social movement organizations (Oberschall 1973; McCarthy and Zald 1977; Minkoff 1997).[10]

This consideration of how national contexts shape the opportunities for citizens to participate in transnational political associations generates the following hypotheses:

> H1: Participation in global civil society (as indicated by TSMO memberships) will be higher in countries with stronger democracies.

> H2: Participation in TSMOs will be higher in countries with comparatively higher levels of economic development.

While it is important to distinguish national-level factors from transnational ones, we emphasize that these ostensibly national conditions are often strongly influenced by global processes, particularly in the global south. World-system and dependency theories postulate that internal grievances, as well as the availability of resources to address them, are affected by a country's position in the world-system, among other factors. Thus, a country's position in the world economic hierarchy is likely to have an important influence on people's decisions about whether to participate in transnational collective action. It is to the system of international economic relations that we now turn our attention.

Structural Relationship to the World-system

The relationship of a state to the capitalist world economy has been identified as an important causal factor in the emergence and spread of rebellion (see Jenkins and Schock 1992). It both shapes the opportunities for domestic challengers to organize and engage in collective action against the state and constrains the state's capacity to respond to popular challenges (Maney 2002; Muñoz 2002). Two key arguments have been forwarded to explain this relationship. First, the practices of expanding states and empires, such as the imposition of private property and coerced labor, have been linked to protest and rebellion of various kinds. Second, colonialism and postcolonial dependency have contributed to conditions such as widening inequality, slowed economic growth, and urbanization. These factors increase the mobilization potential of lower classes while dividing elites, increasing dependency on foreign capital, and weakening the legitimacy of the state (Jenkins and Schock 1992; Walton and Seddon 1994).

Although the conditions of life in countries of the global south increase the potential for citizens to engage in collective action in order to change their situation, the exclusive and repressive nature of many of the state regimes make doing so very difficult. Poor and working-class people are largely excluded from participating in the political process within many of these countries. Moreover, unconventional attempts to influence state policy (such as public protests) are likely to be repressed by governments that are far less tolerant of political rights that are largely taken for granted in global north countries.

It is important to recognize that the exclusive and repressive nature of state regimes in the global south can be tied to the role these states have historically played—and continue to play—in the global economy. Countries in Africa, Southeast Asia, Central America, and other regions of the global south have played a profound role in maintaining the engine of global capitalism. This is so not only because of the plentiful natural resources (such as gold, diamonds, and timber) found within these regions but, more important, because these areas of the world provide the cheap labor from which multinational corporations, elites in the global south and global north, and consumers in richer countries benefit tremendously. The cheaper the labor, the more attractive a country is to a multinational corporation.

In a globalized economy in which states compete for foreign investment, states are under great pressure to reduce (or even eliminate) basic protections for the working classes, such as minimum wage, social benefits, and workplace laws regarding safety on the job, in order to attract investment. This is far easier to do in places where there is little or no organizing among workers and other groups in society. The colonial pasts of global south countries have given them disproportionately strong military and police forces relative to civil society, making it easier for them to suppress interests of workers and citizens in order to attract foreign investments and loans (see, e.g., Tilly 1990, chap. 7). In short, rather than simply serving as a tool for beneficial economic development, global economic integration—reflected in foreign investment, trade, and loans—also leads to the continued exploitation of the poorest states and people (Timberlake and Williams 1984; Hippler 1995).

Further limiting opportunities for political mobilization in the global south is the fact that core states intervene directly in the domestic political processes of southern states in order to support regimes that are favorable to their economic interests. Ironically, such activity is often legitimated by a claim that the intervention is helping to support democratic development in a subject country. William Robinson (1996) refers to this intervention as the promotion of "low intensity democracy" or "polyarchy," whereby electoral competition and governance are restricted, through a variety of interventions, to those alternatives that do not threaten the economic interests of multinational corporations or powerful Western states. This generally means, for instance, that politicians must agree to open their nation's markets to foreign goods and investments, privatize state industries, and continue making payments on international debts. The consequences of not doing so are often severe, as we can see by examining, for instance, recent U.S. policies toward Cuba, Venezuela, and Iraq.

Not only do global south countries tend to have fewer domestic political opportunities for social movements, but also their domestic contexts are more strongly determined by global-level processes than are those of core countries.[11] In other words, it is much harder for activists in the global south to ignore global processes and institutions than it might be for activists in the core. At the same time, the world-system hierarchy makes both elite and social movement actors in the global south far less able to affect both the domestic and the global decisions that shape their environments than their counterparts in the north.[12] Given the difficulties citizens in the global south confront in any attempt to influence their governments, we might expect an increased demand among them for more transnational ties to citizens in the north, who have greater access to influential states and institutions.

Neoliberal-oriented policy makers and popular discourse (in the global north, at least) either explicitly or implicitly claim that a country's integration into the global economy will produce economic growth that, in turn, will generate other social benefits, such as improved quality of life, environmental preservation, and political openness. We refer to this as the "trickle down" theory of economic globalization. If this theory is accurate, we would expect that higher levels of trade and foreign investment in a country would create wider social benefits such a free and vibrant civil society. We would also expect to find a positive relationship between global economic integration and other forms of global interaction, such as citizen participation in transnational association. Sassen (1998) provides a more elaborated understanding of *how* global economic ties might affect transnational mobilization, and her work leads us to expect that flows of trade and direct foreign investment will positively affect levels of participation in TSMOs, but not as a result of the trickle down of supposed benefits of economic growth. Instead, these economic relations serve as mechanisms that foster transnational social ties, flows of technology, and communications infrastructures. The following hypotheses emerge from the preceding discussion of the world economic system:

> H3: Participation in TSMOs will be highest in the richer, core countries of the world economy.

> H4: Participation in TSMOs will be highest in countries that are most integrated into the global economy, that is, those with comparatively higher levels of global trade and investment.

> H5: Countries that are integrated into the global economy in a highly dependent manner (i.e., the poorest countries) will have higher rates of participation in TSMOs.

We drew from neoliberal and institutional arguments to articulate these hypotheses, but we note that world-systems theorists would argue that the global economy affects countries differently, depending on their position in the world-system hierarchy. So while economic integration may benefit core countries and their citizens, it has detrimental effects on the countries and people outside the core. Thus, our analysis will investigate how world-system position interacts with measures of economic integration to affect TSMO participation.

Levels of Integration into the Global Political System

Despite the emphases in popular discourse on economic forms of globalization, integration of states into a global society also takes on political and social forms. Although the international political arena has not replaced the nation-state as a mobilizing context for social movements, it has become increasingly important by expanding the available political space for building alliances and providing a common focal point for contention. Transnational social movements play an important role not only in the continuing construction of the international political arena but also in the enforcement of internationally generated policies and treaties adopted by states (Keck and Sikkink 1998). Moreover, the extent to which political actors will choose to bring a *particular* grievance to transnational political arenas is also shaped by that country's involvement in the global political order. As Risse-Kappen argues:

> The more the respective issue-area is regulated by international norms of co-operation, the more permeable should state boundaries become for transnational activities. Highly regulated and cooperative structures of international governance tend to legitimize transnational activities and to increase their access to the national polities as well as their ability to form "winning coalitions" for policy change. Transnational relations acting in a highly institutionalized international environment are, therefore, likely to overcome hurdles otherwise posed by state-dominated domestic structures more easily. (1995:6–7)

While national structures continue to present certain obstacles for mobilization, the existence of international norms and the growing authority of supranational structures (such as the United Nations) increase nongovernmental actors' potential for influencing national policy (Risse-Kappen 1995). In the absence of resources and formal mechanisms for enforcing most international treaties, social movement organizations have played an important role in monitoring international agreements. Thus, participation in the transnational social movement sector is more likely in states that have ratified international treaties. Other factors also affect a state's incorporation into a global political order. For instance, Reimann (2002) shows that when a country hosts or otherwise participates in international conferences, its national elites become socialized in international norms that accept nongovernmental organizations as legitimate participants in global conferences, and they begin to at least pay lip service to the idea that civil society deserves a voice in national and international policy debates.[13] This creates opportunities for that country's social movement sector to expand its domestic mobilization as well as its access to national and international political processes.

Participation in international treaties also signals a state's incorporation into what Boli and his colleagues call the "world polity" (Boli and Thomas 1997, 1999; Meyer et al. 1997a, 1997b; Boli, Loya, and Loftin 1999). A state's participation in international organizations serves as evidence of its adoption of a wider system of values, beliefs, and organizing principles (see, e.g., Frank 1999; Frank, Hironaka, and Schofer 2000). These "world cultural values," moreover, reflect the principal tenets of Western ideologies that support individualism, legal-scientific rationalism, and economic liberalism. According to the world cultural perspective, as states become increasingly enmeshed in the world polity (e.g., through participation in international organizations and agreements of all kinds), they begin to internalize world cultural values and to mimic the organizational routines of other actors in their environments. This facilitates transnational association among people from different nations who, as a result of their countries' involvement in the world polity, face very similar structures of opportunity and grievance as well as common cultural tools for interpreting and responding to problems (DiMaggio and Powell 1991; Giugni 2002).

Another institutional dynamic that scholars of global institutions have identified is what we might call the "hypocrisy paradox." This refers to the institutional dynamics that encourage weak states to join international treaties in order to enhance their international legitimacy, even though they have no intention of following such agreements. Notions of what an effective state is come from observations of what other states do, and participating in interstate negotiations and signing treaties is an essential aspect of state action. Moreover, once accepted into the community of states, a country can sign treaties in order both to attempt to influence the course of negotiations and to draw on the symbolic and concrete resources of international institutions, which can enhance its capacities to perform the basic functions of a state (Boli 1999). States might even compete with one another for favorable international standing and whatever material benefits may come from that. Hafner-Burton and Tsutsui (2003) tested this assumption, and they found a negative association between the ratification of international human rights treaties and actual human rights practices. However, they also found that, although in the short term human rights practices did not correspond to treaty requirements, over time human rights practices improved. They associate these improvements with the fact that treaty participation assisted the emergence of civil society groups that advanced human rights claims against the state through international human rights machinery.[14] This interpretation is supported by the work of Patrick Ball, who analyzed the factors associated with the formation of human rights organizations in Latin America. He explains the association he found between treaty participation and rates of organizational founding in these terms:

> Activists exploited the weakness of the hypocritical position required by the international public sphere in order to strengthen claims for justice. In this use of hypocrisy lies an insight: although noble international agreements made by brutal state leaders may seem cynical or meaningless, in the context of a globalizing regime of international human rights, activists have learned how to hold states accountable for these promises. (2000:74)

Below are several hypotheses that emerge from a consideration of world polity dynamics and their likely impacts on the sector:

H6: Participation in TSMOs will be highest in countries that have longer and more extensive involvement in international organizations.

H7: Participation in TSMOs will be highest in countries that are most integrated into the world political order, as represented by international treaty ratifications.

Data and Analysis

We used data from the *Yearbook of International Associations* to test the above hypotheses about which countries' citizens are likely to be most involved in transnational social movement organizations. We asked how *national conditions,* including levels of resources and political openness; *global economic factors,* levels of international trade, investment, and aid; and *global political factors,* including a country's ties to international organizations and participation in international treaties, influence the numbers of TSMOs that report having members in a given country. Table 14.1 displays the average number of TSMOs active in countries with different amounts of wealth, political regimes, and ties to global political and economic institutions. By examining these differences, we can begin to assess the extent to which the preceding theoretical discussion seems to explain the evidence we have here.

Table 14.1 shows that it is indeed wealthier and more democratic countries that are more active in transnational social movement organizations. It also supports arguments that countries with more ties to global political institutions will see more transnational activism within their borders. However, the patterns here don't seem to support claims that more international trade will encourage civil society engagement. Countries with lower levels of trade had somewhat higher levels of participation in TSMOs than those with more extensive amounts of international trade.

Before we say too much about the patterns in table 14.1, however, it is important to note that in the real world all these variables exist together and influence one another. So we need to use a method that allows us to test all the variables *together* in order to determine which of them affects rates of participation in TSMOs, irrespective of the influence of the other variables. For instance, we want to know whether a country with greater participation in international treaties will have more citizen involvement in TSMOs, even if the

Table 14.1. Variation in TSMO Participation According to Country Attributes

Selected Attributes of Countries	Average Number of TSMOs with Members in Country
Domestic Opportunities and Resources	
Low income	115
Middle income	157
High income	329
Nondemocratic*	112
Democratic*	220
Global Economic Ties**	
Low levels of international trade	186
Average or high levels of international trade	162
Global Political Ties	
Low participation in human right treaties	123
Average or high participation in human rights treaties	195
Low involvement in intergovernmental organizations	111
Average or high involvement in intergovernmental organizations	225

Notes: TSMO = transnational social movement organization.
 *Based on classification scheme developed by Jaggers and Gurr (1995).
** Our measure of international trade is the value of international trade relative to the country's economy, controlling for the country's population.

country does not have vast economic resources or a democratic form of government. The method that we used to test this is a form of nonlinear regression called negative binomial regression.[15] Table 14.2 summarizes the multivariate results, indicating which variables significantly influenced rates of TSMO participation across countries.

Table 14.2 shows that domestic factors remain important for explaining which nations' citizens are able to become involved in transnational social movement organizations. Resources and political openings have significant effects on participation rates even when we control for international economic and political factors. In other words, globalization has not meant the end of the nation-state's significance.

Somewhat surprisingly, our study finds that a country's ties to the global economy do not influence its rates of participation in global civil society.

Global trade proponents' claims that expanding global markets will automatically generate other benefits such as greater openness and democratization are not supported by this evidence. However, there is a connection between higher levels of official development assistance (incoming and outgoing) and greater numbers of ties to transnational associations. This is likely due to the fact that more government aid is given to nongovernmental citizens' groups rather than directly to governments. So these aid flows are designed specifically to encourage civil society organizing rather than economic growth specifically, and they appear to be achieving this aim. When we explored the extent to which the poorest countries differed from others, we found that higher levels of trade did matter for this subset of countries, even if it didn't impact rates of transnational participation by middle- or high-income countries. This finding suggests that more global trade may indeed have some

Table 14.2. Summary of Domestic and International Effects on TSMO Participation

Variables	Direction/Sig. (Partial Model)	Direction/Sig. (Partial Model)	Direction/Sig. (Partial Model)	Direction/Sig. (Full Model)
Domestic				
Income level	+/***	+/***	+/***	+/***
Population	+/***	+/***	+/***	+/***
Democracy	+/***	+/***	+/***	+/***
Economic ties				
Trade				
FDI				
ODA		+/***		
Debt				
Low-income trade[1]		+/***		
Political ties				
# IGOs			+/***	+/***
# HR Treaty			+/***	+/***
# Yrs. UN				
Low-income IGO[1]			+/***	+/***

Notes: TSMO = transnational social movement organization; FDI = foreign direct investment; ODA = official development assistance; HR = human rights. Results from negative binomial regression analysis of national counts of TSMO memberships on domestic and international variables (Smith and Wiest 2004).
[1] "Low-income" countries are classified according to World Bank ratings.

positive impacts, and it also tells us that world-systems theorists are correct to argue that a country's position in the world economy affects its opportunities and possibilities for change.

The model containing global political measures shows that these factors are far more influential on rates of participation in transnational association than are a country's ties to the global economy. This model contributes much more to our effort to explain variation in who participates in global civil society, and it shows that countries with more ties to international organizations and human rights treaties are also more likely to have citizens who are active in TSMOs. Again, we find that low-income countries are most likely to be positively affected by their ties to global institutions—that is, the more ties to international organizations, the more participation in TSMOs. When we run the "full model" that contains all the variables in our analysis, we find that, while domestic factors still matter, it is ties to the global political system rather than to the global economy that tell us most about which countries' citizens are participating in global civil society.

Some scholars of globalization argue that the rise of supranational institutions and an increasingly integrated global economy signals the decline of the national state, but our study suggests that such a conclusion is premature at best. The state still matters tremendously in conditioning the possibilities for individuals to engage in political associations that cross national boundaries. Regardless of the availability of resources for political mobilization, countries with stronger democratic traditions are better represented in transnational social movement organizations.

Most notable, our findings challenge predominant assumptions that it is the economic forms of global integration that matter the most. Controlling for other factors, we found no significant effects of important measures of economic integration—amount of foreign direct investment, aid flows, and trade—on participation in TSMOs. Moreover, the models including only economic integration measures were the weakest among those we tested.

Our results provide strong support for our contention that international institutions matter, at least for explaining how people engage in transnational political action. Countries with structured, routine participation in the global polity, measured in terms of memberships in international organizations and treaties, are more likely to become "socialized" into the norms of international society (Finnemore 1996; Riemann 2002). These are the same countries that are likely to have comparatively higher levels of citizen participation in TSMOs. Evidence from other studies suggests that transnational or world cultural processes are becoming more influential over time. For instance, longitudinal studies by Ramirez and his colleagues and by Tsutsui and Wotipka found stronger world cultural effects on the adoption of women's suffrage and on participation in international human rights NGOs, respectively, in more recent years than they found in earlier years (Ramirez, Soysal, and Shanahan 1997; Tsutsui and Wotipka 2003). Thus, if we test our models with data from earlier time periods, we would expect to find much weaker connections between a state's integration into the global polity and its levels of transnational participation.

Global political institutions matter, but we also found that their impact varies according to a country's position in the world-system hierarchy. Low-income countries with higher numbers of ties to intergovernmental organizations tended to be *more* active in transnational associations. This finding corresponds best with an institutional or world polity explanation rather than with the notion that economic globalization drives other forms of transnational interaction. Countries that are more vulnerable to pressures from richer states may find opportunities for enhancing their influence in global affairs through global institutions. Global institutions extend legitimacy to a state, thereby providing incentives for governments to join them. Paradoxically, by using international institutions to bolster their position in the interstate system, low-income countries create internal conditions that encourage civil society mobilization within their borders, and although they may join treaties with few intentions of following them, they may soon face rising internal pressures to conform to international standards.

In short, the size and comprehensiveness of global civil society are strongly related to increased global *political* integration, not economic integration. The "trickle down" theory of global integration—that is, that economic integration will produce economic growth that, in turn, supports and encourages other forms of transnational cooperation—is not supported with the evidence we use here. Instead, it is a country's participation in intergovernmental organizations and in global treaty bodies that encourages its citizens to engage in other forms of transnational association, and this can overcome the disadvantages of a country's position in the world economy. More democratic countries are the most active participants in all forms of transnational association, but the results here show that the direction of influence may be two-way. Institutional norms and pressures can lead nondemocratic states to join international treaties and organizations. Global political integration, in turn, encourages democratization within countries by legitimizing values of pluralism, equality, and tolerance and by creating processes that can socialize states along these values (Boli and Thomas 1999; UNDP 2002). In the aftermath of September 11, multilateral institutions may prove even more central to efforts of all countries to promote their own security interests (despite arguments to the contrary in the United States).

This study has important lessons for policy makers. By showing that participation in these explicitly nonviolent, cooperatively based organizations is directly related to countries' participation in international organizations of all kinds, it says that efforts to increase cooperative international problem-solving are best sought by promoting multilateral institutions. Pressing for stronger or more expansive trade agreements and urging states to open their markets to the world *do not* lead to more open societies. For the United States, this would require a fundamental rethinking of the "war on terror." Instead of pursuing preemptive and unilateral wars and economically motivated versions of democratization in the Middle East, if it is serious about limiting the spread of intolerant, militant fundamentalism it must put multilateralism at the forefront of its policy agenda. Countries will not continue to participate in international organizations and treaties if they see that the United States refuses to abide by the norms of these organizations. If the United States continues to "unsign" treaties like Kyoto and the International Criminal Court, we may see other countries following suit, and this can have negative consequences for transnational citizen engagement. Without strong international ties that enable information and ideas to flow across national boundaries, there are ample opportunities for divisive, fundamentalist mobilizations within countries. And to the extent that economic globalization excludes more and more of the world's poor from partaking in its benefits, efforts to promote economic globalization in the absence of broader political globalization will only facilitate the recruiting efforts of groups promoting political violence.

Notes

This chapter summarizes the research reported in "The Uneven Geography of Global Civil Society: National and Global Influences on Transnational Association," forthcoming in *Social Forces*.

1. For more on the political dynamics of social movements within nested national and interstate politics, see Smith, Pagnucco, and Chatfield (1997), Tarrow (2001b, 2003), and Rothman and Oliver (2002).

2. Many social scientists discuss the importance of networks in contemporary

global settings. Certainly the proliferation of relatively low cost communications and travel-related technologies has enabled more informal and decentralized relations to span an ever widening geographic scope. While we clearly see networks embedded within the organizations we study, we focus here on more formally structured relationships (i.e., organizations) because these are likely to be more durable and predictable than "networks," and they also allow for large-scale and longitudinal comparisons that would be very difficult to do with networks. That said, it is clear that the organizations we analyze operate in ways that are similar to networks, that they build on the technologies and opportunities that also facilitate networks, and that in many ways they are becoming more decentralized and informal like networks.

3. The *Yearbook of International Associations* is edited by the Union of International Associations (UIA), which was formally charged by the United Nations with the task of assembling a regular database of all international and transnational organizations—that is (by UIA's definition), all organizations involving different national governments or citizens (or both) from at least three countries. The UIA makes extensive efforts to identify new groups and to identify inactive or disbanded groups. Once identified, responsible authorities within each organization are asked to complete an annual questionnaire that details the organization's work, its members, and its links with international organizations and NGOs, among other information. The UIA has made systematic efforts to improve its data collection methods, and as a result we can be quite confident about their accuracy for more recent years. While it is not a perfect census of all transnational organizations—and it is likely to be comparatively less accurate in tracking the less formal and more fluid social movement groups we're interested in here—it remains the best record we have over a long period of time of transnational organizational activity.

4. INGOs is the common term used among practitioners and in much of the political science literature and within the United Nations system to refer to voluntary, nonprofit citizens associations. It includes groups as diverse as the International Olympic Committee, Amnesty International, and the International Elvis Presley Fan Club.

5. Although other nongovernmental organizations are important in social movements, existing research suggests that it is those groups that are specifically focused on movement goals that play consistent roles in either mobilizing or introducing innovations into social movements. Thus, we focus on those groups that we expect to be most involved in social movement activity (Smith et al. 1997).

6. Following common practices among scholars and practitioners of global politics, we use the terms "global north" to refer to the Western, postindustrial states (members of the Organisation for Economic Cooperation and Development [OECD]) and "global south" to refer to those postcolonial and later-industrializing states that generally constitute what world-systems scholars call the "periphery" and "semiperiphery."

7. The standard deviation for noncore countries is 74 percent of mean, compared with 23 percent for core countries.

8. However, the work of Tilly (1990), Walton and Seddon (1994), and world-systems theorists argues for a treatment of the state that accounts for its position in the global economic and political order.

9. Our preliminary examination of this hypothesis suggests, however, that transnational human rights groups are not any more likely to be active in repressive contexts, at least not in the sense that they have participants from those regions among their members. In fact, environmental groups—perhaps because their grievances can in some instances be cast in more politically neutral terms—seem somewhat better able to cultivate transnational ties in more repressive settings.

10. We currently lack comparative data on the strength of national voluntary sectors, but existing measures of political openness and democratic practice indicate the extent to which citizens of a country enjoy the right to free association.

11. This is not meant to imply that the domestic politics of core states are not affected by global factors (see, e.g., Knopf 1993; Evangelista 1995) but rather that periphery states are more vulnerable to external influences on a wider range of policy areas.

12. Several respondents to a survey Smith conducted of affiliates of a transnational organization, EarthAction, captured this sentiment as they described a sense of being doubly disenfranchised: they had little effective access to their domestic political leaders, and their governments had little impact on the United Nations, which they saw as being dominated by the United States (Smith 2002).

13. Many international treaties and declarations call explicitly for states to include nongovernmental organizations in various aspects of policy-making and monitoring of international agreements.

14. A similar dynamic is outlined in Risse, Ropp, and Sikkink's (1999) "spiral model" for explaining changes in human rights practices, and in Friedman, Clark, and Hochstetler (forthcoming).

15. For details about the data and methods used in this study, see Smith and Wiest, "The Uneven Geography of Global Civil Society: National and Global Influences on Transnational Association," forthcoming in *Social Forces*.

References

Anheier, Helmut, Marlies Glasius, and Mary Kaldor. 2001. "Global Civil Society 2001." New York: Oxford University Press.

Ball, Patrick. 2000. "State Terror, Constitutional Traditions, and National Human Rights Movements: A Cross-National Quantitative Comparison." Pp. 54–75 in *Globalizations and Social Movements: Culture, Power, and the Transnational Public Sphere*, edited by J. A. Guidry, M. D. Kennedy, and M. N. Zald. Ann Arbor, MI: University of Michigan Press.

Bob, Clifford. 2001. "Marketing Rebellion: Insurgent Groups, International Media, and NGO Support." *International Politics* 38:311–334.

————. 2005. *The Marketing of Rebellion: Insurgents, Media, and International Activism.* Cambridge, MA: Cambridge University Press.

Boli, John. 1999. "Conclusion: World Authority Structures and Legitimation." Pp. 267–302 in *Constructing World Culture: International Nongovernmental Organizations since 1875,* edited by J. Boli and G. M. Thomas. Stanford, CA: Stanford University Press.

Boli, John, Thomas A. Loya, and Teresa Loftin. 1999. "National Participation in World-Polity Organizations." Pp. 50–79 in *Constructing World Culture: International Nongovernmental Organizations since 1865,* edited by J. Boli and G. M. Thomas. Stanford, CA: Stanford University Press.

Boli, John and George Thomas. 1997. "World Culture in the World Polity: A Century of Non-Governmental Organization." *American Sociological Review* 62:171–190.

————, ed. 1999. *Constructing World Culture: International Nongovernmental Organizations since 1875.* Stanford, CA: Stanford University Press.

Chilton, Patricia. 1995. "Mechanics of Change: Social Movements, Transnational Coalitions, and the Transformation Process in Eastern Europe." In *Bringing Transnational Relations Back In: Non-State Actors, Domestic Structures, and International Institutions,* edited by T. Risse-Kappen. New York: Cambridge University Press.

Clark, Ann Marie, Elisabeth J. Friedman, and Kathryn Hochstetler. 1998. "The Sovereign Limits of Global Civil Society: A Comparison of NGO Participation in UN World Conferences on the Environment, Human Rights, and Women." *World Politics* 51:1–35.

Coy, Patrick. 1997. "Protecting Targets of Human Rights Abuse: The Networking Work of Peace Brigades International." In *Transnational Social Movements and World Politics: Solidarity beyond the State,* edited by J. Smith, C. Chatfield, and R. Pagnucco. Syracuse, NY: Syracuse University Press.

Curtis, James E., Douglas E. Baer, and Edward G. Grabb. 2001. "Nations of Joiners: Explaining Voluntary Association Membership in Democratic Countries." *American Sociological Review* 66:783–805.

della Porta, Donatella and Hanspeter Kriesi. 1999. "Social Movements in a Globalizing World: An Introduction." Pp. 3–23 in *Social Movements in a Globalizing World,* edited by D. della Porta, H. Kriesi, and D. Rucht. New York: St. Martin's Press.

DiMaggio, Paul J. and Walter W. Powell. 1991. "The Iron Cage Revisited: Institutional Isomorphism and Collective Rationality in Organization Fields." Pp. 63–82 in *The New Institutionalism in Organizational Analysis,* edited by W. W. Powell and P. J. DiMaggio. Chicago: University of Chicago Press.

Evangelista, Matthew. 1995. "Transnational Relations, Domestic Structures, and Security Policy in the USSR and Russia." Pp. 146–188 in *Bringing Transnational Relations Back In: Non-State Actors, Domestic Structures, and International Institutions,* edited by T. Risse-Kappen. New York: Cambridge University Press.

Finnemore, Martha. 1996. *National Interests in International Society.* Ithaca, NY: Cornell University Press.

Frank, David John. 1999. "The Social Bases of Environmental Treaty Ratification." *Sociological Inquiry* 69:523–550.

Frank, David John, Ann Hironaka, and Evan Schofer. 2000. "The Nation-State and the Natural Environment over the Twentieth Century." *American Sociological Review* 65:96–116.

Friedman, Elisabeth Jay, Ann Marie Clark, and Kathryn Hochstetler. Forthcoming. *The Sovereign Limits of Global Civil Society.* New York: State University of New York Press.

Giugni, Marco. 2002. "The Other Side of the Coin: Explaining Crossnational Similarities between Social Movements." Pp. 11–24 in *Globalization and Resistance: Transnational Dimensions of Social Movements,* edited by J. Smith and H. Johnston. Lanham, MD: Rowman and Littlefield.

Guidry, John A., Michael D. Kennedy, and Mayer N. Zald. 2000. "Globalizations and Social Movements: Introduction." Pp. 1–32 in *Globalizations and Social Movements: Culture, Power, and the Global Public Sphere,* edited by J. A. Guidry, M. D. Kennedy, and M. N. Zald. Ann Arbor, MD: University of Michigan Press.

Hafner-Burton, Emilie M. and Kiyotero Tsutsui. 2003. "Human Rights in a Globalizing World: The Paradox of Empty Promises." Manuscript, Stony Brook, New York.

Hippler, Jochen.1995. "Democratization of the Third World after the End of the Cold War." Pp. 1–31 in *The Democratization of Disempowerment: The Problem of Democracy in the Third World,* edited by J. Hippler. East Haven, CT: Pluto Press.

Imig, Doug and Sidney Tarrow. 2001. *Contentious Europeans: Protest and Politics in an Integrating Europe.* Lanham, MD: Rowman and Littlefield.

Jaggers, Keith and Ted Robert Gurr. 1995. "Tracking Democracy's Third Wave with Polity III Data" *Journal of Peace Research* 4:469–482.

Jenkins, Craig J. and Kurt Schock. 1992. "Global Structures and Political Processes in the Study of Domestic Political Conflict." *Annual Review of Sociology* 18:161–185.

Joppke, C.1992. "Explaining Cross-National Variations of Two Anti-Nuclear Movements: A Political Process Perspective." *Sociology* 26:311–331.

Keck, Margaret and Kathryn Sikkink. 1998. *Activists beyond Borders: Advocacy Networks in International Politics.* Ithaca, NY: Cornell University Press.

Kitchelt, Herbert. 1986. "Political Opportunity Structures and Political Protest: Anti-Nuclear Movements in Four Democracies." *British Journal of Political Science* 16:57–85.

Knopf, Jeffrey W. 1993. "Beyond Two-Level Games: Domestic-International Interaction in the Intermediate Range Nuclear Forces Negotiations." *International Organization* 47:599–628.

Koopmans, Ruud. 1999. "A Comparison of Protests against the Gulf War in Germany, France and the Netherlands." Pp. 57–70 in *Social Movements in a Globalizing World,* edited by D. della Porta, H. Kriesi, and D. Rucht. New York: St. Martin's Press.

Lewis, Tammy L. 2002. "Transnational Conservation Movement Organizations: Shaping the Protected Area Systems of Less Developed Countries." Pp. 75–94 in

Globalizing Resistance: Transnational Dimensions of Social Movements, edited by J. Smith and H. Johnston. Lanham, MD: Rowman and Littlefield.

Liebowitz, Debra J. 2000. "Explaining Absences, Analyzing Change, Looking Toward the Future—U.S. Women's Participation in Transnational Feminist Organizing in North America." Paper presented at the International Studies Association Annual Meeting, Los Angeles.

Maney, Greg. 2002. "Transnational Structures and Protest: Linking Theories and Assessing Evidence." In *Globalization and Resistance: Transnational Dimensions of Social Movements,* edited by Jackie Smith and Hank Johnston Lanham. MD.: Rowman and Littlefield.

Markoff, John. 2003. "Who Will Construct the Global Order?" In *Transnational Democracy,* edited by B. Williamson. London: Ashgate.

McAdam, Doug, John D. McCarthy, and Mayer Zald, eds. 1996. *Comparative Perspectives on Social Movements: Political Opportunities, Mobilizing Structures and Cultural Framings.* New York: Cambridge University Press.

McCarthy, John D. 1996. "Mobilizing Structures: Constraints and Opportunities in Adopting, Adapting and Inventing." In *Comparative Perspectives on Social Movements: Political Opportunities, Mobilizing Structures and Cultural Framings,* edited by D. McAdam, J. McCarthy, and M. Zald. New York: Cambridge University Press.

McCarthy, John D. and Mayer Zald. 1977. "Resource Mobilization in Social Movements: A Partial Theory." *American Journal of Sociology* 82:1212–1241.

Meyer, John W., John Boli, George M. Thomas, and Francisco O. Ramirez. 1997a. "World Society and the Nation-State." *American Journal of Sociology* 103:144–181.

Meyer, John W., David John Frank, Ann Hironaka, Evan Schofer, and Nancy Brandon Tuma. 1997b. "The Structuring of a World Environmental Regime, 1870–1990." *International Organization* 51:623–651.

Minkoff, Deborah. 1997. "Producing Social Capital: National Social Movements and Civil Society." *American Behavioral Scientist* 40:606–619.

Muñoz, Jose. 2002. "The Global Structuring of Collective Action: Zapatistas, Mexico, and the New World Economy." Yale Center for International and Area Studies Working Paper Series. Available at www.cis.yale.edu/ycias/.

Oberschall, Anthony. 1973. *Social Conflict and Social Movements.* Englewood Cliffs, NJ: Prentice-Hall.

Ramirez, Francisco O., Yasemin Soysal, and Suzanne Shanahan. 1997. "The Changing Logic of Political Citizenship: Cross-National Acquisition of Women's Suffrage Rights, 1890–1990." *American Sociological Review* 62:735–745.

Reimann, Kim D. 2002. "Building Networks from the Outside In: International Movements, Japanese NGOs, and the Kyoto Climate Change Conference." In *Globalization and Resistance: Transnational Dimensions of Social Movements,* edited by Jackie Smith and Hank Johnston. Lanham, MD: Rowman and Littlefield.

Risse-Kappen, Thomas. 1995. "Bringing Transnational Relations Back In: Introduction." Pp. 3–33 in *Bringing Transnational Relations Back In: Non-State Actors, Do-*

mestic Structures, and International Institutions, edited by T. Risse-Kappen. New York: Cambridge University Press.

Risse-Kappen, Thomas, Stephen C. Ropp, and Kathryn Sikkink. 1999. *The Power of Human Rights: International Norms and Domestic Change.* New York: Cambridge University Press.

Robinson, William. 1996. *Promoting Polyarchy: Globalization, U.S. Intervention and Hegemony.* Cambridge, UK: Cambridge University Press.

Rootes, Christopher. 2002. "Global Visions: Global Civil Society and the Lessons of European Environmentalism." *Voluntas: International Journal of Voluntary and Nonprofit Organizations* 20:411–429.

Rothman, Franklin Daniel and Pamela E. Oliver. 2002. "From Local to Global: The Anti-Dam Movement in Southern Brazil 1979–1992." In *Globalization and Resistance: Transnational Dimensions of Social Movements,* edited by Jackie Smith and Hank Johnston. Lanham, MD: Rowman and Littlefield.

Sassen, Saskia. 1998. *Globalization and Its Discontents.* New York: New Press.

Schofer, Evan and Marion Fourcade-Gournchas. 2001. "The Structural Contexts of Civic Engagement: Voluntary Association Membership in Comparative Perspective." *American Sociological Review* 66:806–828.

Sikkink, Kathryn. 1993. "Human Rights, Principled Issue-Networks, and Sovereignty in Latin America." *International Organization* 47:411–441.

Smith, Jackie. 2000. "Social Movements, International Institutions, and Local Empowerment." Pp. 65–84 in *Global Institutions and Local Empowerment,* edited by K. Stiles. New York: Macmillan Press.

———. 2002. "Bridging Global Divides? Strategic Framing and Solidarity in Transnational Social Movement Organizations." *International Sociology* 17:505–528.

Smith, Jackie, Ron Pagnucco, and Charles Chatfield. 1997. "Transnational Social Movements and World Politics: Theoretical Framework." Pp. 59–77 in *Transnational Social Movements and Global Politics: Solidarity beyond the State,* edited by J. Smith, C. Chatfield, and R. Pagnucco. Syracuse, NY: Syracuse University Press.

Tarrow, Sidney. 1988. "National Politics and Collective Action." *Annual Review of Sociology* 14:421–440.

———. 2001a. "Contentious Politics in a Composite Polity." Pp. 233–251 in *Contentious Europeans: Protest and Politics in an Emerging Polity,* edited by D. Imig and S. Tarrow. Boulder, CO: Rowman and Littlefield.

———. 2001b. "Transnational Politics: Contention and Institutions in International Politics." *Annual Review of Political Science* 4:1–20.

———. 2003. "'Global' Movements, Complex Internationalism, and North-South Inequality." Paper presented at the Workshop on Contentious Politics, Columbia University, New York.

Tilly, Charles. 1984. "Social Movements and National Politics." Pp. 297–317 in *Statemaking and Social Movements: Essays in History and Theory,* edited by C. Bright and S. Harding. Ann Arbor, MI: University of Michigan Press.

———. 1990. *Coercion, Capital and European States, AD 990–1990.* Cambridge, MA: Blackwell.

Timberlake, Michael and Kirk R. Williams. 1984. "Dependence, Political Exclusion, and Government Repression: Some Cross-National Evidence." *American Sociological Review* 49:141–146.

Tsutsui, Kiyoteru and Christine Min Wotipka. 2003. "Global Civil Society and the Expansion of the International Human Rights Movement." Manuscript, State University of New York, Stony Brook.

Union of International Associations. 2000. *Yearbook of International Organizations.* Vol. 2. Brussels: Union of International Associations.

———. 2004. *Yearbook of International Organizations.* Brussels: Union of International Associations.

UNDP. 2002. *Human Development Report 2002: Deepening Democracy in a Fragmented World.* New York: Oxford University Press.

Walton, John and David Seddon. 1994. *Free Markets and Food Riots: The Politics of Global Adjustment.* Cambridge, MA: Blackwell.

Wapner, Paul. 1996. *Environmental Activism and World Civic Politics.* New York: City University of New York Press.

———. 2002. "Defending Accountability in NGOs." *Chicago Journal of International Law* 3:197–205.

Warkentin, Craig and Karen Mingst. 2000. "International Institutions, the State, and Global Civil Society in the Age of the World Wide Web." *Global Governance* 6:237–257.

VI | Democracy and Democratization

15

Transnational Social Movements and Democratic Socialist
Parties in the Semiperiphery   *On to Global Democracy*

TERRY BOSWELL AND CHRISTOPHER CHASE-DUNN

We contend that the progressive antisystemic movements are likely to find
their greatest support in the semiperiphery. Democratic socialist parties and
regimes that are coming to power in the semiperipheral countries will be the
forereachers that show how the progressive transnational movements (feminism, environmentalism, labor, indigenism) can work together to democratize global governance.

The "semiperipheral development" idea is an important tool for understanding the real possibilities for global social change because semiperipheral
countries are the weakest link in the global capitalist system—the zone where
the most powerful antisystemic movements have emerged in the past and
where vital and transformative developments are likely to occur in the future.

Globalization is producing a backlash, much as it did in the nineteenth
century and in the 1920s. Capitalist globalization, especially the kind that
has occurred since the 1970s, exposes many individuals to disruptive market
forces and increases inequalities within countries and internationally. The
gap between the winners and the losers grows, and the winners use more coercion and less consent in their efforts to stay on top. Polanyi's notion of the
double-movement by which marketization produces defensive reactions and
new forms of regulation is conceptually similar to the notion that expansive
capitalism produces efforts to decommodify labor and communities and that
these then drive capitalism to mobilize on a larger scale in order to overcome
the constraints that political resistance produces. This process has been
metaphorically characterized by Boswell and Chase-Dunn (2000) as the "spiral of capitalism and socialism." This chapter provides a political analysis of
the contemporary period in which capitalist globalization is once again being
challenged.

Amory Starr (2000) has studied 15 transnational social movements that
name corporate capitalism as the enemy. She divides these movements into
three categories: (1) contestation and reform (e.g., human rights, the peace

movement, cyberpunks); (2) globalization from below (populist global governance); and (3) delinking of localities from the global economy to rebuild small-scale communities that are protected from global corporations. Starr herself favors delinking, and several other critics of global capitalism also envision a process of deglobalization as desirable (e.g., Amin 1997; Bello 2002; McMichael 2004).

One of the big challenges is how the different kinds of progressive social movements can work together to struggle against capitalist globalization. The issue of alliances is complicated by the fact that some of the groups in opposition to capitalist globalization are reactionary rather than progressive. So the enemy of my enemy is not always my friend. And even among the progressives there are major contentious issues.

Environmentalists and labor groups have notorious differences. Core and peripheral workers may have different interests regarding issues such as global labor standards. And there are obvious contradictions between those who want to democratize global governance and those who want to abolish it altogether in favor of maximum local autonomy. It is our position that the human species needs both better and more democratic global governance *and* more local autonomy and that the globalization-from-below movements should work together with the local-autonomy movements, or at least with those participants who are progressive and willing. We contend that socialism or anarchism within one country or one community will not work for very long and that we must confront the difficult issues of global governance head-on in order to move toward a more humane and equitable world society. This will not require homogenization and further subordination. Cultural differences and diversity are desirable as long as they are not used as an excuse for domination or exploitation. And we favor the "principle of subsidiarity," whereby problems that are most efficiently and equitably dealt with on a local, regional, or national level need not be the concern of global governance (see below). But some problems (global environmental degradation, warfare among states, reducing international inequalities) cannot be effectively solved by exclusively local jurisdictions. Thus we must envision and eventually create a democratic and collectively rational global government in order to survive and prevail as a species. Some localists will support this project.

One implication of the comparative world-systems perspective (Chase-Dunn and Hall 1997; Hall and Chase-Dunn, Chapter 3, this volume) is that all hierarchical and complex world-systems exhibit a "power cycle" in which political-military power becomes more centralized followed by a phase of decentralization. This is likely to be true of the future of the world-system as well, though the form of the power cycle may change. Our species needs to invent political and cultural institutions that allow adjustments in the global political and economic structures to take place without resort to warfare. This is analogous to the problem of succession within single states, and the solution is obvious—a global government that represents the interests of the majority of the peoples of the Earth and allows for political restructuring to occur by democratic processes.

Capitalist accumulation usually favors a multicentric interstate system because this provides greater opportunities for the maneuverability of capital than would exist in a world state. Big capitals can play national states off against one another and can escape movements that try to regulate investment or redistribute profits by abandoning (and repressing) the national states in which such movements attain political power.

The modern world-system has experienced long waves of economic and political integration over recent centuries. As in Chapter 5 of this volume, we use the term "structural globalization" to denote intercontinental integration and connectedness. The recent waves of global integration are the contemporary incarnations of the pulsations of widening and deepening interaction networks that are an important feature of all regional world-systems for millennia. But since the nineteenth century these have occurred in a single global system. Figure 5.1 in Chapter 5 shows the waves of global trade integration in the nineteenth and twentieth centuries. The crucial comparison is between the late nineteenth century (1890–1914) and recent decades (beginning with 1980). These are the periods when the cycle of globalization makes a qualitative shift upward. The shift is so steep that it changes human consciousness and people become vividly aware of their increasing global interdependence.

Capitalist Globalization

A key feature of the historical development of the modern world-system is the evolution of certain central institutions. The most important institutions in the modern system have been commodification of goods, land, and labor; technologies of production, transportation, and communications; and techniques of power—states and global governance institutions. These institutions have all been shaped by tremendous struggles between classes, between contending states, and between core and peripheral zones. The outcomes of these struggles can be characterized as a series of global orders in which constellations of institutions have evolved.

The story of how global orders have been restructured in order to facilitate capitalist accumulation must be told in world-historical perspective in order to be able to see how the most recent wave of corporate globalization is similar to, or different from, earlier waves of globalization. Of particular interest here is the phenomenon of "world revolutions" and increasingly transnational antisystemic social movements. In order to comprehend the possibilities for the emergence of global democracy we need to understand both the successes and failures of the social movements that have tried to democratize the world-system in the past.

Most immediately relevant to our own era is the world history of the nineteenth century and its huge wave of capitalist globalization under the auspices of British hegemony. The most important transnational antisystemic movements were antislavery, antiserfdom, the labor movement, and the feminist movement. In these struggles slaves, serfs, workers, and women consciously took the up the role of world citizen, organizing local and international movements to bring social justice to an emerging global society. Political and economic elites, especially finance capitalists, had already been consciously operating on an intercontinental scale for centuries, but the degree of international integration of these elites reached a very high level in the late nineteenth century.[1]

The British created the Concert of Europe after defeating Napoleon. This was a Europe-wide alliance of conservative dynasties and politicians who were dedicated to the prevention of any future French revolutions and Napoleonic adventures. The British Royal Navy suppressed the slave trade and encouraged decolonization of the Spanish colonies in the Americas, thus providing an important justification for the hegemony of the United Kingdom. The English Anti-Corn Law League's advocacy of international free trade (carried abroad by British diplomats and businessmen) was adopted by most European and American states in the middle of the century. The gold standard was an important stimulus to increased international trade and investment (O'Rourke and Williamson 1999; Chase-Dunn, Kawano, and Brewer 2000). The expanding Atlantic economy, already firmly attached to the Indian Ocean, was accompanied by an expanding Pacific economy as Japan and China were more completely and directly brought into the trade and investment networks of Europe and North America. American ginseng was harvested in Pennsylvania as an important commodity export that could be used in lieu of silver in the trade for Chinese silks and "china" (porcelain).

The nineteenth-century wave of capitalist globalization was massively contested in a great globalization backlash. The decolonization of Latin

America extended the formal aspects of state sovereignty to a large chunk of the periphery. Slave revolts, abolitionism, and the further incorporation of Africa into the capitalist world-system eventually led to the abolition of slavery almost everywhere, and serfdom was also abolished in Russia and most of eastern Europe. Within Europe socialist and democratic demands for political and economic rights of the nonpropertied classes strongly emerged in the world revolution of 1848, and new religious sects and revitalization movements of indigenous peoples in the Americas and in East Asia widely challenged the rule of states in the middle decades of the nineteenth century.

An important aspect of our model of world-systems evolution is the idea of semiperipheral development (Hall and Chase-Dunn, Chapter 3, this volume). Institutional development in premodern world-systems occurred because innovations and implementations of new techniques and organizational forms have tended to occur in societies that have semiperipheral positions within larger core-periphery hierarchies. Semiperipheral marcher chiefdoms conquered adjacent core polities to create larger paramount chiefdoms. And semiperipheral marcher states conquered adjacent core states to create larger and larger corewide empires (e.g., Chin, Akkad, Assyrian, Achaemenid Persians, Alexander, Rome, Abbasid Caliphate) And semiperipheral capitalist city-states (Dilmun, Phoenician Tyre, Sidon, and Carthage; Venice, Genoa, Malacca, etc.) expanded commercialized trade networks and encouraged commodity production within and between the tributary empires and peripheral regions, linking larger and larger regions together to eventually become the single global economy of today.

The modern hegemons (the Dutch Republic of the seventeenth century, the United Kingdom of Great Britain in the nineteenth century, and the United States in the twentieth century) were all formerly semiperipheral nation-states that rose to the position of hegemony by transforming the institutional bases of economic and political-military power in response to challenges from contenders for hegemony and challenges from popular movements contesting the injustices of capitalism and modern colonial imperialism. The modern world-system has experienced systemwide waves of democracy rather than separate and disconnected sequences of democratization within individual countries (Markoff 1996). These waves have tended to start in semiperipheral countries, and the institutional inventions that have diffused from country to country have disproportionately been invented and implemented in semiperipheral countries first (Markoff, Chapter 16, this volume). Both the Russian and Chinese communist challenges to capitalism emerged from the semiperiphery.

The workers' movement became increasingly organized on an international basis during the nineteenth century. Mass production made working conditions increasingly similar for industrial workers around the world. Labor organizers were able to make good use of cheap and rapid transportation as well as new modes of communication (the telegraph) in order to link struggles in distant locations. And the huge migration of workers from Europe to the New World spread the ideas and the strategies of the labor movement. Socialists, anarchists, and communists challenged the rule of capital while they competed with one another for leadership of an increasingly global antisystemic movement that sought to democratize the world-system.

The decline of British hegemony, and the failure of efforts after World War I to erect an effective structure of global governance, led to the collapse of capitalist globalization during the depression of the 1930s, culminating in World War II. In our perspective capitalist globalization is a cycle as well as a trend. The great wave of the nineteenth century was followed by a collapse in the early twentieth century and then a reemergence in the period after World War II. The global institutions of the post–World War II order, now under the sponsorship of the hegemonic United States, were intended to resolve the problems that were perceived to have caused the military conflagrations and economic disasters of the early twentieth century. The United Nations was a stronger version of a global protostate than the League of Nations had been, though still a long way from the "monopoly of legitimate violence" that is the effective center of a real state.

The Bretton Woods institutions—the World Bank and the International Monetary Fund (IMF)—were originally intended to promote Keynesian national development rather than a globalized market of investment flows. Free trade was encouraged, but important efforts were made to track international investments and to encourage the efforts of national states to use fiscal policy as a tool of national development. The architects of the Bretton Woods institutions were nervous about the effects of volatile waves of international capital flows on economic development and political stability because of what they perceived to have been the lessons of the 1920s. The restarting of the world economy after World War II under the aegis of the Bretton Woods institutions and U.S. support for relatively autonomous capitalism in Europe and Japan succeeded tremendously. But the growing power of unions within the core, and the perceived constraints on U.S. fiscal and financial interests imposed by the Bretton Woods currency regime, along with the oil crisis of the early 1970s, led the United States to abandon Bretton Woods in favor of a free world market of currency trading and capital mobility. The "Washington Consensus" was basically Reaganism-Thatcherism on a global scale—deregulation, privatization, and reneging on the "social contract" with core labor unions and the welfare state. The IMF was turned into a tool for imposing these policies on countries all over the world.

This neoliberal regime of global capitalism led by the United States and Britain (Reaganism-Thatcherism) was a reaction to the successes of the Third World and the core labor movements, not in achieving true global democracy, but in getting a somewhat larger share of the profits of global capitalism. The attack on the institutions of Keynesian national development (labor unions and the welfare state) was also a delayed response to the world revolution of 1968, in which students, women, environmentalists, Third Worldists, indigenous peoples, democracy movements, and radical parts of the labor movement had critiqued the inadequacies of welfare capitalism and business unionism in favor of a more participatory democracy that challenged continuing racism, sexism, and class inequalities. The New Right appropriated some of the ideology and many of the tactics of the 68ers—demonstrations, civil disobedience, guerrilla armies, drug financing, mobilization of subnations, and so on. These tactics have come back to haunt the powers that be. In the recent wave of "blowback," organizations and ideologies formerly supported by the U.S. CIA as instruments against the Soviet Union (e.g., Al Qaeda) have turned against their former sponsors, employing dirty tricks to besmirch symbols of global power and to murder innocent bystanders (Johnson 2000).

We contend that the current historical moment is similar to the end of the nineteenth century. Like British hegemony, U.S. hegemony is declining. Contenders for global economic power have emerged in Germany-led Europe and China-led Asia. Popular movements and institutions have been under attack, especially since the rise to ideological hegemony of the neoliberal "globalization project." Antisystemic movements are struggling to find new paths for dealing with capitalist globalization. New communications technologies such as the Internet provide possibilities for creating coordinated and integrated movements in favor of global democracy. The liberating potential of decentered and democratized communications is great. But cheap interactive and mass communications also facilitate increasing differentiation and specialization of political mobilization, which can undercut efforts to promote intermovement coordination. We hold that the Internet will be, on balance, a liberating force, but the big gains in movement integration will probably come as a response to the economic, political, and ecological disasters that globalized capitalism is likely to produce in the not too distant future.

We expect that the current resistance to global capitalism will, in large part, take the form of local self-reliance, the revitalization of diverse cultural forms and the rejection of the cultural and technological totems of corporate capitalism. Thus the characterization of the recently emergent protest movements (Seattle, Genoa, etc.) as "antiglobalization" movements is partially correct, but it is misleading. Self-reliance may take forms that are progressive or forms that promote divisions among the people based on ethnicity, nation, or race. Self-reliance by itself is not an adequate strategy for transforming capitalism into a more humane and sustainable social system. Rather, the building of self-reliant communities needs also to organize with a coordinated movement of "globalization from below" that will seek to reform, or create de novo, world institutions that will promote social justice and environmental sustainability.

The theorists who have delineated a recent stage of "global capitalism" contend that the latest wave of integration has created a single integrated global bourgeoisie that has overthrown the dynamics of the hegemonic sequence (hegemonic rise and fall and interstate rivalry) (e.g., Robinson 2004). While most world-systems theorists hold that the U.S. hegemony continues the decline that began in the 1970s, many other observers interpret the demise of the Soviet Union and the relatively greater U.S. economic growth in the 1990s as ushering in a renewal of U.S. hegemony. Although some interpret this U.S. upturn in the 1990s as the beginning of another wave of U.S. "leadership" in the global economy based on comparative advantages in information technology and biotechnology, Giovanni Arrighi sees the 1990s as another wave of financialization comparable to the belle epoque or Edwardian Indian summer that occurred in the last decades of the nineteenth century (see Chapter 10, this volume). Much of the expansion in the U.S. economy was due to huge inflows of investment capital from Europe and East Asia during the 1990s. The theorists of global capitalism contend that the U.S. state, and other core states, are now instruments of the integrated global capitalist class rather than of separate and competing groups of national capitalists (Robinson 2004).

We agree with Walter Goldfrank (pers. comm.) that both global capitalism and the hegemonic sequence are operating simultaneously and are interacting with each other in complicated ways. Despite the rather high degree of international integration among economic and political elites, there is quite likely to be another round of rivalry among core states. This can already be seen in the disagreements about the Iraq war. Global elites achieved a rather high degree of international integration during the late nineteenth-century wave of globalization, but this did not prevent the world wars of the twentieth century.

Admitting to some aspects of the "global capitalism" thesis does not require accepting all of its claims. Some global capitalism theorists contend that information technology has changed everything and that we have entered a new stage of global history in which comparisons with what happened before 1960 are completely useless because things have changed so much. This kind of "presentism" is attractive because it means that we do not need to know anything about history. The most important part of the global capitalism thesis is the focus on global elite integration. Indeed, global class formation needs to be analyzed for peasants and workers as well as for elites (Goldfrank 1977). Research is currently under way to compare the nineteenth- and twentieth-century global elites as to their degree of international integration, as well as changes in the patterns of alliances and connections among the wealthiest and most powerful people on Earth (Chase-Dunn and Reifer 2002).

The hegemonic sequence (the rise and fall of hegemonic core powers) is not usefully understood as a cycle that takes the same form each time around. Rather, as Giovanni Arrighi (1994) has so convincingly shown, each "systemic cycle of accumulation" involves a reorganization of the relationships among big capitals and states. And not only do the evolutionary aspects of hegemony adapt to changes in scale, geography, and technology, but they also must solve problems created by resistance from below (Boswell and Chase-Dunn 2000; Silver 2003). Workers and farmers in the world-system are not inert objects of exploitation and domination. Rather, they develop new organizational and institutional instruments of protection and resistance. So the interaction between the powerful and less powerful is a spiral of domination and resistance that is one of the most important driving forces of the developmental history of modern capitalism.

The discourse produced by world-systems scholars about "the family of antisystemic movements" is an important contribution to our understanding of how different social movements act vis-à-vis one another on the terrain of the whole system (Arrighi, Hopkins, and Wallerstein 1989). It is unfortunate that public discourse about globalization has characterized recent protest movements in terms of "antiglobalization." This has occurred because, in the popular mind, globalization has been associated primarily with what Phil McMichael (1996) has termed the "globalization project"—the neoliberal policies of the "Washington Consensus" and the hegemony of corporate capitalism. This is the political ideology of Reaganism-Thatcherism—

market magic, deregulation, privatization, and allegedly no alternative to submitting to the "realities" of global capitalist competition.[2]

The terminology of "antiglobalization" is unfortunate because it conflates two different meanings of "globalization" and implies that the only sensible form of resistance to globalization involves the construction of local institutions to defend against the forces of global capitalism. Structural globalization means economic, political, and cultural international and transnational integration. This should be analytically separated from the political ideology of the "globalization project."

The "neoliberal globalization project" is what the demonstrators are protesting, but the term "antiglobalization" also implies that they are against international integration and global institutions. The term "antisystemic movements" needs to be carefully clarified so that it does not add to this confusion.

Local protectionism will undoubtedly be an important component of the emerging resistance to corporate globalization and neoliberal policies. But one lesson we can derive from earlier efforts to confront and transform capitalism is that local resistance cannot, by itself, overcome the strong forces of modern capitalism. What is needed is globalization from below. Global politics has mainly been the politics of the powerful because they have had the resources to establish long-distance connections and to structure global institutions. But waves of elite transnational integration have been accompanied by upsurges of transnational linkages, strategies, and institutions formed by workers, farmers, and popular challenges to the logic of capitalist accumulation. Globalization from below means the transnationalization of antisystemic movements and the active participation of popular movements in global politics and global citizenship.

An analysis of earlier waves of the spiral of domination and resistance demonstrates that "socialism in one country" and other strategies of local protection have not been capable of overcoming the negative aspects of capitalist development in the past, and they are even less likely to succeed in the more densely integrated global system of the future. Strategies that mobilize people to organize themselves locally must be complemented by and coordinated with transnational strategies to democratize or replace existing global institutions and to create new organizational structures that facilitate collective rationality for all the peoples of the world.

The major transnational antisystemic movements are the labor movement, the women's movement, the environmental movement, and the indigenous movement. Of these, the environmental movement and the women's movement have had the most recent successes in forming transnational linkages and confronting the difficult issues posed by regional, national, and core-periphery differences. But the labor and indigenous movements have made important efforts to catch up. Cross-border organizing efforts and support for demonstrations against corporate globalization show that the AFL-CIO is interested in exploring new approaches. One important task for world-systems scholars is to study these movements and to help devise initiatives that can produce tactical and strategic transnational alliances.

Bruce Podobnik's (2002) careful and systematic study of globalization protests shows how these have emerged over the past decade in the core and the noncore countries. There was an important wave of anti-IMF struggles in the 1980s researched by John Walton and David Seddon (1994). Podobnik's research shows that between 1900 and June 2002, 44 percent of the globalization protests occurred in core (developed) countries and 56 percent occurred in noncore (less developed) countries. The percentage of protesters injured, arrested, and killed was far higher in the noncore than in the core countries. Podobnik also shows that these protests were temporarily dampened by the events of September 11, 2001, but that they rebounded in the months following. Contrary to popular opinion, the globalization protests were not stopped by the events of September 11.

Growing Inequalities

Growing inequalities (both within and between countries) were an important source of globalization backlash in the late nineteenth century (O'Rourke and Williamson 1999) and are already shaping up to be an important driving force in the coming world revolution. Mike Davis's (2001) analysis of late Victorian drought-famine disasters in Brazil, India, and China shows how these were partly caused by newly expanded market forces impinging on regions that were subject to international political-military coercion. He also documents how starving peasants created millenarian movements that promised to end the domination of the foreign devils or restore the rule of the good king. *Islamic fundamentalism is a contemporary functional equivalent.*

Huge and visible injustices provoke people to resist, and in the absence of true histories and theories, they utilize whatever ideological apparatus is at hand. The world-systems perspective offers a useful systematic understanding of history that cannot be found elsewhere.

The phenomenon of semiperipheral development suggests that social organizational innovations that can transform the predominant logic of accumulation will continue to emerge from the semiperiphery. The Russian and Chinese revolutions of the twentieth century were efforts to restructure capitalist institutions and developmental logic that succeeded mainly in spurring the U.S. hegemony and the post–World War II expansion of capitalism. The Soviet and Chinese efforts were compromised from the start by their inability to rely on participatory democracy. In order to survive in a world still strongly dominated by capitalist states they were forced to construct authoritarian socialism, a contradiction in terms.

We can expect that democratic socialist regimes will come to state power in the semiperiphery by electoral means, as already happened in Allende's Chile. Brazil, Mexico, and Korea are strong candidates, and India, Argentina, Indonesia, and China are possibilities. Democratic socialism in the semiperiphery is a good strategy for fending off many of the worst aspects of corporate globalization. The transnational antisystemic movements will want to support and be supported by these new socialist democracies.

The ability of capitalist core states to destabilize democratic socialist regimes in the semiperiphery is great, and this is why support movements within the core are so important. Information technology can certainly be a great aid to transborder organizing. Issues such as sweatshop exploitation can help to make students aware of core-periphery inequalities and to link them with activists far away. The emergence of democratically elected challengers to global corporate capitalism will strain the ideologues of "polyarchy" and facilitate the contestation of narrow definitions of democracy. The emergence of a World Party to educate activists about the world-historical dimensions of capitalism and the lessons of earlier world revolutions will add the leaven that may move the coming backlash against corporate globalization in a progressive direction. A world-historical perspective will help political campaigns and organizing efforts make tactical and strategic decisions and will provide a structurally informed basis for the building of a democratic and collectively rational global commonwealth.

Imagining Global Democracy

What might global democracy look like? And how could we get from here to there? A consideration of global democracy must confront two main issues: huge and growing inequalities within and between countries; and the grave problems of environmental sustainability that capitalist (and communist) industrialization has produced.

Rather than drawing the blueprint of a global utopia and then arguing the fine points, it makes more sense to learn from the heritages of earlier efforts. Utopias may be useful for those who are unable to imagine any possible improvement over existing institutions. But they also function to delegitimize efforts to make social change because they often appear to be unattainable. A more useful approach is to imagine a historically apt next step, one that the relevant constituencies can agree is a significant improvement and that is plausibly attainable.

Global democracy means real economic, political, and cultural rights and influence for the majority of the world's people over the local and global institutions that affect their lives. Local and national democracy is part of the problem, but not the whole problem. Global democracy requires that local institutions and national states be democratic and the building of democratic institutions of global governance.

We support the proposals for radically reforming the United Nations and for establishing an institutional framework for global finance proposed by Camilleri, Malhotra, and Tehranian (2000).[3] Their principles and thoughtful step-by-step proposals for democratizing global governance address most of the issues quite well. The *principle of subsidiarity* proposes the decentralization of control over all issues that can be effectively resolved at the decentralized level (2000:46). This principle is similarly applied to the national and international regional levels, so that global-level institutions deal with problems that can find effective solutions only at the global level. We agree with this important principle.

Camilleri, Malhotra, and Tehranian (2000:25) abjure the term "global government" and prefer terms such as "interlocking institutions" and "international regimes" for describing global governance. Alberto Martinelli's (2002) insightful discussion of democratizing global governance also categorically rejects the notion of global government. We understand the political sensitivities involved in this choice of terms, and we agree that it is important to use language wisely. There is a lot of resistance to the idea of an emerging world state because people understandably fear that such an institution might become an instrument of repression or exploitation. But we are concerned that careful rhetoric might obscure or paper over issues that need to be confronted explicitly. The main reason that the United Nations has been largely ineffective at stopping interstate warfare is that it is not a state in the Weberian sense—a monopoly of legitimate violence. International law is not truly law according to Weber because it is not backed up by institutionalized sanctions.

Our position is that the human species needs to establish a real global government that is legitimate, effective, and democratic. This does not require the centralization of everything. As stated above, we agree with the principle of subsidiarity, according to which everything that can effectively be left to local, national, and regional bodies should be. But inequality, environmental problems, population pressure, and peace are all global problems that can be effectively solved only by a democratic global government with the power to enforce the law.

Thus, reforming the United Nations must move in the direction of the establishment of a democratic global government. This is in the interest of all the people of the Earth, but especially the dispossessed. The Westphalian interstate system has allowed powerful capitalists to repeatedly escape the institutional controls that have emerged from antisystemic movements that have sought to protect workers and communities from exploitation. Only a democratic world state can produce institutions that can guarantee social justice.

We also support the establishment of new institutions to provide a framework for global financial relations that can support local and national development, as well as increased oversight of these by the United Nations (Patomaki, Teivainen, and Ronkko 2002). And we see a need to go beyond polyarchy at both the national and the global levels.

Bill Robinson (1996) examines the struggle over the concept of democracy. He redefines the meaning of the term "polyarchy," which was coined by Robert Dahl to signify pluralism. In Robinson's usage *polyarchy* means a system in which a small group actually rules and mass participation in decision-making is confined to leadership choice in elections carefully managed by competing elites. Institutionalized polyarchy prevents the emergence of more egalitarian popular democracy that would threaten the rule of those who hold power and property. The notion of popular democracy stresses human equality, participatory forms of decision-making, and a holistic integration of political, social, and economic realms that are artificially kept separate in the polyarchic definition of democracy.

We are not satisfied with polyarchy (parliamentary democracy) at the national level. We contend that real democracy must address the issue of wealth and property, rather than defining these as beyond the bounds of political discourse. This said, we can also learn much from those failed experiments with collective property that were carried out in the socialist and communist states in the twentieth century. State ownership works well for major infrastructure, such as utilities, health, and education. But for the production of most goods and services, even when the state is itself truly democratic, state ownership creates grave economic problems because of the problem of "soft budget constraints." This is because state-owned firms are usually bailed out by the state for their economic mistakes, and they mainly respond to political exigencies rather than to consumer demand. In order to achieve a reasonable level of efficiency large firms need to compete with one another in markets, and they should also compete for financing by showing that they can make a profit.

We support John Roemer's (1994) advocacy of a kind of market socialism in which ownership shares of large firms are distributed to all adult citizens, who then invest their shares in a stock market that is the main source of capital for large firms. All citizens receive a set number shares at the age of majority, and when they die, their shares revert to the public weal. So there is no inheritance of corporate property, though personal property can be inherited. Firms, large and small, produce for markets, and labor is rewarded in competitive labor markets. Small firms can be privately owned. This kind of market socialism equalizes income, though some inequalities due to skill differences will still exist. The economy will still be a market economy, but the democratic state will provide security and due process and oversee the redistribution of corporate shares across generations.

This model of public market socialism incentivizes technological change and efficiency without producing increasing inequalities. It will probably work well, especially in the core countries, for which Roemer has intended it. But when we think about the global economy, there are certain problems that are not addressed in Roemer's model. One of the main problems in the global economy is the huge difference in productivity between core and peripheral labor. This is why labor standards in international economic agreements are anathema to workers and unions in peripheral countries. A single worldwide minimum wage standard sounds good, but it would tend to function as a protectionist agreement for core workers and undercut the ability of peripheral firms and workers to sell their products in core markets. Wage and other standards have to take into account local conditions, but their enforcement is the key to preventing the race to the bottom pursued by many transnational corporations. The real solution to this is to raise the level of productivity of peripheral labor. So global democracy needs to create institutions that can do this. Banning child labor worldwide while supporting the children's families to speed the demographic transition would be a giant first step in this direction.

This is why we need effective institutions of global governance. Antisystemic movements cannot simply dismantle such institutions as the World

Bank and the International Monetary Fund. These must either be reformed (democratized and empowered) or be replaced. Market socialism in the core will not be enough. A movement for economic democracy in the core needs also to mobilize for economic democracy at the global level.

Support for both more democratic national regimes and global socialist institutions is likely to come from the semiperiphery. We expect that some of the most potent efforts to democratize global capitalism will come out of movements and democratic socialist regimes that emerge in semiperipheral countries. As in earlier epochs, semiperipheral countries have the "advantages of backwardness"—they are not already heavily invested in the existing organizational and political institutions and technologies—and so they have both the maneuverability and the resources to invest in new institutions.

Peripheral countries could also do this, but they are more completely dependent on the core and are not able to mobilize sufficient resources to overcome this dependency. The large semiperipheral countries, such as Mexico, Brazil, Argentina, India, Indonesia, and China, have opportunities that neither core nor peripheral countries have. If a democratic socialist regime is able to come to state power by legal means, and if this regime has the political will to mobilize the popular sectors in favor of democratic socialism, an experiment in Roemerian market socialism could be carried out. We expect that regimes of this type will in fact emerge in the near future as the options of kowtowing to the megacorps or demagoguing the popular sectors become more obviously bankrupt.

The smaller semiperipheral countries (South Korea, Taiwan, South Africa, Israel) may also opt for democratic socialism, but we expect that these will be able to do so only after earlier efforts have been made in the large semiperipheral countries. Much also depends on what happens in the contest for hegemony. Continued U.S. primacy will likely strengthen the resistance to democratizing global governance, while the rise of the European Union, which has stronger social democratic traditions, will likely provide greater core support for democratizing global institutions and for emerging democratic socialist movements in the semiperiphery.

The semiperipheral democratic socialist regimes will be the strongest organizational entities that can forge the links between the global antisystemic movements and produce a network for bringing forth the institutions of global socialism.

Globalization from below and the formation of global socialist institutions will need to be facilitated by an organized network of world citizens. We have adopted the name given to such a confederation by Warren Wagar

(1996)—the World Party. But this is not a party in the old sense of the Third International—a vanguard party of the world proletariat. Rather, the World Party we propose would be a network of individuals and representatives of popular organizations from all over the world who agree to help create a democratic and collectively rational global commonwealth.

The Postmodern Prince and the World Party

Stephen Gill (2000, 2003) has advocated the building of a World Party, a peoples' international, that could help to coordinate the several antisystemic movements emerging in resistance to global corporate capitalist and neoliberal policies. Gill invokes Gramci's characterization of the Italian Communist Party as the "modern prince," a network of organic intellectuals and workers who would challenge the hegemony of capital. Gill is careful to distance his idea from the putative errors of the left parties of old—hierarchy, dogmatism, and so on. He says, "The multiple and diverse political forces that form the postmodern Prince combine both defensive and forward-looking strategies" (2000:131). This is an appropriate stance, especially in light of what happened to the New Left in the 1970s. A period of broad social movement activism morphed into a bevy of small sectarian parties yelling slogans at potential organizees and at one another. The sectarian model is obviously not one to emulate, and Gill is careful in this regard.

Warren Wagar (1992, 1996) has also had the temerity to suggest that an organized group of political actors making use of and further developing the world-systems perspective might come together in what he calls the World Party. The angle here would be the use of a world-historical and comparative perspective on the development of capitalism to help the family of antisystemic movements see the big picture and to cooperate with one another on feasible projects.

The World Party will actively recruit people of all nations and religions and will seek to create the institutional bases for a culturally pluralistic, socially just, and ecologically sustainable world society. This is what we mean by global democracy.[4]

Notes

1. The Institute for Research on World-Systems (IROWS) at the University of California, Riverside, is carrying out a research project to compare the degree and contours of international integration of nineteenth-century and twentieth-century

global elites (Chase-Dunn and Reifer 2002). See http://irows.ucr.edu/research /glbelite/globelite.htm.

2. Giovanni Arrighi has recently been advocating the position that the globalization project that emerged in the 1970s was importantly a reaction to the world revolution of 1968 that appropriated the antistate ideology and many of the tactics of the New Left. In the latest installment of global ideological history the *Wall Street Journal* has declared that the Washington Consensus is dead, and Jeffrey Sachs, a former leading light of neoliberalism, has urged a new concern for the global poor (Sachs 2005).

3. Patomaki, Teivainen and Ronkko (2002) provide a valuable review of proposals for democratizing global governance that includes the United Nations, the Bretton Woods institutions, and the system of international courts.

4. On the World Party, see http://wsarch.ucr.edu/archive/praxis.htm.

References

Amin, Samir. 1997. *Capitalism in an Age of Globalization.* London: Zed Books.

Arrighi, Giovanni. 1994. *The Long Twentieth Century.* London: Verso.

Arrighi, Giovanni, Terence K. Hopkins, and Immanuel Wallerstein. 1989. *Antisystemic Movements.* London: Verso.

Bello, Walden. 2002. *Deglobalization: Ideas for a New World Economy.* London: Zed Books.

Boswell, Terry and Christopher Chase-Dunn. 2000. *The Spiral of Capitalism and Socialism: Toward Global Democracy.* Boulder, CO: Lynne Rienner.

Camilleri, Joseph A., Kamal Malhotra, and Majid Tehranian. 2000. *Reimagining the Future: Toward Democratic Government.* Bundoora, Victoria, Australia: La Trobe University Department of Politics.

Chase-Dunn, Christopher and Thomas Hall. 1997. *Rise and Demise: Comparing World-Systems.* Boulder, CO: Westview.

Chase-Dunn, Christopher, Yukio Kawano, and Benjamin Brewer. 2000. "Trade Globalization since 1795: Waves of Integration in the World-System." *American Sociological Review* 65:77–95 (February).

Chase-Dunn, Christopher and Bruce Podobnik. 1995. "The Next World War: World-System Cycles and Trends." *Journal of World-Systems Research* 1 (6).

Chase-Dunn, Christopher and Thomas E. Reifer. 2002. "Globalization Backlash: Integration and Conflict since 1840." Research proposal submitted to the National Science Foundation. http://irows.ucr.edu/research/glbelite/globeliteprop03.htm.

Davis, Mike. 2001. *Late Victorian Holocausts.* London: Verso.

Gill, Stephen. 2000. "Toward a Postmodern Prince? The Battle in Seattle as a Moment in the New Politics of Globalisation." *Millennium* 29 (1): 131–141.

———. 2003. *Power and Resistance in the New World Order.* London: Palgrave.

Goldfrank, Walter L. 1977. "Who Rules the World: Class Formation at the International Level." *Quarterly Journal of Ideology* 1 (2): 32–37.

Johnson, Chalmers A. 2000. *Blowback: The Costs and Consequences of American Empire.* New York: Metropolitan Books.

Markoff, John. 1996. *Waves of Democracy.* Thousand Oaks, CA: Pine Forge.

Martinelli, Alberto. 2002. "Markets, Governments, Communities and Global Governance." Presidential address to the World Congress of Sociology, Brisbane, Australia, July 7.

McMichael, Philip. 1996. *Development and Social Change: A Global Perspective.* Thousand Oaks, CA: Pine Forge.

———. 2004. *Development and Social Change.* 2nd ed. Thousand Oaks, CA: Pine Forge.

O'Rourke, Kevin H. and Jeffrey G. Williamson. 1999. *Globalization and History: The Evolution of a 19th Century Atlantic Economy.* Cambridge, MA: MIT Press.

Patomaki, Heikki and Teivo Teivainen, with Mike Ronkko. 2002. *Global Democracy Initiatives: The Art of the Possible.* Hakapaino, Finland: Finland Network Institute for Global Democratization.

Podobnik, Bruce. 2002. "The Globalization Protest Movement: An Analysis of Broad Trends and the Impact of September 11." Presented at the Annual Meeting of the American Sociological Association, Chicago, August 16–19.

Robinson, William I. 1996. *Promoting Polyarchy.* Cambridge, UK: Cambridge University Press.

———. 2004 *A Theory of Global Capitalism.* Baltimore, MD: Johns Hopkins University Press.

Roemer, John. 1994. *A Future for Socialism.* Cambridge, MA: Harvard University Press.

Sachs, Jeffrey. 2005. *The End of Poverty.* New York: Penguin Press.

Shiva, Vandana. 1997. *Biopiracy: The Plunder of Nature and Knowledge.* Boston: South End Press.

Silver, Beverly. 2003. *Forces of Labor: Workers' Movements and Globalization since 1870.* Cambridge, UK: Cambridge University Press.

Starr, Amory. 2000. *Naming the Enemy: Anti-corporate Movements Confront Globalization.* London: Zed Books.

Wagar, W. Warren. 1992. *A Short History of the Future.* Chicago: University of Chicago Press.

———. 1996. "Toward a Praxis of World Integration." *Journal of World-Systems Research* 2 (2).

Walton, John and Michael Seddon. 1994. *Free Markets and Food Riots: The Politics of Global Adjustment.* Cambridge, MA: Blackwell.

Wallerstein, Immanuel. 1998. *Utopistics.* New York: New Press.

16

Globalization and the Future of Democracy

JOHN MARKOFF

Writing on the eve of the democratic breakthrough of the late eighteenth century, Jean-Jacques Rousseau gave vivid voice to a critique of the political institutions across the Channel that were admired by so many French reformers of the day. Commenting scornfully on British electoral practice, he observed in 1762, "The people of England regards itself as free, but it is gravely mistaken. It is free only during the election of Parliament. As soon as they are elected, slavery overtakes it, and it is nothing. The use it makes of the short moments of liberty it enjoys merits losing them" (Rousseau 1943:340). Rousseau's contention about the limitations of electoral institutions was in no way superseded by the age of democratic revolution that followed. From the 1790s to the present, there have been recurrent complaints about the depth of popular involvement in political life, the reality of popular control over power holders, and the possibility that the existence of some form of institutional channel for participation could blind publics to the inadequacy of that participation. Rousseau's critique has repeatedly reappeared in one form or another and has informed movements for a more genuine democratization.

But as a matter of simple, empirical observation, Rousseau was utterly mistaken about the British political practice he so eloquently despised, for even the occasional contests for a Parliament of uncertain authority in which only a narrowly constituted stratum had the right to vote provided occasions for the political involvement of much larger numbers, often in ways that overflowed the bounds of electoral and even legal practice. Local elites mobilized large numbers for festive parades, the distribution of leaflets, and the display of enthusiasm, not to mention the occasional attempt to intimidate the partisans of rival candidates. Not only did a larger target public need to be courted than had the right to vote, but an opportunity for popular forces to bargain with elites was institutionalized. Elections could easily be a time of disturbance as well as celebration, a moment for challenge as well as a ritual of orderliness (O'Gorman 1989). And parliamentary representation created a framework for the petitioning of representatives, including the organizing of petition drives by the representatives themselves. Only one year after Rousseau's complaint, in fact, the expulsion of John Wilkes from the British Parliament set off a long campaign fought out in the journalistic, judicial, electoral, and parliamentary arenas—and in the streets—that was an early prototype of the modern social movement (Rudé 1962).

If some of the political institutions of early modern Europe already presented opportunities for popular action, the democratic breakthrough of the late eighteenth century linked together

- elites claiming to rule on the basis of popular consent;

- the creation of new formal institutions through which the will of the people was to be shaped, made known, and asserted;

- the proliferation of organizational networks to influence parliaments (in the form of territorially, occupationally, or issue-based associations);

- the explosion of journalism, as citizens sought up-to-date information on what was happening on high, those on high sought equally up-to-date information on what was happening down below, and some of those on high sought information on the doings of each other;

- and the flowering of new forms of political struggle for those outside the centers of wealth and power.

The Uneven Trajectory of Democratization

The late eighteenth century seems to be a crucial moment in forging the linkages between democratic claims of legitimation, new forms of popular mobilization, and new institutions of governance that eventually came to be summed up by the catchall term "democracy." It is symptomatic that the 1780s appear to be the moment when the word "democrat" entered political discourse (Palmer 1953:203–226; Shoemaker 1966:83–95; Christophersen 1968; Conze and Koselleck 1984:821–899; Dippel 1986:57–97; Rosanvallon 1995:140–154) as a term of praise or (probably more frequently) abuse because people were engaged in attempting to imagine, and realize, new institutions here and now. After North American settlers defeated the greatest maritime power of the age, French revolutionary armies dominated Europe, and Haitian former slaves fought off the armies of three empires, the power of democratic claims to legitimation were clear to all, and many states began to make claims that they ruled as the deputies of, with the assent of, or in the interests of "the people" as never before. Even conservative states were coming to do so by the time the French forces went down to defeat.[1]

Although multicontinental in scope and extending across two centuries since the late eighteenth century, democratization has not been a smooth or uniform process either temporally or spatially. A look at the Europe of 1815 would have suggested that conservatism as much as radicalism was a legacy of the revolutionary era. In the twentieth century, there have been three major democratizing moments. Struggles about parliamentary powers over ministers and budgets and over the extension and equalization of suffrage rights were tremendously accelerated as World War I went on and on. Although dissenting voices were initially stifled, wartime labor shortages eventually gave increased clout to workers and women (as many women became workers), and postwar fears of revolution led elites to find nonrevolutionary routes to meet working-class aspirations. The word "democracy" was used more frequently in public discourse than ever before (Pool 1952), and one major power, the United States, even defined the war as about democracy. The Western democracies emerged with their political systems more or less intact, despite the vast wartime suffering in some of them. The new states formed on the ruins of empire in central Europe frequently opted for democratic structures, those freed from colonial domination (Iceland and the Irish Republic) also adopted the triumphant model, and other states emerged from revolutionary turmoil, like Mexico and Turkey, to take on democratic elements.

But in the 1920s and 1930s, a wide variety of antidemocratic monarchs, militaries, and mass movements subverted or overthrew the new democracies in continental Europe; by the early 1940s the fascists' armies had overrun most of the older ones while antidemocratic regimes were common in Latin America as well (sometimes including fascist elements as in Brazil's "New State"). The defeat of fascism provided the opportunity for a new, and geographically broader, democratizing wave, as Western armies remade western Europe and Japan, decolonization in Asia and Africa opened the way for democratic constitutions, and, joining the trend, a number of Latin American states followed suit.

This wave, too, generated powerful counterforces, and during the Cold War antidemocratic currents allied to and supported by one or the other side in the U.S.-Soviet struggle challenged hopes for a democratic future. While Russian arms supported communist rule in Eastern Europe, the United States encouraged the near universal rule of anticommunist generals in South America, and both sides supported antidemocratic directions in postcolonial Asia and Africa. So the democratization of the states was not a smooth, uniform process temporally. Nor was it uniform spatially.

As of the early 1970s, democratic institutions tended to be characteristic of countries with high standards of living and unusual (although not unknown) elsewhere. If about 1970 the core of the world-economy could be said to have largely (in some places recently) democratized, in the next multicontinental wave the locus of the democratizing transformation was, approximately, the semiperiphery (Korzeniewicz and Awbrey 1992:609–640). In the 1970s the military overthrow of Portugal's long-standing authoritarian regime launched the most recent wave of democratization, which has by now embraced other southern European states, most of Latin America, Eastern Europe, several Asian cases (South Korea, the Philippines, Taiwan), and South Africa and continued into the 1990s with struggles for democratization in Kenya, Nigeria, Burma, Hong Kong, Indonesia, and elsewhere. In geographic range this has been the most extensive wave of democratization thus far.

At the beginning of a new millennium, more people in more countries than ever before in human history had a voice in the selection of the incumbents of political office in the states of which they are citizens. Some observers were so carried away by the sudden surge as to make millenarian pronouncements to the effect that history is now over and the democratization of the remaining states will be simply anticlimactic (Fukuyama 1989:3–18; Tilly 2004).

If we try to understand the current moment in relation to democracy's history, however, it seems to me that this is an occasion on which democrats should be not complacently celebratory but concerned, perhaps even alarmed. Democracy's future is deeply threatened in several ways. Let me sum up the past 200 years of democratic history. The intertwined histories of democratic legitimations, social movement activism, and institutional changes generated, in some of the world's states, a significant democratization of the institutions of government (Markoff 1996; Tilly 2004). Despite antidemocratic countertrends (Markoff 1996:71–99), the long-run direction of change in some of the states was a democratization of state power. What I suggest about the current moment is threefold.

First, there are in fact very significant countercurrents that threaten, as in the past, the democratization of the states.

Second, the current moment is one in which it is becoming evident that the democratization of (some of) the states is not remotely enough to assure a more democratic world.

And third, the mechanisms that were so important in achieving the (very imperfect) democratization of (some of) the states are very unlikely to be capable of achieving the democratization of the emerging new structures of power.

The Challenges of Globalization

The question of new structures of power is crucial. The interplay of democratizing institutions, democratic legitimations of power, and social movements was born out of an epochal redeployment of power from local to national arenas. The late twentieth century may have seen the beginning of another such epochal moment of redeployment of power, from national states to a variety of trans-statal structures, which are probably still only in embryonic form. This much discussed globalization presents some significant challenges to the democratization of the states, some of which I shall touch on here. But these transnational processes are raising in a very stark way an issue beyond the democratization of the states, for we must recognize that the entire modern history of democratization has been, and continues to be, precisely the democratization of some, but not other, states. Democratization has given some people, but not others, some measure of control over those on high. Globalization is not only a challenge to the democratization of the states. It also raises the issue of whether the democratization of the states is even going to continue to be meaningful in a world of transnational connection. What will be at stake, in the twenty-first century's history of democracy, if there be any to reflect on at the next century's end, will be the question of what a more democratic world might look like. I shall first examine the threats to the democratization thus far achieved of the national states and then turn to the limitations of that achievement. I shall consider this first group of issues under four broad heads: the meaningfulness of electoral accountability to citizens; the nature of citizenship; the reinvigoration of exclusionary politics; and, last but hardly least, the continued effectiveness of social movements as a force for democratization. These issues are all intertwined, but I shall not attempt to map out all the interconnections here.

Although distant places have often had significant economic linkages, the volume and diversity of these linkages have enormously expanded as capital investments, goods and services, and (although to a significantly lesser extent) labor have become mobile as never before. Giant corporate actors and otherwise atomized individuals alike can enter into near instantaneous contact with distant interlocutors through fax and e-mail. Governments, partly as a consequence, have been losing their capacity to control the economic and cultural life of the territories vulnerable to their authority, but additionally they now often seem eager to shed some of their traditional responsibilities in the name of the allegedly superior efficiencies of the globalizing marketplace.

And now we enter a realm of claims and counterclaims about this web of transnational connection whose students have made the most varied arguments (Sklair 1991; Wallerstein 1991:24–55; Ganley 1992; Robertson 1992; Castells 1994:18–32; Sassen 1994; Held 1995; Tilly 1995:1–23; Appadurai 1996; Hannerz 1996; Keohane and Milner 1996; Wade 1996: 60–88; Albrow 1997; Piven and Cloward 1997:3–14; Weiss 1997:3–27; Chase-Dunn, Kawano, and Nikitin 1998). For some, phenomena such as the sheer quantity of global financial transactions, the flows of immigrants (legal and otherwise), the economic clout of transnational criminal enterprises, and the geographic reach of pop music amount to an overwhelming case that we are entering an utterly novel era, in which the states are less weighty players, utterly unable to control these diverse flows. The world-system argument suggests a very different response, one to the effect that the capitalist world-system has always involved separate states enmeshed in a transnational economy subject to their influence to some extent but securely beyond their effective control. Others argue that use of the grand term "globalization" to include transborder connections that might be merely dyadic or that might be regionally circumscribed is deeply misleading. Others yet again contend that some of those misleading claims are deliberately misleading, that they are ideological defenses for attacking worker rights in the name of the tough measures that are allegedly necessary in the face of the inevitably global marketplace (claims that run much stronger in the United States than in most of Europe). And still others argue that the central change is an increased awareness of cross-border processes, some of which are not in themselves of especially recent vintage; an important variant of this last contention goes on to point out that this newfangled global awareness can itself be the motor of further change. So some see epochal change, and others write of "the globalization hoax" or even "globaloney"; some in France speak of "globalitarianism."

Distinguishing trends in the web of transnational connection from changes that are cyclical in character; distinguishing both trends and cycles from transnational phenomena of long standing that have been mistakenly thought to be new; distinguishing increasing transnational flows of people, goods, and ideas from increasing awareness of such flows; and distinguishing statements that are true of one or several locations from those that are true of the world as a whole constitute a very large but urgent research agenda. I believe the available evidence suggests that there are both frequently exaggerated claims of novelty that are simply mistaken and purposeful attacks on social programs in the name of the global marketplace—both of which are important to correct and challenge. Nonetheless, I also believe the available evidence to indicate that there are both cycles and trends whose character may be clarified as systematic research catches up to anecdote and hype.[2] Among those trends is a proliferation of transnational mechanisms for economic decision-making.[3]

The impulse toward transnational structures for decision-making is multiply motivated, rooted in various forms of cross-border connection that generate threats from which even powerful elites may be unable to protect themselves without new structures of governing. These include the invention and subsequent diffusion of nuclear weapons and globe-circling missiles; the more insidious long-term challenge of potential global environmental devastation; and the possibly ruinous consequences of uncontrolled global economic markets. These have all impelled the powerful to begin to create new mechanisms of cross-border coordination.

The Meaningfulness of Electoral Accountability to Citizens

In this emerging world of transnational connection, the abilities of national governments to manage many important things are diminishing.[4] Control over flows of capital is proving especially elusive, but the movement of goods and even of the relatively less mobile individual workers has proved hard to control as well. Effective decision-making power over parts of the transnationalized economies is becoming established at levels other than the state level and in several forms:

There are formally constituted trans-statal quasi governments of which the European Union (EU) is the most powerful within its formal jurisdiction and the United Nations the geographically broadest in its scope. The European Union's executive agencies have an enormous capacity to issue a myriad of binding regulations affecting business and consumer interests, but the EU is also involved in the redefinition of welfare rights, environmental concerns, educational practice, and even human rights issues. For its part, the United Nations' recent propensity to dispatch various combinations of relief workers and armed soldiers in the name of human rights to various places defined as "failed states" (as in Somalia, Zaire, or Bosnia-Herzegovina) suggests a new tendency of trans-statal organizations to regard national "sovereignty" as less sacrosanct than heretofore. As the post–World War II norm that all should live in sovereign states came to approximate fruition with decolonization and the breakup of Soviet Europe, sovereignty itself became blurrier.

There are also formally constituted agreements for regulating the levels and nature of economic integration without other quasi-governmental trappings; models of such agreements include the North American Free Trade Agreement (NAFTA) between Canada, the United States, and Mexico and South America's Mercosur. Agreements of this sort have the potential to significantly constrain not only economic policy, narrowly conceived, in the signatory states but a whole range of other concerns, including environmental and even human rights issues. It might, for example, be claimed that such and such a conservation measure violates the free-market provisions of some agreement. It seems merely a matter of time before some powerful economic interest launches a lawsuit claiming that some government's public education system constitutes an improper subsidy of economic rivals.

And then there are agreements between financial interests to make major decisions about the geography of capital flows; of these, the International Monetary Fund (IMF) and the World Bank are by far the most consequential. Successful agreements between a state and those organizations are taken by other financial interests as the transnational equivalent of a good credit rating. A full survey would include the various forms of multinational corporations, the subcontracting corporate relationships centered in Japan, and the Asian business networks linked through kinship ties, as well as the transnational networks that move falsely labeled commodities ranging from clothing with fake labels to pirated CDs and the vast trade in illicit psychoactive substances. Among such hidden structures of cross-border negotiation, perhaps we ought not to omit some of the activity of governments themselves, in particular some of the secretive meetings between finance ministers of the major industrial countries, currently constituted as the G-8.

The simple but very important consequence: At the historical moment when more citizens of more states than ever before in human history have been acquiring some control over the incumbents in office of the national states, the capacity of those incumbents to function as autonomous national policy makers has been seriously eroding. Few governments in the world today risk a serious confrontation with the economic policies dear to the IMF and World Bank, for example.[5] No government seems able to prevent its police forces from supplementing their salaries from the treasuries of transnational criminal enterprises. The relationship between the wishes of elected politicians and the rule makers of the European Union is exceedingly complex. Cross-border infusions of money now seem a feature of U.S. presidential election campaigns, suggesting that the use of foreign funds to influence elections would no longer be exclusively a tool of U.S. interests operating abroad but could run in the other direction as well.[6] We could sum this up as a diminution of national sovereignty.

In short, states are weaker in the global marketplace. This particular challenge to democracy is very profound: Publics, to an unprecedented extent—if far from everywhere—can choose incumbents, but it hardly follows from that fact that they thereby can choose policy, especially on central matters of economic life.

Withdrawal of States from Commitments to Welfare

An important aspect of these diminished state capacities is the degree to which states are doing it to themselves.[7] Students of contemporary Western European polities, for example, speak of a hollowing-out of the state, as all sorts of functions pass upward to transnational bodies (like the European Union), downward to reinvigorated local or regional organs of government, and outward in the form of privatization (which may be accomplished via deregulation, sale of assets, or the replacement of bureaucratically supervised public services by contracting out to private agencies). In the United States in recent years we have seen the federal government turning over much of its poor relief to the states and some of its vast population of imprisoned people (by far the largest such population in the world) to private prison providers. In other parts of the world, we have seen the collapse of European communist regimes, the embrace of the market by their Asian counterparts, and a general retreat from commitments to state-led developmentalism in many poorer countries. Most Western European states have moved, with varying misgivings, to give up the economic leverage afforded by control over their own currency in favor of the common Euro.

So there is an ideological dimension to restricting the sphere of state action, in which even holders of state power are participating. The belief in the superiority of "the market" over "the state" has many components ranging from ethical claims about human freedom to technical claims about efficiency, so there are many arguments that devalue central political institutions in favor of "the private sector," the "local community," "the family," "the individual," or "the free market." Champions of such positions maintain that the agents of states have been responsible for many evils, including hindering the wealth-generating capacities of less regulated economic enterprises.

In this view, those who saw states as agents for either the generation of wealth or its more just redistribution were, at best, well meaning but mistaken. The untrammeled marketplace will augment aggregate wealth, and the interplay of market forces will on its own, in the fullness of time, redistribute that wealth and relieve the crushing poverty in which many live. Redistributionist state actions are folly and accumulationist state actions even worse. Not to worry—rising tide raises all boats.

In fact, the empirical evidence suggests that on a world scale this particular rising tide merely raises all yachts. In the recent period of state retreat and concomitant acceptance of the global market as the central social institution to which all other institutions need accommodate themselves, the income gap between the poorest and richest has been growing apace (Braun 1997; Korzeniewicz and Moran 1997:1000–1039; Rodrik 1997).

Of course, there is nothing especially new in some people being much poorer than other people. What is striking about the current moment, however, is how issues of poverty have become marginal in political debates in some of the richer countries. In the United States and in Great Britain, for example, the major parties vie with each other for the votes and support of everyone but the poor.[8] And should recent global trends in income distribution continue—to be sure this is a speculative matter about which much controversy swirls[9]—it is not hard to wonder whether poorer people in democratic countries will indefinitely continue to assent to a political system in which the major parties compete in ignoring them. In the new economic order lifetime careers may be giving way to part-time, temporary jobs. Enhanced freedom from state regulation for owners of capital means downsizing, flexible specialization, outsourcing, capital mobility across interstate frontiers, and rapid technological change—all of which threaten economic insecurity for many. Even middle-class homes are threatened with economic insecurity as a permanent state of affairs. It is hard to see why political challenges to the constitutional order will not eventually be heard.

In this connection, let us consider the recent, widespread reversals of social welfare policies. Many students of politics since World War II simply assumed an inevitable connection of expanded rights of democratic participation and expanded social rights (Marshall 1950; Turner 1993; Steenbergen 1994; Offe 1996; Tilly 1996; Piven 1997; Hanagan 1998). If all adults have the vote, so the argument went, of course the large numbers of people who feel economically threatened by potential medical costs, old age, expensive education for their children, and so forth would support programs of social provision. Such programs in turn would attach large numbers of people to the current constitutional order. Thus democratization would promote social provision, and social provision in turn would assure large majorities favoring democracy. But the first half of this relationship has suddenly and rapidly eroded—raising important questions about the second half.

Let us briefly consider the unexpected withdrawal of the wealthier democratic states from social provision. Relevant aspects of the current climate, some already discussed, include

widespread embrace of notions of priority for the market over other human institutions;

the weakening of labor as a political force;

pressures to reduce government expenditures coming from transnational financial networks;

expedient concern for competitiveness in the global marketplace;

and the invocation of the global marketplace by the powerful in order to convince democratic publics to acquiesce in an increase of profits at the expense of labor.

Late Twentieth-Century Exclusionary Politics

Part of what gives antiwelfare positions their special force today is a fragmentation of political identities. To the extent that poorer people are identifiable as ethnically distinctive, a category that includes an identity as recent immigrants, some political parties are able to denounce welfare as taking from "us" to give to "them." With millions of North African Muslims in France, Turks in Germany, and Albanians and Africans moving to Italy, the mobilization of xenophobic sentiment is readily linkable to an attack on welfare. When Surinamese or Indonesians show up on Dutch welfare roles, the Dutch rethink their generous unemployment insurance. Moreover, the weakening of labor in the transnational marketplace reduces the likelihood that a collective identity as workers will effectively override this fragmentation. The shift among a portion of France's workers from voting for the communists to voting for the anti-immigrant National Front is an important sign of the power of anti-immigrant politics in an age of globalized economics.

In the absence of policies directed at their inclusion, in the absence of notions of minimal acceptable standards of life guaranteed by a national community, will large numbers of poorer people feel materially or symbolically excluded from national life and simply opt out of support for a democratic practice that no longer aspires to both their inclusion and material advance? Such a possibility may be more profoundly corrosive of democracy than the direct exclusionary notions of xenophobic parties.

But xenophobic politics is by no means insignificant. Patterns of economic, political, and cultural transformation have made political conflict over national identities dramatically salient—for example, the fragmentation of the Soviet Union, Yugoslavia, and Czechoslovakia and the unification of Germany; with the murderous violence in former Yugoslavia and some of the fragments of the former Soviet Union and massacres in Rwanda; with the cycles of violence and counterviolence surrounding the rights of groups in Ethiopia, Sri Lanka, India, Turkey, and Northern Ireland; with the increasing significance of political conflict over immigration policy in the wealthier countries, including Germany, France, Italy, and the United States; and with continuing challenges to the present national state in Canada and Belgium.[10] Current social transformations assure that conflicts defined by the participants in ethnic terms will continue to be a highly significant part of political life in many countries. Such conflicts in themselves are hardly unprecedented; what is to the point in the present context is the challenge conflicts structured around such identities pose for democracy.

For at least three reasons, many students of democracy regard such conflicts as very difficult to address within the confines of democratic procedures. All three deserve extended discussion; here I only comment briefly on each.

First of all, strongly held identities may challenge the very existence of a national state. To those for whom such identities are a more significant matter than the procedures followed by the alien and inherently oppressive state under which they feel they live, it may be a matter of indifference how that state is governed: Indeed, to the extent that democracy seems to secure the allegiance of citizens, including citizens of the nationality for which the nationalists claim to speak, democracy itself may be held to be a target to be destroyed if possible. The actions of some parts of the Basque separatist movement in the post-Franco period have been in this vein.

Second, it is often suggested that conflicts framed in terms of collective identities are far less subject to negotiated compromises than conflicts framed in class terms.[11] Where the conflict of labor and capital dominates, one can imagine all sorts of compromises: at the crudest level, labor accepts certain levels of profit, and capital accepts certain levels of wages. Conflicts over the claims of minorities to distinct educational systems, distinct public use of language, and public displays of religious affiliation often do not have any very obvious intermediary position.

Third, democratic protections for free speech and free association permit political mobilization around ethnocultural questions that may sometimes be successfully stifled under authoritarian political systems. A transition toward democracy may also be a transition toward open expression of inflammatory positions. The murderous violence in former Yugoslavia in significant part derives from the capacities of political elites in Serbia and Croatia to mobilize nationalist appeals within a partially democratizing context. But it is not merely a matter of the limited character of the democratization. The violent intimidation of the Czech Republic's gypsy population since the 1990s is happening in a state whose democratic features are far more developed than those of former Yugoslavia. In former communist Europe, indeed, the expression of ethnically defined hostilities is part and parcel of the experience of recent liberation from coercive states defining the limits of acceptable public discourse. Anti-Russian speech (and legislation) in Latvia and Estonia, anti-Gypsy violence in the Czech Republic, Hungary, and Romania, and anti-Jewish speech (without legislation) in a near Judenrein Poland are part and parcel of those countries' democratizations.

The Future of Social Movements as Democratizing Forces

Let me turn now to the continued effectiveness of social movements as a force for democratization.[12] Recall that as power passed from local lords and local officials in Europe to central authority, people engaged in conflicts began to develop new techniques to press that new authority to act on their behalf. The emerging movements became a critical element in the democratization of the states, and democratization encouraged further movements. Indeed, the movements became an element that shaped the very contours of state power, as those states took on vastly expanded welfare and police activity partly in response to pressure and threat from below.

We appear to be at another such epochal moment of reconfigured power —away from national states and toward transnational actors. It is far from obvious that social movements as we have come to know them over the past two centuries will be able to operate with the same effectiveness in relation to transnational structures of power as they have in relation to national ones. Of all the issues I am discussing here, the most serious in my view is the possibility that there may be no forms of social action for the effective democratization of reconfigured power. But we need to review what is happening to movements in the present in order to speculate about the future.

The attention that scholars of social movements have been devoting to the transnational aspects of movements has been expanding so rapidly that virtually anything one says based on current research might have to be rethought in the future (and the forms of political action may themselves be in flux). Nonetheless, I believe this recent research (Markoff 1996:27–31; Smith, Chatfield, and Pagnucco 1997; Keck and Sikkink 1998; Tarrow 1998a, 1998c:176–195) thus far suggests three points.

First, throughout the entire modern history of social movements, notions of strategy and tactics, models of organizational forms, general notions of social justice, and participants in social movement activism have frequently crossed national frontiers.

Second, in the past few decades, a wide variety of transnationally organized activists have made intermittently effective use of international organizations, NGO resources, and the governments of some national states to address issues in other national states or transnational institutions. In large part, the activities of such transnational activist networks do not include the collective, public, mass mobilizations that some see as among the defining hallmarks of social movements.

Third, although the institutions of transnational power have been targets of mass mobilizations (as well as of the lobbying campaigns of transnational advocacy networks), for the most part social movement activism has continued to address national states, although sometimes with an eye on having that state take some action on some transborder matter.

There are several distinct levels on which social movements might respond to the shift in power from national states to transnational structures. We might look for analyses by activists that recognize the transnational character of issues. We might look for the development of transnational organizations. We might look for the deployment of tactics that address transnational sources of power. Instances of all of these are not hard to find. People in the environmental movement have often spoken of the global context of environmental issues, have held international conferences to exchange ideas among themselves, and sometimes have acted across national frontiers. The human rights movement also has a strong tendency to organize across state boundaries. The very notion that we have rights as human beings, not only as citizens, and that as fellow human beings we need to support one another against abusive governments is in itself a challenge to notions of national sovereignty. Women's rights activists have made some effective use of international organizations. Popular protest on several continents has been mobilized around actions of the IMF and World Bank.

Nonetheless, it seems fair to say that, thus far, the principal way social movements have acted in the transnational arena is to deploy their own traditional techniques of political action in national arenas. People moved by some transnational issue have been, on the whole, inclined to challenge their own national governments to take some position in the transnational arena.[13] Environmentalists, for example, demand that their governments sign some treaty between governments protecting the sea or the air; human rights groups demand that their governments stop supporting other governments that violate human rights. And when it comes to economic policy, challenging one's own government is overwhelmingly the main arena of action of today's movements. Margaret Keck and Kathryn Sikkink have shown a rapid increase in the number of organizations engaging in transnational political activism (by their figures, from 102 in 1953 to 569 in 1993), but they have persuasively shown that these organizations are, for the most part, not engaged in mobilizing transnational collective action (Keck and Sikkink 1998:184–195).

Not only do social movements still largely move in their own national arenas, but the gains they have made over the past 200 years have largely been at the level of the national state. The labor movement, for example, so important in the history of democratization, has largely achieved its successes through national labor legislation. But with the rapid transnational deployment of power, the capacity of labor's traditional modes of action and organization to advance the interests of workers has declined with remarkable rapidity in the traditional industrial heartlands. If owners of capital can easily move their investments to another country, it is extraordinarily difficult for the labor movement to take effective countermeasures. Its traditional means of engaging in conflict, which we may summarize as striking, demonstrating, and voting, have all been reduced in effectiveness. Strikes are a riskier business when capital is so mobile, and mounting demonstrations as well as effective use of the ballot have been weakened by the fragmentation of a worker identity. The environmental movement has the proud slogan "Think globally, act locally." But for many issues there may be no effective local actions.

This does not mean that social movements have no effectiveness at all in relation to transnational power. Even acting locally, the environmental movement has made significant achievements. European farmers or truckers demanding that their governments take particular actions within the governing structures of the European Union have sometimes had considerable impact. And human rights protesters challenging their own governments to withdraw support from South Africa in the 1970s and 1980s helped bring about an international climate that encouraged the dramatic abandonment of that country's racially organized governing structure. Jackie Smith's quantitative inventory of the growth of "transnational social movement organizations" between 1973 and 1993 finds that more than half of such organizations at that latter date can be grouped under three broad rubrics: "human rights," "environment," and "women's rights," (Smith et al. 1997:47), which suggests that an exclusive focus on the labor movement may miss much of the transnationally coordinated collective action at the turn of the new century (and some labor issues may be pursued under these other labels). The forms of pressure so finely anatomized by Keck and Sikkink have had their successes, too.[14] For the most part, however, it does seem that social movements are not acting directly on the new centers of power and that there is (as yet?) only limited movement in that direction. When we consider the webs of transnational finance, not only does the element of democratic accountability vanish completely (George and Sabelli 1994), but the points of possible leverage for democratization are far from obvious. The inner processes of the World Bank and IMF, to take two conspicuously significant examples, are hardly publicized, and positions taken by many national representatives to those organizations are not even made publicly available.[15] Rather than legitimacy, it is invisibility that is sought. How such power might be democratized is the challenge of the twenty-first century.

Beyond the National States

The democratization of the states, geographically extensive as it is, can therefore hardly be regarded as secure. But let us take a geographically yet more extensive view. Although successive waves of state democratizations have left a legacy of expanded accountability of governments to citizens in increasing numbers of states, very large numbers of the residents of the planet have not benefited. Democracy has always been deeply exclusionary.

As late eighteenth-century legislators, at the moment of revolutionary democratic breakthrough, planned their new political systems, the question of to whom, precisely, governments were to be responsible came to the fore, and democratizing states adopted a distinction between citizens with and citizens without voting rights. Women, those with little property, children, and domestic servants were commonly excluded, and at various times and places since some have been excluded for ethnic criteria, criminality, mental deficiencies, illiteracy, and membership in the clergy or military. The common expression "universal suffrage" has been and continues to be one of the most obfuscating terms in the vocabulary of modern political life. Tocqueville, for example, set himself the task of explaining the remarkable universal suffrage of the United States, at a moment when women could vote nowhere and free blacks in the North, even when not legally barred from voting, confronted threats of violence if they attempted to do so.[16]

In the late twentieth-century democratizing waves, countries claiming the mantle of democracy have something that might properly be called near universal adult suffrage, with children constituting the largest category of excluded citizens. What stands most starkly revealed, therefore, is the distinction of citizen/noncitizen. To the extent that we see democratization as a series of successful attempts by social movements to secure rights, we also see that those rights were largely secured for citizens of particular national states and largely secured within those states. Toward the beginning of the era of modern democracy the very title of the revolutionary French Declaration of the Rights of Man and Citizen encapsulated a very important ambiguity: Did one have rights because one was a human being, or because one was a French citizen? To the extent that rights are claims that are empty unless they constitute an obligation on some party with the resources to actually meet that claim, for the most part what rights a person had were obligatory only for the state of which that person was a citizen. In addition, interstate treaties might sometimes grant reciprocal rights of various sorts, and multilateral interstate documents might speak of other, "universal" rights, which courts in some states might sometimes take to constitute state obligations. But generally speaking, rights are connected to citizenship and enforceable in relation to the state of which one is a citizen. This includes, importantly, political rights.

By the late twentieth century, pervasive notions of democratic legitimation within states and multilateral human rights treaties between states seemed to be creating new challenges for some legal systems confronting long-term resident noncitizens, asylum seekers of various sorts, and transnationally mobile workers. Some see the emergence of new kinds of rights claims not anchored in national citizenship (Soysal 1994). So issues of inclusion/exclusion along the citizen/noncitizen fault line are highly salient. In addition we have, following Keck and Sikkink, pointed to the rapid proliferation of organized activism (but not taking the form of social movements) in which participants attempt to influence the policies of states not their own.

That such advocacy networks have some significant successes still doesn't amount to any routinized rights of participation.

Despite such developments, we may say that an important aspect of the history of modern democracy has been that institutional mechanisms for holding the powerful of the world responsible for their actions have never been available to much of the world's population. For the most part, the more securely established democratizations up to the current wave meant that citizens of the wealthier and more powerful states had some control over the incumbents in office of their states. Very much to the point are Immanuel Wallerstein's (1995:24–27) observations to the effect that the democratization of some of the states since the late eighteenth century to a large degree incorporated the working class of the wealthier countries into the system of global inequality on relatively favorable terms. With some economic security in the form of social rights; some say with a voice in public affairs in the form of political rights, as exemplified by the suffrage; and with rights of association, speech, petition, and so forth that undergird the capacity to engage in social movement activism, and the consequent dignity that goes with such empowerment, large numbers of people in a small part of the world came to participate in what has still been profoundly exclusionary democracy. The exclusionary character of such democracy is in plain sight yet unnoticed as long as we cast our gaze only on the governance of the states, separately.

There was no necessary incompatibility at all between the democratization of the core states of the world-economy in the nineteenth century and the extension of colonial rule by those same states. Democratizing movements might come to secure rights at home, while state violence was projected outward onto other continents.[17] In the nineteenth century, workers in the centers of world economic and military power obtained rights at home but also manufactured the guns and warships, built and staffed the communications networks, and enlisted in (or were conscripted into) the armies that fostered and maintained colonial rule over subject peoples (Conklin 1998:419–442).

Perhaps even a stronger statement is warranted. It may be that the democratization of the core of the world-economy owes a great deal to the control of sufficient resources to pay for the extension of rights, while that extension helped secure democratic popular assent for global domination. The correlation of high national income and democratic political practice is one of the best-attested regularities in the literature on democratization (Lipset 1981:27–63, although many have attempted to explain this relationship differently). This important role of the core in the world history of democracy intersects the social struggles within, and between, the states out of which the actual institutions of democracy emerged in temporally clustered bursts of increasing geographic range. But we must bear in mind that this has never been a process strictly confined to the core. In the period, for example, when conservative forces dominated Europe, stretching from the Congress of Vienna until the tumultuous early 1830s, the world centers of democratization were in the western hemisphere. And, as indicated above, not only have major institutional innovations been pioneered in the semiperiphery, but many of the instances of democratization in the late twentieth century wave have also been semiperipheral.

The uneven democratization of the states at the dawn of a new century confronts new challenges. The recent combination of extended—but hardly "global"—geographic range and potential trivialization, which together characterize the most recent wave of democratizations, raises anew questions of political power beyond the national states. The density of economic and cultural interconnection across national frontiers now threatens to trivialize the democratization of those states that have achieved significant democratization, raising the question of whether there is a meaningful future for the democracy of the states that does not address democracy beyond the states. The democracy of the states has always been a profoundly unfinished thing, as movements have utilized democratic legitimations and institutions to push further democratization. The democratization of the world beyond the states has yet to begin.

The present moment in the history of democracy is therefore an occasion not for triumphal celebration but for concern. To summarize: The remarkable and radical geographic extension of democratic practices coincides with a number of serious threats. The leaching of power out of the national states, in part toward a variety of transnational institutions, raises the specter of a trivialization of the very real democratization of the states. The mobility of capital and workers on a transnational scale reenergizes political conflicts around inclusion and exclusion. And last, but hardly least, the future of social movements, a major source of the democratization of the states for the past 200 years, is in serious doubt, at least as far as their capacity to democratize the emerging global order is concerned. In the past, as labor actions threatened, investors have relocated outward, often re-creating the labor conflicts they had fled (Silver 1998:41–69). But as the focus of power shifts upward beyond the bounds of the state, any state, it is not obvious that labor movements, or other movements, will be able to generate countervailing power.

Past democratizations have sometimes generated elite efforts, some successful, to sidestep the new challenge to themselves. For example, one of the institutional bases of early modern slavery in the British Caribbean had been the considerable autonomy of planter-run local government. British island plantocracies tenaciously demanded their freedom from central dictate. In the wake of nineteenth-century slave emancipation, and further challenged by metropolitan notions of expanding suffrage rights, the planter elite of places like Montserrat and Dominica now shifted to supporting direct crown rule and the disempowerment of a local legislature in which nonwhites had a voice (Stinchcombe 1995:276–277). On the edge of the twenty-first century, the unrivaled democratization of the states is now challenged by a new redeployment of power. The actions of people in rural villages and urban workshops played a major role in the history of early modern states; the emerging social movements of the nineteenth century played a major role in the democratization of some of them. It remains to be seen whether the construction of the world order of the twenty-first century continues as a nearly exclusively elite project or whether social movements (or new forms of contestation to be invented) can inject a more democratic element into the emerging structures of global governance (for further discussion, see Markoff 2004).

In short, many challenges remain. Despite the wavelike pattern of ebb and flow of democratic history, the geographic extensiveness of the present diffusion of democratic forms should not mislead us, like Bryce at the end of World War I (Bryce 1921:4–5), to see the major challenge as one of further geographic range. Extending the current democratic institutions of some of the states to still other states embedded in the global marketplace will not be adequate to deal with the challenge of what a more democratic world might be like. Yet the strength of the core notion of a self-ruling people that has repeatedly, if intermittently, galvanized institutional change for two centuries remains. Democratic legitimations are now widespread and may energize new movements in many states. More important, this may lead to pressures to democratize emerging structures of transnational power. And the challenges posed by globalization may be complemented by new possibilities as well. If, for example, I referred repeatedly to the political clout of labor, we may well ask if the movement of a great deal of manufacturing out of the traditional industrial heartlands might be the prelude to a new wave of labor activism in new places. On the historical record, indeed, the places where the new institutions of a renewed democracy will be pioneered—if anywhere—are likely not to be in the old centers where past success leads people to think the rest of the world need only copy them. The democratic challenge for the twenty-first century, if democracy is not to become trivialized, will demand more than the extension of a known, completed, fixed model to new territories. If democracy is to have a meaningful future, it will have to be redefined and reinvented, as it always has been.

Notes

This is an edited and heavily abridged version of an article that originally appeared in 1999 in the *Journal of World-Systems Research* (vol. 5, no. 2, pp. 277–309). For a fuller treatment, readers are encouraged to download the original article, which is available for no charge from www.jwsr.org.

1. Consider the constitution issued by the restored French monarchy in 1814, announced in its royal preamble as in recognition "of the wishes of our subjects." See "Charte constitutionelle" (1960:80).

2. For an exemplary study of cycles and trends, see Chase-Dunn, Kawano, and Brewer (1999).

3. These assertions rest, I hope not too precariously, on the accumulated data put forward in the works cited in the previous notes. What is needed is a demonstration (a) that significant social interactions are happening across greater distances than in the past; (b) that such an increase in recent decades is more than the current upswing of a recurrent cyclical pattern and instead represents a trend; and (c) that these first two conditions hold for the globe as a whole rather than some limited part of it. No one has conclusively demonstrated any such thing, but I believe the evidence points in this direction. If this proves mistaken, much of what follows here would need to be rethought.

4. There is surely considerable variation from place to place in this regard. The United States, for example, has far more influence on the making of transnationally consequential decisions than many other places and is less at the mercy of market forces. One important symptom of the ideologically driven utility for some of the claims that global competitiveness mandates dismantling First World social safety nets is how much more prevalent such claims are in the United States than anywhere else in the First World when the plausibility of such arguments is actually weaker there.

5. As I wrote the first draft of this essay in May 1998, the Indonesian government was wavering from one day to the next, between claiming to adhere to the demands of transnational finance and placating vast urban crowds of angry Indonesians who—

along with the friends and relatives of both the recently deposed and the newly elevated presidents—would be injured by such adherence.

I will not take up here the important question of the relationship of the United States to the IMF and the World Bank.

6. The extent of cross-border financing of political parties generally (and in the 1990s in particular) seems to be scholarly terra incognita.

7. A valuable collection of essays may be found in Suleiman and Waterbury (1990).

8. The extent to which confronting unemployment is a serious political strategy in, say, France (where it played an important role in the Left's electoral victory in 1997) again suggests a range of variation that I ignore here.

9. For bibliography, see Korzeniewicz and Moran (1997).

10. For an especially compelling treatment of these issues in the new Eastern Europe, see Brubaker (1996).

11. On such grounds, for example, Diamond, Linz, and Lipset contend that ethnic conflicts are "the most difficult type of cleavage for a democracy to manage." See Diamond, Linz, and Lipset (1995:42).

12. Important discussions of the issues treated here include Brysk (1994); Tarrow (1994); Smith (1995:185–219); Tilly (1995); Smith, Chatfield, and Pagnucco (1997); Hanagan (1998); Keck and Sikkink (1998); Tarrow (1998b, 1998c:176–210).

13. For some quantitative data from Europe, see Tarrow 1998a.

14. Keck and Sikkink (1998) examine the sources of variation in the effectiveness of transnational advocacy networks.

15. George and Sabelli (1994:214). The extremely complex formal rules for IMF decision-making have been described in the literature (Lister 1984). What seems to have escaped scrutiny, however, is the political process of reaching actual decisions by the bank and the fund.

16. Tocqueville (1945:57, 197, 199). If voting rights were universal in the United States Tocqueville visited in 1831, it was but a short step to urge: "At the present day the principle of the sovereignty of the people has acquired in the United States all the practical development that the imagination can conceive" (p. 57).

17. Movements involving working-class people in core countries on behalf of the rights of people in colonies, like the British antislavery movement, demand more systematic attention from students of social movements than they have received. For example, see Drescher (1987).

References

Albrow, Martin. 1997. *The Global Age: State and Society beyond Modernity*. Stanford, CA: Stanford University Press.

Appadurai, Arjun. 1996. *Modernity at Large: Cultural Dimensions of Globalization*. Minneapolis, MN: University of Minnesota Press.

Braun, Denny. 1997. *The Rich Get Richer: The Rise of Income Inequality in the United States and the World*. Chicago: Nelson-Hall Publishers.

Brubaker, Rogers. 1996. *Nationalism Reframed: Nationhood and the National Question in the New Europe*. Cambridge, UK: Cambridge University Press.

Bryce, James. 1921. *Modern Democracies*. New York: Macmillan.

Brysk, Alison. 1994. "Acting Globally: Indian Rights and International Politics in Latin America." Pp. 29–51 in *Indigenous Peoples and Democracy in Latin America*, edited by Donna Lee Van Cott. New York: St. Martin's.

Castells, Manuel. 1994. "European Cities, the Informational Society, and the Global Economy." *New Left Review* 204:18–32.

"Charte constitutionelle de 4 juin 1814." 1960. In Maurice Duverger, *Constitutions et documents politiques*. Paris: Presses Universitaires de France.

Chase-Dunn, Christopher, Yukio Kawano, and Benjamin Brewer. 1999. "Economic Globalization since 1795: Structures and Cycles in the Modern World-System." Paper presented at the meetings of the International Studies Association, Washington, DC, February.

Chase-Dunn, Christopher, Yukio Kawano, and Denis Nikitin. 1998. "Globalization: A World-Systems Perspective." Paper presented at the World Congress of Sociology, Montreal.

Christophersen, Jens A. 1968. *The Meaning of "Democracy" As Used in European Ideologies from the French to the Russian Revolutions: An Historical Study of Political Language*. Oslo: Universitetsforlaget.

Conklin, Alice. 1998. "Colonialism and Human Rights, a Contradiction in Terms? The Case of France and West Africa, 1895–1914." *American Historical Review* 103.

Conze, Werner and Reinhart Koselleck, eds. 1984. *Geschichtliche Grundbegriffe*. Stuttgart: Klett Verlag.

Diamond, Larry, Juan J. Linz, and Seymour Martin Lipset. 1995. Introduction to *Politics in Developing Countries: Comparing Experiences with Democracy*, 2nd ed., edited by Larry Diamond, Juan J. Linz, and Seymour Martin Lipset. Boulder, CO: Lynne Rienner.

Dippel, Horst. 1986. "Démocratie, Démocrates." In *Handbuch politsch-sozialer Grundbegriffe in Frankreich 1680–1920*, edited by Rolf Reichardt and Eberhard Schmitt. Munich: Oldenbourg.

Drescher, Seymour. 1987. *Capitalism and Antislavery: British Mobilization in Comparative Perspective*. New York: Oxford University Press.

Fukuyama, Francis. 1989. "The End of History?" *National Interest* 16:3–18.

Ganley, Gladys. 1992. *The Exploding Political Power of Personal Media*. Norwood, NJ: Ablex.

George, Susan and Fabrizio Sabelli. 1994. *Faith and Credit: The World Bank's Secular Empire*. Boulder, CO: Westview Press.

Hanagan, Michael. 1998. "Transnational Social Movements, Deterritorialized Migrants, and the State System: A Nineteenth-Century Case Study." In *How Move-*

ments Matter, edited by Marco Giugni, Doug McAdam, and Charles Tilly. Minneapolis, MN: University of Minnesota Press.

Hannerz, Ulf. 1996. *Transnational Connections: Culture, People, Places.* London: Routledge.

Held, David. 1995. *Democracy and the Global Order: From the Modern State to Cosmopolitan Government.* Stanford, CA: Stanford University Press.

Keck, Margaret and Kathryn Sikkink. 1998. *Activists beyond Borders: Advocacy Networks in International Politics.* Ithaca, NY: Cornell University Press.

Keohane, Robert and Helen Milner, eds. 1996. *Internationalization and Domestic Politics.* New York: Cambridge University Press.

Korzeniewicz, Roberto P. and Kimberley Awbrey. 1992. "Democratic Transitions and the Semiperiphery of the World-Economy." *Sociological Forum* 7.

Korzeniewicz, Roberto P. and Timothy P. Moran. 1997. "World-Economic Trends in the Distribution of Income, 1965–1992." *American Journal of Sociology* 102:1000–1039.

Lipset, Seymour Martin. 1981. "Economic Development and Democracy." In Lipset, *Political Man: The Social Bases of Politics.* Baltimore, MD: Johns Hopkins University Press.

Lister, Frederick K. 1984. *Decision-Making Strategies for International Organization: The IMF Model.* Vol. 20, bk. 4 of *Monograph Series in World Affairs.* Denver, CO: University of Denver, Graduate School of International Affairs.

Markoff, John. 1996. *Waves of Democracy: Social Movements and Political Change.* Thousand Oaks, CA: Pine Forge Press.

———. 2004. "Who Will Construct the Global Order?" In *Transnational Democracy in Critical and Comparative Perspective: Democracy's Range Reconsidered,* edited by Bruce Morrison. London: Ashgate Publishing.

Marshall, T. H. 1950. *Citizenship and Social Class and Other Essays.* Cambridge, UK: Cambridge University Press.

Offe, Claus. 1996. *Modernity and the State: East, West.* Cambridge, MA: MIT Press.

O'Gorman, Frank. 1989. *Voters, Patrons, and Parties: The Unreformed Electoral System of Hanoverian England, 1734–1832.* Oxford: Clarendon Press.

Palmer, Robert R. 1953. "Notes on the Use of the Word 'Democracy,' 1789–1799." *Political Science Quarterly* 68.

Piven, Frances Fox and Richard Cloward. 1997. *The Breaking of the American Social Compact.* New York: New Press.

Pool, Ithiel de Sola. 1952. *Symbols of Democracy.* Stanford, CA: Stanford University Press.

Robertson, Roland. 1992. *Globalization: Social Theory and Global Culture.* London: Sage.

Rodrik, Dani. 1997. *Has Globalization Gone Too Far?* Washington, DC: Institute for International Economics.

Rosanvallon, Pierre. 1995. "The History of the Word Democracy in France." *Journal of Democracy* 6.

Rousseau, Jean-Jacques. 1943. *Du Contrat Social, Book III*. Paris: Aubier-Montaigne.

Rudé, George. 1962. *Wilkes and Liberty: A Social Study of 1763 to 1774*. Oxford: Clarendon Press.

Sassen, Saskia. 1994. *Cities in a World Economy*. Thousand Oaks, CA: Pine Forge Press.

Shoemaker, Robert W. 1966. "'Democracy' and 'Republic' As Understood in Late Eighteenth Century America." *American Speech* 41.

Silver, Beverly. 1998. "Turning Points in Workers' Militancy in the World Automobile Industry, 1930s–1990s." In *Research in the Sociology of Work*, vol. 6, edited by Randy Hodson. Greenwich, CT: JAI Press.

Sklair, Leslie. 1991. *Sociology of the Global System*. Baltimore, MD: Johns Hopkins University Press.

Smith, Jackie. 1995. "Transnational Political Processes and the 'Human Rights Movement.'" Pp. 185–219 in *Research in Social Movements, Conflicts and Change*, vol. 18, edited by Michael Dobkowski, Isidor Wallimann, and Christo Stojanov. Greenwich, CT: JAI Press.

Smith, Jackie, Charles Chatfield, and Ron Pagnucco, eds. 1997. *Transnational Social Movements and Global Politics: Solidarity beyond the State*. Syracuse, NY: Syracuse University Press.

Soysal, Yasemin. 1994. *Limits of Citizenship: Migrants and Postnational Membership in Europe*. Chicago: University of Chicago Press.

Steenbergen, Bart van, ed. 1994. *The Condition of Citizenship*. London: Sage.

Stinchcombe, Arthur L. 1995. *Sugar Island Slavery in the Age of Enlightenment: The Political Economy of the Caribbean World*. Princeton, NJ: Princeton University Press.

Suleiman, Ezra N. and John Waterbury. 1990. *The Political Economy of Public Sector Reform and Privatization*. Boulder, CO: Westview Press.

Tarrow, Sidney. 1994. "Social Movements in Europe: Movement Society or Europeanization of Conflict?" European University Institute Working Paper RSC No. 94/8.

———. 1998a. "Building a Composite Polity: Popular Contention in the European Union." Cornell University Institute for European Studies Working Paper 98.3.

———. 1998b. "Fishnets, Internets and Catnets: Globalization and Transnational Collective Action." Pp. 228–244 in *Challenging Authority: The Historical Study of Contentious Politics*, edited by Michael Hanagan, Leslie Page Moch, and Wayne Ph Te Brake. Minneapolis, MN: University of Minnesota Press.

———. 1998c. *Power in Movement: Social Movements and Contentious Politics*. Cambridge, UK: Cambridge University Press.

Tilly, Charles. ed. 1996. *Citizenship, Identity and Social History*. Cambridge, UK: Cambridge University Press.

———. 1995. "Globalization Threatens Labor's Rights." *International Labor and Working-Class History* 47:1–23 (with responses by Immanuel Wallerstein, Aristide R. Zolberg, E. J. Hobsbawm, and Lourdes Benería, pp. 24–55).

———. 2004. *Social Movements, 1768–2004*. Boulder, CO: Paradigm Publishers.

Tocqueville, Alexis de. 1945. *Democracy in America.* Vol. 1. New York: Knopf.

Turner, Bryan, ed. 1993. *Citizenship and Social Theory.* London: Sage.

Wade, Robert. 1996. "Globalization and Its Limits: Reports of the Death of the National Economy Are Greatly Exaggerated." Pp. 60-88 in *National Diversity and Global Capitalism,* edited by Suzanne Berger and Ronald Dore. Ithaca, NY: Cornell University Press.

Wallerstein, Immanuel. 1991. *Unthinking Social Science: The Limits of Nineteenth-Century Paradigms.* Cambridge: Polity Press.

Weiss, Linda. 1997. "Globalization and the Myth of the Powerless State." *New Left Review* 225:3–27.

Giovanni Arrighi is Professor of Sociology at the Johns Hopkins University. He is the author of *The Long Twentieth Century* (Verso, 1994) and coauthor of *Chaos and Governance in the Modern World System* (University of Minnesota Press, 1999). His most recent book is *The Resurgence of East Asia: 500, 150 and 50 Year Perspectives,* coedited with T. Hamashita and M. Selden (Routledge, 2003).

Salvatore J. Babones is Assistant Professor of Sociology, Public Health, and Public and International Affairs at the University of Pittsburgh. He received his Ph.D. from the Johns Hopkins University in 2003. His work focuses on the levels and trajectories of income inequality both within and between countries. He is currently researching the relationship between societal inequality and population health.

Frederick H. Buttel was Professor of Sociology and Environmental Studies at the University of Wisconsin–Madison. He made important contributions to rural sociology, environmental sociology, and the sociology of agriculture. He coauthored and edited several books, including *The Sociology of Agriculture* (Greenwood Press, 1990), *Environment and Global Modernity* (Sage, 2000), *Hungry for Profit* (New York University Press, 2000), *Environment, Energy and Society* (Wadsworth, 2001), *Sociological Theory and the Environment* (Rowman and Littlefield, 2002), and *The Environmental State under Pressure* (JAI Press, 2002). He lost his long battle with cancer in 2005.

Christopher Chase-Dunn is Distinguished Professor of Sociology and Director of the Institute for Research on World-Systems at the University of California–Riverside. His studies of economic and political globalization in the modern world-system over the past 200 years are supported by the National Science Foundation. Chase-Dunn is the founder and coeditor of the electronic *Journal of World-Systems Research*. With Bruce Lerro he is writing a textbook entitled *Social Change: World Historical Transformations* (Allyn and Bacon).

Kenneth A. Gould is Professor of Sociology at St. Lawrence University. He is the coauthor of *Environment and Society: The Enduring Conflict* (St. Martin's Press, 1994; Blackburn Press, 2000) and *Local Environmental Struggles: Citizen Activism in the Treadmill of Production* (Cambridge University Press, 1996). He is completing a book to be titled "The Treadmill of Production: Injustice and Unsustainability in the Global Economy" (with David Pellow and Allan Schnaiberg) and another on labor-environmentalist coalitions (with Tammy L. Lewis and J. Timmons Roberts).

Peter Gowan is Professor of International Relations at London Metropolitan University. He is a member of the editorial board of the *New Left Review* and is a member of the America Discussion Group at the Royal Institute of International Affairs. Since the late 1990s he has been working on American capitalism and the external orientations of the United States as well as on transatlantic relations. He is the author of *The Global Gamble* (Verso, 1999) and *The Twisted Road to Kosovo* (Manifest, 2000).

Thomas D. Hall is Lester M. Jones Professor of Sociology and University Professor at DePauw University in Greencastle, Indiana. His recent works include *A World-Systems Reader* (Rowman and Littlefield, 2000) and *Rise and Demise: Comparing World-Systems,* with Christopher Chase-Dunn (Westview, 1997). Recently he has published a number of articles with James V. Fenelon on indigenous peoples, and they are completing a book on indigenous peoples and globalization.

Alf Hornborg is an anthropologist and Professor of Human Ecology at Lund University, Sweden. He is the author of *The Power of the Machine: Global Inequalities of Economy, Technology, and Environment* (AltaMira, 2001) and editor of *World System History and Global Environmental Change* (AltaMira, in press) as well as *The World System and the Earth System: Global Socio-Environmental Change and Sustainability 3000 BC–AD 2000* (Left Coast Books, in press).

Andrew K. Jorgenson is Assistant Professor of Sociology at Washington State University. His current research involves analyses of the environmental impacts of sector-level foreign investment and the structure of international trade. Recent and forthcoming publications appear in such journals as *Social Forces, Social Problems, Sociological Perspectives, International Journal of Comparative Sociology, Human Ecology Review,* and the *Journal of World-Systems Research.* He is the coeditor of the forthcoming volume to be entitled *Globalization and the Environment* (Brill Academic Press).

John Markoff is Professor of Sociology, History, and Political Science at the University of Pittsburgh. His books include *Abolition of Feudalism: Peasants, Lords and Legislators in the French Revolution* (Penn State University Press, 1996), *Waves of Democracy: Social Movements and Poltical Change* (Pine Forge Press, 1996), and (with Gilbert Shapiro) *Revolutionary Demands: A Content Analysis of the Cahiers de Doleance of 1789* (Stanford University Press, 1998). His current research is on the history of democracy.

Valentine M. Moghadam works for UNESCO in Paris, as Chief of the Gender Equality and Development in the Social and Human Sciences Sector. She was previously Director of Women's Studies and Professor of Sociology at Illinois State University, and is the author of *Globalizing Women: Transnational Feminist Networks* (Johns Hopkins University Press, 2005), *Modernizing Women: Gender and Social Change in the Middle East* (Lynne Rienner, 2003, 2nd ed.) and *Women, Work and Economic Reform in the Middle East and North Africa* (Lynne Rienner, 1998). She is currently researching women's movements in the Middle East.

Bruce Podobnik is Associate Professor of Sociology at Lewis and Clark College. He is the author of *Global Energy Shifts: Fostering Sustainability in a Turbulent Age* (Temple, 2005) and coeditor (with Thomas Reifer) of *Transforming Globalization: Challenges and Opportunities in the Post 9/11 Era* (Brill, 2005).

Leslie Sklair is Professor Emeritus of Sociology at the London School of Economics and Political Science. His recent publications include *The Transnational Capitalist Class* (Blackwell, 2001) and *Globalization: Capitalism and Its Alternatives* (Oxford University Press, 2002). Forthcoming from his recent project is "Iconic Architecture and Capitalist Globalization."

Jackie Smith is Associate Professor of Sociology and Peace Studies at the University of Notre Dame. She is the author of a forthcoming book to be entitled Changing the World: Social Movements in a Global System, and she has coedited three other books on the ways globalization affects civil society and political movements. The most recent of these collections is *Coalitions across Borders: Transnational Protest and the Neoliberal Order* (Rowman and Littlefield, 2005). Smith teaches courses on globalization, popular politics, and the United Nations.

Jonathan H. Turner is Distinguished Professor of Sociology at the University of California–Riverside. He is the author of 29 books and many articles on theoretical and substantive issues. His most recent books are *Human Institutions: A Theory of Societal Evolution* (Rowman and Littlefield, 2003), *The Sociology of Emotions*

(Cambridge University Press, 2005), and *Face-to-Face: A Sociological Theory of Interpersonal Behavior* (Stanford University Press, 2002). He has long been interested in societal stratification, and his chapter in the present volume represents an extension of this interest to the global system of inequality.

Dawn Wiest is a Ph.D. candidate at Stony Brook University. Currently she is teaching at Notre Dame. She is the coauthor of "The Uneven Geography of Global Civil Society: National and Global Influences on Transnational Association," which will be published in the December 2005 issue of *Social Forces*. She is also writing a book with Jackie Smith and Kiyoteru Tsutsui on the relationship between global political-economic changes and changes in the the transnational social movement organizational sector. Her dissertation focuses on geographic patterns of collaboration in transnational social movement networks and coalitions.